Knife Laws
of the U.S.

Evan F. Nappen
Attorney at Law

Published by

Krause Publications, a division of F+W Media, Inc.
700 East State Street • Iola, WI 54990-0001
715-445-2214 • 888-457-2873
www.krausebooks.com

To order books or other products call toll-free 1-800-258-0929
or visit us online at www.krausebooks.com

ISBN-13: 978-1-4402-4493-3
ISBN-10: 1-4402-4493-6

Cover Design by Kevin Ulrich
Designed by Rachael Wolter
Edited by Chad Love

For more titles in knives and knife making, visit www.shopblade.com

Printed in United States of America

10 9 8 7 6 5 4 3 2 1

DEDICATION

This book is dedicated to the Knife Rights Movement.

May all knife laws that turn honest citizens into criminals be repealed and tossed in the dust bin of history.

ACKNOWLEDGMENTS

Appreciation goes to the following people who helped make this book possible:

SENATOR ROBERT CLEGG

DAVID W. HUANG, ESQ.

MARGARET D. LEEDOM

MICHELLE MADDOX

ABIGAIL Y. NAPPEN

BARBARA F. NAPPEN

BEVERLY C. NAPPEN

DR. ENOCH L. NAPPEN

ETHAN F. NAPPEN

LOUIS P. NAPPEN, ESQ.

NATHANAEL B. NAPPEN

DOUG RITTER

JEFFREY A. SKIENDZIIUL, ESQ.

KATY SOLSKY

TABLE OF CONTENTS

PREFACE

"...always keep an edge on yr knife, son, always keep an edge on yr knife - cuz a good sharp edge is a man's best hedge against the vague uncertainties of life..."
Corb Lund

By Evan F. Nappen, Attorney at Law

Knife Laws of the U.S. contains over 5000 answers to general knife law legal questions regarding all 50 States, the District of Columbia and the United States of America. This book is intended to help law-abiding citizens better protect themselves from becoming victims of arbitrary knife laws. It is also intended to illuminate a path toward greater knife liberty and help the fast growing Knife Rights Movement.

It was an honor for me to write this book. It was a labor of love. The book furthers my dedication in the fight for greater knife rights freedom. By identifying the knife laws of each state, the places that need change become evident. The rating system used in the book makes it clear how any given jurisdiction can do better in expanding knife liberty. It is up to you to help fight for these changes.

We must stop turning law-abiding citizens into criminals in the false name of public safety by repealing archaic knife laws. Maturity, logic, and experience have taught us that knife bans do nothing to stop crime. Criminals ignore any such laws and only honest citizens suffer.

No knife is intrinsically "dangerous", "deadly" or "serves no lawful purpose." It is people, not inanimate objects that are either good or bad. Banning a knife by feature or characteristic is absurd. It is often merely a political gimmick by grandstanding politicians selling the public a "boogeyman."

Knives have been part of humanity since the first human made a cut with a sharp rock. Knives have helped mankind survive and thrive. They are used every day, every hour, and every second by people in the world who could not accomplish their given task without a trusty blade.

From a Boy Scout pocket knife to a Navy Seal combat knife, from a short order cook's paring knife to a gourmet chef's knife, from a hunter's skinning knife to someone lost in the woods with a survival knife, from a stock clerk's box cutter to an astronaut's knife, from a historical reenactor's dirk to a movie action hero's dagger, from an antique collector's bowie knife to a museum's 12th century stiletto, from someone's everyday carry assisted-opener to an EMT's life saving automatic, from a fisherman's fillet knife to a deep sea sportsman's knife, from a Swiss Army knife on one's keychain to a machete on one's hip, blades are indispensable tools that deserve a place of respect in our system of laws.

Knife rights are human rights.

Evan F. Nappen, Esq.
Concord, New Hampshire
April 19, 2015

FOREWORD

By Doug Ritter, Chairman – Knife Rights

When my good friend and colleague Evan Nappen first called to tell me he was writing a book on U.S. Knife Law, I was both excited that someone of his caliber was taking on the challenge, and somewhat sorry for him. Making sense of the myriad knife laws in the U.S. was going to be a tough challenge and, besides that, I was dedicated to making his book obsolete as soon as possible. Unfortunately, for many law-abiding knife owners "as soon as possible" is still going to be years down the road, so the need for this book is not going to diminish much anytime too soon.

Evan has delivered on his promise; this is a book every knife owner needs. One thing we have learned as Knife Rights rewrites knife law in America is that the majority of citizens don't even know what a legal knife is and what's not. There's no "three finger" law;" there's no "width of the palm" law. They may think they know the law, but then seem too often surprised when we start work to repeal knife restrictions in their state, restrictions of which they were unaware. Most of the time that ignorance is not a problem—until it becomes one.

All it takes is a simple traffic stop and that knife in your pocket or in the car can turn into a serious crime in too many places in this country, potentially a felony is some states and in some circumstances! Travelers who carry knives must deal with not only differing and confusing state laws, but in the majority of states without knife law preemption, even within their state's borders. Knowledge of the law is your only protection. Evan's work means you don't need to keep a lawyer on staff; just leaf through the book for most of your knife law answers.

Hardly a day goes by that I don't receive a heart-rending call from an unlucky knife owner, or their spouse or parent, who has come face-to-face with the harsh realities of a restrictive knife law. "I had no idea," is a steady refrain. That doesn't elicit much sympathy from cops, prosecutors and many judges. Evan has written the antidote to that refrain, just read it!

Evan's considerable experience as a renowned criminal law attorney working in states with some of the very worst knife (and gun) laws is no more evident than in the chapters "Secrets to Avoid Knife Law Problems" and "What to Do if You are Arrested." The first step is avoiding trouble by not being stupid and by following the law. However, even when your knife is perfectly legal, you can still find yourself accosted by a cop or arrested, let alone if the law is gray and fuzzy in a particular area. How you conduct yourself can determine whether you come out on top or not. Follow Evan's advice and avoid an arrest altogether or at least make it much easier for your attorney. If you carry a knife, YOU NEED TO READ THESE CHAPTERS!

In his dedication, Evan writes, "may all knife laws that turn honest citizens into criminals be repealed and tossed in the dustbin of history." We are working on that, but in the meantime, Evan has gifted the knife community with a tremendous resource to help keep us all out of handcuffs.

Doug Ritter
Gilbert, Arizona
May 6, 2015

BE SURE TO READ THIS!
WARNING / DISCLAIMER:

Knife Laws of the U.S.: Loopholes, Pitfalls, and Secrets provides a knowledge base of the fundamental laws that affect and concern knives and edged weapons. U. S. Knife Law is for general informational use ONLY.

IT IS NOT LEGAL ADVICE. This book is NOT a substitute for professional legal advice. If you have a legal question, issue, scenario or problem, see an attorney who understands and is experienced with knife and weapon laws in your jurisdiction.

LAWS CONSTANTLY CHANGE and are subjected to different interpretations by courts, state agencies, and other attorneys. Legislatures also frequently change laws.

This book focuses only on state and federal knife laws and laws that affect knife and edged weapon owners. Local jurisdictions may have different laws controlling knives and edged weapons.

CHAPTER 1
THE SECOND AMENDMENT
& KNIVES

A well regulated militia, being necessary for the security of a free state, the right of the people to keep and bear arms, shall not be infringed.

— Second Amendment to the United States Constitution

On June 26, 2008, the SUPREME COURT OF THE UNITED STATES (SCOTUS) decided DISTRICT OF COLUMBIA, ET AL., PETITIONERS v. DICK ANTHONY HELLER which found as follows:

"We start therefore with a strong presumption that the Second Amendment right is exercised individually and belongs to all Americans."

Heller further states: "In the colonial and revolutionary war era, [small-arms] weapons used by militiamen and weapons used in defense of person and home were one and the same." (State v. Kessler, 289 Ore. 359, 368, 614 P. 2d 94, 98 (1980) (citing G. Neumann, Swords and Blades of the American Revolution 6-15, 252-254 (1973)).

Kessler found that "…defendant's possession of a billy club in his home was protected by right to bear arms provision of Oregon Constitution." The full quote from Kessler as cited in Heller reads as follows:

"B. The meaning of the term "arms" : The term "arms" is also subject to several interpretations. In the colonial and revolutionary war era, weapons used by militiamen and weapons used in defense of person and home were one and the same. A colonist usually had only one gun which was used for hunting, protection, and militia duty, plus a hatchet, sword, and knife. G. Neumann, Swords and Blades of the American Revolution, 6-15, 252-254 (1973). When the revolutionary war began, the colonists came equipped with their hunting muskets or rifles, hatchets, swords, and knives. The colonists suffered a severe shortage of firearms in the early years of the war, so many soldiers had to rely primarily on swords, hatchets, knives, and pikes (long staffs with a spear head). W. Moore, Weapons of the American Revolution, 8 (1967)."

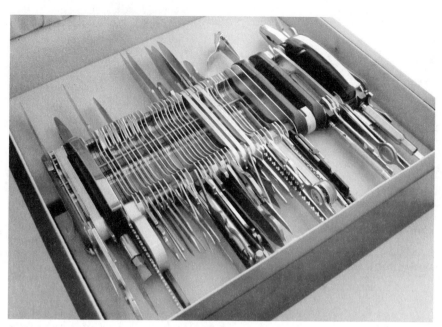

Guinness Book of World Records Swiss Army Knife

Kessler was followed by the Oregon Supreme Court in another case, State v. Delgado, 298 Or. 395 (1984), which in relying upon Kessler found that, "defendant's constitutional right to bear arms was violated by prohibition of mere possession and mere carrying of a switch-blade knife."

Here is partially what the Delgado court had to say about knives in a brilliant opinion by Justice Berkeley "Bud" Lent, 24 years before the Heller decision:

"The state argues that a switch-blade is not a weapon "commonly used for personal defense," and is therefore not an "arm" within the meaning of the Oregon Constitution. It insists that the switch-blade is an offensive weapon used primarily by criminals. In support of this argument we are referred to various authorities, especially the Federal Anti Switchblade Act, 15 USC §§ 1241-44 (Supp IV, 1980), which is aimed at prohibiting the introduction of switch-blade knives into interstate commerce because they are "almost exclusively the weapon of the thug and the delinquent." S. Rep. No. 1980, 85th Cong., 2d Sess., reprinted in 1958 U.S. Code Cong & Ad News 3435, 3437.

We note, first, that that material offers no more than impressionistic observations on the criminal use of switchblades. More importantly, however, we are unpersuaded by this distinction which the state urges of "offensive" and "defensive" weapons. All hand-held weapons necessarily share both characteristics. A kitchen knife can as easily be raised in attack as in defense. The spring mechanism does not, instantly and irrevocably, convert the jackknife into an "offensive" weapon (fn4). Similarly, the clasp feature of the common jackknife does not mean that it is incapable of aggressive and violent purposes. It is not the design of the knife but the use to which it is put that determines its "offensive" or "defensive" character."

There are statutes now on the books that concern the manner in which weapons are carried, the intent with which they are carried, the use to which they may not be put and the status of a person that results in forbidding his possessing a weapon.

The appropriate inquiry in the case at bar is whether a kind of weapon, as modified by its modern de-

Ed Fowler Pronghorn –
Author's EDC (Every Day Carry)

sign and function, is of the sort commonly used by individuals for personal defense during either the revolutionary and post-Revolutionary era (fn5), or in 1859 when Oregon's constitution was adopted. In particular, it must be determined whether the drafters would have intended the word "arms" to include the switch-blade knife as a weapon commonly used by individuals for self defense. To answer that question we must journey briefly into the history of knives. We have resorted primarily to three books by H. Peterson for that history: Arms and Armour in Colonial America, 1526-1783 (1956); American Knives (1958); Daggers and Fighting Knives of the Western World (1968). What we have to say generally in the next few paragraphs is drawn from those works.

The popularity of the fighting knife has had an uneven history, even to today. During the Roman civilization and for several centuries thereafter, for example, the knife was little appreciated as a tool of combat, but during the Viking Period of the 9th and 10th centuries large knives (scramasax), used for general purposes as well as for war, were popular among the Northmen, Germans, Franks and Anglo-Saxons. It was during the Middle Ages that the real flowering of the fighting knife and dagger occurred. New shapes appeared and the knife became part of the standard dress for all classes: from the knights and their men-at-arms as an adjunct to the sword, to the laborer and peasant for protection and convenience. During the 16th century the dagger came to be used by the aristocracy, mainly in conjunction with the sword, and was used primarily for combat; indeed, during the early part of that century the technique of fighting with sword and dagger developed, thus giving rise to the modern school of knife fighting. Through the 16th and 17th centuries knives and daggers declined in importance and were no longer an important part of the daily civilian costume.

In early colonial America the sword and dagger were the most commonly used edged weapons. During the American colonial era every colonist had a knife. As long as a man was required to defend his life, to obtain or produce his own food or to fashion articles from raw materials, a knife was a constant necessity. Around 1650 one form of dagger popular in the colonies was the "plug bayonet," so called because it fit into the muzzle of a musket. It was used both as a dagger or as a general utility knife. Other knives became popular during the 17th and 18th centuries. The American frontiersman used a large knife to ward off danger from Indian attacks and to hunt and trap; along with that he carried a smaller knife, the blade being three to four inches long, in his rifle bag.

In the 19th century, daggers remained popular, but in the west the renowned Bowie knife became the weapon favored by the lawless and law-abiding alike. These were violent times, particularly from the 1820s through the Civil War, when a weapon might be needed at a moment's notice. In response, "the well-equipped gentleman carried a pistol in his pocket and a knife beneath his coattails."

Of the many varieties of knives, none has been a more constant or enduring companion to man than the pocket knife. Specimens of folding pocket knives have been discovered in Roman archeological sites, indicating that such knives were popular at least from the first century A.D. They have been manufactured for their utility as both instruments of labor and combat. One of the most common of the specific named knives is the jackknife, a word of uncertain origin, which was a large single-bladed folding knife, ranging in size from four to seven inches when closed. By the early 1700s, when the eastern seaboard had become a highly settled area with large towns and cities and relatively good roads, men normally carried a folding pocket knife. Even when they joined the American army during the revolution, the knife they carried was the jack-knife, which was mentioned frequently in colonial records. During the American Revolution at least two states, New Hampshire and New York, required their militiamen to carry a jackknife. Even during the mid-18th century, some of these "jackknives" were rather more lethal than their name suggests, measuring two feet long with the blade extended, and designed solely for fighting (G. Neumann, Swords and Blades of the American Revolution 247 (1973). Some others had blades over 16 inches long, extending well beyond the hilt even when folded, and were designed to be used open or closed.

Commemorative Reproduction of the Rezin Bowie Knife.

**Case XX WWII Survival
Machine**

"Gentlemen" and officers during this same era often carried canes with slender daggers mounted inside which could be drawn with a quick tug and were used for personal defense (Neumann, Swords and Blades of the American Revolution, supra, at 239). In the early 19th century a special form of dagger also developed, the pocket or folding dagger, with blades ranging in size from four to sixteen inches; they were intended to be carried in the pocket or in special sheathes.

It is clear, then, that knives have played an important role in American life, both as tools and as weapons. The folding pocketknife, in particular, since the early 18th century has been commonly carried by men in America and used primarily for work, but also for fighting.

This brings us to the switchblade knife. A switchblade is defined as a "pocketknife having the blade spring operated so that pressure on a release catch causes it to fly open" (Webster's Third International Dictionary,1971).

If ORS 166.510(1) proscribed the possession of mere pocketknives, there can be no question but that the statute would be held to conflict directly with Article I, section 27. The only difference is the presence of the spring-operated mechanism that opens the knife. We are unconvinced by the state's argument that the switch-blade is so "substantially different from its historical antecedent" (the jackknife) that it could not have been within the contemplation of the constitutional drafters. They must have been aware that technological changes were occurring in

**Randall Model 18
Attack Survival Knife**

110 NRA Commemorative Knife

weaponry as in tools generally. The format and efficiency of weaponry was proceeding apace. This was the period of development of the Gatling gun, breech-loading rifles, metallic cartridges and repeating rifles. The addition of a spring to open the blade of a jackknife is hardly a more astonishing innovation than those just mentioned.

On June 28, 2010 SCOTUS decided OTIS MCDONALD, ET AL., PETITIONERS, V. CITY OF CHICAGO, ILLINOIS, ET AL. which found as follows:

"After the Civil War, many of the over 180,000 African Americans who served in the Union Army returned to the States of the old Confederacy, where systematic efforts were made to disarm them and other blacks. See Heller, …; E. Foner, Reconstruction: America's Unfinished Revolution 1863–1877, p. 8 (1988) (hereinafter Foner). The laws of some States formally prohibited African-Americans from possessing firearms. For example, a Mississippi law provided that "no freedman, free negro or mulatto, not in the military service of the United States government, and not licensed so to do by the board of police of his or her county, shall keep or carry fire-arms of any kind, or any ammunition, dirk or bowie knife." Certain Offenses of Freedmen, 1865 Miss. Laws p. 165, § 1, in 1 Documentary History of Reconstruction 289 (W. Fleming ed.1950); see also Regulations for Freedmen in Louisiana, in id., at 279–280; H.R. Exec. Doc. No. 70, 39th Cong., 1st Sess., 233, 236 (1866) (describing a Kentucky law); E. McPherson, The Political History of the United States of America During the Period of Reconstruction 40 (1871) (describing a Florida law); id., at 33 (describing an Alabama law)."

McDonald incorporated the protections of the Second Amendment to the states and localities so that the Second Amendment applies throughout all of the United States. Here in the McDonald decision an historic example of racist knife laws is referenced. To this day, many states with large populations of minorities have some of the worst knife laws. Whether unintentional or by design, it is an example of institutionalized racism which can be traced back to the racist roots of the infamous Black Codes. The Black Codes were laws passed in the southern states after the Civil War ended to take away freedom from the newly freed blacks, including the ownership of knives.

Although SCOTUS has not issued a decision specifically dealing with knives and the Second Amendment, it is plain to see that knives are most certainly "arms." It is the "right to keep and bear arms" not the "right to keep and bear guns." Knife rights can be linked to civil rights, as McDonald strongly illustrates. In the future, we will surely see Constitutional challenges to knife laws. The Delgado Court was ahead of its time, but that time is coming.

CHAPTER 2
WHAT TO DO
IF YOU ARE ARRESTED

A trial is still an ordeal by battle. For the broadsword there is the weight of evidence; for the battle-ax, the force of logic; for the sharp spear, the blazing gleam of truth; for the rapier, the quick and flashing knife of wit.

— Lloyd Paul Stryker

You have NO need to read this article because it could never happen to you. Right? This article must have been written for knife-wielding thugs or street gang members. Right? Why would law enforcement authorities ever come after you? Right?

WRONG! Merely because you possess or carry a knife, knife law enforcers may try to justify their existence by turning you into an accused "law-abiding" criminal. Even though you are a careful, honest knife owner, with no intent to do any harm, and would never knowingly break the law, this can easily happen to you. I have plenty of criminal case files of examples of innocent, unsuspecting, law-abiding folks having to fight their way through the justice system to "prove their innocence."

Perhaps you know how to defend yourself with a knife against an unprovoked assault. However, do you know what to do to protect yourself from false arrest and a malicious prosecution? Do you know how to keep your knife, stay out of jail, and not become a convicted felon? Do you know your Constitutional rights and how to invoke their shield of protection?

What I am about to tell you may save your freedom, your reputation, your property, and attorney's fees. I am going to reveal secrets from almost 30 years of criminal defense experience defending honest gun, knife, and weapon owners. You can learn from my client's mistakes and learn the steps people must follow to stay out of the legal system. These steps will at least mitigate the damages and give you the best chance for legal survival in the face of an aggressive, anti-knife prosecution.

Assorted Credit Card Knives

SAC

The fundamental criminal due process protections which are of the most use and vital importance to knife owners may be summed up as three simple Constitutional concepts. These three primary rights can be remembered by the acronym: S.A.C.

A Strategic Air Command (SAC) base provided the nuclear-based defense to the United States from 1946-1992 (most of you are hopefully old enough to remember). If stopped or arrested by law enforcement on a knife violation, the S.A.C. Constitutional mnemonic provides a basic legal defense foundation for the honest knife owner:

S - Remain SILENT - "I assert my right to remain silent."

A - ASK for your attorney - "I want my/an attorney."

C - Do NOT CONSENT to any search. Do not make or sign any statements without your attorney's approval.

ALWAYS be RESPECTFUL, POLITE and COOPERATIVE. DO NOT PHYSICALLY RESIST under any circumstances.

You will have to REMAIN SILENT and YOU MUST REASSERT YOUR REQUEST FOR AN ATTORNEY over and over again during the arrest and interrogation process. DO NOT RELENT! Remember: SAC.

#1: Remain SILENT (The "S" in SAC)

The Fifth Amendment protection against self-incrimination, also known as the "Right to Remain Silent," is one of the most important Constitutional protections Americans have, that many other countries do not grant. Yet, naive people in the United States routinely ignore Fifth Amendment protections and bury themselves with "explanations." When it comes to a criminal violation, most law-abiding citizens are ignorant about the details of the law and its many loopholes and defenses. By opening their mouths, they remove all doubt about their ignorance and usually give the state something not just to use against them, but to twist against them.

**CRKT Blade
Show Knife**

By remaining silent, a person avoids inadvertently incriminating oneself, wiping out potential legal defenses, and assisting the state in its often unjustified case. ALWAYS remain silent after being arrested for any reason. Remaining silent is the purest form of self-protection. Remember the old saying: The fish that opens its mouth is the one that gets caught!

If you are approached or stopped by a law enforcement officer and asked: "Do you have a weapon/knife on your person?" then the only safe response is to ask, "Am I free to go?" If the response is "Yes," then walk away. If the response is "No," then you are in custody and the above rights apply. You then respond per S.A.C., starting with remain SILENT, saying, "I assert my right to remain silent." (See below under #2 for the exception if you are stopped in your vehicle).

You might want to view the video "Don't Talk to Police" by Regent Law School Professor James Duane, which goes into further depth about how to legally and safely respond to a law enforcement officer in order to protect your rights:

It can be viewed online at: www.youtube.com/watch?v=6wXkI4t7nuc

#2: ASK for your ATTORNEY (The "A" in SAC)

The Sixth Amendment guarantees an individual's right to an attorney. By asking for your/an attorney and remaining silent, honest knife owners provide themselves with a fundamental foundation for a strong legal defense. Defense attorneys smile when they learn their clients stood firm on their rights.

Say, "I want my attorney." If you do not already have an attorney, say, "I want an attorney."

Requesting an attorney does much more than simply getting legal counsel. Simply requesting an attorney causes a wall of Constitutional protection to spring up around you. This wall prevents further interrogation by the authorities. After demanding an attorney, statements obtained from further interrogation made without the defendant's attorney present cannot be used by the state as evidence, as long as the person continues to verbally ask for an attorney. This holds true unless defendants foolishly waive their right to an attorney (see rule #3 below). The Sixth Amendment protections often apply even if information is obtained by "dirty tricks" without one's attorney being present.

Recent court decisions require you to reassert your request for an attorney at every opportunity where you are asked a question. Do NOT relent. Continue to remain silent and ask for your attorney.

#3: Do not CONSENT to waiving ANY rights (The "C" in SAC)

A right given up is a right lost. DO NOT CONSENT TO A SEARCH WITHOUT A WARRANT. DO NOT SIGN ANY DOCUMENTS OR STATEMENTS WITHOUT AN ATTORNEY'S ADVICE. All citizens have a Fourth Amendment right to a warrant being issued before their person or premises are searched.

There are exceptions to the necessity for a warrant, and there is a large body of law that exists as to when law enforcement officers have justification or probable cause for a warrantless search.

However, whether an exception for the warrantless search exists or not, YOU SHOULD NEVER CONSENT TO A WARRANTLESS SEARCH.

Spyderco Police Model Knife

The key here is consent. If a law enforcement officer insists on searching you, DO NOT RESIST being searched. Just make it verbally clear that you are not consenting to this search; say "I do not consent to this search."

Additionally, do not sign any consent form or, for that matter, any document, without the advice of your attorney. In some cases the officer may be allowed to ask you to sign that you received the summons. This is done so that you don't have to be formally arrested. Additionally, if stopped while driving, you may be required by law to produce your driver's license, registration, and insurance card. Refusal of blood alcohol testing is usually unlawful as well. Check your jurisdiction's laws for specifics.

If a search is done without adequate probable cause, then the court will suppress evidence obtained after a hearing handled by your attorney, and the state will not be able to use it against you.

When people consent to a search, then anything found may be used as evidence against them - whether there was probable cause or not! Although honest knife owners may feel that they have nothing to hide, consider that people may nonetheless possess contraband which they otherwise believed to be legal or that others may have left or planted in their cars, in their houses, or even in their clothing.

NOT giving consent is NOT probable cause for a search. Some people feel that if they do not consent to the search, the officer will suspect them. People are afraid of the inappropriate question: "What do you have to hide?"

Randall Model 12 Smithsonian Bowie

The actual legal question, which must be answered by the state at court, is: "Why did this law enforcement officer feel it was necessary to invade your privacy and conduct a search?" This question properly shifts the burden of proof to the police, as was our founding fathers' intention.

Remember, the Fourth Amendment is there to protect our privacy from government intrusion.

Law-abiding citizens frequently ask me about what to do when pulled over in a vehicle while transporting knives. There are two basic steps. First, make sure all items are being transported lawfully. Secondly, be polite. Hopefully the reason for being pulled over is simply a traffic matter and will be handled as such without it blowing up into a full-fledged car/person search. The key indicator as to whether this stop is going further than a potential traffic summons will be revealed by the officer's questions and actions.

If asked whether or not there are any weapons in the car, immediately be aware that you are in danger of becoming a victim of an anti-knife arrest. This question may be handled in many ways.

However, my personal response is to ask the officer why I am being asked that question. The answer to this question goes directly to the issue of probable cause. Why are you being asked whether you have weapons in the car? Is this simply a fishing expedition on behalf of the officer or is it because a knife is in plain view on the front seat?

If it is a fishing expedition, then that question is clearly unjustified. If there is a knife on the seat, then regardless of your answer, you are probably looking at having your vehicle and person searched. The key here is not to give any excuses for a vehicle search (e.g., items left in plain view, expired motor vehicle licenses, odd behaviors, etc.) If you obey the law and act in a practical and intelligent manner, you should be able to avoid vehicle/person searches.

THE BOTTOM LINE

We have all heard the Miranda Rights given on various TV cop shows and movies. We have heard them so often that many folks do not even pay attention to what these rights truly mean. The media has so belittled our Constitutional rights that many naive citizens simply ignore them. Knife owners cannot afford to ignore them.

Always remain polite when asserting your rights, but the key is to assert them. Do not be embarrassed or intimidated into giving up your rights. If you give up your rights (apart from making my job defending you that much tougher), you will have substantially increased your chance of becoming the next horror story victim of an anti-knife arrest that your friends will be talking about while you sit in jail.

CHAPTER 3
SECRETS TO AVOID KNIFE LAW PROBLEMS

After a recent knife show, a state trooper pulled a motorist over and proceeded to search the poor fellow's vehicle. The trooper opened the trunk and saw a vast array of hunting knives, kitchen knives, machetes, daggers, hatchets, short swords and other miscellaneous edged tools and weapons. He demanded to know why the motorist had all the knives. The nervous guy told him that he was a juggler in the circus and used the items in his act. The trooper said, "Now I've heard everything!" The guy said "No, really!" and proceeded to start juggling. Soon there was a circle of flying steel in the air. Just about then a husband and wife drove by and the husband blurted out to his wife, "Wow, drunk driving tests are getting tough!"

The above, of course, is a joke, but it does raise questions that many knife enthusiasts have considered, specifically, "What do I do if a knife I have is questioned by a police officer? Whether it's a search of my vehicle, my house, or my person, what can I, as a law-abiding knife owner, do to protect myself?" Constitutional protections are a knife owner's first line of defense if he or she has a potential legal problem (See Chapter 2 for details).

L.L. Bean Stag Bullet Knife

Always remain polite when asserting your rights, but the key is to assert them. Do not be embarrassed, and do not allow yourself to be intimidated into giving up your rights. If you give up your rights (apart from making my job of defending you that much harder), you will have substantially increased your chance of becoming the next horror-story victim of anti-knife laws.

Here are some other tips to avoid problems.

1. BEWARE OF POCKET CLIPS

Never carry your knife clipped to your pocket where the clip might be seen. Sight of a pocket clip is often used as probable cause to stop, search, and arrest someone for a knife. This has particularly been a problem in New York City. Even when covered by a jacket, simply moving the jacket aside to get to a wallet has been enough to get folks arrested.

2. BE AN OFFICIAL KNIFE COLLECTOR

Often, knife laws require that one be able to demonstrate a lawful intent for possessing the knife or knives in question. Sometimes these laws take the form of a reputable presumption or an affirmative defense that places the burden of proof on you, the defendant.

Many times, the burden is actually on the state to prove the unlawful purpose. Being able to present oneself as an "official knife collector" can be extremely valuable as a defense when facing knife charges. Proving that one is, in fact, a genuine collector can be done in various ways.

Most importantly, one should belong to various collector groups. Local arms collector clubs and national knife associations can provide good credentials. Having an extensive knife information library and subscriptions to knife magazines and periodicals can also be presented as evidence. It is a good idea to save receipts for subscriptions to help show one is a bona fide collector.

3. HAVE A COLLECTOR INVENTORY

It is vital to have a collector inventory of the knives that one possesses. The best collector inventory consists of photos and descriptions, which indicate the history, providence, significance and value of each piece in a collection. In today's high-tech world, accomplishing this with a digital camera and a computer is not complex, yet extremely worthwhile.

Having a collector inventory will also provide valuable information in case of theft and can provide detailed descriptions for insurance claims or for an estate to identify the knives and their values in a collection.

Keep your collector inventory list in a place other than with your collection. The list is also valuable if your knives are seized by the government. Also, carefully describing the knives in your collection can make the key difference in how a knife is regarded. Detailing each knife in writing shows one's intent concerning the possession. The following are some examples of knives described, first in a negative manner that might construe them as weapons, then in a positive manner that might show them as the collectibles that they are:

- Is the knife a "dagger," or is it an early World War II British military issue F/S Commando Knife in very good condition?

- Is the knife a "switchblade," or is it a World War II U.S. military issue Schrade Presto Paratrooper Knife?

- Is the knife a "gravity knife," or is it a World War II German military issue Takedown Paratrooper Knife with Third Reich proof marks?

- Is the knife a "dirk," or is it an excellent-condition, early-production, serial-numbered Gerber Mark I Survival Knife?

- Is the knife a "stiletto," or is it a Vietnam War Randall Model 2 Fighting Knife in excellent condition with an 8-inch forged stainless steel blade owned by a Marine Corps Lieutenant?

I am sure you get the idea.

Nowadays, governments are quick to seize collections of weapons, be it knives or guns, so the powers-that-be can do a dog-and-pony show for the media. Make sure that your valuable knives are in protective enclosures or cases. Various coverings are available, from silicon-impregnated cloth sacks, to knife rolls to hard and soft cases.

If the knives were improperly stored when seized, arguments can be made to compensate for damages caused by the government's possible mistreatment of your property. The government will most likely store knives in their original holders, which if properly cased, will protect property while it sits in generally overpopulated evidence rooms.

I had one case involving a valuable collection ($25,000-plus) of automatic knives seized by the police. The authorities, who called these knives "switchblades," ended up returning them because we were able to show that the defendant was a bona fide, genuine, actual, true, recognized, authentic "official knife collector," utilizing many of the techniques described above.

Many members of law enforcement are not familiar with the knife laws. I frequently hear myths and false beliefs concerning what is legal or illegal. I have actually heard law enforcement officers say that a pocketknife cannot be bigger than the palm of their hand and proceed to measure a blade across the palm of their hand. This presents the absurd proposition that at some point that legislature passed a law saying no knife blade can be bigger than the cop's palm!

4. BE DISCREET AND KNOW YOUR RIGHTS

Just being discreet can go a long way in protecting oneself from initiating involvement with the authorities. Do not flash your knives in public. Do not talk about what you possess, carry, or collect in inappropriate environments. In today's anti-knife, anti-gun, anti-weapon, politically correct society, the authorities frequently overreact to any claims by do-gooders regarding these items. You do not need the unwanted attention!

It is extremely important to keep with you the name and telephone number of an attorney familiar with that jurisdiction's knife laws, the criminal justice system and, of course, the technical aspects of knives. Give this information to people you might have to contact should you find yourself charged with a knife-law violation.

By having the laws with you, it may be possible to present (in a non-ego-threatening manner) what you believe the law to be, or simply give the laws to the officer to read for himself. This is where this book could be a big help.

This is particularly of note when alleging a false arrest. Imagine being able to tell the civil jury on your false arrest civil suit that not only were you falsely arrested, but also you gave the arresting officer a copy of the law before he arrested you!

If the law-abiding collector does not give up his or her Constitutional rights and has taken the above measures, that person and their knives will have significant added protection from an unjust prosecution and property confiscation. The best way to avoid becoming a victim of anti-knife laws is to avoid being arrested in the first place and being prepared if you are arrested.

Colt Barry Woods
Folding Knife

CHAPTER 4
FACTS & LAW
ABOUT "SWITCHBLADES"

Switchblade knives in the hands of criminals are, of course poten-
tially dangerous weapons. However, since they serve useful and even
essential purposes in the hands of persons such as sportsmen, ship-
ping clerks, and others engaged in lawful pursuits, the committee
may deem it preferable that they be regulated at the state rather than
the federal level.

— William P. Harris, deputy attorney general for the United States Department of Justice in a letter to the chair of the House Committee considering the 1958 Switchblade Law, appendix to the committee report.

The term "switchblade" is somewhat outdated; however, many laws still use the term. Today, knives that open by way of assistance from a spring – with no manual action, such as the flick of a thumb on a stud or peg near the base of the blade – are generally referred to as automatic.

The legal definition of switchblade does not include all automatics, depending upon how the specific jurisdiction statutorily defines the term switchblade. And, of course, not all automatics are switch-blades. State law definitions are often different from federal law definitions. Historically, the federal government has officially recognized switchblades as having sporting and utilitarian applications. The quote cited above came about in response to the ill-advised congressional proposals to enact federal restrictions on switchblades in the late 1950s.

Given the vilification of switchblades, some people might be surprised to learn that the U.S. Department of Justice opposed this law. The agency honestly recognized the lawful uses of switchblades. Additionally, the Department of Commerce also opposed the law and stated as follows:

Al Mar Auto-SERE
First Production
Automatic Knife

"To us, this [switchblade law] ignores the needs of those who derive and augment their livelihood from the outdoor pursuits of hunting, fishing, trapping, and of the country's sportsmen, and many others. In our opinion, there are sufficient of these that their needs must be considered." – Sinclair Weeks, secretary of the Department of Commerce.

Even though both the Department of Justice and the Department of Commerce opposed the law, political correctness still won the day in the legislature, and the law was passed. In doing so, a valuable tool for the worker and outdoorsman was unjustly defamed and stigmatized. Of course, this law, like all other "feel good laws" has had little or no effect on crime.

Unfortunately, many states followed the federal government's misguided efforts and passed switchblade laws. In some jurisdictions, an automatic is a "per se weapon" in which the burden of proof is shifted to the possessor to prove that he or she had a lawful purpose for the knife's possession. This places the knife owner at risk of being criminally charged and having to defend one's possession of a switchblade. It creates a "presumption of illegality."

Because of the variety of automatic knife mechanisms and the technical aspect of each statutory definition, some knives may qualify as automatics even though they are not readily recognizable as such.

Other knives may appear to be automatics, yet they lack key legal characteristics for making them such. A good example of this is assisted-opening folders that use a "torsion bar" mechanism, for quick extraction of the blade. These knives have no button in the handle for releasing the blade, but once the user of the folding knife begins opening the blade via the thumb stud or other means, the spring assists in opening the blade the rest of the way. These knives do not qualify as switchblades under federal law.

In 2009 the federal law was amended to clarify that assisted opening knives are not switchblades. This was in response to an attempt by U.S. Customs to wrongly declare them as switchblades.

Some individual jurisdictions still might take a different view and try to "push the envelope". I've personally handled a case where the state tried to allege that the classic Buck 110 hunting knife was prohibited as a "switchblade and/or gravity knife" because it had been well-used by its owner, and the blade could be opened with one hand by applying what the state called "centrifugal force." The case was eventually dismissed.

TYPES OF SWITCHBLADES

Whether or not a particular folding knife meets the given statutory definition for "switchblade" is often the determining legal issue. Modern automatics utilize a variety of spring mechanisms and locking devices. These include:

Coil spring: In which a spring is wound around a pivot pin and attached to the blade on one end, and the handle on the other. The button on the knife locks the blade open and closed against the pressure from the spring.

Curved spring: more or less a classic spring mechanism with a leaf-type spring that curves upward, presses against the tang of the knife blade and propels it outward.

Compressed spring - aptly named because the blade compresses a spring and must be "cocked" prior to use. This type propels the blade straight out the front of the handle.

Straight-line spring or end-line spring - with a blade that fires both in and out, which utilizes a unique mechanism that simultaneously compresses the spring and releases the blade on each up-and-down movement of the button on the knife. This is often referred to as an "out the front" or OTF.

Pull-spring - a term that refers to a spring that pulls the blade open by way of a coil running down the length of the knife.

This is not an exhaustive list of every type of spring mechanism but rather a sampling of the types of spring mechanisms generally encountered.

A relatively new development, which has gained popularity, is the double-action automatic, a switchblade that opens and closes like a traditional lock-back folder (with a locking mechanism on the spine of the handle), yet conceals a secret release that also opens the knife automatically. Double-action automatics open by way of a hidden button, a bolster release, or even a handle-scale release. The number of types of double-action, secret openers are only limited to the creativity of knife makers.

Regardless of the type of mechanism, switchblades have been produced for specific lawful purposes. One noted example of a sporting switchblade incorporated a hilt that doubles as a shell puller for a 16-gauge shotgun on one side and for a 12-gauge on the other. This automatic knife was clearly made as a trusty pocketknife for a shotgun hunter.

Automatics have been made in every conceivable blade shape for every kind of purpose. There are automatic knives with bowie blades, drop-point blades, serrated edges, sheepsfoot blades, can opener blades, screwdrivers, files, florist square points, budding, pruning, and combination blades with cap lifter and wire benders.

Whatever mechanism a given automatic employs, the question becomes, "Does a pocketknife with a blade that opens automatically have a lawful purpose?" Not only does such a knife have the same lawful purpose as any other folding knife, an automatic knife has special features that make it even more suitable for a variety of lawful uses.

It is obvious that an automatic knife can be used to skin a deer, clean a fish, cut a stern line, chop bait or other general sporting tasks called for by an outdoorsman. The advantages with an automatic come in the form of performance accomplished with the use of only one hand (same as with a fixed blade), yet the ability to have the convenience and the safety of a folding pocketknife.

Falling from a tree stand with a fixed blade knife could cause the blade to penetrate the sheath and injure its owner. A folding knife poses no such danger. Imagine a bow hunter working his or her way hauling line up the tree stand, holding it with on hand and having to cut through twigs caught in the pulley. With an automatic knife, the bow hunter can retrieve the knife, open the blade, keep a firm grip on the hauling line and maintain balance on the tree stand. The bow hunter thereby effectively experiences convenience and safety.

How many countless times has a fisherman made an intricate knot with his monofilament line while holding his fishing rod and reel with one hand, and suddenly realized the need to cut off excess line? Again, an automatic

*Dalton Crusader Out
the Front Automatic Knife*

knife allows for one-hand operation without losing a grip on
the fishing pole, the line or the
knot. How many times has a boater
needed to hold a line and cut it without letting go? Accomplishing
this task with an automatic knife is easy, safe, and efficient.

How about the hunter who has just shot a trophy big-game animal on a freezing cold winter
day and needs to do the initial field dressing? With an automatic knife, the hunter can access the
knife without ever having to remove winter gloves and risk exposure to the elements. Try opening a
traditional pocket knife blade with winter gloves on! Additionally, when dressing game, an outdoorsman often needs one hand to manipulate and control the carcass and another hand to access and
open a blade.

Lawful activities are not limited to hunting and fishing. How many outdoor emergencies can one
imagine in which having the availability of a folding knife that opens automatically can mean the difference between life and death? Skydivers, hang gliders, and other aerial sportsmen have a need to both
control their craft and access a folding knife with one hand. Mountain climbers clearly need one-hand
access to a pocketknife when pursuing their sport.

Having a folding knife protects the safety of its owner because, when closed, the knife blade is safely
contained within its handle. A switchblade is safer than many other folding knives because it can lock
closed and most have an extra safety lock further securing it so it stays closed.

An exposed blade is never present unless the owner has consciously opened the knife. It is for this
reason that the U.S. government issued Schrade Cutlery Co. Presto switchblades to American para-
troopers during World War II. The U.S. Armed Forces still issue and utilize automatic knives for many
of the same practical reasons that make them an appropriate choice for outdoorsmen.

The lawful uses of an automatic knife go far beyond those of traditional pocketknives, yet the honest
citizen is still left to deal with the laws concerning switchblades, which are counter-intuitive and illogical. Even though an automatic is clearly an ideal choice for a pocketknife, the laws and undeserved
stigma associated with the switchblade have created a legally perilous situation.

There are many who recognize the inherent technological advantage of an automatic knife. Unfortunately, the risk of being prosecuted under unjustified switchblade laws plainly outweighs the advantages of carrying one.

The Federal Switchblade Act was enacted on August 12, 1958. The Senate committee recommended that the bill be passed to control the "SWITCHBLADE MENACE." The Senate committee found
juvenile delinquents carry switchblade knives as "frequently part of the perpetrator's equipment." The
Senate committee declared:

*"The switchblade knife is, by design and use, almost exclusively the weapon of the thug and the de-
linquent. Such knives are not particularly adapted to the requirements of the hunter or fisherman, and
sportsmen generally do not employ them. It was testified that, practically speaking, there is no legitimate
use for the switchblade to which a conventional sheath or jackknife is not better suited."*

Over 50 years later, the impact of the act is now ripe for analysis. Was the Senate committee justified in its findings and recommendations? One can hardly go to a gun or knife show today and not encounter switchblades of all types. Many of these switchblade knives are made in the United States and are of the highest quality in both design and manufacture. There are handmade, custom variations; high-end factory production; and imported variations that range from gems to junk.

In order to do a proper analysis, one must first understand the federal switchblade laws. The best method which I have found to explain any subject of law is by way of a question and answer format.

Q. How is a "switchblade knife" defined under federal law?
A. In order for a knife to qualify as a switchblade, it must have the following features:

1. It must be a knife.

2. It must have a blade which opens automatically.

3. It must open automatically by either A. hand pressure on a button or other device in the handle of the knife or B. by operation of inertia, gravity, or both.

Q. Are all one-hand opening knives defined as a "switchblade knife" under federal law?
A. No. A qualifying knife must open "automatically" by way of a "button or other device" which is in the "handle." Alternately, a qualifying knife must open by "inertia, gravity, or both." Assisted opening knives are specifically not "switchblades" under federal law, which excludes "a knife that contains a spring, detent, or other mechanism designed to create a bias toward closure of the blade and that requires exertion applied to the blade by hand, wrist, or arm to overcome the bias toward closure to assist in opening the knife."

Q. Who is exempt under federal law?
A. The federal law prohibits interstate commerce in switchblade knives; however, there are specific exceptions under 15 U.S.C. 1244 in which the prohibitions do not apply. These exceptions are as follows: transportation of switchblade knives by any common carrier or contract carrier in the ordinary course of business; pursuant to contract with the armed forces; armed forces members or employees thereof acting in the performance of his duty; or individuals with only one arm (blade length of three inches or less.)

Q. Are law enforcement officers exempt under federal law?
A. 15 U.S.C. 1244 does not specifically exempt law enforcement officers. One must go to 18 U.S.C. 1716 to even find an argument that law enforcement officers might be exempt. 18 U.S.C. 1716 is a U.S. Postal Service law, which elaborates on mailing switchblades.

The following persons are allowed to "convey" switchblades via the U.S. Mail:
(1) civilian or armed forces supply or procurement officers and employees of the federal government in connection with the activities of the federal government; (2) to supply or procurement officers of

**Al Mar
Cigar Cutter
Automatic Knife**

the National Guard, the Air National Guard, or militia of a state in connection with the activities of such organizations; (3) to supply or procurement officers or employees of any state, or any political subdivision of a state or territory, in connection with the activities of such government.

Law enforcement officers could arguably be considered federal or state employees and therefore might qualify as exempt.

Q. Are manufacturers or dealers exempt under federal law?

A. Manufacturers of such knives or bona fide dealers are exempt in connection with any shipment made pursuant to an order from any qualified person designated in the exemptions. The U.S. Postal Service may require that any person proposing to mail switchblades explain in writing to the satisfaction of the U.S. Postal Service that same will not be in violation.

Q. Is it unlawful to advertise "switchblade knives" under federal law?

A. Under certain conditions it is unlawful. Any advertising, promotional, or sales matter, which solicits or induces the mailing of switchblade knives, is likewise nonmailable. Whoever knowingly deposits for mailing anything declared nonmailable (unless in accordance with the rules and regulations authorized to be prescribed by the U.S. Postal Service) shall be fined or imprisoned not more than one year, or both.

Q. How come there are plenty of knives available which do qualify as a "switchblade knife" under federal law?

A. Commerce in switchblades dramatically increased after 1984 when the State of Oregon's Supreme Court found in the case of State v. Delgado that switchblades were protected under Oregon's state constitutional right to keep and bear arms. Manufacturers began to make and distribute these knives in Oregon. Manufacturers and dealers in other states began to look at their states' laws, and production was started in other jurisdictions as well.

A broad position was taken by the manufacturers and dealers relying upon the exceptions of 18 U.S.C 1716 and Title 15, who set up dealer networks in these knives. Once the knife leaves the manufacturer and goes to a dealer, there is no actual control upon the dealer for the knife's distribution beyond the dealer sale. Hence, the American switchblade market exploded, and the time has now come to revisit the "wisdom" of the anti-switchblade laws.

*WWII German
Paratrooper
Gravity Knife*

CHAPTER 5:
FACTS & LAW ABOUT "BALLISTIC KNIVES"

"¿COMO ESTA?" asks Arnold Schwarzenegger in the 1985 movie "Commando," as he fires a ballistic knife into the chest of the bad guy, which amazingly causes immediate death. Hollywood never misses a chance to help fuel a misguided weapons ban, and the ballistic knife was no exception. In May 1986, Francis Ford Coppola's son and Ryan O'Neal's son were in an automobile accident in which Coppola's son died. O'Neal's son was charged with reckless driving and possession of a ballistic knife. Hollywood elitism and hypocrisy is nothing new.

Schrade Vietnam Era Parachute Automatic Knife

What made the ballistic knife so frightening to career politicians, media talking heads and assorted hoplophobes (those who irrationally fear weapons) is that it's a knife that shoots! A ballistic knife is essentially a blade attached to a hollow handle that fits inside of another outer hollow handle that contains a coil spring. The coil spring compresses inside the handle, and a latch holds the knife blade down against the spring pressure. When the latch is released, the knife and attached inner handle launch and "go ballistic".

Politically, the ballistic knife helped fill the gap between guns and knives. It enabled knife haters to join ranks with gun haters and both had a common inanimate object to wail and screech about.

Sure enough, one year after "Commando" was released, the Ballistic Knife Prohibition Act of 1986 was signed into federal law by President Ronald Reagan, as part of the Anti-Drug Abuse Act of 1986.

In addition to the ballistic knife being slandered and falsely linked to drug abuse, this was the newest national attack on knives since the 1958 Federal Switchblade Laws. Republican Sen. Alfonse M. D'Amato held a news conference pushing for and spinning the proposed ban. He announced that a ballistic knife "is a favored weapon used by drug dealers." He further proclaimed, "Ballistic knives are

Fixed blade knife with sheath that goes in and out.

**Microtech HALO
Out the Front
Automatic Knife**

at least as dangerous as switchblade knives that have been banned since 1958.

The hype surrounding ballistic knives did not help matters. The knives were advertised for sale in *Soldier of Fortune* Magazine with the pitch "The Commies Had It. We Stole It. Now You Can Buy It!!!!" Ballistic knives were advertised as being able to "kill swiftly and silently." Sen. D'Amato claimed a ballistic knife to be a "dangerous weapon, a terrorist weapon." He further declared, "Ballistic knives have no legitimate sporting purpose. They are sought by professional criminals because they are easily concealed and capable of penetrating a policeman's bulletproof vest."

Democrat Rep. Mario Biaggi (a well-known anti-gun politician and a sponsor of the so-called "Cop Killer" bullet ban) appeared at the news conference and asserted that ballistic knives were the "latest in cop-killer technology," and that the ballistic knife can "…fire its blade like a bullet," and "penetrate police bullet-resistant vests."

He stated he had bought his ballistic knife via mail order from the Florida Knife Corp. by putting the $79.95 on his credit card. Biaggi stated "… there were no questions asked. I could have been anybody. The ballistic knife is totally accessible to anyone who wants it." At the news conference the typical "dog and pony show" was conducted by a New York police officer who fired a ballistic knife from 30 feet at a silhouette target of a person.

Of course, there were no known cases at that time of anybody ever being killed by a ballistic knife, no less any reported cases of a police officer being shot at by a "drug dealer or terrorist" (or anybody else for that matter) with a ballistic knife. Furthermore, I could not find any Gallup Poll taken of drug dealers inquiring as to whether a ballistic knife was their "preferred weapon" of the 1980s, but somehow I doubt it considering the ready availability of cheaper and more effective black market arms.

The Florida Knife Corp. issued a statement that their ballistic knives do NOT penetrate bulletproof vests, but noted that any ice pick could penetrate a bulletproof vest. Bulletproof vests are NOT ice pick proof, however banning ice picks is not as politically correct or headline grabbing. A ballistic knife has as much "sporting purpose" as any throwing knife. Since when is the "sporting purpose test" applied to knives, anyway? What sporting purpose does an 8-inch chef's knife have? Then again, why should facts get in the way of a feel-good knife ban?

The ballistic knife is also known as the K96 knife, the Spetznan knife, the KGB knife, the Pillum ballistic knife, the Spy knife, the Special Forces knife, the Florida knife, the Bloody Mary knife and the Flying Dutchman knife. That's a lot of names for one knife! Some claim that the knife was developed for the KGB. Others claim it was made for the Soviet Special Forces, called the "Spetznaz." All seem to agree that the ballistic knife design is Russian in origin. With enough vodka anything is possible.

Federal law defines a ballistic knife under 15 U.S.C. § 1245 (d), "Ballistic knife" defined: As used in this section, the term "ballistic knife" means a knife with a detachable blade that is propelled by a spring-operated mechanism.

A question: Which of the following weapons is legally impossible for an average law-abiding citizen to lawfully acquire in interstate commerce under federal law?

1. Live hand grenade

2. Suppressed (silenced) .22 pistol

3. Short-barrel (sawed off) shotgun

4. An UZI submachine gun

5. Browning .50 M2 machine gun

6. Howitzer

7. Ballistic knife

You guessed it! A ballistic knife is utterly impossible for an average law-abiding citizen to acquire in interstate commerce. All of the other items listed are heavily regulated by federal law, but are technically obtainable with the proper paperwork, investigation and approval by the federal government.

Federal law prohibits a ballistic knife under 15 U.S.C. § 1245 as follows:

(a) Prohibition and penalties for possession, manufacture, sale, or importation.

Whoever in or affecting interstate commerce, within any territory or possession of the United, States, within Indian country (as defined in section 1151 of title 18), or within the special maritime and territorial jurisdiction of the United States (as defined in section 7 of title 18), knowingly possesses, manufactures, sells, or imports a ballistic knife shall be fined as provided in title 18, or imprisoned not more than 10 years, or both.

Ballistic Knife

(b) Prohibition and penalties for possession or use during commission of federal crime of violence.

Whoever possesses or uses a ballistic knife in the commission of a Federal crime of violence shall be fined as provided in title 18, or imprisoned not less than 5 years and not more than 10 years, or both.

(c) Exceptions.

The exceptions provided in paragraphs (1), (2), and (3) of section 1244 of this title with respect to switchblade knives shall apply to ballistic knives under subsection (a) of this section. The exceptions for ballistic knives under 15 U.S.C. § 1244 are as follows:

(1) any common carrier or contract carrier, with respect to any switchblade knife shipped, transported, or delivered for shipment in interstate commerce in the ordinary course of business;

(2) the manufacture, sale, transportation, distribution, possession, or introduction into interstate commerce, of switchblade knives pursuant to contract with the Armed Forces;

(3) the Armed Forces or any member or employee thereof acting in the performance of his duty."

The federal law on ballistic knives is very similar to federal law on switchblades, except that the switchblade law exception for "the possession, and transportation upon his person, of any switchblade knife with a blade three inches or less in length by any individual who has only one arm" does not apply to ballistic knives. One-armed individuals are forced by federal law to have to throw their knives by hand just like everyone else.

There are many books that deal with the subject of knife throwing for both fun and combat. A knife can be thrown with substantially more power and accuracy than can be achieved by firing a ballistic knife. This fact alone makes the ballistic knife ban patently absurd and useless. Any decent fixed-blade knife can be thrown (although throwing your handmade, Damascus, ivory-handled bowie is not recommended).

But why should facts and logic stand in the way of any headline-grabbing politician pushing a weapons ban and holding news conferences? Even Arnold Schwarzenegger, in "Commando," first dispatches two bad guys at the same time by THROWING two knives at them before he resorts to utilizing his ballistic knife on a third antagonist.

Okay, the law is ridiculous, so what's the problem? Who needs to own a ballistic knife anyway, right? Well, here is the problem: the ballistic knife ban is a KNIFE BAN, and just because it isn't your ox being gored does not mean you should ignore it. This ban paves the way for more knife bans. The politicians see our knife rights as "easy pickings." They can look like they are doing something about crime, terrorism or drug dealing, when in reality it's just another hit on our knife rights.

Ballistic knife bans lay the groundwork for further knife bans and for activist courts to be judicially dishonest and to prohibit other lawful knives and weapons that are not ballistic knives.

Don't believe it? Then you have obviously not read State of Florida, Appellant, v. Pariya Darynani, Appellee, 4th District, Case No. 4D99-4172. In this case, the Florida Court banned formerly lawful automatic/switchblade knives under the guise of Florida's ballistic knife ban. The case is a classic example of anti-knife bias and the abuse of our knife rights that a wrongful knife ban can cause.

Guardfather
Out the Front
Automatic Spike.

New Jersey's ballistic knife ban has even more potential for abuse. The New Jersey ballistic knife ban was signed into law by Republican Gov. Thomas Kean, who stated, "We have to restrict the flow of knives that serve no useful or lawful purpose." If the animal rights activists wanted to push it, New Jersey's ballistic knife law is so overly broad that archery and bow hunting are threatened and could be banned. New Jersey Law defines a ballistic knife as follows:

"Ballistic knife" means any weapon or other device capable of lethal use and which can propel a knife blade."

Bows and crossbows can all shoot broadhead arrows. Broadheads are and/or contain razor-sharp knife blades. Is a compound bow with a broadhead arrow a "weapon or other device capable of lethal use and which can propel a knife blade?" Of course it is! Sure, it was not the intent of the New Jersey Legislature to ban archery and bow hunting, but it was not the intent of the Florida Legislature to ban switchblades/automatics, either, and yet the Darynani court did just that!

Unfortunately, knife aficionados were not organized, prepared, or ready for the ballistic knife fight in the mid-1980s. We were never warned about the future effect and ramifications of ballistic knife bans on our knife rights. We dramatically lost on the ballistic knife issue and are now paying the price. It is time to join knife rights organizations, educate others and not repeat our mistakes. ¿Comprende?

**Italian Kris Blade
Stiletto Stag Handle
Automatic Knife**

**Lighter with
Automatic Knife**

**Barrel
Take-down
Folding Knife**

CHAPTER 6:
FACTS & LAW ABOUT "KNUCKLE KNIVES"

Knuckle knives are not a topic on "Quick Points" charts found in the federal and state guides in this book because only two jurisdictions specifically ban knuckle knives: Delaware and New York. However, most states ban metal knuckles, brass knuckles, iron knuckles, plastic knuckles, wood knuckles, etc. by themselves, without reference to knives. So, in all those states knuckle knives would be a gray area of the law. Here is Delaware's ban on knuckle knives:

11 D.C. § 1452. Unlawfully dealing with knuckles-combination knife; class B misdemeanor

A person is guilty of unlawfully dealing with a knuckles-combination knife when the person sells, offers for sale or has in possession a knife, the blade of which is supported by a knuckle ring grip handle. Unlawfully dealing with a knuckles-combination knife is a class B misdemeanor.

Delaware's ban might cover Karambit style knives as well depending how a "ring grip handle" is determined to mean by the courts. New York's definition reads as follows:

§ 265.00 Definitions.

5-b. "Metal knuckle knife" means a weapon that, when closed, cannot function as a set of plastic knuckles or metal knuckles, nor as a knife and when open, can function as both a set of plastic knuckles or metal knuckles as well as a knife.

Dalton "IRA Interrogator" Automatic Knuckle Knife

New York's definition specifically includes folding knives that have knuckles. Both laws ignore the historic value and interest that make knuckle knives a fascinating collectable and their utilitarian uses.

While looking through a vintage Bannerman Catalog of Military Goods, it was amusing to see all the armament that citizens could freely purchase back in 1927. Bannerman sold handguns, cannons, Gatling guns, artillery shells, spears, crossbows, swords, bayonets, and strange weapons of all types from around the world with no questions asked and no paperwork required. All except for the World War I knuckle knife. For purchase of that item, a warning in the old Bannerman catalog advised:

"PLEASE NOTE that the restrictions regarding dangerous weapons apply to sale of these trench knives. We must have permit from your chief of police with your order."

I could not find any law back then requiring or authorizing a so-called "knuckle knife permit," and, frankly, I never heard of such a thing. Unfortunately, this same ignorance and discrimination of the past continues today in regard to the knuckle knife.

A knuckle knife is no more or less deadly than other fixed blade, including a 6-inch chef's knife. But knuckle knives look mean. That's all that matters in the illogical mind of someone suffering from hoplophobia. Hoplophobia is an irrational fear of weapons, a term coined by the late Lt. Col. John Dean "Jeff" Cooper. Hoplophobia-driven bans of knuckle knives failed to recognize the following:

1). The important historical and collector significance of knuckle knives;

2). The utilitarian function of knuckle knives;

3). The added safety afforded to the users of a knuckle knives.

As noted above, the state of New York has just such a law specifically defining and of course prohibiting knuckle knives. According to a letter to the Village of Walden from Laura Etlinger, NY assistant solicitor general in charge of opinions, this law even prevents a town or museum from possessing or displaying such a knife. The following is from her letter:

"In sum, none of the exemptions …covers possession by a local government, municipal agency, or museum for display purposes. Nor are we aware of any other state law that exempts possession of per se illegal weapons when displayed for educational, cultural, or historical purposes."

Although this letter was written primarily concerning display of switchblades, it nonetheless covers knuckle knives. It is a sad day indeed when political correctness and anti-knife ignorance prevent historical and educational displays. It is particularly a shame when such

WWI Trench
D-Guard
Knuckle Spike

WWI Trench L. F. &C.
Knuckle Knife

laws directly affect a town like Walden, whose history is so intimately tied to America's cutlery industry. From the 1890's through the 1950's, Walden was home to prominent knife companies, including Schrade Cutlery Company, Press Button Knife Company, New York Knife Company, and Walden Knife Company.

Some of the earliest descendants of knuckle knives in Western civilization can be traced to the 1500s, when common knuckle knives were often referred to as "left-hand daggers" or "main gauches," and primarily used in conjunction with rapier dueling. The knives typically sported large, curved and triangular-shaped knuckle guards, and were often extravagantly engraved.

Soldiers employed the knives in close-quarter combat as supplements to their swords. Duelists used the knuckle guards for striking, as well as for protecting the weaker hand. A blade-catching technique was also employed with the guards of main gauches. Original examples of the knives are highly valuable, yet absurd laws prevent a collector from owning and enjoying such a prize collectible.

As dueling with swords faded into history with the prevalence of firearms, knives took on other roles as both defensive weapons and indispensable tools.

In addition to the utilitarian value of edged tools for skinning animals, cutting food, and general tasks, knives always had the advantage of "never running out of ammunition."

Col. James Bowie's exploits popularized the style of knife that later bore his name – the bowie knife – for defense. The southern states became known for adopting a version of the bowie with a knuckle guard. Knuckle knives became a symbol of Civil War rebels and are commonly referred to today as Confederate D-guard bowies.

The Confederate D-guard bowie generally consists of a large, clip-point blade and a handle with an integral knuckle guard curving around from the pommel to the hilt, forming a "D." Soldiers often made broken swords into D-guard bowie knives, and Gen. Robert E. Lee carried one made from his own lopped-off weapon.

The knuckle knife's association with the Confederacy is readily apparent today, as Browning's knife division sold an impressive "Living History" Robert E. Lee Commemorative D-guard bowie knuckle knife. The 8 ½-inch bladed knife has a wooden handle with a solid brass knuckle guard. The handle is fashioned from wood taken directly from a black oak that still grows on the grounds of Lee's former estate in Arlington, VA.

This knife was actually made by Buck Knives for Browning. Just as Confederate rebels cherished D-guard bowies in the past, the knives are highly sought after by collectors today.

As America entered World War I, the knuckle knife took on a prominent role in the trenches. American trench knuckle knives were the grandsons of Confederate D-guard bowies. The World War I Model U.S. M1917 and M1918 models had triangular blades and D-guards that sported spikey protrusions.

Though the American Cutlery Company manufactured most trench knives, Landers, Frary & Clark (L.F. & C.) and the Oneida Community Ltd. (O.C.L.) also made them.

The U.S. Model 1918 Mark I Trench Knife also made its debut during World War I. The model is instantly recognizable for its set of brass knuckles, "skull crusher" pommel and double-edged blade. It is a fearsome-looking knife, but looks don't kill and no knuckle knife has ever attacked anyone by itself. As far as World War I knuckle knives are concerned, L.F. & C. built most of them, with others made by Henry Disston & Sons, O.C.L. and the French manufacturer Au Lion.

Because World War I knuckle knives are so desirable, there are many modern reproductions. Accordingly, collectors should exercise care when investing in any knuckle knife supposedly dating back to that time period.

Knuckle knives also enjoyed popularity during World War II. By grinding the guards level to the handles for close-to-the-body fits, soldiers and other end users modified many World War I-era U.S. Model 1918 Mark I Trench Knives in the early 1940s. Modified in such a manner, the knife blades slid seamlessly into leather sheaths. Custom knife makers and several manufacturers produced knuckle knives during World War II. Custom knuckle knife makers included Taylor Huff, W.H. Messenger, Eugene Stone, and one of my heroes, M.H. Cole. Cole not only produced 300 magnificent handmade knuckle knives for the war effort, but he later wrote and illustrated the bible of military knife collecting – U.S. Military Knives, Bayonets and Machetes.

The World War II allied forces had a love affair with knuckle knives. The well-known British manufacturer Robbins and Dudley produced several variations of knuckle knives during World War I. The firms of Clements, Brown, J. Hibbert & Sons, Sotherland & Rhoden, Ibberson & Co. also manufactured knuckle knives. Such British knuckle knife manufacturers influenced the production design of the highly collectable BC-41 commando knuckle knife of World War II. The BC-41 was simply a set of brass knuckles with a blade protruding from the "palm" area. The BC-41 was soon replaced by the famous Fairbairn-Sykes commando knife.

The Australians also produced a large-bladed knuckle knife, often referred to as the "Ranger," with a jagged, brass D-guard. Though it's doubtful the U.S. Rangers employed the knives in World War II, Australian knives are frequently found marked "U.S." Nevertheless, Ranger knives are formidable and impressive knuckle knives of high collector value.

New Zealand also produced a knife that many U.S. troops purchased and carried during World War II. The New Zealand knuckle knife had a squared-off D-guard and leather sheath.

Formed from one piece of steel, the Middle East Commando Knuckle Knife is a fascinating World War II-era example. Referred to as a "Death Head" pattern, the knuckle guard is in the form of the upper region of a human skull, and the finger holes in the handle form the skull's eye sockets.

HideAway Knife

Dalton "Pay Up Sucker"
Automatic Brass
Knuckle Knife

The Middle East Commando combines art and function in a macabre way. The blade was available in clip-point or double-edged dagger configurations, and the "Death Head" knuckle knife pattern was even utilized for a ceremonial knife in 1950, honoring the wedding of the Princess of Jodhpur!

During the Vietnam conflict, Kevin Parsons produced a cast-aluminum-handled knuckle knife, and Eight Dollar Mountain Foundry (EDMF) did its part in the Gulf War effort by manufacturing D-guard bowies and other knuckle knives. EDMF combined classic blade shapes with heavy D-guard handles, including a large-blade smatchet, kukri and bowie. Such pieces are well-made knives, just as suitable for combat as for tackling vigorous camping chores.

The market also offers a number of inexpensive folding knuckle knives with one-hand-opening blades. Blade protrusions aid in one-hand operation and double as guards when the blades lock into the open position.

Another modern manufacturer, Dalton Combat Cutlery, came out with a well-made and beautiful switchblade in a brass knuckle pattern. The hook-shaped blade opens via a button on the handle, and the overall craftsmanship is top notch.

Knuckle knives are creatively designed, historic and fascinating to collect, and they all have that desirable "Wow!" factor. Their role in history is indisputable. Anti-knife "do-gooders" do bad by passing, supporting, and maintaining laws that declare inanimate objects intrinsically evil without consideration of their historic significance, artistic beauty, or usefulness. This is particularly true of the knuckle knife.

Hand protection, a surer, non-slip grip and less-than-lethal striking ability are the primary advantages of a knuckle knife. When cutting with any knife, the hand is in motion and therefore vulnerable to accidental cuts. Knuckle guards protect your hands. Scuba diving knives have been made with "knuckles" for just this reason.

Arguably, holes in the grips of common handsaws protect the hands. Shouldn't the handles of knives do the same? Accidental, self-inflicted knife wounds frequently reflect poor design or non-existent guards. A typical knuckle knife has one of the largest and most comprehensive guards found on any type of knife. It is not uncommon for a knuckle knife to incorporate a guard designed to protect each individual finger!

Traditional knuckle knife guards have the additional advantage of creating a more secure grip. With each finger locked in place, one's grip is solid and assured. Sliding up or down on the handle is impossible when using a knuckle knife. Dropping a knuckle knife takes deliberate effort. What knife could be safer?

Some folks, however, argue that a knuckle knife is too restrictive and lends itself to a "fencing" grip or other uncommon knife holds. These criticisms hold some merit. Ultimately it becomes a trade-off of safety versus flexibility. This is why knife users must ultimately choose what best suits their needs. Banning knuckle knives prohibits this choice and forces people to consider less safe and secure knives.

Knuckle knives allow for striking without cutting or stabbing. This type of action can often be less than lethal. Any knife can cut or stab with potentially deadly effect, but knuckle knife users are able to subdue opponents without necessarily killing them. Knuckle knife prohibitions absurdly ensure that only knives capable of death or serious bodily injury are used defensively.

In sum, knuckle knife bans remove the less-than-lethal option and force knife enthusiasts to have less safe knives that are more likely to slip or cut the users. These restrictions ignore the rich history of knuckle knives and punish law-abiding collectors while criminals simply ignore the law. Because the knuckle knife is no more deadly than any other pattern, any knife is in jeopardy of being banned under the same flawed anti-knife logic. If knife laws were invalidated based on illogic, knuckle knife bans would be one of the first to go.

Belt Buckle Knife

Jodhpur City India Ceremonial Royal Wedding Knuckle Knife

CHAPTER 7
FACTS & LAW
ABOUT "DAGGERS"

The view that daggers have only one purpose and that purpose is to kill people demonstrates a profound ignorance about the history and use of daggers. A dagger can mean the difference between life and death when facing outdoor challenges.

It is well established that daggers are and have been used by outdoorsmen in hunting, fishing, scuba diving, trapping, camping, hiking, backpacking, mountain climbing, skydiving, farming, and ranching. Utilization of daggers is common in any outdoor activity that involves or necessitates a reliable cutting tool.

Your humble writer has personally hunted and killed wild boar in South Carolina using only a Randall Model 2 knife with an 8-inch, double-edged blade. The 350-pound hog dropped faster when downed with the blade than if it had been shot. The Randall was particularly effective because it penetrated the wild boar's thick hide with ease and made for a quick and humane kill. A single-edge knife would not have been as effective.

Other personal examples of "sporting" daggers include: (1) my scuba diving knife, a well-worn, double-edge Wenoka that I have had since I was 13 years old; (2) my Tru-Bal double-edge throwing knife called to action when

German
Healthways
Skin Diving Knife

Buck Custom Shop Dagger

I informally compete in knife-throwing contests; (3) a double-edge Gerber Mark II that a good friend of mine never goes camping without, and that he carried in Vietnam; and (4) my Randall Model 12 "Arkansas Toothpick" with a 12-inch, double-edge blade (it beats flossing every time).

To thoroughly explore this topic, one must first define "dagger." There are various definitions that vary between sources. The A.G. Russell Online Knife Encyclopedia defines "dagger" as a "double-edge sheath knife with a symmetrical blade intended for stabbing." This is a fair and common view of what is generally thought of as a "dagger."

A hidden agenda can often be found in legal and statutory definitions that reflect an anti-knife bias. The problem is that false or unclear definitions of edged tools are employed to lump together dissimilar knives into one category. The same technique is used by the anti-gun crowd to exploit a "scary" gun, and use it as a "strawman" to ban several firearms falling under one umbrella definition. A great example of this is the state of California's definition of "dagger".

"Dagger" is broadly defined as "a knife or other instrument with or without a handguard that is capable of ready use as a stabbing weapon that may inflict great bodily injury or death."

Therefore, just about every knife without a handguard is prohibited from concealed carry, including other items as well, like chef knives, ice picks, knitting needles, and scissors. Hopefully no little old ladies carry their knitting needles and scissors in their handbag in California. What do "hand guards," or a lack thereof, have to do with the price of fish? Then, the intrinsically evil "knife" only has to be "capable of ready use as a stabbing weapon." Gee, that's a rather broad definition, wouldn't you say? Now the courts have to sort it out while the law-abiding knife owner suffers.

New Jersey takes another approach that makes the honest dagger owner "guilty until proven innocent." The Garden State's dagger law says: "Any person who knowingly has in his possession any gravity knife, switchblade knife, dagger, dirk, stiletto, billy, blackjack, metal knuckle, sandclub, slingshot, cestus or similar leather band studded with metal filings or razor blades imbedded in wood, ballistic knife, without any explainable purpose, is guilty of a crime of the fourth degree."

This contradicts fundamental fairness for the dagger owner by switching the burden of proof from the prosecution to the defendant. The law-abiding knife owner must prove an "explainable lawful purpose" as an affirmative defense to a jury of 12 folks who the prosecution will try to "pump up" about "why anyone would need such a knife." But what would one expect from a state that also makes possession of a "slingshot" a felony (in the same law cited above), thereby turning Bart Simpson and Dennis the Menace into felons.

Now compare California and New Jersey to Montana, which prohibits a person who "carries or bears concealed upon his person a dirk, dagger...sword cane...knife having a blade 4 inches long or longer," but then has the following exceptions for all persons who are "lawfully engaged in hunting, fishing, trapping, camping, hiking, backpacking, farming, ranching, or other outdoor activity in which weapons are of-

Randall Arkansas Toothpick Model 13

ten carried for recreation and protection."

At least Montana law specifically recognizes the sporting use of daggers. These exceptions say it loud and clear. Whether it is hunting, fishing, trapping, camping, hiking, backpacking, farming, ranching or other outdoor activity, Montana's legislators know that knives save lives and are an important tool of the outdoorsman.

Oklahoma also prohibits "any person to carry upon or about his or her person, or in a purse or other container belonging to the person "any dagger." However, Oklahoma, like Montana, also recognizes the sporting use of daggers. Oklahoma has important exceptions to this prohibition, even including historical reenactment! Oklahoma's insightful exceptions acknowledge:

1) The proper use of guns and knives for hunting, fishing, educational or recreational purposes;

2) The carrying or use of weapons in a manner otherwise permitted by statute or authorized by the Oklahoma Self-Defense Act;

3) The carrying, possession and use of any weapon by a peace officer or other person authorized by law to carry a weapon in the performance of official duties and in compliance with the rules of the employing agency; or

4) The carrying and use of firearms and other weapons provided in this subsection when used for the purpose of living history reenactment. For purposes of this paragraph, "living history reenactment" means depiction of historical characters, scenes, historical life, or events for entertainment, educations or historical documentation through the wearing or use of period, historical, antique or vintage clothing, accessories, firearms, weapons and other implements of the historical period."

Gerber Mark II Fighting Knife

Oklahoma has legislatively declared a "proper use" of knives for recreational purposes. The modern dagger serves an important role as today's man pushes the envelope with greater outdoor and survival challenges. The views expressed by Montana and Oklahoma reflect a practical understanding of the use of daggers and, significantly, the importance of daggers in history.

The dagger has a lineage reaching back to ancient times and has been a constant tool of man. The history of daggers demonstrates an established use of the knives for everything from daily utilitarian tasks to man's survival against nature.

Considered by many to be the preeminent authority on daggers, the legendary Bashford Dean wrote in his classic 332-page book, *The Metropolitan of Art Catalogue of European Daggers* that, "during these epochs, the dagger, partly because it could be used as a knife, was worn oftener than any other arm, and as it increased in usefulness, its forms multiplied. In a general way, it played a role which the swords in their own lines of specialization could not fill. It was par excellence an instrument of convenience and precision."

It is for this fact that the dagger holds a special place in the world of knives, and its sporting uses are undeniable.

Second only to the club as man's earliest weapon, edged instruments have been part of man's existence since the first chipped stone cut the hide of a hunter's kill. The use of two edges by primitive man can be seen in spears, arrowheads and handheld cutting tools, with these being the earliest known "daggers".

The earliest flint daggers had hilts made of wrapped natural material, like animal hide or skins. Such knives have been discovered in Egypt and date back to approximately 3,000 B.C. Similar pieces in Scandinavia date to between 1800 and 1500 B.C.

**Chris Reeve
Kathathu
Dagger**

According to *Daggers & Fighting Knives of the Western World from the Stone Age to 1900*. written by Harold L. Peterson, the Scandinavian daggers were so popular and vital during this time that archaeologists have actually named the period Dolktid or Dagger Period of Scandinavian history. The daggers were used for a multitude of purposes including hunting, skinning, butchering and many other tasks when a sharp edge was demanded.

Although flint and stone could take and hold a sharp edge, it was brittle, could break easily, and was difficult to repair. The advent of metal made a huge difference in the evolution of daggers.

One of the earliest metals to be utilized is believed to be copper. Daggers made of copper have been found in Mesopotamia, Egypt, India, and the Great Lakes region of North America. Copper worked better than stone as a knife blade, but being relatively soft, would bend easily and not hold an edge as well as desired. It was eventually discovered that if tin was added to copper, a harder allow could be created.

This then-new alloy, known as bronze, became one of the most significant technological achievements of ancient times.

The Bronze Age, as it was known, saw a tremendous growth in the production and use of daggers. As early as 2500 B.C., bronze daggers were being made in Mesopotamia. Bronze allowed the blades to be thinner and longer without the risk of failure.

After the Bronze Age, a new metal was used in the manufacture of daggers. Called "iron," it was sometimes left behind by meteors, and the Egyptians even called iron "black copper from the skies." Ancient iron was wrought by heating the metal in a fire and hammering it into a desired shape. Sometimes the iron picked up carbon from the fire and turned into a type of steel. Steel is technically iron with a percentage of carbon added to it.

This technique of "steeling iron" was first learned by the bladesmiths of the Hittite Empire around 1500 B.C., and it became a highly protected military and commercial secret.

Eventually, the secret became known and the popularity of steel in knives lives on to this day. Of course, modern forging techniques can be used to accomplish incredible things with high-tech steels. The ancients would surely marvel in awe at the quality and consistency of high-tech steels.

Modern-day daggers that utilize advanced technology give the outdoorsman a special edge in facing sporting challenges. From edge-holding ability to corrosion resistance, to the durability of the steel itself, a wide range of choices for individual application is available to the ordinary person.

The ability to choose a dagger as one's edged companion is a freedom that should not be taken away from law-abiding knife owners. It is particularly disturbing when the reason for the loss of liberty is pure politics, focused on selling a "bill of goods" to a gullible public by dishonest politicians.

The utilitarian and sporting use of daggers is a historical and provable fact. To defame the dagger as "only designed to kill people" is at best hyperbole, and at worst, an attempt to turn otherwise honest knife owners into criminals.

Any politician who promotes banning inanimate objects as a cure for crime fails to address the real problem — the criminals. Instead, the liberty-sucking politician has made the inanimate object the symbol and the scapegoat for the government's failure to tackle the hard issue.

Whether it is used for hunting, fishing, scuba diving, trapping, camping, hiking, backpacking, mountain climbing, skydiving, farming or ranching, the dagger is a useful outdoor tool. The use of daggers has been around for as long as there have been such double-edged knives in the hands of man.

Unfortunately, sometimes those daggers have been used to kill other men, but it is not the dagger's fault, but rather the fault of the hand that holds it.

CHAPTER 8
KNIVES AND THE INTERNET

The Internet is a wonderful tool that can help you research the history of a knife, the manufacturers' specifications of a knife, the value of a knife and, even to a certain degree, the legality of a knife. The Internet allows knife aficionados to keep up with the latest news on knife forums and to follow websites dedicated to their favorite makers, knife history, and knife rights. Never before have knife owners been able to respond so quickly to a threat against knife rights or to encourage efforts to repeal anti-knife laws.

However, there are legal issues to be concerned with when dealing with knives on the Internet. A number of companies and individuals sell knives on the Internet. There are auction sites for knives and various other means of listing knives for sale. When selling over the Internet, one's audience is virtually the world. International laws on knives can be complex. Receiving and shipping knives in and out of the United States has its own legal issues, including dealing with customs, and import or export restrictions.

Assuming one is staying within the boundaries of the United States, there are still plenty of pitfalls one must avoid. If the knife qualifies as a switchblade, gravity knife, or ballistic knife, placing it into interstate commerce could lead to legal troubles.

Buying or selling knives on the Internet may still require that certain taxes be paid. Shipping certain knives into jurisdictions that may prohibit them could lead to the shipper and the receiver being criminally charged.

Erickson
Women's Legs
Butterfly Knife

Al Mar Combat Smatchet

German Telescope in Handle Knife

WWII US M3 Boker with M6 Scabbard Fighting Knife

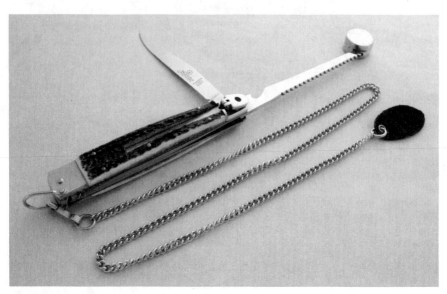

Hubertus Fishing Automatic Knife.

This is true even if the shipper warns that it is the recipient's responsibility to know if the knife is lawful.

Federal law does have certain narrow exemptions such as military and government contracts (see chapter on facts and law about switchblades). Additionally, federal law allows bona fide dealers to receive switchblades in interstate commerce if it is pursuant to the permitted exemptions.

This, of course, raises an issue because plenty of prohibited knives are flowing in interstate commerce that do not fall within exemptions. There is so much business in the transaction of these "prohibited" knives that essentially people are engaging in widespread civil disobedience. The irony is that as these knives become more and more mainstream, particularly with states that no longer prohibit them, it is helping to bring about the demise of these archaic laws.

I am not advocating breaking the law, but merely pointing out that various prohibitions throughout American history have been eliminated because of widespread disobedience to laws. The civil rights movement in America is full of these examples. The end of prohibition of alcohol came about in no small part due to so many people ignoring the law. Marijuana decriminalization and/or legalization, gay rights and Uber are just a few examples of how ignoring laws can help bring about change.

No matter how you feel about these issues, people's behavior often determines whether a law will be prosecuted or repealed.

Assisted-opening knives are not switchblades due to very specific legal features. Yes, they are one-hand opening knives that utilize a spring, but technically they are not switchblades. However, with assisted opening knives being sold mainstream in Wal-Mart, Home Depot, and giant sporting goods retailers throughout America, it gets extremely difficult to justify why switchblades would be singled out and prohibited.

Seriously, what is the big deal if a knife opens with one hand by way of a button or because I have to push the blade with my thumb?

The legal distinction, though actual, is downright silly. Every day millions of Americans use one-hand opening knives for lawful tasks, yet somehow a switchblade or gravity knife is still regulated under the law.

Civil disobedience and the blurring of what is legal verses illegal helps remove laws that have outlived any alleged usefulness. The Internet, which is largely a social media, is quicker to accept a social norm as being legal when it is not. This could be a trap for folks who admit to crimes online even though the law is irrational.

The Internet can be a gold mine for researching the history of a knife or a knife's providence. The history of any given model of knife, particularly in identifying any military pedigree, has been greatly aided by the Internet. Even identifying a particular knife by using for example, Google Images, can get a person on the right track to discovering all about a particular knife.

For example, a knife that can be traced to a certain person because a name is engraved on it can open up a wealth of information about that person and what they may have done with it. One can only imagine the experiences that accompanied that person's possession of that particular knife.

The Internet has also made it substantially easier for individuals to get involved with the knife rights movement. Organizations that fight for knife liberty have websites that make joining easy. With one click of a mouse, a person can go to a sign up page and participant in the fight for knife rights.

Of course, our adversaries can try to do the same thing, but knives, like guns in America, attract far more interest from those who love and appreciate them, then from those who hate them or irrationally fear them.

The Internet boils down to a form of communication. This form of communication is incredibly far-reaching, extremely affordable for the average person, and simple to use. Because of the special characteristics of the Internet, such communication can be an amazing bonanza of information that would have been virtually impossible to achieve 20 years ago. Yet on the other hand, the ability to get into trouble is far easier than it has ever been.

When selling knives over the Internet, one still must be careful not to break state or federal laws. Regardless of how irrational, illogical or just plain stupid any given knife law may be, you don't want to end up as a court case. The Internet has a lot of freedom and can prove invaluable when it comes to knives. However, one must be cognizant of the risks and always proceed with caution.

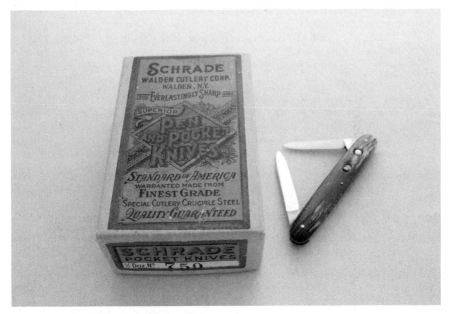

Original Schrade Push Button Box and Knife.

CHAPTER 9
THE ANTI-KNIFE RIGHTS MOVEMENT

> *The prestige of government has undoubtedly been lowered considerably by the prohibition law. For nothing is more destructive of respect for the government and the law of the land than passing laws which cannot be enforced. It is an open secret that the dangerous increase of crime in this country is closely connected with this.*
>
> — Albert Einstein, "My First Impression of the USA," 1921

From kitchen knives to swords, from pocketknives to priceless museum pieces, no sharp piece of metal is safe from prohibition in the United Kingdom. Doctors in the UK have gone so far as to demand a ban on pointy kitchen knives. Unfortunately, crackpot schemes that start across the pond often arrive on the shores of America. It is just a matter of time before our homegrown do-gooders try to impose the same insanity on Americans.

The modern gun control movement started in England around World War One, and at the time American gun owners scoffed at the ridiculousness of such an idea. "It will never happen here" was heard in many gun clubs and hunting lodges in the U.S. However, over 20,000 U.S. gun laws later, our gun rights have never been more "infringed."

So, fellow knife aficionados, do not take lightly the threat of "Knife Control." We must be fully aware of what the UK is doing as they destroy individual freedoms in the name of public safety.

Physicians writing for the *British Medical Journal* have actually called for a ban on pointy kitchen knives. They based their published research on interviews with all of ten chefs who felt points were not necessary on kitchen knives and that "long pointed kitchen knives…have little practical value in the kitchen."

After one stops laughing at this absurdity and after praying never to receive medical treatment from any such doctor foolish enough to publish such a "study," do NOT dismiss this as silly. This should be a warning sign that the UK knife ban propaganda effort is having the desired effect.

The UK newspaper *The Blackpool Gazette* announced, "A campaign to ban the sale of knives to under 18s …" In the UK, newspapers are blatant about their political efforts and do not even try to appear to be "fair and balanced." The *BBC News* blasted the following headline, "Mothers want tougher knife laws". The article goes on to state:

"The mothers' campaign is being backed by a national organization - the Victims of Crime Trust. Trust director Norman Brennan said: "Each year more people are murdered by knives than guns." … Mrs. Hadfield said: "Knives are instruments that can kill with a single stab, the same as a gun can with a bullet." Home Secretary David Blunkett announced last month that he was examining whether carrying a knife should carry equivalent penalties to firearms offences. "

It never fails. Bring in a bunch of hysterical, do-gooder "mums" and logic goes out the window. Focus on the inanimate object. Make it the "Bogey Man." And the media will make you their darling and support your "noble" goal. Another UK paper, *The Sunday Sun* reported that:

"Some parents criticized the Government's action on knife crime, and the press conference at a central London hotel also heard of fears that civil unrest could result if spiraling violence was not controlled. The group have set a three-month deadline for action, before they embark on "the largest petition this country has ever seen". The Knives Destroy Lives campaign, led by the victims of Crime Trust, has written to Lord Chief Justice Woolf and Chief Constables and delivered a letter to Downing Street."

The Knives Destroy Lives campaign is well established and making "progress" in the UK. What The Brady Campaign to Prevent Gun Violence is to guns in the U. S., the Knives Destroy Lives campaign is to knives in the UK.

Strikingly, their tactics are similar. The Brady Campaign had a Law Enforcement Relations (LER) Department that conned police into supporting their movement. The Brady Campaign is "working closely" with law enforcement throughout the country, "implementing programs to reduce gun violence in schools and communities…" and the Brady Campaign claims that "law enforcement has been critical to the success of the Brady Law…"

The Knives Destroy Lives campaign has also brought cops onto their side. For example, the North Wales Police proudly announces on their website "Only Cowards Carry Knives." They provide a "news release" which states in part:

"This anti knife campaign was launched for the first time at the Bay View shopping centre in Colwyn Bay, the campaign is being fully supported by the Welsh Football team. Knives and other sharp or bladed items can inflict serious injury or death…."However, as part of our ongoing strategy of reducing incidents of violence, this initiative is aimed at removing knives and sharply pointed objects from the streets of the area." … We are determined to tackle this and need the help and support of the public during this on-going campaign." … Anyone found in possession of such articles could face up to four years behind bars. … During the campaign, officers will also be using education as a tool in informing the youngsters of the dangers and consequences…Disposable bins will also be placed

Spyderco Vallotton
Double Action Hidden
Release Automatic Knife

Gil Hibben Silver Shadow dagger.

in various locations giving individuals an opportunity to dispose of such items or hand them in to the police station."

The Metropolitan Police in London also promoted anti-knife turn-in program with "Bins." An issue of *The Job* newspaper had an article entitled: "Southwark promotes a 'walk-in' knife amnesty." The piece went on to state:

"A knife amnesty in Southwark aims to reduce the number of offensive weapons on the streets of the borough. Bins have been placed in the foyers of Southwark's five police stations for six weeks since September 6 to enable residents to hand in knives anonymously."

Do you have any knives you wish to dispose of or hand in to the police? If so, feel free to send them to your humble author who will gladly take any such "sharply-pointed objects" and make good use of them. Better get rid of them now! The knives may attack by themselves at any moment and "inflict serious injury or death" on someone.

The UK's war on knives has specifically focused on propagandizing the young. There is a new British video game by an organization called Crimestoppers. Crimestoppers "is targeting young people (aged 13 – 16) with a new interactive campaign against knife crime, Game Over for Knives - for this year's Crimestoppers Week (19 – 25 September)."

The *BBC News* announced, that "Youngsters get anti-knives awards". The story goes on to state: "Nine youngsters who entered an anti-knives poster competition are to be given awards…"

The BBC also has a children's website called *Newsround* that is dedicated to influencing children into the anti-knife campaign. They boldly solicit "Your Views " on knives from children with their biased theme being "*Newsround* has been investigating why young people carry knives and what can be done to stop it." One such response came from Josie, age 10, of Christchurch who said, "I think knives should be banned and would feel really worried if I knew a friend who had a knife, they are really dangerous!"

As with most bans on inanimate objects, the UK's anti-knife movement has caused additional losses of other civil rights. The UK's War on Knives led to successful passage of a law known as the "Knife Act." This law has completely done away with any remaining privacy protections against unreasonable searches in the UK. The police are now empowered to search anyone, at any time, for any reason in order to check for knives.

Do not think for a moment that the anti-knife movement is going to stay in the UK. Like any cancer on freedom, it's going to spread. American knife owners must prepare to battle this cancer NOW or our knife rights surely will be in jeopardy. The UK may want to be a society of hoplophobes, but the U.S. must remain strong and free.

CHAPTER 10
THE KNIFE RIGHTS MOVEMENT

Imagine a state in America where ANY knife (regardless of blade length, design or operation) may be freely bought and sold (even no sales tax), owned, possessed, carried open or concealed, transported, displayed, collected, made, manufactured, produced, given, loaned, acquired, transferred, bequeathed, or inherited under state law with the only exception being possession in a courthouse and possession by a felon.

Imagine further that such a state accomplished this feat by repealing its knife laws which had been on the books for over 50 years that had banned switchblades, daggers, dirks, and stilettos.

Now consider that not one of its 425 politicians in the state's Democrat-controlled government (400 House members with Democrat majority, 24 Senators with Democrat majority and 1 Democrat governor) opposed the repeal. Then imagine that same government unanimously voting again to prohibit all local towns and municipalities from passing or enforcing any knife laws.

Believe it or not, on May 18, 2010, a unanimously passed HB1665 was signed into law which repealed New Hampshire's knife laws and on June 9, 2011, a unanimously passed HB 544 was signed into law which preempts New Hampshire cities, towns or political subdivisions from passing or enforcing any knife laws. This is the story of how a few dedicated activists and knife rights groups helped make it happen and how you can do the same in your state.

The above may sound politically impossible. When do 425 people agree on anything, much less agree twice? However, the above is 100% true and it shows that reforming archaic knife laws can be done anywhere and party affiliation is irrelevant.

Now is the window of opportunity for knife rights. There is no major national anti-knife movement or anti-knife group in America. Although in the United Kingdom there is such a movement, it has not yet crossed the pond. I am sure it eventually will because that is exactly what happened in Great Britain

**Vintage Philippine
Balisong Knife and Sheath**

Randall Miniature Model 27 Trailblazer Knife

Buck 110 purchased in 1974 for the author by his mother. Sheath made at Boy Scout Camp.

with their anti-gun push after World War One. There are important parallels between gun and knife rights issues. Knife owners must learn from the mistakes of gun owners so as not to repeat them.

The first national gun laws in the United States took place in the 1930's with the passage of the 1934 National Firearms Act (NFA). The NFA was passed largely due to media hype about gangland violence (Al Capone, Machine Gun Kelly, Bonnie and Clyde, etc.) The NFA was the only federal gun law until the passage of the 1968 Gun Control Act ('68 GCA). During the 1950's America was extremely gun cultured, and guns were no big deal. Having recently come out of World War Two, most men and many women were experienced and trained in the use of guns, including machine guns. Many schools had rifle teams and bringing your gun to school for hunting afterward was commonplace. This was the lost window of opportunity to repeal the 1934 National Firearms Act.

However, during the 1950's a new media hype arose making the switchblade its symbol, in the same way the submachine gun was the symbol of society's menace in the 1930's.

A magazine article in Women's Home Companion magazine came out in 1950 called "The Toy That Kills." It was a hyped up anti-knife propaganda piece designed to scare naïve housewives, and it worked.

Microtech / Terzuola Hand-Ground
Double Action Hidden Release
Automatic Knife

This fear-mongering was combined with movies like *Rebel Without a Cause, West Side Story* and similar movies and news stories constantly portraying violent youths with switchblades. This helped lead to the passage of the Federal 1958 Switchblade Act and many states passing their own knife bans as well.

Now is our chance to regain lost knife rights. America is generally not anti-knife. Many of our returning soldiers have direct positive experience with knives, including automatics. Although many public schools have a "zero tolerance" policy (I prefer to call it a "zero intelligence policy") for knives, just about every household has a knife.

What the 1950's were to guns, the 2010's are to knives. Switchblades are no longer the symbol of youth violence that they were made out to be in the 1950's. As Second Amendment activist Jeff Knox, Director of Operations for The Firearms Coalition, said in support of the New Hampshire knife rights effort: "I think that the people of New Hampshire can safely lower their guard now that the youngest members of the Sharks and the Jets are in their 80's."

At the 2009 Gun Rights Policy Conference in St. Louis, Jeff Knox submitted Resolution 6, which stated:

"Whereas: The banning of any personal tool or weapon has never resulted in increased public safety. Now therefore be it resolved by the delegates assembled at the Gun Rights Policy Conference in St. Louis, Missouri, this 27th day of September, 2009 that: We support the repeal of the Federal Switchblade Act and any other federal, state or local laws and regulations banning tools and weapons rather than addressing behavior."

The resolution adopted without discussion.

This was really a benchmark moment. It was the first time the repeal of all switchblade laws was unanimously supported by a national group of Second Amendment activists. Realizing that attitudes have changed since the 1950's regarding knives, I decided to fight for change in New Hampshire. Many people assisted in that effort, and we succeeded beyond belief.

Here are the steps to success:

1. Find dedicated legislators who believe in the cause of knife rights to sponsor a bill. They have to be committed and educated on the issue.

2. Get groups and individuals to support it. (Be aware that gun groups do not always support knife rights. In the past, knives have been banned to politically save guns from being banned.) Here are some of the supporters we got in New Hampshire: Knife Rights, Inc., Blade Magazine, American Knife and Tool Institute, Benchmade Knives, Ed Fowler, Suzanna Hupp, Sandra Froman, Citizens Committee for the Right To Keep and Bear Arms, Jews for the Preservation Of Firearms Ownership, Pro-Gun NH, New Hampshire Wildlife Federation, Sword Forum, Firearms Coalition, Cam and Company, Bloomfield Press, Americans for Tax Reform, NH Liberty Alliance, NH Arms Collectors Association, The New Gun Week, Guns Magazine, American Handgunner Magazine, Women & Guns Magazine, Knife World, Cut-

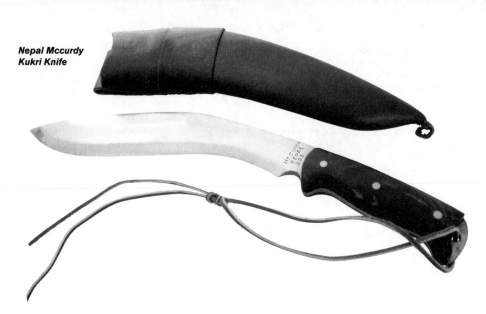

Nepal Mccurdy Kukri Knife

lery News, US Military Knives.com, Al Kulas, Smith & Wesson, Ethan Becker of Becker Knife and Tool Company, Classic Cutlery, Capital Copy, House Republican Alliance, NH Chiefs of Police Association, Radio Show Host Brian "Bulldog" Tilton, and Survival Topics.com.

3). Create a dedicated website for the bill where you can publicize supporters, promote the bill and give news updates. This can be done very inexpensively. Buy your domain name for as little as $10 from a provider and then get a free website from Weebly.com. This is exactly what we did. The New Hampshire website was www.knifelawonline.com. The page headings on the website included the following, which anyone is free to copy:

a. Home: (This page gives an introduction to website).

b. The Bill (post the actual bill along with sponsors).

c. How to contact your representative (include email and phone info)..

d. News Updates.

e. What People are Saying: (This page contains endorsements from famous supporters).

f. Articles, Blogs and Radio.

g. People to Know.

h. Resolution Six.

i. Contact (Very important page so supporters can get involved).

j. 125 Honest Citizens Who Use A "Switchblade, Dirk, Dagger, or Stiletto."

k. Knife Rights Raffle: (Our fund raiser which helped pay for our expenses).

l. The NEW LAW! (A celebration page after passage).

4. Hire a lobbyist. Working with Knife Rights, Inc., we were able to get a lobbyist to help with the bill's passage. Our lobbyist was former State Senator Bob Clegg, who was indispensable. We would not have succeeded without Bob's guidance and skill.

5) Prepare for the legislative committee hearings. This is a great chance to educate the public about knives. Bring in law-abiding people who have suffered under the knife ban. For example, we had one gun dealer testify that he was arrested and all his knives seized because he sold a switchblade to a

law enforcement officer, who he knew was a law enforcement officer, and he specifically sold him the knife because he was a law enforcement officer! Another dealer did a great job of showing the committee members the differences between various knives and how outdated and absurd the ban was.

6. Try to get law enforcement on your side. The New Hampshire Chiefs of Police Association supported the New Hampshire Knife Rights Bill. The modern automatic knife is a valuable tool for law enforcement, EMT's, firefighters and honest citizens who have a job that needs a knife. Because of New Hampshire's knife ban, a dealer could not sell a prohibited knife even to a cop!

7. Be ready to challenge and deal with any opposition. It may come from unexpected sources. It may be based on emotion stemming from an anti-knife bias. It might come from personality issues.

8). Get supporters to send letters, email, and call their legislators. This can be done inexpensively by email blasts from the supporting groups to their members. Flyers at gun shows and shops are also effective. Grassroots support really helps make a difference.

New Hampshire leads the U.S. by having the first presidential primary in the nation. New Hampshire also leads the U.S. by being the first state to repeal all of its anti-knife laws. It is a wonderful experience to have total knife freedom. I love knowing that I can enjoy my knives without worrying about being turned into a criminal due to some outdated foolish law that makes an inanimate object a crime. The more states that reform their knife laws, the more protected our knives will be from an anti-knife push in the future. Total knife freedom is possible. New Hampshire proves it beyond any doubt.

American knife aficionados have suffered long enough under bad laws. Through selective enforcement of laws which are unenforceable in practical terms, they exist only as a political memorial to symbolism over substance. The even greater wrong is that many of these laws knowingly perpetrated a fraud upon the American people. They were enacted for purely political purposes and promoted with blatant lies and a cover up of the facts that they did not want the American people to know.

The switchblade laws particularly defy logic. There are plenty of one-hand opening folding knives which do not legally qualify as a switchblade. These include stud-peg opening knives in which a stud/peg is in the blade; hole in the blade (e.g., Spiderco), spring-assisted blade (Kershaw), and the cam-type action (e.g. Camillus Cuda) just to name a few. Of course, most lock blades can be opened one-handed by using numerous techniques including the "snap-down", "whip wrist", "pinched blade", the "pocket catch" and the "stiff wrist". Lock blades can also be modified to open with one hand via the old "flickit", a screw on stud, or even friction tape on the blade. Plus assisted openers open with one hand and use a spring! With all these one-handers available, does a switchblade ban have any rational purpose?

Of course, fixed blades don't have to be opened at all! In addition to the huge variety of alternatives and the large number of imported switchblades, which make it past customs, there is now an active, growing market in American manufactured switchblades.

Buck 110 Converted to an Automatic Knife

By focusing on "loopholes" in the federal law and utilizing various state jurisdiction advantages, the American manufacturing of switchblades is alive and well. Some of the finest quality switchblades ever produced in the history of switchblade production are being made today in America.

So, why are there switchblade bans if it is useless, illogical and only represents a fraud sold to the American people in the name of fighting "crime" or "juvenile delinquency"?

These laws have clearly outlived any arguable use. The current federal switchblade law makes it a crime to possess, transport or manufacture "in interstate commerce" a switchblade. One faces five years in federal prison for a violation. No exemption or consideration is given to sportsmen, knife collectors, law enforcement officers, emergency rescue personnel, firefighters, sailors or any law-abiding civilian with the exception of a one-armed person. We must demand repeal of the Federal Switchblade Law.

The juvenile gang symbol is no longer a leather jacket tough guy with a switchblade. If we do not take action now, when we face future proposed laws which will add more knives to the banned list, we will wish that we had seized the opportunity to change the course of history. If we fail to try, we only have ourselves to blame. Yet, by trying, we will, at a minimum, raise the awareness of the foolhardiness of switchblade laws and other anti-knife laws.

Now is our opportunity to undue this wrong. We are stronger than ever before. We have knife publications, knife organizations and knife shows. We currently have the best political opportunity for success.

Knife owners, politically speaking, are similarly situated to gun owners in the 1950's. Gun owners had the political advantage in the '50's and could have fought for repeal/reform of the 1934 National Firearm Act (NFA). The 1934 NFA laid the legal groundwork for the 1968 Gun Control Act and other subsequent gun laws. Consider the following comparisons between knife owners of today and gun owners in the '50's.

1. Knife owners have no organized opposition, for example, no "Moms Against Knives" or billionaires with an axe to grind. Likewise, gun owners in the '50's had no organized opposition either.

2). Knife owners have pro-knife communications such as magazines, books, newsletters, CD's, Internet forums and chat rooms that discuss legislative issues. Gun owners in the 1950's had the NRA, whose primary focus was target shooting, marksmanship and gun safety. There was no NRA-ILA, which is the political arm of NRA. Magazines and books in the 1950's focused on shooting not on politics.

Dalton Assassin
Damascus Double Edge
Automatic Knife

ACA Campolin
Italian Stag Shotshell
Puller Automatic Knife

3. Knife owners have pro-knife political organizations and collector clubs which have ore political awareness than ever before. Gun owners had shooting and hunting clubs that were primarily focused on the enjoyment of firearms.

4. Knife owners have knife shows, bladesmithing seminars and exhibitions. Gun owners also had some gun shows and exhibitions, plus target-shooting matches, but politics was not a main area of anyone's concern.

5. Knife owners have a vested financial interest (we own blades). Gun owners also have a vested financial interest (we own guns); however, without a threat to these interests people did not take action.

6. The Second Amendment to the U.S. Constitution protects our right to keep and bear arms. Arms include knives. This right had not been yet been affirmed or applied in any meaningful way by the courts in the 1950's. No legal challenge to the NFA was brought.

7. The one thing that gun owners and knife owners absolutely have on their side is the truth. There are no bad knives just as there are no bad firearms. There are bad people, but laws that ban objects instead of behavior end up punishing the innocent.

US Air Force Survival Knife

Randall Set Model 12 and Model 5

Following is a battle plan to help you fight for your knife rights:

1. Educate yourself about the issue. Promote your position based on facts. Oppose the lies and misinformation about sharpened steel. Counter the "let's-ban-the-inanimate-objects" crowd with a line of reasoning about targeting criminals, not items having important lawful uses.

2. Talk first to your friends and family members. These are people who will listen to your opinion and give you a chance to sharpen your arguments and test your position. If you can convince your wife or husband, for instance, convincing a congressman should be a piece of cake.

3. Communicate with your elected officials. Write to your senator, congressman and the President and respectfully ask for repeal. Use both mail and e-mail. Explain that you're are a voting constituent and why the anti-knife laws must go.

4. Communicate with your local newspaper by sending a letter to the editor. More folks read letters to the editor than the professional op-ed pieces. Keep your letters rational, concise, clear and focused.

5. Communicate via knife publications, for example, letters to the editor. Such missives aren't always "preaching to the choir." Many knife owners don't understand the dynamics and importance of this issue. Let fellow knife owners know that they aren't alone in their beliefs. Let them know that they must take lawful actions for change and that the responsibility for protecting their knife rights is "yours, mine and ours".

6. Communicate via the Internet through websites, e-mail, forums, chat rooms, etc. Also, use the Internet to research and stay on top of knife rights issues.

7. Communicate on talk radio and cable television. Call-in shows are more popular than ever. Get on the air and promote the cause. Many of these shows have open-line days when any topic can be discussed. Warning: Don't be used by the host as a "straw man." Hosts may try to paint you as an extremist in the way they do with gun-rights advocates. Always be personable and rational in your presentation. Otherwise, a loss of credibility may occur. Remember, the idea is to win folks over to our side.

8. Communicate with knife organizations and collector clubs to fight for repeal of the knife laws and to protect our knife rights. Let directors, officers and members know how you feel about the cause. Vote for those who will stand up for our knife rights.

9. Circulate fact sheets and flyers at gun shows. Circulate petitions for the repeal of knife laws at knife and gun shows.

Repealing the useless political sham of anti-knife laws is not only possible but a morally worthy cause. These laws are a violation of our Constitutional right to keep and bear arms (see the chapter "Knives and the Second Amendment"). We must seize the moment and take the offensive!

CHAPTER 11
FEDERAL KNIFE LAW GUIDE

HOW TO USE THIS GUIDE

The "Quick Points" chart for each jurisdiction contains 100 legal questions answered by either "Legal", "Prohibited," or "Gray".

"Legal" means that it is generally lawful.

"Prohibited" means that it is generally unlawful.

"Gray" means that it is neither generally lawful nor unlawful and that there are ambiguities, conflicting law, exceptions, requirements or special considerations that may determine legality.

The laws provided have been selected because of their relevance to knives. Sections of the law may have been edited. It is also possible that some laws may have been inadvertently omitted due to legal research not revealing same. In other words, your author tried his best, but he is not perfect.

KNIFE RIGHTS MOVEMENT RATING SYSTEM

The Knife Rights Movement rating system grades the States, the District of Columbia, and the United States of America on a scale from one to five.

The highest rating is a five, which means that jurisdiction stands out for knife liberty. A rating of one means that jurisdiction has a disdain for knives and individual rights, and has arbitrary laws that treat honest citizens like criminals. Ratings of two, three, or four show where that jurisdiction is in regards to its respect for knife rights freedom. If a place has a rating lower than five, then there is work to be done there restoring knife liberty and continuing the Knife Rights Movement.

UNITED STATES OF AMERICA
KNIFE RIGHTS MOVEMENT RATING

★ ★ ★ ★ ☆

CUTTING TO THE CHASE

The United States of America restricts switchblades, gravity knives and ballistic knives. Federal law prohibits possession of switchblades or gravity knives within a territory or possession of the U.S., within Indian country or within the special maritime and territorial jurisdiction of the U.S. In the 50 states one is prohibited from introducing, or manufacturing for introduction, into interstate commerce switchblades or gravity knives. Ballistic knife possession, manufacture, sale, or importation "in or affecting interstate commerce" or within a territory or possession of the U.S., within Indian country or within the special maritime and territorial jurisdiction of the U.S. is prohibited.

Quick Points Concerning Federal Knife Law*

KNIFE TYPE	POSSESSION	(Open/Concealed) CARRY	SALE	MANUFACTURE
Assisted Opening	Legal	Legal/Legal	Legal	Legal
Automatic/Switchblade	Prohibited	Prohibited/Prohibited	Prohibited	Prohibited
Ballistic	Prohibited	Prohibited/Prohibited	Prohibited	Prohibited
Bayonets	Legal	Legal/Legal	Legal	Legal
Bowie	Legal	Legal/Legal	Legal	Legal
Butterfly/Balisong	Gray	Gray	Gray	Gray
Combat/Survival	Legal	Legal/Legal	Legal	Legal
Dagger	Legal	Legal/Legal	Legal	Legal
Dirk	Legal	Legal/Legal	Legal	Legal
Disguised	Legal	Legal/Legal	Legal	Legal
Fixed	Legal	Legal/Legal	Legal	Legal
Folding	Legal	Legal/Legal	Legal	Legal
Gravity	Prohibited	Prohibited/Prohibited	Prohibited	Prohibited
Hunting/Fishing	Legal	Legal/Legal	Legal	Legal
Machete	Legal	Legal/Legal	Legal	Legal
Razor	Legal	Legal/Legal	Legal	Legal
Stiletto	Legal	Legal/Legal	Legal	Legal
Sword	Legal	Legal/Legal	Legal	Legal
Throwing	Legal	Legal/Legal	Legal	Legal
Undetectable	Legal	Legal/Legal	Legal	Legal

Note: Some federal prohibitions do not necessarily apply to activity strictly occuring within a state (intrastate versus interstate).
*See all information above and below for more details.

SHARP TIPS ABOUT FEDERAL KNIFE LAWS

In 2009 the Federal law was amended to clarify that assisted openers were not switchblades. There are important exceptions to the federal knife laws including "manufacturers of such knives or bona fide dealers therein in connection with any shipment made pursuant to an order ... to civilian or armed forces supply or procurement officers and employees of the federal government ordering, procuring, or purchasing such knives in connection with the activities of the federal government; to supply or procurement officers of the National Guard, the Air National Guard, or militia of a State ordering, procuring, or purchasing such knives in connection with the activities of such organizations; to supply or procurement officers or employees of any State, or any political subdivision of a State or Territory, ordering, procuring, or purchasing such knives in connection with the activities of such government." U.S. Customs bars the import of balisongs.

EDGE –U- CATIONAL --- FEDERAL KNIFE LAWS
15 U.S.C. § 1241. Definitions
As used in this chapter--

(a) The term "interstate commerce" means commerce between any State, Territory, possession of the United States, or the District of Columbia, and any place outside thereof.

(b) The term "switchblade knife" means any knife having a blade which opens automatically--

(1) by hand pressure applied to a button or other device in the handle of the knife, or

(2) by operation of inertia, gravity, or both.

15 U.S.C. § 1242. Introduction, manufacture for introduction, transportation or distribution in interstate commerce; penalty
Whoever knowingly introduces, or manufactures for introduction, into interstate commerce, or transports or distributes in interstate commerce, any switchblade knife, shall be fined not more than $2,000 or imprisoned not more than five years, or both.

15 U.S.C. § 1243. Manufacture, sale, or possession within specific jurisdictions; penalty
Whoever, within any Territory or possession of the United States, within Indian country (as defined in section 1151 of Title 18), or within the special maritime and territorial jurisdiction of the United States (as defined in section 7 of Title 18), manufactures, sells, or possesses any switchblade knife, shall be fined not more than $2,000 or imprisoned not more than five years, or both.

15 U.S.C. § 1244. Exceptions
Sections 1242 and 1243 of this title shall not apply to--

(1) any common carrier or contract carrier, with respect to any switchblade knife shipped, transported, or delivered for shipment in interstate commerce in the ordinary course of business;

(2) the manufacture, sale, transportation, distribution, possession, or introduction into interstate commerce, of switchblade knives pursuant to contract with the Armed Forces;

(3) the Armed Forces or any member or employee thereof acting in the performance of his duty;

(4) the possession, and transportation upon his person, of any switchblade knife with a blade three inches or less in length by any individual who has only one arm; or

(5) a knife that contains a spring, detent, or other mechanism designed to create a bias toward closure of the blade and that requires exertion applied to the blade by hand, wrist, or arm to overcome the bias toward closure to assist in opening the knife.

15 U.S.C. § 1245. Ballistic knives
(a) Prohibition and penalties for possession, manufacture, sale, or importation

Whoever in or affecting interstate commerce, within any Territory or possession of the United States, within Indian country (as defined in section 1151 of Title 18), or within the special maritime and territorial jurisdiction of the United States (as defined in section 7 of Title 18), knowingly possesses, manufactures, sells, or imports a ballistic knife shall be fined as provided in Title 18, or imprisoned not more than ten years, or both.

(b) Prohibition and penalties for possession or use during commission of Federal crime of violence

Whoever possesses or uses a ballistic knife in the commission of a Federal crime of violence shall be fined as provided in Title 18, or imprisoned not less than five years and not more than ten years, or both.

(c) Exceptions. The exceptions provided in paragraphs (1), (2), and (3) of section 1244 of this title with respect to switchblade knives shall apply to ballistic knives under subsection (a) of this section.

(d) "Ballistic knife" defined

As used in this section, the term "ballistic knife" means a knife with a detachable blade that is propelled by a spring-operated mechanism.

18 U.S.C. § 1716. Injurious articles as nonmailable

(g) All knives having a blade which opens automatically (1) by hand pressure applied to a button or other device in the handle of the knife, or (2) by operation of inertia, gravity, or both, are nonmailable and shall not be deposited in or carried by the mails or delivered by any officer or employee of the Postal Service. Such knives may be conveyed in the mails, under such regulations as the Postal Service shall prescribe--

(1) to civilian or Armed Forces supply or procurement officers and employees of the Federal Government ordering, procuring, or purchasing such knives in connection with the activities of the Federal Government;

(2) to supply or procurement officers of the National Guard, the Air National Guard, or militia of a State ordering, procuring, or purchasing such knives in connection with the activities of such organizations;

(3) to supply or procurement officers or employees of any State, or any political subdivision of a State or Territory, ordering, procuring, or purchasing such knives in connection with the activities of such government; and

(4) to manufacturers of such knives or bona fide dealers therein in connection with any shipment made pursuant to an order from any person designated in paragraphs (1), (2), and (3).

The Postal Service may require, as a condition of conveying any such knife in the mails, that any person proposing to mail such knife explain in writing to the satisfaction of the Postal Service that the mailing of such knife will not be in violation of this section.

(h) Any advertising, promotional, or sales matter which solicits or induces the mailing of anything declared nonmailable by this section is likewise nonmailable unless such matter contains wrapping or packaging instructions which are in accord with regulations promulgated by the Postal Service.

(i)(1) Any ballistic knife shall be subject to the same restrictions and penalties provided under subsection (g) for knives described in the first sentence of that subsection.

(2) As used in this subsection, the term "ballistic knife" means a knife with a detachable blade that is propelled by a spring-operated mechanism.

(j)(1) Whoever knowingly deposits for mailing or delivery, or knowingly causes to be delivered by mail, according to the direction thereon, or at any place at which it is directed to be delivered by the person to whom it is addressed, anything declared nonmailable by this section, unless in accordance with the rules and regulations authorized to be prescribed by the Postal Service, shall be fined under this title or imprisoned not more than one year, or both.

(2) Whoever knowingly deposits for mailing or delivery, or knowingly causes to be delivered by mail, according to the direction thereon or at any place to which it is directed to be delivered by the person to whom it is addressed, anything declared nonmailable by this section, whether or not transmitted in accordance with the rules and regulations authorized to be prescribed by the Postal Service, with intent to kill or injure another, or injure the mails or other property, shall be fined under this title or imprisoned not more than twenty years, or both.

(3) Whoever is convicted of any crime prohibited by this section, which has resulted in the death of any person, shall be subject also to the death penalty or to imprisonment for life.

(k) For purposes of this section, the term "State" includes a State of the United States, the District of Columbia, and any commonwealth, territory, or possession of the United States.

46 U.S.C. § 11506. Carrying sheath knives

A seaman in the merchant marine may not wear a sheath knife on board a vessel without the consent of the master. The master of a vessel of the United States shall inform each seaman of this prohibition before engagement. A master failing to advise a seaman is liable to the United States Government for a civil penalty of $50.

49 U.S.C. § 46505. Carrying a weapon or explosive on an aircraft

(b) General criminal penalty.--An individual shall be fined under title 18, imprisoned for not more than 10 years, or both, if the individual--

(1) when on, or attempting to get on, an aircraft in, or intended for operation in, air transportation or intrastate air transportation, has on or about the individual or the property of the individual a concealed dangerous weapon that is or would be accessible to the individual in flight;

(c) Criminal penalty involving disregard for human life.--An individual who willfully and without regard for the safety of human life, or with reckless disregard for the safety of human life, violates subsection (b) of this section, shall be fined under title 18, imprisoned for not more than 20 years, or both, and, if death results to any person, shall be imprisoned for any term of years or for life.

(d) Nonapplication.--Subsection (b)(1) of this section does not apply to--

(1) a law enforcement officer of a State or political subdivision of a State, or an officer or employee of the United States Government, authorized to carry arms in an official capacity;

(2) another individual the Administrator of the Federal Aviation Administration or the Under Secretary of Transportation for Security by regulation authorizes to carry a dangerous weapon in air transportation or intrastate air transportation; or

(3) an individual transporting a weapon (except a loaded firearm) in baggage not accessible to a passenger in flight if the air carrier was informed of the presence of the weapon.

(e) Conspiracy.--If two or more persons conspire to violate subsection (b) or (c), and one or more of such persons do any act to effect the object of the conspiracy, each of the parties to such conspiracy shall be punished as provided in such subsection.

CHAPTER 12
STATE KNIFE LAW GUIDE A-D

HOW TO USE THIS GUIDE

The "Quick Points" chart for each jurisdiction contains 100 legal questions answered by either "Legal", "Prohibited," or "Gray".

"Legal" means that it is generally lawful.

"Prohibited" means that it is generally unlawful.

"Gray" means that it is neither generally lawful nor unlawful and that there are ambiguities, conflicting law, exceptions, requirements or special considerations that may determine legality.

The laws provided have been selected because of their relevance to knives. Sections of the law may have been edited. It is also possible that some laws may have been inadvertently omitted due to legal research not revealing same. In other words, your author tried his best, but he is not perfect.

KNIFE RIGHTS MOVEMENT RATING SYSTEM

The Knife Rights Movement rating system grades the States, the District of Columbia, and the United States of America on a scale from one to five.

The highest rating is a five, which means that jurisdiction stands out for knife liberty. A rating of one means that jurisdiction has a disdain for knives and individual rights, and has arbitrary laws that treat honest citizens like criminals. Ratings of two, three, or four show where that jurisdiction is in regards to its respect for knife rights freedom. If a place has a rating lower than five, then there is work to be done there restoring knife liberty and continuing the Knife Rights Movement.

✦ ALABAMA ✦

Knife Rights Movement Rating

★ ★ ★ ★ ☆

CUTTING TO THE CHASE

Alabama does not prohibit possession of knives by type. However, carrying knives concealed can be a problem, specifically Bowie knives. Also prohibited from concealed carry are "...knife or instrument of like kind..." This is vague and an aggressive prosecutor could push this to cover many other knives.

Quick Points Concerning Alabama's Knife Law*

KNIFE TYPE	POSSESSION	CARRY *(Open/Concealed)*	SALE	MANUFACTURE
Assisted Opening	Legal	Legal/Gray	Legal	Legal
Automatic/Switchblade	Legal	Legal/Gray	Legal	Legal
Ballistic	Legal	Legal/Gray	Legal	Legal
Bayonets	Legal	Legal/Gray	Legal	Legal
Bowie	Legal	Legal/Prohibited	Legal	Legal
Butterfly/Balisong	Legal	Legal/Gray	Legal	Legal
Combat/Survival	Legal	Legal/Prohibited	Legal	Legal
Dagger	Legal	Legal/Gray	Legal	Legal
Dirk	Legal	Legal/Gray	Legal	Legal
Disguised	Legal	Legal/Gray	Legal	Legal
Fixed	Legal	Legal/Gray	Legal	Legal
Folding	Legal	Legal/Gray	Legal	Legal
Gravity	Legal	Legal/Gray	Legal	Legal
Hunting/Fishing	Legal	Legal/Gray	Legal	Legal
Machete	Legal	Legal/Prohibited	Legal	Legal
Razor	Legal	Legal/Gray	Legal	Legal
Stiletto	Legal	Legal/Gray	Legal	Legal
Sword	Legal	Legal/Gray	Legal	Legal
Throwing	Legal	Legal/Gray	Legal	Legal
Undetectable	Legal	Legal/Gray	Legal	Legal

Pre-emption (Only State Law May Regulate, No Local Laws Permitted) – NO
*See all information above and below for more details.

SHARP TIPS ABOUT ALABAMA'S KNIFE LAWS

Other than carrying certain concealed knives, Alabama's knife laws primary focus is on having bad intent. Selling a "bowie knife, or other "knife of like kind" to a minor is prohibited. No pre-emption, so watch out for local laws.

EDGE –U- CATIONAL --- ALABAMA'S KNIFE LAWS

1975 § 13A-1-2. Definitions.

Unless different meanings are expressly specified in subsequent provisions of this title, the following terms shall have the following meanings:

(5) Dangerous instrument. Any instrument, article, or substance which, under the circumstances in which it is used, attempted to be used, or threatened to be used, is highly capable of causing death

or serious physical injury. The term includes a "vehicle," as that term is defined in subdivision (15).

(7) Deadly weapon. A firearm or anything manifestly designed, made, or adapted for the purposes of inflicting death or serious physical injury. The term includes, but is not limited to, a pistol, rifle, or shotgun; or a switch-blade knife, gravity knife, stiletto, sword, or dagger; or any billy, black-jack, bludgeon, or metal knuckles.

1975 § 13A-11-50. Carrying concealed weapons.
Except as otherwise provided in this Code, a person who carries concealed about his person a bowie knife or knife or instrument of like kind or description or a pistol or firearm of any other kind or an air gun shall, on conviction, be fined not less than $50.00 nor more than $500.00, and may also be imprisoned in the county jail or sentenced to hard labor for the county for not more than six months.

1975 § 13A-11-55. Indictment for carrying weapons unlawfully; proof.
In an indictment for carrying weapons unlawfully, it is sufficient to charge that the defendant carried concealed about his person a pistol, or other description of firearms, on premises not his own, or a bowie knife, or other knife or instrument of the like kind or description, or other forbidden weapon, describing it, as the case may be; and the excuse, if any, must be proved by the defendant on the trial, to the satisfaction of the jury; and if the evidence offered to excuse the charge raises a reasonable doubt of the defendant's guilt, the jury must acquit him.

1975 § 13A-11-57. Selling, etc., pistol or bowie knife to minor.
Any person who sells, gives or lends to any minor any pistol or bowie knife, or other knife of like kind or description, shall, on conviction, be fined not less than $50.00 nor more than $500.00.

1975 § 13A-11-72. Certain persons forbidden to possess pistol.
(c) Subject to the exceptions provided by Section 13A-11-74, no person shall knowingly with intent to do bodily harm carry or possess a deadly weapon on the premises of a public school.

(d) Possession of a deadly weapon with the intent to do bodily harm on the premises of a public school in violation of subsection (c) of this section is a Class C felony.

(e) School security personnel and school resource officers qualified under subsection (a) of Section 16-1-44.1, employed by a local board of education, and authorized by the employing local board of education to carry a deadly weapon while on duty are exempt from subsection (c) of this section. Law enforcement officers are exempt from this section, and persons with pistol permits issued pursuant to Section 13A-11-75, are exempt from subsection (c) of this section.

(f) The term "school resource officer" as used in this section means an Alabama Peace Officers' Standards and Training Commissioner-certified law enforcement officer employed by a law enforcement agency who is specifically selected and specially trained for the school setting.

(g) The term "public school" as used in this section applies only to a school composed of grades K-12 and shall include a school bus used for grades K-12.

(h) The term "deadly weapon" as used in this section means a firearm or anything manifestly designed, made, or adapted for the purposes of inflicting death or serious physical injury, and such term includes, but is not limited to, a bazooka, hand grenade, missile, or explosive or incendiary device; a pistol, rifle, or shotgun; or a switch-blade knife, gravity knife, stiletto, sword, or dagger; or any club, baton, billy, black-jack, bludgeon, or metal knuckles.

1975 § 40-12-143. Pistols, revolvers, bowie and dirk knives, etc.; gun and knife shows.
Persons dealing in pistols, revolvers, maxim silencers, bowie knives, dirk knives, brass knucks or knucks of like kind, whether principal stock in trade or not shall pay the following license tax: In cities and towns of 35,000 inhabitants and over, $150; and in all other places, $100. The required license amounts shall be paid for each place of business from which sales of such items are made. In addition to any other required licens-

es, a person may organize and conduct a gun and knife show of no more than seven days, by paying the maximum license tax prescribed in this section, as well as the maximum license taxes provided in Sections 40-12-158 and 40-12-174(d), for each such show. Participants shall not be required to pay the license taxes provided in this section, nor in Section 40-12-158 or 40-12-174 for participating in such shows, provided the organizer has paid the license taxes prescribed in this section prior to the commencement of the event. It shall be the duty of the organizer of such show to determine if each participant is licensed under the sales tax laws of this state as well as the particular county and municipality in which the show is conducted. The organizer shall be responsible for providing a list of participants to the county and municipality in which the gun show is held and for collecting and remitting all state and local sales taxes for any participant not licensed under state or local sales tax laws. In the event the organizer does not provide the information required herein or pay the license taxes prescribed in this section, prior to the commencement of the event, each participant shall be responsible for his or her applicable licenses. The organizer and all participants shall abide by applicable federal, state, and local laws and regulations. All persons dealing in pistols, revolvers, and maxim silencers shall be required to keep a permanent record of the sale of every pistol, revolver, or maxim silencer, showing the date of sale, serial number, or other identification marks, manufacturer's name, caliber and type, and also the name and address of the purchaser. The records shall always be open for inspection by any peace officer of the State of Alabama or any municipality thereof. The failure to keep such record shall subject such person to having his or her license revoked by the probate judge of the county where such license was issued on motion of any district attorney of the State of Alabama.

⚔ ALASKA ⚔
KNIFE RIGHTS MOVEMENT RATING
★ ★ ★ ★ ★

CUTTING TO THE CHASE
Alaska is one of best states for knife rights freedom in the United States. Alaska was one of nine other states to join the Knife Rights Movement and repeal their knife prohibition laws and pass pre-emption.

Quick Points Concerning Alaska's Knife Law*

KNIFE TYPE	POSSESSION	(Open/Concealed) CARRY	SALE	MANUFACTURE
Assisted Opening	Legal	Legal/Legal	Legal	Legal
Automatic/Switchblade	Legal	Legal/Legal	Legal	Legal
Ballistic	Legal	Legal/Legal	Legal	Legal
Bayonets	Legal	Legal/Legal	Legal	Legal
Bowie	Legal	Legal/Legal	Legal	Legal
Butterfly/Balisong	Legal	Legal/Legal	Legal	Legal
Combat/Survival	Legal	Legal/Legal	Legal	Legal
Dagger	Legal	Legal/Legal	Legal	Legal
Dirk	Legal	Legal/Legal	Legal	Legal
Disguised	Legal	Legal/Legal	Legal	Legal
Fixed	Legal	Legal/Legal	Legal	Legal
Folding	Legal	Legal/Legal	Legal	Legal
Gravity	Legal	Legal/Legal	Legal	Legal
Hunting/Fishing	Legal	Legal/Legal	Legal	Legal

KNIFE TYPE	POSSESSION	(Open/Concealed) CARRY	SALE	MANUFACTURE
Machete	Legal	Legal/Legal	Legal	Legal
Razor	Legal	Legal/Legal	Legal	Legal
Stiletto	Legal	Legal/Legal	Legal	Legal
Sword	Legal	Legal/Legal	Legal	Legal
Throwing	Legal	Legal/Legal	Legal	Legal
Undetectable	Legal	Legal/Legal	Legal	Legal

Pre-emption (Only State Law May Regulate, No Local Laws Permitted) — YES
*See all information above and below for more details.

SHARP TIPS ABOUT ALASKA'S KNIFE LAWS

When carrying a concealed knife in Alaska and contacted by a peace officer, make sure to immediately inform the officer and let him secure it. Certain laws apply to those under 16, 18 and 21 years old. Do not possess knives in schools or courts.

EDGE –U- CATIONAL --- ALASKA'S KNIFE LAWS
§ 11.81.900. Definitions

(b) In this title, unless otherwise specified or unless the context requires otherwise,

(15) "dangerous instrument" means

(A) any deadly weapon or anything that, under the circumstances in which it is used, attempted to be used, or threatened to be used, is capable of causing death or serious physical injury; or

(17) "deadly weapon" means any firearm, or anything designed for and capable of causing death or serious physical injury, including a knife, an axe, a club, metal knuckles, or an explosive;

(20) "defensive weapon" means an electric stun gun, or a device to dispense mace or a similar chemical agent, that is not designed to cause death or serious physical injury;

(29) "gravity knife" means any knife that has a blade that opens or releases a blade from its handle or sheath by the force of gravity or by the application of centrifugal force; "gravity knife" does not include a knife that has a spring, detent, or other mechanism designed to create a bias toward closure that requires a person to apply exertion to the blade by hand, wrist, or arm to overcome the bias toward closure and open or release the blade;

(53) "public place" means a place to which the public or a substantial group of persons has access and includes highways, transportation facilities, schools, places of amusement or business, parks, playgrounds, prisons, and hallways, lobbies, and other portions of apartment houses and hotels not constituting rooms or apartments designed for actual residence;

(62) "switchblade" means any knife that has a blade that folds, closes, or retracts into the handle or sheath that opens automatically by pressure applied to a button or other device located on the handle or sheath; "switchblade" does not include a knife that has a spring, detent, or other mechanism designed to create a bias toward closure that requires exertion applied to the blade by hand, wrist, or arm to overcome the bias toward closure and open the blade;

§ 11.61.220. Misconduct involving weapons in the fifth degree

(a) A person commits the crime of misconduct involving weapons in the fifth degree if the person

(1) is 21 years of age or older and knowingly possesses a deadly weapon, other than an ordinary pocket knife or a defensive weapon,

(A) that is concealed on the person, and, when contacted by a peace officer, the person fails to (i)

immediately inform the peace officer of that possession; or

(ii) allow the peace officer to secure the deadly weapon, or fails to secure the weapon at the direction of the peace officer, during the duration of the contact;

(B) that is concealed on the person within the residence of another person unless the person has first obtained the express permission of an adult residing there to bring a concealed deadly weapon within the residence;

(3) being an unemancipated minor under 16 years of age, possesses a firearm, switchblade, or gravity knife without the consent of a parent or guardian of the minor;

(6) is less than 21 years of age and knowingly possesses a deadly weapon, other than an ordinary pocket knife or a defensive weapon, that is concealed on the person.

(b) In a prosecution under (a)(6) of this section, it is an affirmative defense that the defendant, at the time of possession, was

(1) in the defendant's dwelling or on land owned or leased by the defendant appurtenant to the dwelling; or

(2) actually engaged in lawful hunting, fishing, trapping, or other lawful outdoor activity that necessarily involves the carrying of a weapon for personal protection.

(e) For purposes of this section, a deadly weapon on a person is concealed if it is covered or enclosed in any manner so that an observer cannot determine that it is a weapon without removing it from that which covers or encloses it or without opening, lifting, or removing that which covers or encloses it; a deadly weapon on a person is not concealed if it is an unloaded firearm encased in a closed container designed for transporting firearms.

(g) Misconduct involving weapons in the fifth degree is a class B misdemeanor.

(h) The provisions of (a)(1) and (6) of this section do not apply to a

(1) peace officer of this state or a municipality of this state acting within the scope and authority of the officer's employment;

(2) peace officer employed by another state or a political subdivision of another state who, at the time of the possession, is

(A) certified as a peace officer by the other state; and

(B) acting within the scope and authority of the officer's employment; or

(3) police officer of this state or a police officer or chief administrative officer of a municipality of this state; in this paragraph, "police officer" and "chief administrative officer" have the meanings given in AS 18.65.290.

(j) In (a)(1) of this section, "contacted by a peace officer" means stopped, detained, questioned, or addressed in person by the peace officer for an official purpose.

§ 11.61.210. Misconduct involving weapons in the fourth degree

(a) A person commits the crime of misconduct involving weapons in the fourth degree if the person

(4) manufactures, possesses, transports, sells, or transfers metal knuckles;

(5) sells or transfers a switchblade or a gravity knife to a person under 18 years of age without the prior written consent of the person's parent or guardian;

(6) knowingly sells a firearm or a defensive weapon to a person under 18 years of age;

(7) other than a preschool, elementary, junior high, or secondary school student, knowingly possesses a deadly weapon or a defensive weapon, without the permission of the chief administrative officer of the school or district or the designee of the chief administrative officer, within the buildings of, on the grounds of, or on the school parking lot of a public or private preschool, elementary, junior high, or secondary school, on a school bus while being transported to or from school or a school-sponsored event, or while participating in a school-sponsored event, except that a person 21 years of age or older may possess

(A) a deadly weapon, other than a loaded firearm, in the trunk of a motor vehicle or encased in a closed container in a motor vehicle;

(B) a defensive weapon; … or

(8) being a preschool, elementary, junior high, or secondary school student, knowingly possesses a deadly weapon or a defensive weapon, within the buildings of, on the grounds of, or on the school parking lot of a public or private preschool, elementary, junior high, or secondary school, on a school bus while being transported to or from school or a school-sponsored event, or while participating in a school-sponsored event, except that a student may possess a deadly weapon, other than a firearm as defined under 18 U.S.C. 921, or a defensive weapon if the student has obtained the prior permission of the chief administrative officer of the school or district or the designee of the chief administrative officer for the possession.

(c) The provisions of (a)(7) of this section do not apply to a peace officer acting within the scope and authority of the officer's employment.

(d) Misconduct involving weapons in the fourth degree is a class A misdemeanor.

§ 29.35.145. Regulation of firearms and knives

(a) The authority to regulate firearms and knives is reserved to the state, and, except as specifically provided by statute, a municipality may not enact or enforce an ordinance regulating the possession, ownership, sale, transfer, use, carrying, transportation, licensing, taxation, or registration of firearms or knives.

(b) Municipalities may enact and enforce ordinances

(1) that are identical to state law and that have the same penalty as provided for by state law;

(2) restricting the discharge of firearms in any portion of their respective jurisdictions where there is a reasonable likelihood that people, domestic animals, or property will be jeopardized; ordinances enacted or enforced under this paragraph may not abridge the right of the individual guaranteed by art. I, sec. 19, Constitution of the State of Alaska, to bear arms in defense of self or others;

(3) restricting the areas in their respective jurisdictions in which firearms or knives may be sold; a business selling firearms or knives may not be treated more restrictively than other businesses located within the same zone; and

(4) prohibiting the possession of firearms or knives in the restricted access area of municipal government buildings; the municipal assembly shall post notice of the prohibition against possession of firearms or knives at each entrance to the restricted access area.

(d) This section applies to home rule and general law municipalities.

(e) In this section, (2) "restricted access area" means the area beyond a secure point where visitors are screened and does not include common areas of ingress and egress open to the general public.

Rules Governing the Administration of All Courts, Rule 26.2. Court Security

(a) Except as otherwise provided by this rule, no person may possess a weapon on the premises of any court facility, or in the portion of any other building occupied by the court system, unless the weapon is to be used as evidence in a court proceeding. The term weapon includes firearms, knives, and chemical agents such as mace and pepper spray. This prohibition does not apply to:

(1) a peace officer;

(2) a private uniformed security guard employed by a financial institution or private security service who is transporting money or other valuables;

(3) a private security guard under contract with the court system to provide security services within a court facility who possesses a weapon authorized under the contract;

(4) a judicial officer;

(5) a person who has written authorization from the administrative director to possess a weapon on court premises. This authorization will be given only upon a showing of good cause and only for a specified period of time;

(6) court system employees, who may possess on the premises of any court facility, or in the portion of any other building occupied by the court system: (a) small knives or multitools (like Swiss Army-type or Leatherman-type tools) provided that any knife blade may not exceed 4 inches in length; and (b) small chemical agent canisters for personal safety purposes; or

(7) court system facility construction contractors, who may possess on the premises of court facilities knives and knife-like tools that are necessary for their work.

(b) The exemptions listed in (a)(1)-(3) and (a)(6)-(7) apply only to persons acting within the scope and authority of their employment. A peace officer ,private security guard, court system employee, or court system contractor who is participating in or attending a court proceeding outside the scope of his or her employment, whether as a party, witness, victim, or other interested person, is not permitted to bring a weapon onto court premises unless authorized to do so under (a)(5).

(d) Weapons to be used as evidence in court proceedings must be marked and prepared as directed by the administrative director by administrative bulletin. Each presiding judge may prescribe procedures for courts within that judge's district requiring prior notification to designated court personnel before weapons to be used as evidence may be brought onto court premises.

⊹⊢ ARIZONA ⊣⊹
KNIFE RIGHTS MOVEMENT RATING
★ ★ ★ ★ ★

CUTTING TO THE CHASE
Arizona is a great state for knife freedom. It has few knife laws and respects the Second Amendment.

Quick Points Concerning Arizona's Knife Law*

KNIFE TYPE	POSSESSION	(Open/Concealed) CARRY	SALE	MANUFACTURE
Assisted Opening	Legal	Legal/Legal	Legal	Legal
Automatic/Switchblade	Legal	Legal/Legal	Legal	Legal
Ballistic	Legal	Legal/Legal	Legal	Legal
Bayonets	Legal	Legal/Legal	Legal	Legal
Bowie	Legal	Legal/Legal	Legal	Legal
Butterfly/Balisong	Legal	Legal/Legal	Legal	Legal
Combat/Survival	Legal	Legal/Legal	Legal	Legal

KNIFE TYPE	POSSESSION	(Open/Concealed) CARRY	SALE	MANUFACTURE
Dagger	Legal	Legal/Legal	Legal	Legal
Dirk	Legal	Legal/Legal	Legal	Legal
Disguised	Legal	Legal/Legal	Legal	Legal
Fixed	Legal	Legal/Legal	Legal	Legal
Folding	Legal	Legal/Legal	Legal	Legal
Gravity	Legal	Legal/Legal	Legal	Legal
Hunting/Fishing	Legal	Legal/Legal	Legal	Legal
Machete	Legal	Legal/Legal	Legal	Legal
Razor	Legal	Legal/Legal	Legal	Legal
Stiletto	Legal	Legal/Legal	Legal	Legal
Sword	Legal	Legal/Legal	Legal	Legal
Throwing	Legal	Legal/Legal	Legal	Legal
Undetectable	Legal	Legal/Legal	Legal	Legal

Pre-emption (Only State Law May Regulate, No Local Laws Permitted) – YES
*See all information above and below for more details.

SHARP TIPS ABOUT ARIZONA'S KNIFE LAWS

"Deadly weapon" means anything that is designed for lethal use. This could potentially cover many types of knives. Carrying a deadly weapon, concealed on one's person or in a vehicle, except a pocket knife, is prohibited IF it's carried in furtherance of a crime, failing to tell a law enforcement officer about it when asked, or if you are under 21 years old. Carrying a "deadly weapon" is also unlawful on school grounds, at election polling places, in vehicles and buildings possessed by the state, at public events and at power plants. Prohibited possessors are also barred from possessing "deadly weapons."

EDGE –U- CATIONAL --- ARIZONA'S KNIFE LAWS
§ 13-3101. Definitions

A. In this chapter, unless the context otherwise requires:

1. "Deadly weapon" means anything that is designed for lethal use. The term includes a firearm.

7. "Prohibited possessor" means any person:

(a) Who has been found to constitute a danger to self or to others or to have persistent or acute disabilities or grave disabilities pursuant to court order pursuant to § 36-540, and whose right to possess a firearm has not been restored pursuant to § 13-925.

(b) Who has been convicted within or without this state of a felony or who has been adjudicated delinquent for a felony and whose civil right to possess or carry a gun or firearm has not been restored.

(c) Who is at the time of possession serving a term of imprisonment in any correctional or detention facility.

(d) Who is at the time of possession serving a term of probation pursuant to a conviction for a domestic violence offense as defined in § 13-3601 or a felony offense, parole, community supervision, work furlough, home arrest or release on any other basis or who is serving a term of probation or parole pursuant to the interstate compact under title 31, chapter 3, article 4.1.1

(e) Who is an undocumented alien or a nonimmigrant alien traveling with or without documentation in this state for business or pleasure or who is studying in this state and who maintains a foreign residence abroad. This subdivision does not apply to:

(i) Nonimmigrant aliens who possess a valid hunting license or permit that is lawfully issued by a state in the United States.

(ii) Nonimmigrant aliens who enter the United States to participate in a competitive target shooting event or to display firearms at a sports or hunting trade show that is sponsored by a national, state or local firearms trade organization devoted to the competitive use or other sporting use of firearms.

(iii) Certain diplomats.

(iv) Officials of foreign governments or distinguished foreign visitors who are designated by the United States department of state.

(v) Persons who have received a waiver from the United States attorney general.

(f) Who has been found incompetent pursuant to rule 11, Arizona rules of criminal procedure, and who subsequently has not been found competent.

(g) Who is found guilty except insane.

§ 13-3102. Misconduct involving weapons; defenses; classification; definitions

A. A person commits misconduct involving weapons by knowingly:

1. Carrying a deadly weapon except a pocket knife concealed on his person or within his immediate control in or on a means of transportation:

(a) In the furtherance of a serious offense as defined in § 13-706, a violent crime as defined in § 13-901.03 or any other felony offense; or

(b) When contacted by a law enforcement officer and failing to accurately answer the officer if the officer asks whether the person is carrying a concealed deadly weapon; or

2. Carrying a deadly weapon except a pocket knife concealed on his person or concealed within his immediate control in or on a means of transportation if the person is under twenty-one years of age; or

4. Possessing a deadly weapon or prohibited weapon if such person is a prohibited possessor; or

5. Selling or transferring a deadly weapon to a prohibited possessor; or

6. Defacing a deadly weapon; or

7. Possessing a defaced deadly weapon knowing the deadly weapon was defaced; or

8. Using or possessing a deadly weapon during the commission of any felony offense included in chapter 34 of this title;1 or

10. Unless specifically authorized by law, entering any public establishment or attending any public event and carrying a deadly weapon on his person after a reasonable request by the operator of the establishment or the sponsor of the event or the sponsor's agent to remove his weapon and place it in the custody of the operator of the establishment or the sponsor of the event for temporary and secure storage of the weapon pursuant to § 13-3102.01; or

11. Unless specifically authorized by law, entering an election polling place on the day of any election carrying a deadly weapon; or

12. Possessing a deadly weapon on school grounds; or

13. Unless specifically authorized by law, entering a nuclear or hydroelectric generating station carrying a deadly weapon on his person or within the immediate control of any person; or

15. Using, possessing or exercising control over a deadly weapon in furtherance of any act of terrorism as defined in § 13-2301 or possessing or exercising control over a deadly weapon knowing or having reason to know that it will be used to facilitate any act of terrorism as defined in § 13-2301; or

16. Trafficking in weapons or explosives for financial gain in order to assist, promote or further the inter-

ests of a criminal street gang, a criminal syndicate or a racketeering enterprise.

B. Subsection A, paragraph 2 of this section shall not apply to:

1. A person in his dwelling, on his business premises or on real property owned or leased by that person or that person's parent, grandparent or legal guardian.

2. A member of the sheriff's volunteer posse or reserve organization who has received and passed firearms training that is approved by the Arizona peace officer standards and training board and who is authorized by the sheriff to carry a concealed weapon pursuant to § 11-441.

C. Subsection A, paragraphs 2, 3, 7, 10, 11, 12 and 13 of this section shall not apply to:

1. A peace officer or any person summoned by any peace officer to assist and while actually assisting in the performance of official duties; or

2. A member of the military forces of the United States or of any state of the United States in the performance of official duties; or

3. A warden, deputy warden, community correctional officer, detention officer, special investigator or correctional officer of the state department of corrections or the department of juvenile corrections; or

4. A person specifically licensed, authorized or permitted pursuant to a statute of this state or of the United States.

D. Subsection A, paragraph 10 of this section does not apply to an elected or appointed judicial officer in the court facility where the judicial officer works if the judicial officer has demonstrated competence with a firearm as prescribed in § 13-3112, subsection N, except that the judicial officer shall comply with any rule or policy adopted by the presiding judge of the superior court while in the court facility. For the purposes of this subsection, appointed judicial officer does not include a hearing officer or a judicial officer pro tempore that is not a full-time officer.

E. Subsection A, paragraphs 3 and 7 of this section shall not apply to:

1. The possessing, transporting, selling or transferring of weapons by a museum as a part of its collection or an educational institution for educational purposes or by an authorized employee of such museum or institution, if:

(a) Such museum or institution is operated by the United States or this state or a political subdivision of this state, or by an organization described in 26 United States Code section 170(c) as a recipient of a charitable contribution; and

(b) Reasonable precautions are taken with respect to theft or misuse of such material.

2. The regular and lawful transporting as merchandise; or

3. Acquisition by a person by operation of law such as by gift, devise or descent or in a fiduciary capacity as a recipient of the property or former property of an insolvent, incapacitated or deceased person.

F. Subsection A, paragraph 3 of this section shall not apply to the merchandise of an authorized manufacturer of or dealer in prohibited weapons, when such material is intended to be manufactured, possessed, transported, sold or transferred solely for or to a dealer, a regularly constituted or appointed state, county or municipal police department or police officer, a detention facility, the military service of this or another state or the United States, a museum or educational institution or a person specifically licensed or permitted pursuant to federal or state law.

G. Subsection A, paragraph 10 of this section shall not apply to shooting ranges or shooting events, hunting areas or similar locations or activities.

H. Subsection A, paragraph 3 of this section shall not apply to a weapon described in § 13-3101, subsection A, paragraph 8, subdivision (a), item (v), if such weapon is possessed for the purposes of preparing for, conducting or participating in lawful exhibitions, demonstrations, contests or athletic events involving the use of such weapon. Subsection A, paragraph 12 of this section shall not apply to a weapon if such weapon is possessed for the purposes of preparing for, conducting or participating in hunter or firearm safety courses.

J. Subsection A, paragraphs 2, 3, 7 and 13 of this section shall not apply to commercial nuclear generating station armed nuclear security guards during the performance of official duties or during any security training exercises sponsored by the commercial nuclear generating station or local, state or federal authorities.

K. The operator of the establishment or the sponsor of the event or the employee of the operator or sponsor or the agent of the sponsor, including a public entity or public employee, is not liable for acts or omissions pursuant to subsection A, paragraph 10 of this section unless the operator, sponsor, employee or agent intended to cause injury or was grossly negligent.

M. Misconduct involving weapons under subsection A, paragraph 15 of this section is a class 2 felony. Misconduct involving weapons under subsection A, paragraph 9, 14 or 16 of this section is a class 3 felony. Misconduct involving weapons under subsection A, paragraph 3, 4, 8 or 13 of this section is a class 4 felony. Misconduct involving weapons under subsection A, paragraph 12 of this section is a class 1 misdemeanor unless the violation occurs in connection with conduct that violates § 13-2308, subsection A, paragraph 5, § 13-2312, subsection C, § 13-3409 or § 13-3411, in which case the offense is a class 6 felony. Misconduct involving weapons under subsection A, paragraph 1, subdivision (a) of this section or subsection A, paragraph 5, 6 or 7 of this section is a class 6 felony. Misconduct involving weapons under subsection A, paragraph 1, subdivision (b) of this section or subsection A, paragraph 10 or 11 of this section is a class 1 misdemeanor. Misconduct involving weapons under subsection A, paragraph 2 of this section is a class 3 misdemeanor.

N. For the purposes of this section:

1. "Contacted by a law enforcement officer" means a lawful traffic or criminal investigation, arrest or detention or an investigatory stop by a law enforcement officer that is based on reasonable suspicion that an offense has been or is about to be committed.

2. "Public establishment" means a structure, vehicle or craft that is owned, leased or operated by this state or a political subdivision of this state.

3. "Public event" means a specifically named or sponsored event of limited duration that is either conducted by a public entity or conducted by a private entity with a permit or license granted by a public entity. Public event does not include an unsponsored gathering of people in a public place.

4. "School" means a public or nonpublic kindergarten program, common school or high school.

5. "School grounds" means in, or on the grounds of, a school.

§ 13-3120. Knives regulated by state; state preemption; definitions
A. Except as provided in subsections C and D, a political subdivision of this state shall not enact any ordinance, rule or tax relating to the transportation, possession, carrying, sale, transfer, purchase, gift, devise, licensing, registration or use of a knife or knife making components in this state.

B. A political subdivision of this state shall not enact any rule or ordinance that relates to the manufacture of a knife and that is more prohibitive than or that has a penalty that is greater than any rule or ordinance that is related to the manufacture of any other commercial goods.

C. This section does not prohibit a political subdivision of this state from enacting and enforcing any ordinance or rule pursuant to state law, to implement or enforce state law or relating to imposing any privilege or use tax on the retail sale, lease or rental of, or the gross proceeds or gross income from the sale, lease or rental of, a knife or any knife components at a rate that applies generally to other items of tangible personal property.

D. This section does not prohibit a political subdivision of this state from regulating employees or independent contractors of the political subdivision who are acting within the course and scope of their employment or contract.

E. A political subdivision's rule or ordinance that relates to knives and that is inconsistent with or more restrictive than state law, whether enacted before or after the effective date of this amendment to this section, is null and void.

F. For the purposes of this section:

1. "Knife" means a cutting instrument and includes a sharpened or pointed blade.

2. "Political subdivision" includes any county, city, including a charter city, town, municipal corporation or special district, any board, commission or agency of a county, city, including a charter city, town, municipal corporation or special district or any other local public agency.

⊰— ARKANSAS —⊱
KNIFE RIGHTS MOVEMENT RATING
★ ★ ★ ★ ☆

CUTTING TO THE CHASE

Arkansas is a great state for knife rights freedom. It has no bans on knife possession by type. If Arkansas had pre-emption, it would have a five rating.

Quick Points Concerning Arkansas's Knife Law*

KNIFE TYPE	POSSESSION	(Open/Concealed) CARRY	SALE	MANUFACTURE
Assisted Opening	Legal	Legal/Legal	Legal	Legal
Automatic/Switchblade	Legal	Legal/Legal	Legal	Legal
Ballistic	Legal	Legal/Legal	Legal	Legal
Bayonets	Legal	Legal/Legal	Legal	Legal
Bowie	Legal	Legal/Legal	Legal	Legal
Butterfly/Balisong	Legal	Legal/Legal	Legal	Legal
Combat/Survival	Legal	Legal/Legal	Legal	Legal
Dagger	Legal	Legal/Legal	Legal	Legal
Dirk	Legal	Legal/Legal	Legal	Legal
Disguised	Legal	Legal/Legal	Legal	Legal
Fixed	Legal	Legal/Legal	Legal	Legal
Folding	Legal	Legal/Legal	Legal	Legal
Gravity	Legal	Legal/Legal	Legal	Legal
Hunting/Fishing	Legal	Legal/Legal	Legal	Legal
Machete	Legal	Legal/Legal	Legal	Legal
Razor	Legal	Legal/Legal	Legal	Legal
Stiletto	Legal	Legal/Legal	Legal	Legal
Sword	Legal	Legal/Legal	Legal	Legal
Throwing	Legal	Legal/Legal	Legal	Legal
Undetectable	Legal	Legal/Legal	Legal	Legal

Pre-emption (Only State Law May Regulate, No Local Laws Permitted) – NO
*See all information above and below for more details.

SHARP TIPS ABOUT ARKANSAS KNIFE LAWS

Sales to minors are prohibited. Carrying a knife is prohibited if it is done with an unlawful purpose. Do not bring knives to public buildings or state capital grounds. Also, there is no pre-emption, beware of local laws.

EDGE –U- CATIONAL --- ARKANSAS KNIFE LAWS

§ 5-1-102. Definitions

As used in the Arkansas Criminal Code:

(4) "Deadly weapon" means:

(B) Anything that in the manner of its use or intended use is capable of causing death or serious physical injury;

(21) "Serious physical injury" means physical injury that creates a substantial risk of death or that causes protracted disfigurement, protracted impairment of health, or loss or protracted impairment of the function of any bodily member or organ; and

§ 5-73-109. Minors, furnishing deadly weapons

(a) A person commits the offense of furnishing a deadly weapon to a minor if he or she sells, barters, leases, gives, rents, or otherwise furnishes a firearm or other deadly weapon to a minor without the consent of a parent, guardian, or other person responsible for general supervision of the minor's welfare.

(b)(1) Furnishing a deadly weapon to a minor is a Class A misdemeanor.

(2) However, furnishing a deadly weapon to a minor is a Class B felony if the deadly weapon is:

(G) Metal knuckles;

(I) Another implement for the infliction of serious physical injury or death that serves no common lawful purpose.

§ 5-73-120. Carrying a weapon

(a) A person commits the offense of carrying a weapon if he or she possesses a handgun, knife, or club on or about his or her person, in a vehicle occupied by him or her, or otherwise readily available for use with a purpose to attempt to unlawfully employ the handgun, knife, or club as a weapon against a person.

(b) As used in this section:

(3) "Journey" means travel beyond the county in which a person lives; and

(4) "Knife" means any bladed hand instrument three inches (3) or longer that is capable of inflicting serious physical injury or death by cutting or stabbing, including a dirk, a sword or spear in a cane, a razor, an ice pick, a throwing star, a switchblade, and a butterfly knife.

(d) Carrying a weapon is a Class A misdemeanor.

§ 5-73-122. Possession of deadly weapons in publicly owned buildings and facilities

(a)(1) Except as provided in § 5-73-322, it is unlawful for any person other than a law enforcement officer or a security guard in the employ of the state or an agency of the state, or any city or county, or any state or federal military personnel, to knowingly carry or possess a loaded firearm or other deadly weapon in any publicly owned building or facility or on the State Capitol grounds.

(2) It is unlawful for any person other than a law enforcement officer or a security guard in the employ of the state or an agency of the state, or any city or county, or any state or federal military personnel,

to knowingly carry or possess a firearm, whether loaded or unloaded, in the State Capitol Building or the Justice Building in Little Rock.

(3) However, the provisions of this subsection do not apply to a person carrying or possessing a firearm or other deadly weapon in a publicly owned building or facility or on the State Capitol grounds for the purpose of participating in a shooting match or target practice under the auspices of the agency responsible for the building or facility or grounds or if necessary to participate in a trade show, exhibit, or educational course conducted in the building or facility or on the grounds.

(4) As used in this section, "facility" means a municipally owned or maintained park, football field, baseball field, soccer field, or another similar municipally owned or maintained recreational structure or property.

(b)(1) Any person other than a law enforcement officer, officer of the court, or bailiff, acting in the line of duty, or any other person authorized by the court, who possesses a handgun in the courtroom of any court of this state is guilty of a Class D felony.

(2) Otherwise, any person violating a provision of this section is guilty of a Class A misdemeanor.

⚔ CALIFORNIA ⚔
KNIFE RIGHTS MOVEMENT RATING

★ ☆ ☆ ☆ ☆

CUTTING TO THE CHASE

California is one of the worst states for knife liberty. It bans possession of ballistic knives, balisongs, air gauge knives, shobi-zues, belt buckle knives, throwing stars, cane swords, gravity knives, lipstick case knives, and undetectable knives. One cannot conceal carry dirks or daggers. "Dirk" or "dagger" is broadly defined as "a knife or other instrument with or without a handguard that is capable of ready use as a stabbing weapon that may inflict great bodily injury or death." Therefore, just about every knife without a handguard is prohibited from concealed carry and other items as well, like chef knives, ice picks, knitting needles, and scissors. (I hope no little old ladies carry their knitting needles and scissors in their handbag in California.)

Quick Points Concerning California's Knife Law*

KNIFE TYPE	POSSESSION	(Open/Concealed) CARRY	SALE	MANUFACTURE
Assisted Opening	Legal	Legal/Gray	Legal	Legal
Automatic/Switchblade	Gray	Gray/Gray	Gray	Gray
Ballistic	Prohibited	Prohibited/Prohibited	Prohibited	Prohibited
Bayonets	Gray	Legal/Gray	Gray	Gray
Bowie	Gray	Legal/Gray	Gray	Gray
Butterfly/Balisong	Gray	Gray/Gray	Gray	Gray
Combat/Survival	Legal	Legal/Gray	Legal	Legal
Dagger	Legal	Legal/Prohibited	Legal	Legal
Dirk	Gray	Legal/Prohibited	Legal	Legal
Disguised	Prohibited	Prohibited/Prohibited	Prohibited	Prohibited
Fixed	Legal	Legal/Gray	Legal	Legal
Folding	Gray	Gray/Gray	Gray	Gray
Gravity	Gray	Gray/Gray	Gray	Gray
Hunting/Fishing	Legal	Legal/Gray	Legal	Legal

KNIFE TYPE	POSSESSION	(Open/Concealed) CARRY	SALE	MANUFACTURE
Machete	Legal	Legal/Gray	Legal	Legal
Razor	Legal	Legal/Gray	Legal	Legal
Stiletto	Legal	Legal/Gray	Legal	Legal
Sword	Gray	Gary/Gray	Gray	Gray
Throwing	Gray	Gray/Gray	Gray	Gray
Undetectable	Prohibited	Prohibited/Prohibited	Prohibited	Prohibited

Pre-emption (Only State Law May Regulate, No Local Laws Permitted) – NO
*See all information above and below for more details.

SHARP TIPS ABOUT CALIFORNIA'S KNIFE LAWS

Concealed carry is also prohibited of a "…nonlocking folding knife, a folding knife that is not prohibited by Section 21510, or a pocketknife is capable of ready use as a stabbing weapon that may inflict great bodily injury or death only if the blade of the knife is exposed and locked into position." Concealed or open carry of folding knives (other than switchblades with blades over 2") like box cutters, pocket knives, Swiss Army knives and utility knives is lawful, so long as they're closed and not in a locked position. Knives which fall into the family of dirks, daggers, stilettos, ice picks, and the like, may be carried but only openly. Switchblades (with blades 2 inches or longer) are legal to possess unless one: (a) Possesses the knife in the passenger's or driver's area of any motor vehicle in any public place or place open to the public.(b) Carries the knife upon the person. (c) Sells, offers for sale, exposes for sale, loans, transfers, or gives the knife to any other person. One cannot bring a knife into public buildings, any meetings open to the public, schools, colleges, courthouses, city halls, and airports. No pre-emption, so beware of local laws as well.

EDGE –U- CATIONAL --- CALIFORNIA'S KNIFE LAWS

§ 16140. Air gauge knife defined
As used in this part, "air gauge knife" means a device that appears to be an air gauge but has concealed within it a pointed, metallic shaft that is designed to be a stabbing instrument which is exposed by mechanical action or gravity which locks into place when extended.

§ 16220. Ballistic knife defined
As used in this part, "ballistic knife" means a device that propels a knifelike blade as a projectile by means of a coil spring, elastic material, or compressed gas. Ballistic knife does not include any device that propels an arrow or a bolt by means of any common bow, compound bow, crossbow, or underwater speargun.

§ 16260. Belt buckle knife defined
As used in this part, "belt buckle knife" is a knife that is made an integral part of a belt buckle and consists of a blade with a length of at least two and one-half inches.

§ 16340. Cane sword defined
As used in this part, "cane sword" means a cane, swagger stick, stick, staff, rod, pole, umbrella, or similar device, having concealed within it a blade that may be used as a sword or stiletto.

§ 16420. Dagger defined
Use of the term "dagger" is governed by Section 16470.

§ 16430. Deadly weapon defined
As used in Division 4 (commencing with Section 18250) of Title 2, "deadly weapon" means any weapon, the possession or concealed carrying of which is prohibited by any provision listed in Section 16590.

§ 16470. Dirk defined; dagger defined
As used in this part, "dirk" or "dagger" means a knife or other instrument with or without a handguard

that is capable of ready use as a stabbing weapon that may inflict great bodily injury or death. A non-locking folding knife, a folding knife that is not prohibited by Section 21510, or a pocketknife is capable of ready use as a stabbing weapon that may inflict great bodily injury or death only if the blade of the knife is exposed and locked into position.

§ 16590. Generally prohibited weapon defined

As used in this part, "generally prohibited weapon" means any of the following:

(a) An air gauge knife, as prohibited by Section 20310.

(c) A ballistic knife, as prohibited by Section 21110.

(d) A belt buckle knife, as prohibited by Section 20410.

(h) A cane sword, as prohibited by Section 20510.

(i) A concealed dirk or dagger, as prohibited by Section 21310.

(n) A lipstick case knife, as prohibited by Section 20610.

(s) A shobi-zue, as prohibited by Section 20710.

(u) A shuriken, as prohibited by Section 22410.

(y) A writing pen knife, as prohibited by Section 20910.

§ 16600. Great bodily injury defined

As used in Chapter 2 (commencing with Section 25100) of Division 4 of Title 4, "great bodily injury" means a significant or substantial physical injury.

§ 16830. Lipstick case knife defined

As used in this part, a "lipstick case knife" means a knife enclosed within and made an integral part of a lipstick case.

§ 17160. Shobi-zue defined

As used in this part, a "shobi-zue" means a staff, crutch, stick, rod, or pole concealing a knife or blade within it, which may be exposed by a flip of the wrist or by a mechanical action.

§ 17200. Shuriken defined

As used in this part, a "shuriken" means any instrument, without handles, consisting of a metal plate having three or more radiating points with one or more sharp edges and designed in the shape of a polygon, trefoil, cross, star, diamond, or other geometric shape, for use as a weapon for throwing.

§ 17235. Switchblade knife defined

As used in this part, "switchblade knife" means a knife having the appearance of a pocketknife and includes a spring-blade knife, snap-blade knife, gravity knife, or any other similar type knife, the blade or blades of which are two or more inches in length and which can be released automatically by a flick of a button, pressure on the handle, flip of the wrist or other mechanical device, or is released by the weight of the blade or by any type of mechanism whatsoever. "Switchblade knife" does not include a knife that opens with one hand utilizing thumb pressure applied solely to the blade of the knife or a thumb stud attached to the blade, provided that the knife has a detent or other mechanism that provides resistance that must be overcome in opening the blade, or that biases the blade back toward its closed position.

§ 17290. Undetectable knife defined

As used in this part, "undetectable knife" means any knife or other instrument, with or without a hand-guard, that satisfies all of the following requirements:

(a) It is capable of ready use as a stabbing weapon that may inflict great bodily injury or death.

(b) It is commercially manufactured to be used as a weapon.

(c) It is not detectable by a metal detector or magnetometer, either handheld or otherwise, which is set at standard calibration.

§ 17350. Writing pen knife defined
As used in this part, "writing pen knife" means a device that appears to be a writing pen but has concealed within it a pointed, metallic shaft that is designed to be a stabbing instrument which is exposed by mechanical action or gravity which locks into place when extended or the pointed, metallic shaft is exposed by the removal of the cap or cover on the device.

§ 18010. Weapons constituting nuisance; actions to enjoin; destruction of weapons
(a) The Attorney General, district attorney, or city attorney may bring an action to enjoin the manufacture of, importation of, keeping for sale of, offering or exposing for sale, giving, lending, or possession of, any item that constitutes a nuisance under any of the following provisions:

(2) Section 20390, relating to an air gauge knife.

(3) Section 20490, relating to a belt buckle knife.

(4) Section 20590, relating to a cane sword.

(5) Section 20690, relating to a lipstick case knife.

(6) Section 20790, relating to a shobi-zue.

(7) Section 20990, relating to a writing pen knife.

(8) Section 21190, relating to a ballistic knife.

(9) Section 21890, relating to metal knuckles.

(12) Section 22490, relating to a shuriken.

(b) These weapons shall be subject to confiscation and summary destruction whenever found within the state.

(c) These weapons shall be destroyed in the same manner described in Section 18005, except that upon the certification of a judge or of the district attorney that the ends of justice will be served thereby, the weapon shall be preserved until the necessity for its use ceases.

§ 20200. Knife carried in sheath worn openly deemed not concealed
A knife carried in a sheath that is worn openly suspended from the waist of the wearer is not concealed within the meaning of Section 16140, 16340, 17350, or 21310.

§ 20310. Manufacture, import, sale, supply or possession of air gauge knife; punishment
Except as provided in Chapter 1 (commencing with Section 17700) of Division 2 of Title 2, any person in this state who manufactures or causes to be manufactured, imports into the state, keeps for sale, or offers or exposes for sale, or who gives, lends, or possesses any air gauge knife is punishable by imprisonment in a county jail not exceeding one year or imprisonment pursuant to subdivision (h) of Section 1170.

§ 20390. Air gauge knife as nuisance subject to Section 18010
Except as provided in Chapter 1 (commencing with Section 17700) of Division 2 of Title 2, any air gauge knife is a nuisance and is subject to Section 18010.

§ 20410. Manufacture, import, sale, supply or possession of belt buckle knife; punishment
Except as provided in Chapter 1 (commencing with Section 17700) of Division 2 of Title 2, any person in this state who manufactures or causes to be manufactured, imports into the state, keeps for sale, or offers or exposes for sale, or who gives, lends, or possesses any belt buckle knife is punishable by imprisonment

in a county jail not exceeding one year or imprisonment pursuant to subdivision (h) of Section 1170.

§ 20490. Belt buckle knife deemed nuisance; exceptions
Except as provided in Chapter 1 (commencing with Section 17700) of Division 2 of Title 2, any belt buckle knife is a nuisance and is subject to Section 18010.

§ 20510. Manufacture, import, sale, supply or possession of cane sword; punishment
Except as provided in Chapter 1 (commencing with Section 17700) of Division 2 of Title 2, any person in this state who manufactures or causes to be manufactured, imports into the state, keeps for sale, or offers or exposes for sale, or who gives, lends, or possesses any cane sword is punishable by imprisonment in a county jail not exceeding one year or imprisonment pursuant to subdivision (h) of Section 1170.

§ 20590. Cane sword deemed nuisance; exceptions
Except as provided in Chapter 1 (commencing with Section 17700) of Division 2 of Title 2, any cane sword is a nuisance and is subject to Section 18010.

§ 20610. Manufacture, import, sale, supply or possession of lipstick case knife; punishment
Except as provided in Chapter 1 (commencing with Section 17700) of Division 2 of Title 2, any person in this state who manufactures or causes to be manufactured, imports into the state, keeps for sale, or offers or exposes for sale, or who gives, lends, or possesses any lipstick case knife is punishable by imprisonment in a county jail not exceeding one year or imprisonment pursuant to subdivision (h) of Section 1170.

§ 20690. Lipstick case knife deemed nuisance; exceptions
Except as provided in Chapter 1 (commencing with Section 17700) of Division 2 of Title 2, any lipstick case knife is a nuisance and is subject to Section 18010.

§ 20710. Manufacture, import, sale, supply or possession of shobi-zue; punishment
Except as provided in Chapter 1 (commencing with Section 17700) of Division 2 of Title 2, any person in this state who manufactures or causes to be manufactured, imports into the state, keeps for sale, or offers or exposes for sale, or who gives, lends, or possesses any shobi-zue is punishable by imprisonment in a county jail not exceeding one year or imprisonment pursuant to subdivision (h) of Section 1170.

§ 20790. Shobi-zue deemed nuisance; exceptions
Except as provided in Chapter 1 (commencing with Section 17700) of Division 2 of Title 2, any shobi-zue is a nuisance and is subject to Section 18010.

§ 20810. Undetectable knives; commercial manufacture, import for commercial sale, export or offer for commercial, dealer, wholesaler, or distributor sale; misdemeanor; manufacture of knives or other instruments to include detectable metal
(a) Any person in this state who commercially manufactures or causes to be commercially manufactured, or who knowingly imports into the state for commercial sale, or who knowingly exports out of this state for commercial, dealer, wholesaler, or distributor sale, or who keeps for commercial sale, or offers or exposes for commercial, dealer, wholesaler, or distributor sale, any undetectable knife is guilty of a misdemeanor.

(b) Notwithstanding any other provision of law, commencing January 1, 2000, all knives or other instrument with or without a handguard that is capable of ready use as a stabbing weapon that may inflict great bodily injury or death that are commercially manufactured in this state that utilize materials that are not detectable by a metal detector or magnetometer, shall be manufactured to include materials that will ensure they are detectable by a metal detector or magnetometer, either handheld or otherwise, that is set at standard calibration.

§ 20815. Undetectable knives for sale to law enforcement or military entity
Section 20810 does not apply to the manufacture or importation of any undetectable knife for sale to a law enforcement or military entity with a valid agency, department, or unit purchase order, nor does Section 20810 apply to the subsequent sale of any undetectable knife to a law enforcement or military entity.

§ 20820. Undetectable knives for sale to historical society, museum, or institutional collection

Section 20810 does not apply to the manufacture or importation of any undetectable knife for sale to a federal, state, or local historical society, museum, or institutional collection that is open to the public, provided that the undetectable knife is properly housed and secured from unauthorized handling, nor does Section 20810 apply to the subsequent sale of the knife to any of these entities.

§ 20910. Manufacture, import, sale, supply or possession of writing pen knife; punishment

Except as provided in Chapter 1 (commencing with Section 17700) of Division 2 of Title 2, any person in this state who manufactures or causes to be manufactured, imports into the state, keeps for sale, or offers or exposes for sale, or who gives, lends, or possesses any writing pen knife is punishable by imprisonment in a county jail not exceeding one year or imprisonment pursuant to subdivision (h) of Section 1170.

§ 20990. Writing pen knife deemed nuisance; exceptions

Except as provided in Chapter 1 (commencing with Section 17700) of Division 2 of Title 2, any writing pen knife is a nuisance and is subject to Section 18010.

§ 21110. Manufacture, import, sale, supply or possession of ballistic knife; punishment

Except as provided in Chapter 1 (commencing with Section 17700) of Division 2 of Title 2, any person in this state who manufactures or causes to be manufactured, imports into the state, keeps for sale, or offers or exposes for sale, or who gives, lends, or possesses any ballistic knife is punishable by imprisonment in a county jail not exceeding one year or imprisonment pursuant to subdivision (h) of Section 1170.

§ 21190. Ballistic knife deemed nuisance; exceptions

Except as provided in Chapter 1 (commencing with Section 17700) of Division 2 of Title 2, any ballistic knife is a nuisance and is subject to Section 18010.

§ 21310. Carrying of concealed dirk or dagger; punishment

Except as provided in Chapter 1 (commencing with Section 17700) of Division 2 of Title 2, any person in this state who carries concealed upon the person any dirk or dagger is punishable by imprisonment in a county jail not exceeding one year or imprisonment pursuant to subdivision (h) of Section 1170.

§ 21390. Unlawful concealed carrying of dirk or dagger deemed nuisance

The unlawful concealed carrying upon the person of any dirk or dagger, as provided in Section 21310, is a nuisance and is subject to Sections 18000 and 18005.

§ 21510. Possession, carrying, sale, loan or transfer of switchblade knife prohibited

Every person who does any of the following with a switchblade knife having a blade two or more inches in length is guilty of a misdemeanor:

(a) Possesses the knife in the passenger's or driver's area of any motor vehicle in any public place or place open to the public.

(b) Carries the knife upon the person.

(c) Sells, offers for sale, exposes for sale, loans, transfers, or gives the knife to any other person.

§ 21590. Unlawful possession or carrying of switchblade knife deemed nuisance

The unlawful possession or carrying of any switchblade knife, as provided in Section 21510, is a nuisance and is subject to Sections 18000 and 18005.

§ 22410. Manufacture, import, sale, supply or possession of shuriken; punishment

Except as provided in Chapter 1 (commencing with Section 17700) of Division 2 of Title 2, any person in this state who manufactures or causes to be manufactured, imports into the state, keeps for sale, or offers or exposes for sale, or who gives, lends, or possesses any shuriken is punishable by imprisonment in a county jail not exceeding one year or imprisonment pursuant to subdivision (h) of Section 1170.

§ 22490. Shuriken as nuisance subject to § 18010

Except as provided in Chapter 1 (commencing with Section 17700) of Division 2 of Title 2, any shuriken is a nuisance and is subject to Section 18010.

§ 17505. Advertising of unlawful weapons or devices prohibited

It shall be unlawful for any person, as defined in Section 16970, to advertise the sale of any weapon or device, the possession of which is prohibited by Section 18710, 20110, 30315, 30320, 32625, or 33410, by Article 2 (commencing with Section 30600) of Chapter 2 of Division 10 of Title 4, or by any provision listed in Section 16590, in any newspaper, magazine, circular, form letter, or open publication that is published, distributed, or circulated in this state, or on any billboard, card, label, or other advertising medium, or by means of any other advertising device.

§ 626.10. Bringing or possessing weapons on school grounds; exceptions

(a)(1) Any person, except a duly appointed peace officer as defined in Chapter 4.5 (commencing with Section 830) of Title 3 of Part 2, a full-time paid peace officer of another state or the federal government who is carrying out official duties while in this state, a person summoned by any officer to assist in making arrests or preserving the peace while the person is actually engaged in assisting any officer, or a member of the military forces of this state or the United States who is engaged in the performance of his or her duties, who brings or possesses any dirk, dagger, ice pick, knife having a blade longer than 2 ½ inches, folding knife with a blade that locks into place, razor with an unguarded blade, taser, or stun gun, as defined in subdivision (a) of Section 244.5, any instrument that expels a metallic projectile, such as a BB or a pellet, through the force of air pressure, CO2 pressure, or spring action, or any spot marker gun, upon the grounds of, or within, any public or private school providing instruction in kindergarten or any of grades 1 to 12, inclusive, is guilty of a public offense, punishable by imprisonment in a county jail not exceeding one year, or by imprisonment pursuant to subdivision (h) of Section 1170.

(2) Any person, except a duly appointed peace officer as defined in Chapter 4.5 (commencing with Section 830) of Title 3 of Part 2, a full-time paid peace officer of another state or the federal government who is carrying out official duties while in this state, a person summoned by any officer to assist in making arrests or preserving the peace while the person is actually engaged in assisting any officer, or a member of the military forces of this state or the United States who is engaged in the performance of his or her duties, who brings or possesses a razor blade or a box cutter upon the grounds of, or within, any public or private school providing instruction in kindergarten or any of grades 1 to 12, inclusive, is guilty of a public offense, punishable by imprisonment in a county jail not exceeding one year.

(b) Any person, except a duly appointed peace officer as defined in Chapter 4.5 (commencing with Section 830) of Title 3 of Part 2, a full-time paid peace officer of another state or the federal government who is carrying out official duties while in this state, a person summoned by any officer to assist in making arrests or preserving the peace while the person is actually engaged in assisting any officer, or a member of the military forces of this state or the United States who is engaged in the performance of his or her duties, who brings or possesses any dirk, dagger, ice pick, or knife having a fixed blade longer than 2 ½ inches upon the grounds of, or within, any private university, the University of California, the California State University, or the California Community Colleges is guilty of a public offense, punishable by imprisonment in a county jail not exceeding one year, or by imprisonment pursuant to subdivision (h) of Section 1170.

(c) Subdivisions (a) and (b) do not apply to any person who brings or possesses a knife having a blade longer than 2 ½ inches, a razor with an unguarded blade, a razor blade, or a box cutter upon the grounds of, or within, a public or private school providing instruction in kindergarten or any of grades 1 to 12, inclusive, or any private university, state university, or community college at the direction of a faculty member of the private university, state university, or community college, or a certificated or classified employee of the school for use in a private university, state university, community college, or school-sponsored activity or class.

(d) Subdivisions (a) and (b) do not apply to any person who brings or possesses an ice pick, a knife having a blade longer than 2 ½ inches, a razor with an unguarded blade, a razor blade, or a box cutter upon the grounds of, or within, a public or private school providing instruction in kindergarten or any of grades 1 to 12, inclusive, or any private university, state university, or community college for a lawful purpose within the scope of the person's employment.

(e) Subdivision (b) does not apply to any person who brings or possesses an ice pick or a knife having a fixed blade longer than 2 ½ inches upon the grounds of, or within, any private university, state university, or community college for lawful use in or around a residence or residential facility located upon those grounds or for lawful use in food preparation or consumption.

(g) Any certificated or classified employee or school peace officer of a public or private school providing instruction in kindergarten or any of grades 1 to 12, inclusive, may seize any of the weapons described in subdivision (a), and any certificated or classified employee or school peace officer of any private university, state university, or community college may seize any of the weapons described in subdivision (b), from the possession of any person upon the grounds of, or within, the school if he or she knows, or has reasonable cause to know, the person is prohibited from bringing or possessing the weapon upon the grounds of, or within, the school.

(h) As used in this section, "dirk" or "dagger" means a knife or other instrument with or without a handguard that is capable of ready use as a stabbing weapon that may inflict great bodily injury or death.

(i) Any person who, without the written permission of the college or university president or chancellor or his or her designee, brings or possesses a less lethal weapon, as defined in Section 16780, or a stun gun, as defined in Section 17230, upon the grounds of, or within, a public or private college or university campus is guilty of a misdemeanor.

§ 4502. Possession or manufacture of weapon; punishment

(a) Every person who, while at or confined in any penal institution, while being conveyed to or from any penal institution, or while under the custody of officials, officers, or employees of any penal institution, possesses or carries upon his or her person or has under his or her custody or control any instrument or weapon of the kind commonly known as a blackjack, slungshot, billy, sandclub, sandbag, or metal knuckles, any explosive substance, or fixed ammunition, any dirk or dagger or sharp instrument, any pistol, revolver, or other firearm, or any tear gas or tear gas weapon, is guilty of a felony and shall be punished by imprisonment pursuant to subdivision (h) of Section 1170 for two, three, or four years, to be served consecutively.

(b) Every person who, while at or confined in any penal institution, while being conveyed to or from any penal institution, or while under the custody of officials, officers, or employees of any penal institution, manufactures or attempts to manufacture any instrument or weapon of the kind commonly known as a blackjack, slungshot, billy, sandclub, sandbag, or metal knuckles, any explosive substance, or fixed ammunition, any dirk or dagger or sharp instrument, any pistol, revolver, or other firearm, or any tear gas or tear gas weapon, is guilty of a felony and shall be punished by imprisonment pursuant to subdivision (h) of Section 1170 for 16 months, or two or three years, to be served consecutively.

(c) For purposes of this section, "penal institution" means the state prison, a prison road camp, prison forestry camp, or other prison camp or farm, or a county jail or county road camp.

⊶ COLORADO ⊷
KNIFE RIGHTS MOVEMENT RATING
★ ★ ☆ ☆ ☆

CUTTING TO THE CHASE

Colorado bans certain knives by type and prohibits carrying of certain knives concealed. It allows for the carry of hunting and fishing knives, but this is an affirmative defense in which one charged with carrying a knife has the burden of proof. A carrier of a hunting or fishing knife is essentially guilty until proven innocent.

Quick Points Concerning Colorado's Knife Law*

KNIFE TYPE	POSSESSION	(Open/Concealed) CARRY	SALE	MANUFACTURE
Assisted Opening	Legal	Legal/Gray	Legal	Legal
Automatic/Switchblade	Prohibited	Prohibited/Prohibited	Prohibited	Prohibited
Ballistic	Prohibited	Prohibited/Prohibited	Prohibited	Prohibited
Bayonets	Legal	Legal/Prohibited	Legal	Legal
Bowie	Legal	Legal/Prohibited	Legal	Legal
Butterfly/Balisong	Gray	Gray/Gray	Gray	Gray
Combat/Survival	Legal	Legal/Prohibited	Legal	Legal
Dagger	Legal	Legal/Prohibited	Legal	Legal
Dirk	Legal	Legal/Prohibited	Legal	Legal
Disguised	Legal	Legal/Prohibited	Legal	Legal
Fixed	Legal	Legal/Gray	Legal	Legal
Folding	Legal	Legal/Gray	Legal	Legal
Gravity	Prohibited	Prohibited/Prohibited	Prohibited	Prohibited
Hunting/Fishing	Legal	Legal/Legal	Legal	Legal
Machete	Legal	Legal/Gray	Legal	Legal
Razor	Legal	Legal/Gray	Legal	Legal
Stiletto	Legal	Legal/Gray	Legal	Legal
Sword	Legal	Legal/Gray	Legal	Legal
Throwing	Legal	Legal/Gray	Legal	Legal
Undetectable	Legal	Legal/Gray	Legal	Legal

Pre-emption (Only State Law May Regulate, No Local Laws Permitted) – YES
*See all information above and below for more details.

SHARP TIPS ABOUT COLORADO'S KNIFE LAWS

Knives with blades under 3 ½ are excluded from the definition of a "knife" and are therefore not prohibited. "Per se" knives such as switchblades, gravity knives and ballistic knives are banned regardless of blade size. Certain convicted persons are prohibited from knife possession.

EDGE –U- CATIONAL --- COLORADO'S KNIFE LAWS
§ 18-1-901. Definitions

(1) Definitions set forth in any section of this title apply wherever the same term is used in the same sense in another section of this title unless the definition is specifically limited or the context indicates that it is inapplicable.

(2) The terms defined in section 18-1-104 and in section 18-1-501, as well as the terms defined in

subsection (3) of this section, are terms which appear in various articles of this code. Other terms which need definition but which are used only in a limited number of sections of this code are defined in the particular section or article in which the terms appear.

(c) "Bodily injury" means physical pain, illness, or any impairment of physical or mental condition.

(d) "Deadly physical force" means force, the intended, natural, and probable consequence of which is to produce death, and which does, in fact, produce death.

(e) "Deadly weapon" means:

(II) A knife, bludgeon, or any other weapon, device, instrument, material, or substance, whether animate or inanimate, that, in the manner it is used or intended to be used, is capable of producing death or serious bodily injury.

(p) "Serious bodily injury" means bodily injury which, either at the time of the actual injury or at a later time, involves a substantial risk of death, a substantial risk of serious permanent disfigurement, a substantial risk of protracted loss or impairment of the function of any part or organ of the body, or breaks, fractures, or burns of the second or third degree.

§ 18-12-101. Definitions--peace officer affirmative defense

(1) As used in this article, unless the context otherwise requires:

(a) "Adult" means any person eighteen years of age or older.

(a.3) "Ballistic knife" means any knife that has a blade which is forcefully projected from the handle by means of a spring-loaded device or explosive charge.

(e) "Gravity knife" means any knife that has a blade released from the handle or sheath thereof by the force of gravity or the application of centrifugal force.

(f) "Knife" means any dagger, dirk, knife, or stiletto with a blade over three and one-half inches in length, or any other dangerous instrument capable of inflicting cutting, stabbing, or tearing wounds, but does not include a hunting or fishing knife carried for sports use. The issue that a knife is a hunting or fishing knife must be raised as an affirmative defense.

(j) "Switchblade knife" means any knife, the blade of which opens automatically by hand pressure applied to a button, spring, or other device in its handle.

(2) It shall be an affirmative defense to any provision of this article that the act was committed by a peace officer in the lawful discharge of his duties.

§ 18-12-102. Possessing a dangerous or illegal weapon--affirmative defense

(1) As used in this section, the term "dangerous weapon" means a firearm silencer, machine gun, short shotgun, short rifle, or ballistic knife.

(2) As used in this section, the term "illegal weapon" means a blackjack, gas gun, metallic knuckles, gravity knife, or switchblade knife.

(3) A person who knowingly possesses a dangerous weapon commits a class 5 felony. Each subsequent violation of this subsection (3) by the same person shall be a class 4 felony.

(4) A person who knowingly possesses an illegal weapon commits a class 1 misdemeanor.

(5) It shall be an affirmative defense to the charge of possessing a dangerous weapon, or to the charge of possessing an illegal weapon, that the person so accused was a peace officer or member of the armed forces of the United States or Colorado National Guard acting in the lawful discharge of his duties, or that said person has a valid permit and license for possession of such weapon.

§ 18-12-105. Unlawfully carrying a concealed weapon--unlawful possession of weapons

(1) A person commits a class 2 misdemeanor if such person knowingly and unlawfully:

(a) Carries a knife concealed on or about his or her person; or

(2) It shall not be an offense if the defendant was:

(a) A person in his or her own dwelling or place of business or on property owned or under his or her control at the time of the act of carrying; or

(b) A person in a private automobile or other private means of conveyance who carries a weapon for lawful protection of such person's or another's person or property while traveling; or

(c) A person who, at the time of carrying a concealed weapon, held a valid written permit to carry a concealed weapon issued pursuant to section 18-12-105.1, as it existed prior to its repeal, or, if the weapon involved was a handgun, held a valid permit to carry a concealed handgun or a temporary emergency permit issued pursuant to part 2 of this article; except that it shall be an offense under this section if the person was carrying a concealed handgun in violation of the provisions of section 18-12-214; or

(d) A peace officer, as described in section 16-2.5-101, C.R.S., when carrying a weapon in conformance with the policy of the employing agency as provided in section 16-2.5-101(2), C.R.S.; or

(f) A United States probation officer or a United States pretrial services officer while on duty and serving in the state of Colorado under the authority of rules and regulations promulgated by the judicial conference of the United States.

§ 18-12-105.5. Unlawfully carrying a weapon--unlawful possession of weapons--school, college, or university grounds

(1) A person commits a class 6 felony if such person knowingly and unlawfully and without legal authority carries, brings, or has in such person's possession a deadly weapon as defined in section 18-1-901(3)(e) in or on the real estate and all improvements erected thereon of any public or private elementary, middle, junior high, high, or vocational school or any public or private college, university, or seminary, except for the purpose of presenting an authorized public demonstration or exhibition pursuant to instruction in conjunction with an organized school or class, for the purpose of carrying out the necessary duties and functions of an employee of an educational institution that require the use of a deadly weapon, or for the purpose of participation in an authorized extracurricular activity or on an athletic team. (3) It shall not be an offense under this section if:

(a) The weapon is unloaded and remains inside a motor vehicle while upon the real estate of any public or private college, university, or seminary; or

(b) The person is in that person's own dwelling or place of business or on property owned or under that person's control at the time of the act of carrying; or

(c) The person is in a private automobile or other private means of conveyance and is carrying a weapon for lawful protection of that person's or another's person or property while traveling; or

(d) The person, at the time of carrying a concealed weapon, held a valid written permit to carry a concealed weapon issued pursuant to section 18-12-105.1, as said section existed prior to its repeal; except that it shall be an offense under this section if the person was carrying a concealed handgun in violation of the provisions of section 18-12-214(3); or

(e) The person is a school resource officer, as defined in section 22-32-109.1(g.5), C.R.S., or a peace officer, as described in section 16-2.5-101, C.R.S., when carrying a weapon in conformance with the policy of the employing agency as provided in section 16-2.5-101(2), C.R.S.; or

(h) The person has possession of the weapon for use in an educational program approved by a school which program includes, but shall not be limited to, any course designed for the repair or maintenance of weapons.

§ 18-12-105.6 Limitation on local ordinances regarding firearms in private vehicles

(1) The general assembly hereby finds that:

(a) A person carrying a weapon in a private automobile or other private means of conveyance for hunting or for lawful protection of such person's or another's person or property, as permitted in sections 18-12-105(2)(b) and 18-12-105.5(3)(c), may tend to travel within a county, city and county, or municipal jurisdiction or in or through different county, city and county, and municipal jurisdictions, en route to the person's destination;

(b) Inconsistent laws exist in local jurisdictions with regard to the circumstances under which weapons may be carried in automobiles and other private means of conveyance;

(c) This inconsistency creates a confusing patchwork of laws that unfairly subjects a person who lawfully travels with a weapon to criminal penalties because he or she travels within a jurisdiction or into or through another jurisdiction;

(d) This inconsistency places citizens in the position of not knowing when they may be violating local laws while traveling within a jurisdiction or in, through, or between different jurisdictions, and therefore being unable to avoid committing a crime.

(2)(a) Based on the findings specified in subsection (1) of this section, the general assembly concludes that the carrying of weapons in private automobiles or other private means of conveyance for hunting or for lawful protection of a person's or another's person or property while traveling into, through, or within, a municipal, county, or city and county jurisdiction, regardless of the number of times the person stops in a jurisdiction, is a matter of statewide concern and is not an offense.

(b) Notwithstanding any other provision of law, no municipality, county, or city and county shall have the authority to enact or enforce any ordinance or resolution that would restrict a person's ability to travel with a weapon in a private automobile or other private means of conveyance for hunting or for lawful protection of a person's or another's person or property while traveling into, through, or within, a municipal, county, or city and county jurisdiction, regardless of the number of times the person stops in a jurisdiction.

§ 18-12-108. Possession of weapons by previous offenders

(1) A person commits the crime of possession of a weapon by a previous offender if the person knowingly possesses, uses, or carries upon his or her person a firearm as described in section 18-1-901(3)(h) or any other weapon that is subject to the provisions of this article subsequent to the person's conviction for a felony, or subsequent to the person's conviction for attempt or conspiracy to commit a felony, under Colorado or any other state's law or under federal law.

(2)(a) Except as otherwise provided by paragraphs (b) and (c) of this subsection (2), a person commits a class 6 felony if the person violates subsection (1) of this section.

(b) A person commits a class 5 felony, as provided by section 18-12-102, if the person violates subsection (1) of this section and the weapon is a dangerous weapon, as defined in section 18-12-102(1).

(c) A person commits a class 5 felony if the person violates subsection (1) of this section and the person's previous conviction was for burglary, arson, or any felony involving the use of force or the use of a deadly weapon and the violation of subsection (1) of this section occurs as follows:

(I) From the date of conviction to ten years after the date of conviction, if the person was not incarcerated; or

(II) From the date of conviction to ten years after the date of release from confinement, if such person was incarcerated or, if subject to supervision imposed as a result of conviction, ten years after the date of release from supervision.

(d) Any sentence imposed pursuant to this subsection (2) shall run consecutively with any prior sentences being served by the offender.

(3) A person commits the crime of possession of a weapon by a previous offender if the person knowingly possesses, uses, or carries upon his or her person a firearm as described in section 18-1-901(3)(h) or any other weapon that is subject to the provisions of this article subsequent to the person's adjudication for an act which, if committed by an adult, would constitute a felony, or subsequent to the person's adjudication for attempt or conspiracy to commit a felony, under Colorado or any other state's law or under federal law.

(4)(a) Except as otherwise provided by paragraphs (b) and (c) of this subsection (4), a person commits a class 6 felony if the person violates subsection (3) of this section.

(b) A person commits a class 5 felony, as provided by section 18-12-102, if the person violates subsection (3) of this section and the weapon is a dangerous weapon, as defined in section 18-12-102(1).

§ 22-33-102. Definitions
As used in this article, unless the context otherwise requires:

(4) "Dangerous weapon" means:

(c) A fixed-blade knife with a blade that exceeds three inches in length

(d) A spring-loaded knife or a pocket knife with a blade exceeding three and one-half inches in length; or

(e) Any object, device, instrument, material, or substance, whether animate or inanimate, that is used or intended to be used to inflict death or serious bodily injury.

§ 22-33-106. Grounds for suspension, expulsion, and denial of admission
(1) The following may be grounds for suspension or expulsion of a child from a public school during a school year:

(d) Committing one of the following offenses on school grounds, in a school vehicle, or at a school activity or sanctioned event:

(I) Possession of a dangerous weapon without the authorization of the school or the school district;

§ 12-36-135 Injuries to be reported--penalty for failure to report--immunity from liability
(1)(a)(I) Every licensee who attends or treats any of the following injuries shall report the injury at once to the police of the city, town, or city and county or the sheriff of the county in which the licensee is located:

(A) A bullet wound, a gunshot wound, a powder burn, or any other injury arising from the discharge of a firearm, or an injury caused by a knife, an ice pick, or any other sharp or pointed instrument that the licensee believes to have been intentionally inflicted upon a person;

(II) Any licensee who fails to make a report as required by this section commits a class 2 petty offense, as defined by section 18-1.3-503, C.R.S., and, upon conviction thereof, shall be punished by a fine of not more than three hundred dollars, or by imprisonment in the county jail for not more than ninety days, or by both such fine and imprisonment.

(2) Any licensee who, in good faith, makes a report pursuant to subsection (1) of this section shall have immunity from any liability, civil or criminal, that might otherwise be incurred or imposed with respect to the making of such report, and shall have the same immunity with respect to participation in any judicial proceeding resulting from such report.

(3) Any licensee who makes a report pursuant to subsection (1) of this section shall not be subject to the physician-patient relationship described in section 13-90-107(1)(d), C.R.S., as to the medical examination and diagnosis. Such licensee may be examined as a witness, but not as to any statements made by the patient that are the subject matter of section 13-90-107(1)(d), C.R.S.

⚔ CONNECTICUT ⚔
KNIFE RIGHTS MOVEMENT RATING
★ ★ ★ ☆ ☆

CUTTING TO THE CHASE
Connecticut has a fair degree of knife rights freedom. Its carry laws are complex with various arbitrary exemptions and a bias exists against certain knife features.

Quick Points Concerning Connecticut's Knife Law*

KNIFE TYPE	POSSESSION	(Open/Concealed) CARRY	SALE	MANUFACTURE
Assisted Opening	Legal	Gray/Gray	Legal	Legal
Automatic/Switchblade	Legal	Gray/Gray	Legal	Legal
Ballistic	Legal	Gray/Gray	Legal	Legal
Bayonets	Legal	Gray/Gray	Legal	Legal
Bowie	Legal	Gray/Gray	Legal	Legal
Butterfly/Balisong	Legal	Gray/Gray	Legal	Legal
Combat/Survival	Legal	Gray/Gray	Legal	Legal
Dagger	Legal	Gray/Gray	Legal	Legal
Dirk	Legal	Gray/Gray	Legal	Legal
Disguised	Legal	Gray/Gray	Legal	Legal
Fixed	Legal	Gray/Gray	Legal	Legal
Folding	Legal	Gray/Gray	Legal	Legal
Gravity	Legal	Gray/Gray	Legal	Legal
Hunting/Fishing	Legal	Gray/Gray	Legal	Legal
Machete	Legal	Gray/Gray	Legal	Legal
Razor	Legal	Gray/Gray	Legal	Legal
Stiletto	Legal	Gray/Gray	Legal	Legal
Sword	Legal	Gray/Gray	Legal	Legal
Throwing	Legal	Gray/Gray	Legal	Legal
Undetectable	Legal	Gray/Gray	Legal	Legal

Pre-emption (Only State Law May Regulate, No Local Laws Permitted) – NO
*See all information above and below for more details.

SHARP TIPS ABOUT CONNECTICUT'S KNIFE LAWS
Connecticut focuses its anti-knife rights laws on persons carrying knives and transporting them in vehicles. They have many exemptions listed in the law. No pre-emption so beware of town laws.

EDGE –U- CATIONAL --- CONNECTICUT'S KNIFE LAWS
§ 53-206. Carrying of dangerous weapons prohibited
(a) Any person who carries upon his or her person any BB gun, blackjack, metal or brass knuckles, or any dirk knife, or any switch knife, or any knife having an automatic spring release device by which a blade is released from the handle, having a blade of over one and one-half inches in length, or stiletto, or any knife the edged portion of the blade of which is four inches or more in length, any police baton or nightstick, or any martial arts weapon or electronic defense weapon, as defined in section 53a-3, or any other dangerous or deadly weapon or instrument, shall be guilty of a class E felony. Whenever any person is found guilty of a violation of this section, any weapon or other instrument within the provisions of this section, found upon the body of such person, shall be forfeited to the municipality

wherein such person was apprehended, notwithstanding any failure of the judgment of conviction to expressly impose such forfeiture.

(b) The provisions of this section shall not apply to (1) any officer charged with the preservation of the public peace while engaged in the pursuit of such officer's official duties; (2) the carrying of a baton or nightstick by a security guard while engaged in the pursuit of such guard's official duties; (3) the carrying of a knife, the edged portion of the blade of which is four inches or more in length, by (A) any member of the armed forces of the United States, as defined in section 27-103, or any reserve component thereof, or of the armed forces of the state, as defined in section 27-2, when on duty or going to or from duty, (B) any member of any military organization when on parade or when going to or from any place of assembly, (C) any person while transporting such knife as merchandise or for display at an authorized gun or knife show, (D) any person who is found with any such knife concealed upon one's person while lawfully removing such person's household goods or effects from one place to another, or from one residence to another, (E) any person while actually and peaceably engaged in carrying any such knife from such person's place of abode or business to a place or person where or by whom such knife is to be repaired, or while actually and peaceably returning to such person's place of abode or business with such knife after the same has been repaired, (F) any person holding a valid hunting, fishing or trapping license issued pursuant to chapter 4901 or any saltwater fisherman carrying such knife for lawful hunting, fishing or trapping activities, or (G) any person while participating in an authorized historic reenactment; (4) the carrying by any person enrolled in or currently attending, or an instructor at, a martial arts school of a martial arts weapon while in a class or at an authorized event or competition or while transporting such weapon to or from such class, event or competition; (5) the carrying of a BB. gun by any person taking part in a supervised event or competition of the Boy Scouts of America or the Girl Scouts of America or in any other authorized event or competition while taking part in such event or competition or while transporting such weapon to or from such event or competition; and (6) the carrying of a BB gun by any person upon such person's own property or the property of another person provided such other person has authorized the carrying of such weapon on such property, and the transporting of such weapon to or from such property.

§ 29-38. Weapons in vehicles. Penalty. Exceptions

(a) Any person who knowingly has, in any vehicle owned, operated or occupied by such person, any weapon, any pistol or revolver for which a proper permit has not been issued as provided in section 29-28 or any machine gun which has not been registered as required by section 53-202, shall be guilty of a class D felony, and the presence of any such weapon, pistol or revolver, or machine gun in any vehicle shall be prima facie evidence of a violation of this section by the owner, operator and each occupant thereof. The word "weapon", as used in this section, means any BB. gun, any blackjack, any metal or brass knuckles, any police baton or nightstick, any dirk knife or switch knife, any knife having an automatic spring release device by which a blade is released from the handle, having a blade of over one and one-half inches in length, any stiletto, any knife the edged portion of the blade of which is four inches or more in length, any martial arts weapon or electronic defense weapon, as defined in section 53a-3, or any other dangerous or deadly weapon or instrument.

(b) The provisions of this section shall not apply to: (1) Any officer charged with the preservation of the public peace while engaged in the pursuit of such officer's official duties; (2) any security guard having a baton or nightstick in a vehicle while engaged in the pursuit of such guard's official duties; (3) any person enrolled in and currently attending a martial arts school, with official verification of such enrollment and attendance, or any certified martial arts instructor, having any such martial arts weapon in a vehicle while traveling to or from such school or to or from an authorized event or competition; (4) any person having a BB. gun in a vehicle provided such weapon is unloaded and stored in the trunk of such vehicle or in a locked container other than the glove compartment or console; and (5) any person having a knife, the edged portion of the blade of which is four inches or more in length, in a vehicle if such person is (A) any member of the armed forces of the United States, as defined in section 27-103, or any reserve component thereof, or of the armed forces of the state, as defined in section 27-2, when on duty or going to or from duty, (B) any member of any military organization when on parade or when going to or from any place of assembly, (C) any person while transporting such knife as merchandise or for display at an authorized gun or knife show, (D) any person while lawfully removing such person's household goods or effects from one place to another, or from one residence to another, (E) any person while actually and peaceably engaged in carrying any such knife from such person's place of abode or business to a place or person where or by whom such knife is to be repaired, or while actually and peaceably returning to such person's place of abode or business with such knife after the same has been repaired, (F) any person holding a valid hunting, fishing or trapping license issued pursuant to chapter 4901 or any saltwater fisherman while having such knife in a vehicle for lawful hunting, fishing or trapping activities, or (G) any person participating in an authorized historic reenactment.

§ 53a-3. Definitions

Except where different meanings are expressly specified, the following terms have the following meanings when used in this title:

(4) "Serious physical injury" means physical injury which creates a substantial risk of death, or which causes serious disfigurement, serious impairment of health or serious loss or impairment of the function of any bodily organ;

(5) "Deadly physical force" means physical force which can be reasonably expected to cause death or serious physical injury;

(6) "Deadly weapon" means any weapon, whether loaded or unloaded, from which a shot may be discharged, or a switchblade knife, gravity knife, billy, blackjack, bludgeon, or metal knuckles. The definition of "deadly weapon" in this subdivision shall be deemed not to apply to section 29-38 or 53-206;

(7) "Dangerous instrument" means any instrument, article or substance which, under the circumstances in which it is used or attempted or threatened to be used, is capable of causing death or serious physical injury, and includes a "vehicle" as that term is defined in this section and includes a dog that has been commanded to attack, except a dog owned by a law enforcement agency of the state or any political subdivision thereof or of the federal government when such dog is in the performance of its duties under the direct supervision, care and control of an assigned law enforcement officer;

(21) "Martial arts weapon" means a nunchaku, kama, kasari-fundo, octagon sai, tonfa or chinese star;

§ 53a-174a. Possession of weapon or dangerous instrument in correctional institution: Class B felony

(a) A person is guilty of possession of a weapon or dangerous instrument in a correctional institution when, being an inmate of such institution, he knowingly makes, conveys from place to place or has in his possession or under his control any firearm, weapon, dangerous instrument, explosive, or any other substance or thing designed to kill, injure or disable.

(b) Possession of a weapon or dangerous instrument in a correctional institution is a class B felony.

§ 53a-217b. Possession of a weapon on school grounds: Class D felony

(a) A person is guilty of possession of a weapon on school grounds when, knowing that such person is not licensed or privileged to do so, such person possesses a firearm or deadly weapon, as defined in section 53a-3, (1) in or on the real property comprising a public or private elementary or secondary school, or (2) at a school-sponsored activity as defined in subsection (h) of section 10-233a.

(b) The provisions of subsection (a) of this section shall not apply to the otherwise lawful possession of a firearm (1) by a person for use in a program approved by school officials in or on such school property or at such school-sponsored activity, (2) by a person in accordance with an agreement entered into between school officials and such person or such person's employer, (3) by a peace officer, as defined in subdivision (9) of section 53a-3, while engaged in the performance of such peace officer's official duties, or (4) by a person while traversing such school property for the purpose of gaining access to public or private lands open to hunting or for other lawful purposes, provided such firearm is not loaded and the entry on such school property is permitted by the local or regional board of education.

(c) Possession of a weapon on school grounds is a class D felony.

§ 2-1e. Interference with the legislative process; firearms; dangerous or deadly weapons; explosives; felony

(a) A person is guilty of interfering with the legislative process when he, alone or in concert with others, either by force, physical interference, fraud, intimidation or by means of any independently unlawful act, prevents or attempts to prevent any member, officer or employee of the general assembly, either house thereof or any committee of the general assembly or either house thereof, from performing any of his official functions, powers or duties.

(b) A person is guilty of coercing performance when he, alone or in concert with others, either by force, physical interference, fraud, intimidation or by means of any unlawful act, compels or induces any member, officer or employee of the general assembly, either house thereof or any committee of the general assembly or either house thereof to perform any acts as a member, officer or employee against his will.

(c) Notwithstanding the provisions of sections 29-35 and 53-206, (1) a person, other than a state or local police officer, a member of the Office of State Capitol Police or a police officer of any other state or of the federal government, who is carrying out official duties in this state, or any person summoned by any such officer to assist in making arrests or preserving the peace while he is actually engaged in assisting such officer, while such officer is in the performance of his official duties or any member of the armed forces of the United States, as defined by section 27-103, or of this state, as defined by section 27-2, in the performance of official duties, or any veteran, as defined by section 27-103, performing in uniform as a member of an official ceremonial unit, is guilty of interfering with the legislative process when he, alone or in concert with others, brings into, or possesses within, any building in which the chamber of either house of the General Assembly is located or in which the official office of any member, officer or employee of the General Assembly or the office of any committee of the General Assembly or either house thereof is located or any building in which a committee of the General Assembly is holding a public hearing, any weapon, whether loaded or unloaded, from which a shot may be discharged, or a billy; and (2) any person is guilty of interfering with the legislative process when he, alone or in concert with others, brings into, or possesses within, any such building, a switchblade, gravity knife, blackjack, bludgeon, metal knuckles or any other dangerous or deadly weapon or instrument, or any explosive or incendiary or other dangerous device.

(d) The violation of any provision of this section is a class D felony.

✢ DELAWARE ✢
KNIFE RIGHTS MOVEMENT RATING
★ ★ ☆ ☆ ☆

CUTTING TO THE CHASE
The only knife that may be carried concealed is a pocket knife with a blade less than 3". Delaware bans knives by type as well. Not a good state for knife rights.

Quick Points Concerning Delaware's Knife Law*

KNIFE TYPE	POSSESSION	(Open/Concealed) CARRY	SALE	MANUFACTURE
Assisted Opening	Legal	Gray	Legal	Legal
Automatic/Switchblade	Prohibited	Prohibited/Prohibited	Prohibited	Prohibited
Ballistic	Gray	Gray/ Prohibited	Gray	Gray
Bayonets	Legal	Legal/ Prohibited	Legal	Legal
Bowie	Legal	Legal/ Prohibited	Legal	Legal
Butterfly/Balisong	Gray	Gray/ Prohibited	Gray	Gray
Combat/Survival	Legal	Legal/ Prohibited	Legal	Legal
Dagger	Legal	Legal/ Prohibited	Prohibited	Prohibited
Dirk	Legal	Legal/ Prohibited	Prohibited	Prohibited
Disguised	Legal	Legal/ Prohibited	Legal	Legal
Fixed	Legal	Legal/ Prohibited	Legal	Legal
Folding	Legal	Legal/ Prohibited	Legal	Legal
Gravity	Prohibited	Prohibited/Prohibited	Prohibited	Prohibited
Hunting/Fishing	Legal	Legal/ Prohibited	Legal	Legal
Machete	Legal	Legal/ Prohibited	Legal	Legal
Razor	Legal	Legal/ Prohibited	Legal	Legal
Stiletto	Legal	Legal/ Prohibited	Legal	Legal
Sword	Legal	Legal/ Prohibited	Legal	Legal
Throwing	Legal	Legal/ Prohibited	Legal	Legal
Undetectable	Prohibited	Prohibited/Prohibited	Prohibited	Prohibited

Pre-emption (Only State Law May Regulate, No Local Laws Permitted) – NO
*See all information above and below for more details.

SHARP TIPS ABOUT DELAWARE'S KNIFE LAWS
Delaware bans knuckle knives as well as switchblades, undetectables, and gravity knives. Certain convicted persons are prohibited from knife possession. No knives in schools. No pre-emption so beware of local laws.

EDGE –U- CATIONAL --- DELAWARE'S KNIFE LAWS
11 D.C. § 222. General definitions
When used in this Criminal Code:

(4) "Dangerous instrument" means any instrument, article or substance which, under the circumstances in which it is used, attempted to be used or threatened to be used, is readily capable of causing death or serious physical injury, or any disabling chemical spray, as defined in paragraph (6) of this section or any electronic control devices including but not limited to a neuromuscular incapacitation device designed to incapacitate a person.

(5) "Deadly weapon" includes a "firearm", as defined in paragraph (12) of this section, a bomb, a knife of any sort (other than an ordinary pocketknife carried in a closed position), switchblade knife, billy, blackjack, bludgeon, metal knuckles, slingshot, razor, bicycle chain or ice pick or any "dangerous instrument", as defined in paragraph (4) of this section, which is used, or attempted to be used, to cause death or serious physical injury. For the purpose of this definition, an ordinary pocketknife shall be a folding knife having a blade not more than 3 inches in length.

11 D.C. § 1442. Carrying a concealed deadly weapon; class G felony; class D felony

A person is guilty of carrying a concealed deadly weapon when the person carries concealed a deadly weapon upon or about the person without a license to do so as provided by § 1441 of this title. Carrying a concealed deadly weapon is a class G felony, unless the deadly weapon is a firearm, in which case it is a class D felony.

It shall be a defense that the defendant has been issued an otherwise valid license to carry a concealed deadly weapon pursuant to terms of § 1441 of this title, where:

(1) The license has expired,

(2) The person had applied for renewal of said license within the allotted time frame prior to expiration of the license, and

(3) The offense is alleged to have occurred while the application for renewal of said license was pending before the court.

11 D.C. § 1443 Carrying a concealed dangerous instrument; class A misdemeanor

(a) A person is guilty of carrying a concealed dangerous instrument when the person carries concealed a dangerous instrument upon or about the person.

(b) It shall be a defense that the defendant was carrying the concealed dangerous instrument for a specific lawful purpose and that the defendant had no intention of causing any physical injury or threatening the same.

(c) For the purposes of this section, disabling chemical spray, as defined in § 222 of this title, shall not be considered to be a dangerous instrument.

(d) Carrying a concealed dangerous instrument is a class A misdemeanor

11 D.C. § 1446. Unlawfully dealing with a switchblade knife; unclassified misdemeanor

A person is guilty of unlawfully dealing with a switchblade knife when the person sells, offers for sale or has in possession a knife, the blade of which is released by a spring mechanism or by gravity. Unlawfully dealing with a switchblade knife is an unclassified misdemeanor.

11 D.C. § 1446A. Undetectable knives; commercial manufacture, import for commercial sale, or offers for commercial sale; or possession

(a) Any person in this state who commercially manufactures or causes to be commercially manufactured, or who knowingly imports into the state for commercial sale, keeps for commercial sale, or offers or exposes for commercial sale, or who possesses any undetectable knife is guilty of a class G felony. As used in this section, an "undetectable knife" means any knife or other instrument with or without a handguard that is capable of ready use as a stabbing weapon that may inflict serious physical injury or death that is commercially manufactured to be used as a weapon and is not detectable by a metal detector or magnetometer because there is no material permanently affixed that would be detectable by a metal detector or magnetometer, either handheld or otherwise, that is set at standard calibration.

(b) Notwithstanding any other provision of law, all knives or other instruments with or without a handguard that are capable of ready use as a stabbing weapon that may inflict serious physical injury or death that are commercially manufactured in this state that utilize materials that are not detectable by a metal detector or magnetometer, shall be manufactured to include permanently installed materials that will ensure they are detectable by a metal detector or magnetometer, either handheld or otherwise, that is set at standard calibration.

(c) This section shall not apply to the manufacture or importation of undetectable knives for sale to a law enforcement or military entity nor shall this section apply to the subsequent sale of these knives to law enforcement or military entity.

(d) This section shall not apply to the manufacture or importation of undetectable knives for sale to federal, state, and local historical societies, museums, and institutional collections which are open to the public, provided that the undetectable knives are properly housed and secured from unauthorized handling, nor shall this section apply to the subsequent sale of the knives to these societies, museums, and collections.

11 D.C. § 1448. Possession and purchase of deadly weapons by persons prohibited; penalties

(a) Except as otherwise provided herein, the following persons are prohibited from purchasing, owning, possessing or controlling a deadly weapon or ammunition for a firearm within the State:

(1) Any person having been convicted in this State or elsewhere of a felony or a crime of violence involving physical injury to another, whether or not armed with or having in possession any weapon during the commission of such felony or crime of violence;

(2) Any person who has ever been committed for a mental disorder to any hospital, mental institution or sanitarium, unless such person can demonstrate that he or she is no longer prohibited from possessing a firearm pursuant to § 1448A of this title;

(3) Any person who has been convicted for the unlawful use, possession or sale of a narcotic, dangerous drug or central nervous system depressant or stimulant as those terms were defined prior to the effective date of the Uniform Controlled Substances Act in June 1973 or of a narcotic drug or controlled substance as defined in Chapter 47 of Title 16;

(4) Any person who, as a juvenile, has been adjudicated as delinquent for conduct which, if committed by an adult, would constitute a felony, unless and until that person has reached their 25th birthday;

(5) Any juvenile, if said deadly weapon is a handgun, unless said juvenile possesses said handgun for the purpose of engaging in lawful hunting, instruction, sporting or recreational activity while under the direct or indirect supervision of an adult. For the purpose of this subsection, a handgun shall be defined as any pistol, revolver or other firearm designed to be readily capable of being fired when held in 1 hand;

(6) Any person who is subject to a Family Court protection from abuse order (other than an ex parte order), but only for so long as that order remains in effect or is not vacated or otherwise terminated, except that this paragraph shall not apply to a contested order issued solely upon § 1041(1)d., e., or h. of Title 10, or any combination thereof;

(7) Any person who has been convicted in any court of any misdemeanor crime of domestic violence.

(b) Any prohibited person as set forth in subsection (a) of this section who knowingly possesses, purchases, owns or controls a deadly weapon or ammunition for a firearm while so prohibited shall be guilty of possession of a deadly weapon or ammunition for a firearm by a person prohibited.

(c) Possession of a deadly weapon by a person prohibited is a class F felony, unless said deadly weapon is a firearm or ammunition for a firearm, and the violation is 1 of paragraphs (a)(1)-(8) of this section, in which case it is a class D felony, or unless the person is eligible for sentencing pursuant to subsection (e) of this section, in which case it is a class C felony. As used herein, the word "ammunition" shall mean 1 or more rounds of fixed ammunition designed for use in and capable of being fired from a pistol, revolver, shotgun or rifle but shall not mean inert rounds or expended shells, hulls or casings.

(d) Any person who is a prohibited person solely as the result of a conviction for an offense which is not a felony shall not be prohibited from purchasing, owning, possessing or controlling a deadly weapon or ammunition for a firearm if 5 years have elapsed from the date of conviction.

(e)(1) Notwithstanding any provision of this section or Code to the contrary, any person who is a prohibited person as described in this section and who knowingly possesses, purchases, owns or controls a firearm or destructive weapon while so prohibited shall receive a minimum sentence of:

a. Three years at Level V, if the person has previously been convicted of a violent felony;

b. Five years at Level V, if the person does so within 10 years of the date of conviction for any violent felony or the date of termination of all periods of incarceration or confinement imposed pursuant to said conviction, whichever is the later date; or

c. Ten years at Level V, if the person has been convicted on 2 or more separate occasions of any violent felony.

(3) Any sentence imposed pursuant to this subsection shall not be subject to the provisions of § 4215 of this title. For the purposes of this subsection, "violent felony" means any felony so designated by § 4201(c) of this title, or any offense set forth under the laws of the United States, any other state or any territory of the United States which is the same as or equivalent to any of the offenses designated as a violent felony by § 4201(c) of this title.

(4) Any sentence imposed for a violation of this subsection shall not be subject to suspension and no person convicted for a violation of this subsection shall be eligible for good time, parole or probation during the period of the sentence imposed.

(f)(1) Upon conviction, any person who is a prohibited person as described in paragraph (a)(5) of this section and who is 14 years of age or older shall, for a first offense, receive a minimum sentence of 6 months of Level V incarceration, and shall receive a minimum sentence of 1 year of Level V incarceration for a second and subsequent offense, which shall not be subject to suspension. Any sentence imposed pursuant to this subsection shall not be subject to §§ 4205(b) and 4215 of this title.

(2) The penalties prescribed by this subsection and subsection (g) of this section shall be imposed regardless of whether or not the juvenile is determined to be amenable to the rehabilitative process of the Family Court pursuant to § 1010(c) of Title 10 or any successor statute.

11 D.C. § 1452. Unlawfully dealing with knuckles-combination knife; class B misdemeanor

A person is guilty of unlawfully dealing with a knuckles-combination knife when the person sells, offers for sale or has in possession a knife, the blade of which is supported by a knuckle ring grip handle. Unlawfully dealing with a knuckles-combination knife is a class B misdemeanor.

11 D.C. § 1457. Possession of a weapon in a Safe School and Recreation Zone; class D, E, or F felony; class A or B misdemeanor

(a) Any person who commits any of the offenses described in subsection (b) of this section, or any juvenile who possesses a firearm or other deadly weapon, and does so while in or on a "Safe School and Recreation Zone" shall be guilty of the crime of possession of a weapon in a Safe School and Recreation Zone.

(b) The underlying offenses in Title 11 shall be:

(1) Section 1442. --Carrying a concealed deadly weapon; class G felony; class D felony.

(2) Section 1444. --Possessing a destructive weapon; class E felony.

(3) Section 1446. --Unlawfully dealing with a switchblade knife; unclassified misdemeanor.

(4) Section 1448. --Possession and purchase of deadly weapons by persons prohibited; class F felony.

(5) Section 1452. --Unlawfully dealing with knuckles-combination knife; class B misdemeanor.

(6) Section 1453. --Unlawfully dealing with martial arts throwing star; class B misdemeanor.

(c) For the purpose of this section, "Safe School and Recreation Zone" shall mean:

(1) Any building, structure, athletic field, sports stadium or real property owned, operated, leased or rented by any public or private school including, but not limited to, any kindergarten, elementary, secondary or vocational-technical school or any college or university, within 1,000 feet thereof; or

(2) Any motor vehicle owned, operated, leased or rented by any public or private school including, but not limited to, any kindergarten, elementary, secondary, or vocational-technical school or any college or university; or

(3) Any building or structure owned, operated, leased or rented by any county or municipality, or by the State, or by any board, agency, commission, department, corporation or other entity thereof, or by any private organization, which is utilized as a recreation center, athletic field or sports stadium.

(d) Nothing in this section shall be construed to preclude or otherwise limit a prosecution of or conviction for a violation of this chapter or any other provision of law. A person may be convicted both of the crime of possession of a weapon in a Safe School and Recreation Zone and of the underlying offense as defined elsewhere by the laws of the State.

(e) It shall not be a defense to a prosecution for a violation of this section that the person was unaware that the prohibited conduct took place on or in a Safe School and Recreation Zone.

(f) It shall be an affirmative defense to a prosecution for a violation of this section that the weapon was possessed pursuant to an authorized course of school instruction, or for the purpose of engaging in any school-authorized sporting or recreational activity. The affirmative defense established in this section shall be proved by a preponderance of the evidence. Nothing herein shall be construed to establish an affirmative defense with respect to a prosecution for any offense defined in any other section of this chapter.

(g) It is an affirmative defense to prosecution for a violation of this section that the prohibited conduct took place entirely within a private residence, and that no person under the age of 18 was present in such private residence at any time during the commission of the offense. The affirmative defense established in this section shall be proved by the defendant by a preponderance of the evidence. Nothing herein shall be construed to establish an affirmative defense with respect to a prosecution for an offense defined in any other section of this chapter.

(h) This section shall not apply to any law enforcement or police officer, or to any security officer as defined in Chapter 13 of Title 24.

(i) For purposes of this section only, "deadly weapon" shall include any object described in § 222(5) or (12) of this title or BB guns.

(j) The penalty for possession of a weapon in a Safe School and Recreation Zone shall be:

(1) If the underlying offense is a class B misdemeanor, the crime shall be a class A misdemeanor;

(2) If the underlying offense is an unclassified misdemeanor, the crime shall be a class B misdemeanor;

(3) If the underlying offense is a class E, F, or G felony, the crime shall be one grade higher than the underlying offense.

(4) If the underlying offense is a class D felony, the crime shall also be a class D felony.

(5) In the event that an elementary or secondary school student possesses a firearm or other deadly weapon in a Safe School and Recreation Zone in addition to any other penalties contained in this section, the student shall be expelled by the local school board or charter school board of directors for a period of not less than 180 days unless otherwise provided for in federal or state law. The local school board or

charter school board of directors may, on a case by case basis, modify the terms of the expulsion.

24 D.C. § 901. License requirement

No person shall engage in the business of selling any pistol or revolver, or stiletto, steel or brass knuckles, or other deadly weapon made especially for the defense of one's person without first having obtained a license therefor, which license shall be known as "special license to sell deadly weapons." No person licensed or unlicensed shall possess, sell or offer for sale any switchblade knife. This section shall not apply to toy pistols, pocket knives or knives used for sporting purposes and in the domestic household, or surgical instruments or tools of any kind.

✦ DISTRICT OF COLUMBIA ✦
KNIFE RIGHTS MOVEMENT RATING
★ ★ ☆ ☆ ☆

CUTTING TO THE CHASE
Any knife is lawful to possess except those banned by federal law including switchblade, gravity and ballistic knives. Federal law covers the District and the District has its own switchblade ban.

Quick Points Concerning District Of Columbia's Knife Law*

KNIFE TYPE	POSSESSION	(Open/Concealed) CARRY	SALE	MANUFACTURE
Assisted Opening	Legal	Gray/Gray	Legal	Legal
Automatic/Switchblade	Prohibited	Prohibited/Prohibited	Prohibited	Prohibited
Ballistic	Prohibited	Prohibited/Prohibited	Prohibited	Prohibited
Bayonets	Legal	Prohibited/Prohibited	Gray	Gray
Bowie	Legal	Gray/Gray	Gray	Gray
Butterfly/Balisong	Gray	Gray/Gray	Gray	Gray
Combat/Survival	Legal	Prohibited/Prohibited	Gray	Gray
Dagger	Legal	Prohibited/Prohibited	Gray	Gray
Dirk	Legal	Prohibited/Prohibited	Gray	Gray
Disguised	Legal	Gray/Gray	Gray	Gray
Fixed	Legal	Gray/Gray	Gray	Gray
Folding	Legal	Gray/Gray	Gray	Gray
Gravity	Prohibited	Prohibited/Prohibited	Prohibited	Prohibited
Hunting/Fishing	Legal	Gray/Gray	Gray	Gray
Machete	Legal	Gray/Gray	Gray	Gray
Razor	Legal	Gray/Gray	Gray	Gray
Stiletto	Legal	Prohibited/Prohibited	Gray	Gray
Sword	Legal	Prohibited/Prohibited	Gray	Gray
Throwing	Legal	Gray/Gray	Gray	Gray
Undetectable	Legal	Gray/Gray	Gray	Gray

Pre-emption (Only State Law May Regulate, No Local Laws Permitted) – NO
*See all information above and below for more details.

SHARP TIPS ABOUT DISTRICT OF COLUMBIA'S KNIFE LAWS
Carrying "dangerous or deadly" knives whether open or concealed is a problem. This is vague and one must err on the side of caution.

EDGE –U- CATIONAL --- DISTRICT OF COLUMBIA'S KNIFE LAWS

§ 22-4514. Possession of certain dangerous weapons prohibited; exceptions.

(a) No person shall within the District of Columbia possess any machine gun, sawed-off shotgun, knuckles, or any instrument or weapon of the kind commonly known as a blackjack, slungshot, sand club, sandbag, switchblade knife, nor any instrument, attachment, or appliance for causing the firing of any firearm to be silent or intended to lessen or muffle the noise of the firing of any firearms; provided, however, that machine guns, or sawed-off shotgun, knuckles and blackjacks may be possessed by the members of the Army, Navy, Air Force, or Marine Corps of the United States, the National Guard, or Organized Reserves when on duty, the Post Office Department or its employees when on duty, marshals, sheriffs, prison or jail wardens, or their deputies, policemen, or other duly-appointed law venforcement officers, including any designated civilian employee of the Metropolitan Police Department, or officers or employees of the United States duly authorized to carry such weapons, banking institutions, public carriers who are engaged in the business of transporting mail, money, securities, or other valuables, wholesale dealers and retail dealers licensed under § 22-4510.

(b) No person shall within the District of Columbia possess, with intent to use unlawfully against another, an imitation pistol, or a dagger, dirk, razor, stiletto, or knife with a blade longer than 3 inches, or other dangerous weapon.

(c) Whoever violates this section shall be punished as provided in § 22-4515 unless the violation occurs after such person has been convicted in the District of Columbia of a violation of this section, or of a felony, either in the District of Columbia or in another jurisdiction, in which case such person shall be imprisoned for not more than 10 years.

(d) In addition to any other penalty provided under this section, a person may be fined an amount not more than the amount set forth in § 22-3571.01.

§ 22-4504. Carrying concealed weapons; possession of weapons during commission of crime of violence; penalty.

(a) No person shall carry within the District of Columbia either openly or concealed on or about their person, a pistol, or any deadly or dangerous weapon capable of being so concealed. Whoever violates this section shall be punished as provided in § 22-4515, except that:

(1) A person who violates this section by carrying a pistol, or any deadly or dangerous weapon, in a place other than the person's dwelling place, place of business, or on other land possessed by the person, shall be fined not more than the amount set forth in § 22-3571.01 or imprisoned for not more than 5 years, or both; or

(2) If the violation of this section occurs after a person has been convicted in the District of Columbia of a violation of this section or of a felony, either in the District of Columbia or another jurisdiction, the person shall be fined not more than the amount set forth in § 22-3571.01 or imprisoned for not more than 10 years, or both.

(a-1) Except as otherwise permitted by law, no person shall carry within the District of Columbia a rifle or shotgun. A person who violates this subsection shall be subject to the criminal penalties set forth in subsection (a)(1) and (2) of this section.

(b) No person shall within the District of Columbia possess a pistol, machine gun, shotgun, rifle, or any other firearm or imitation firearm while committing a crime of violence or dangerous crime as defined in § 22-4501. Upon conviction of a violation of this subsection, the person may be sentenced to imprisonment for a term not to exceed 15 years and shall be sentenced to imprisonment for a mandatory-minimum term of not less than 5 years and shall not be released on parole, or granted probation or suspension of sentence, prior to serving the mandatory-minimum sentence.

(c) In addition to any other penalty provided under this section, a person may be fined an amount not more than the amount set forth in § 22-3571.01.

CHAPTER 13

STATE KNIFE LAW GUIDE E-M

HOW TO USE THIS GUIDE

The "Quick Points" chart for each jurisdiction contains 100 legal questions answered by either "Legal", "Prohibited," or "Gray".

"Legal" means that it is generally lawful.

"Prohibited" means that it is generally unlawful.

"Gray" means that it is neither generally lawful nor unlawful and that there are ambiguities, conflicting law, exceptions, requirements or special considerations that may determine legality.

The laws provided have been selected because of their relevance to knives. Sections of the law may have been edited. It is also possible that some laws may have been inadvertently omitted due to legal research not revealing same. In other words, your author tried his best, but he is not perfect.

KNIFE RIGHTS MOVEMENT RATING SYSTEM

The Knife Rights Movement rating system grades the States, the District of Columbia, and the United States of America on a scale from one to five.

The highest rating is a five, which means that jurisdiction stands out for knife liberty. A rating of one means that jurisdiction has a disdain for knives and individual rights, and has arbitrary laws that treat honest citizens like criminals. Ratings of two, three, or four show where that jurisdiction is in regards to its respect for knife rights freedom. If a place has a rating lower than five, then there is work to be done there restoring knife liberty and continuing the Knife Rights Movement.

⁍— **FLORIDA** —⁌
KNIFE RIGHTS MOVEMENT RATING
★ ★ ★ ★ ☆

CUTTING TO THE CHASE

Florida is basically knife friendly. Florida "relegalized" switchblades in 2006 after a court case determined that Florida's ballistic knife definition included switchblades. The case was obviously wrongly decided, either by ignorance of the judge or by design. Regardless, the Florida legislature fixed it and Governor Jeb Bush signed it.

Quick Points Concerning Florida's Knife Law*

KNIFE TYPE	POSSESSION	(Open/Concealed) CARRY	SALE	MANUFACTURE
Assisted Opening	Legal	Legal/Gray	Legal	Legal
Automatic/Switchblade	Legal	Legal/Gray	Legal	Legal
Ballistic	Prohibited	Prohibited/Prohibited	Prohibited	Prohibited
Bayonets	Legal	Legal/Gray	Legal	Legal
Bowie	Legal	Legal/Gray	Legal	Legal
Butterfly/Balisong	Legal	Legal/Gray	Legal	Legal
Combat/Survival	Legal	Legal/Gray	Legal	Legal
Dagger	Legal	Legal/Gray	Legal	Legal
Dirk	Legal	Legal/Gray	Legal	Legal
Disguised	Legal	Legal/Gray	Legal	Legal
Fixed	Legal	Legal/Gray	Legal	Legal
Folding	Legal	Legal/Gray	Legal	Legal
Gravity	Legal	Legal/Gray	Legal	Legal
Hunting/Fishing	Legal	Legal/Gray	Legal	Legal
Machete	Legal	Legal/Gray	Legal	Legal
Razor	Legal	Legal/Gray	Legal	Legal
Stiletto	Legal	Legal/Gray	Legal	Legal
Sword	Legal	Legal/Gray	Legal	Legal
Throwing	Legal	Legal/Gray	Legal	Legal
Undetectable	Legal	Legal/Gray	Legal	Legal

Pre-emption (Only State Law May Regulate, No Local Laws Permitted) – YES
*See all information above and below for more details.

SHARP TIPS ABOUT FLORIDA'S KNIFE LAWS

Ballistic knives are banned. Concealed carry is regulated, but with a carry license there are exceptions. Open carry is fine for all knives except for the disrespected ballistic knife.

EDGE –U- CATIONAL --- FLORIDA'S KNIFE LAWS
§ 790.001. Definitions

As used in this chapter, except where the context otherwise requires:

(3)(a) "Concealed weapon" means any dirk, metallic knuckles, slungshot, billie, tear gas gun, chemical weapon or device, or other deadly weapon carried on or about a person in such a manner as to conceal the weapon from the ordinary sight of another person.

(13) "Weapon" means any dirk, knife, metallic knuckles, slungshot, billie, tear gas gun, chemical weapon or device, or other deadly weapon except a firearm or a common pocketknife, plastic knife, or blunt-bladed table knife.

(16) "Readily accessible for immediate use" means that a firearm or other weapon is carried on the person or within such close proximity and in such a manner that it can be retrieved and used as easily and quickly as if carried on the person.

(18) "Sterile area" means the area of an airport to which access is controlled by the inspection of persons and property in accordance with federally approved airport security programs.

§ 790.225. Ballistic self-propelled knives; unlawful to manufacture, sell, or possess; forfeiture; penalty

(1) It is unlawful for any person to manufacture, display, sell, own, possess, or use a ballistic self-propelled knife which is a device that propels a knifelike blade as a projectile and which physically separates the blade from the device by means of a coil spring, elastic material, or compressed gas. A ballistic self-propelled knife is declared to be a dangerous or deadly weapon and a contraband item. It shall be subject to seizure and shall be disposed of as provided in s. 790.08(1) and (6).

(2) This section shall not apply to:

(a) Any device from which a knifelike blade opens, where such blade remains physically integrated with the device when open.

(b) Any device which propels an arrow, a bolt, or a dart by means of any common bow, compound bow, crossbow, or underwater spear gun.

(3) Any person violating the provisions of subsection (1) is guilty of a misdemeanor of the first degree, punishable as provided in s. 775.082 or s. 775.083.

§ 790.01. Carrying concealed weapons

(1) Except as provided in subsection (4), a person who carries a concealed weapon or electric weapon or device on or about his or her person commits a misdemeanor of the first degree, punishable as provided in s. 775.082 or s. 775.083.

(3) This section does not apply to a person licensed to carry a concealed weapon or a concealed firearm pursuant to the provisions of s. 790.06.

§ 790.115. Possessing or discharging weapons or firearms at a school-sponsored event or on school property prohibited; penalties; exceptions

(1) A person who exhibits any sword, sword cane, firearm, electric weapon or device, destructive device, or other weapon as defined in s. 790.001(13), including a razor blade, box cutter, or common pocketknife, except as authorized in support of school-sanctioned activities, in the presence of one or more persons in a rude, careless, angry, or threatening manner and not in lawful self-defense, at a school-sponsored event or on the grounds or facilities of any school, school bus, or school bus stop, or within 1,000 feet of the real property that comprises a public or private elementary school, middle school, or secondary school, during school hours or during the time of a sanctioned school activity, commits a felony of the third degree, punishable as provided in s. 775.082, s. 775.083, or s. 775.084. This subsection does not apply to the exhibition of a firearm or weapon on private real property within 1,000 feet of a school by the owner of such property or by a person whose presence on such property has been authorized, licensed, or invited by the owner.

(2)(a) A person shall not possess any firearm, electric weapon or device, destructive device, or other weapon as defined in s. 790.001(13), including a razor blade or box cutter, except as authorized in support of school-sanctioned activities, at a school-sponsored event or on the property of any school, school bus, or school bus stop; however, a person may carry a firearm:

1. In a case to a firearms program, class or function which has been approved in advance by the principal or chief administrative officer of the school as a program or class to which firearms could be carried;

2. In a case to a career center having a firearms training range; or

3. In a vehicle pursuant to s. 790.25(5); except that school districts may adopt written and published policies that waive the exception in this subparagraph for purposes of student and campus parking privileges.

For the purposes of this section, "school" means any preschool, elementary school, middle school, junior high school, secondary school, career center, or postsecondary school, whether public or nonpublic.

(b) A person who willfully and knowingly possesses any electric weapon or device, destructive device, or other weapon as defined in s. 790.001(13), including a razor blade or box cutter, except as authorized in support of school-sanctioned activities, in violation of this subsection commits a felony of the third degree, punishable as provided in s. 775.082, s. 775.083, or s. 775.084.

(c)1. A person who willfully and knowingly possesses any firearm in violation of this subsection commits a felony of the third degree, punishable as provided in s. 775.082, s. 775.083, or s. 775.084.

2. A person who stores or leaves a loaded firearm within the reach or easy access of a minor who obtains the firearm and commits a violation of subparagraph 1. commits a misdemeanor of the second degree, punishable as provided in s. 775.082 or s. 775.083; except that this does not apply if the firearm was stored or left in a securely locked box or container or in a location which a reasonable person would have believed to be secure, or was securely locked with a firearm-mounted push-button combination lock or a trigger lock; if the minor obtains the firearm as a result of an unlawful entry by any person; or to members of the Armed Forces, National Guard, or State Militia, or to police or other law enforcement officers, with respect to firearm possession by a minor which occurs during or incidental to the performance of their official duties.

(3) This section does not apply to any law enforcement officer as defined in s. 943.10(1), (2), (3), (4), (6), (7), (8), (9), or (14).

§ 790.23. Felons and delinquents; possession of firearms, ammunition, or electric weapons or devices unlawful

(1) It is unlawful for any person to own or to have in his or her care, custody, possession, or control any firearm, ammunition, or electric weapon or device, or to carry a concealed weapon, including a tear gas gun or chemical weapon or device, if that person has been:

(a) Convicted of a felony in the courts of this state;

(b) Found, in the courts of this state, to have committed a delinquent act that would be a felony if committed by an adult and such person is under 24 years of age;

(c) Convicted of or found to have committed a crime against the United States which is designated as a felony;

(d) Found to have committed a delinquent act in another state, territory, or country that would be a felony if committed by an adult and which was punishable by imprisonment for a term exceeding 1 year and such person is under 24 years of age; or

(e) Found guilty of an offense that is a felony in another state, territory, or country and which was punishable by imprisonment for a term exceeding 1 year.

(2) This section shall not apply to a person convicted of a felony whose civil rights and firearm authority have been restored.

(3) Except as otherwise provided in subsection (4), any person who violates this section commits a felony of the second degree, punishable as provided in s. 775.082, s. 775.083, or s. 775.084.

(4) Notwithstanding the provisions of s. 874.04, if the offense described in subsection (1) has been committed by a person who has previously qualified or currently qualifies for the penalty enhancements provided for in s. 874.04, the offense is a felony of the first degree, punishable by a term of years not exceeding life or as provided in s. 775.082, s. 775.083, or s. 775.084.

§ 790.10. Improper exhibition of dangerous weapons or firearms
If any person having or carrying any dirk, sword, sword cane, firearm, electric weapon or device, or other weapon shall, in the presence of one or more persons, exhibit the same in a rude, careless, angry, or threatening manner, not in necessary self-defense, the person so offending shall be guilty of a misdemeanor of the first degree, punishable as provided in s. 775.082 or s. 775.083.

§ 790.17. Furnishing weapons to minors under 18 years of age or persons of unsound mind and furnishing firearms to minors under 18 years of age prohibited
(1) A person who sells, hires, barters, lends, transfers, or gives any minor under 18 years of age any dirk, electric weapon or device, or other weapon, other than an ordinary pocketknife, without permission of the minor's parent or guardian, or sells, hires, barters, lends, transfers, or gives to any person of unsound mind an electric weapon or device or any dangerous weapon, other than an ordinary pocketknife, commits a misdemeanor of the first degree, punishable as provided in s. 775.082 or s. 775.083.

(2)(a) A person may not knowingly or willfully sell or transfer a firearm to a minor under 18 years of age, except that a person may transfer ownership of a firearm to a minor with permission of the parent or guardian. A person who violates this paragraph commits a felony of the third degree, punishable as provided in s. 775.082, s. 775.083, or s. 775.084.

(b) The parent or guardian must maintain possession of the firearm except pursuant to s. 790.22.

⊰⊱ GEORGIA ⊰⊱
KNIFE RIGHTS MOVEMENT RATING
★ ★ ★ ★ ★

CUTTING TO THE CHASE
Georgia has a high regard for knife rights. It is one of the top states for knife freedom. One may carry open or concealed any knife with a blade under 5".

Quick Points Concerning Georgia's Knife Law*

KNIFE TYPE	POSSESSION	(Open/Concealed) CARRY	SALE	MANUFACTURE
Assisted Opening	Legal	Legal/Legal	Legal	Legal
Automatic/Switchblade	Legal	Legal/Legal	Legal	Legal
Ballistic	Legal	Legal/Legal	Legal	Legal
Bayonets	Legal	Legal/Legal	Legal	Legal
Bowie	Legal	Legal/Legal	Legal	Legal
Butterfly/Balisong	Legal	Legal/Legal	Legal	Legal
Combat/Survival	Legal	Legal/Legal	Legal	Legal
Dagger	Legal	Legal/Legal	Legal	Legal
Dirk	Legal	Legal/Legal	Legal	Legal
Disguised	Legal	Legal/Legal	Legal	Legal
Fixed	Legal	Legal/Legal	Legal	Legal

KNIFE TYPE	POSSESSION	(Open/Concealed) * CARRY	SALE	MANUFACTURE
Folding	Legal	Legal/Legal	Legal	Legal
Gravity	Legal	Legal/Legal	Legal	Legal
Hunting/Fishing	Legal	Legal/Legal	Legal	Legal
Machete	Legal	Legal/Legal	Legal	Legal
Razor	Legal	Legal/Legal	Legal	Legal
Stiletto	Legal	Legal/Legal	Legal	Legal
Sword	Legal	Legal/Legal	Legal	Legal
Throwing	Legal	Legal/Legal	Legal	Legal
Undetectable	Legal	Legal/Legal	Legal	Legal

<u>Pre-emption</u> (Only State Law May Regulate, No Local Laws Permitted) – YES
*See all information above and below for more details.

SHARP TIPS ABOUT GEORGIA'S KNIFE LAWS

To carry open or concealed knives with blades over 5", one needs a carry license.

Possession of a knife in a courthouse, government building, church, or a jail is highly regulated.

EDGE –U- CATIONAL --- GEORGIA'S KNIFE LAWS

§ 16-11-101. Furnishing weapons to persons under 18

A person is guilty of a misdemeanor of a high and aggravated nature when he or she knowingly sells to or furnishes to a person under the age of 18 years knuckles, whether made from metal, thermoplastic, wood, or other similar material, or a knife designed for the purpose of offense and defense.

§ 16-11-125.1. Definitions

As used in this part, the term:

(2) "Knife" means a cutting instrument designed for the purpose of offense and defense consisting of a blade that is greater than five inches in length which is fastened to a handle.

(3) "License holder" means a person who holds a valid weapons carry license.

(5) "Weapon" means a knife or handgun.

(6) "Weapons carry license" or "license" means a license issued pursuant to Code Section 16-11-129.

§ 16-11-126 Possessing or carrying a handgun or long gun

(a) Any person who is not prohibited by law from possessing a handgun or long gun may have or carry on his or her person a weapon or long gun on his or her property or inside his or her home, motor vehicle, or place of business without a valid weapons carry license.

(e) Any person licensed to carry a handgun or weapon in any other state whose laws recognize and give effect to a license issued pursuant to this part shall be authorized to carry a weapon in this state, but only while the licensee is not a resident of this state; provided, however, that such licensee shall carry the weapon in compliance with the laws of this state.

(g) Notwithstanding Code Sections 12-3-10, 27-3-1.1, 27-3-6, and 16-12-122 through 16-12-127, any person with a valid weapons carry license may carry a weapon in all parks, historic sites, or recreational areas, as such term is defined in Code Section 12-3-10, including all publicly owned buildings located in such parks, historic sites, and recreational areas, in wildlife management areas, and on public transportation; provided, however, that a person shall not carry a handgun into a place where it is prohibited by federal law.

(h)(1) No person shall carry a weapon without a valid weapons carry license unless he or she meets one of the exceptions to having such license as provided in subsections (a) through (g) of this Code section.

(2) A person commits the offense of carrying a weapon without a license when he or she violates the provisions of paragraph (1) of this subsection.

(i) Upon conviction of the offense of carrying a weapon without a valid weapons carry license, a person shall be punished as follows:

(1) For the first offense, he or she shall be guilty of a misdemeanor; and

(2) For the second offense within five years, as measured from the dates of previous arrests for which convictions were obtained to the date of the current arrest for which a conviction is obtained, and for any subsequent offense, he or she shall be guilty of a felony and, upon conviction thereof, shall be imprisoned for not less than two years and not more than five years.

§ 16-11-127. Carrying a weapon in unauthorized locations

(a) As used in this Code section, the term:

(1) "Courthouse" means a building occupied by judicial courts and containing rooms in which judicial proceedings are held.

(2) "Government building" means:

(A) The building in which a government entity is housed;

(B) The building where a government entity meets in its official capacity; provided, however, that if such building is not a publicly owned building, such building shall be considered a government building for the purposes of this Code section only during the time such government entity is meeting at such building; or

(C) The portion of any building that is not a publicly owned building that is occupied by a government entity.

(3) "Government entity" means an office, agency, authority, department, commission, board, body, division, instrumentality, or institution of the state or any county, municipal corporation, consolidated government, or local board of education within this state.

(4) "Parking facility" means real property owned or leased by a government entity, courthouse, jail, prison, or place of worship that has been designated by such government entity, courthouse, jail, prison, or place of worship for the parking of motor vehicles at a government building or at such courthouse, jail, prison, or place of worship.

(b) Except as provided in Code Section 16-11-127.1 and subsection (d) or (e) of this Code section, a person shall be guilty of carrying a weapon or long gun in an unauthorized location and punished as for a misdemeanor when he or she carries a weapon or long gun while:

(1) In a government building;

(2) In a courthouse;

(3) In a jail or prison;

(4) In a place of worship, unless the governing body or authority of the place of worship permits the carrying of weapons or long guns by license holders;

(5) In a state mental health facility as defined in Code Section 37-1-1 which admits individuals on an involuntary basis for treatment of mental illness, developmental disability, or addictive disease; provided, however, that carrying a weapon or long gun in such location in a manner in compliance with paragraph (3) of subsection (d) of this Code section shall not constitute a violation of this subsection;

(6) On the premises of a nuclear power facility, except as provided in Code Section 16-11-127.2, and the punishment provisions of Code Section 16-11-127.2 shall supersede the punishment provisions of this Code section; or

(7) Within 150 feet of any polling place, except as provided in subsection (i) of Code Section 21-2-413.

(c) A license holder or person recognized under subsection (e) of Code Section 16-11-126 shall be authorized to carry a weapon as provided in Code Section 16-11-135 and in every location in this state not listed in subsection (b) or prohibited by subsection (e) of this Code section; provided, however, that private property owners or persons in legal control of private property through a lease, rental agreement, licensing agreement, contract, or any other agreement to control access to such private property shall have the right to exclude or eject a person who is in possession of a weapon or long gun on their private property in accordance with paragraph (3) of subsection (b) of Code Section 16-7-21, except as provided in Code Section 16-11-135. A violation of subsection (b) of this Code section shall not create or give rise to a civil action for damages.

(d) Subsection (b) of this Code section shall not apply:

(1) To the use of weapons or long guns as exhibits in a legal proceeding, provided such weapons or long guns are secured and handled as directed by the personnel providing courtroom security or the judge hearing the case;

(2) To a license holder who approaches security or management personnel upon arrival at a location described in subsection (b) of this Code section and notifies such security or management personnel of the presence of the weapon or long gun and explicitly follows the security or management personnel's direction for removing, securing, storing, or temporarily surrendering such weapon or long gun; and

(3) To a weapon or long gun possessed by a license holder which is under the possessor's control in a motor vehicle or is in a locked compartment of a motor vehicle or one which is in a locked container in or a locked firearms rack which is on a motor vehicle and such vehicle is parked in a parking facility.

(e)(1) A license holder shall be authorized to carry a weapon in a government building when the government building is open for business and where ingress into such building is not restricted or screened by security personnel. A license holder who enters or attempts to enter a government building carrying a weapon where ingress is restricted or screened by security personnel shall be guilty of a misdemeanor if at least one member of such security personnel is certified as a peace officer pursuant to Chapter 8 of Title 35; provided, however, that a license holder who immediately exits such building or immediately leaves such location upon notification of his or her failure to clear security due to the carrying of a weapon shall not be guilty of violating this subsection or paragraph (1) of subsection (b) of this Code section. A person who is not a license holder and who attempts to enter a government building carrying a weapon shall be guilty of a misdemeanor.

(2) Any license holder who violates subsection (b) of this Code section in a place of worship shall not be arrested but shall be fined not more than $100.00. Any person who is not a license holder who violates subsection (b) of this Code section in a place of worship shall be punished as for a misdemeanor.

§ 16-11-127.1. Weapons on school safety zones, school buildings or grounds or at school functions

(a) As used in this Code section, the term:

(1) "Bus or other transportation furnished by a school" means a bus or other transportation furnished by a public or private elementary or secondary school.

(2) "School function" means a school function or related activity that occurs outside of a school safety zone and is for a public or private elementary or secondary school.

(3) "School safety zone" means in or on any real property or building owned by or leased to:

(A) Any public or private elementary school, secondary school, or local board of education and used for elementary or secondary education; and

(B) Any public or private technical school, vocational school, college, university, or other institution of postsecondary education.

(4) "Weapon" means and includes any pistol, revolver, or any weapon designed or intended to propel a missile of any kind, or any dirk, bowie knife, switchblade knife, ballistic knife, any other knife having a blade of two or more inches, straight-edge razor, razor blade, spring stick, knuckles, whether made from metal, thermoplastic, wood, or other similar material, blackjack, any bat, club, or other bludgeon-type weapon, or any flailing instrument consisting of two or more rigid parts connected in such a manner as to allow them to swing freely, which may be known as a nun chahka, nun chuck, nunchaku, shuriken, or fighting chain, or any disc, of whatever configuration, having at least two points or pointed blades which is designed to be thrown or propelled and which may be known as a throwing star or oriental dart, or any weapon of like kind, and any stun gun or taser as defined in subsection (a) of Code Section 16-11-106. This paragraph excludes any of these instruments used for classroom work authorized by the teacher.

(c) The provisions of this Code section shall not apply to:

(3) Persons participating in military training programs conducted by or on behalf of the armed forces of the United States or the Georgia Department of Defense;

(4) Persons participating in law enforcement training conducted by a police academy certified by the Georgia Peace Officer Standards and Training Council or by a law enforcement agency of the state or the United States or any political subdivision thereof;

(5) The following persons, when acting in the performance of their official duties or when en route to or from their official duties:

(A) A peace officer as defined by Code Section 35-8-2;

(B) A law enforcement officer of the United States government;

(C) A prosecuting attorney of this state or of the United States;

(D) An employee of the Georgia Department of Corrections or a correctional facility operated by a political subdivision of this state or the United States who is authorized by the head of such correctional agency or facility to carry a firearm;

(E) A person employed as a campus police officer or school security officer who is authorized to carry a weapon in accordance with Chapter 8 of Title 20; and

(F) Medical examiners, coroners, and their investigators who are employed by the state or any political subdivision thereof;

(6) A person who has been authorized in writing by a duly authorized official of a public or private elementary or secondary school or a public or private technical school, vocational school, college, university, or other institution of postsecondary education or a local board of education as provided in Code Section 16-11-130.1 to have in such person's possession or use within a school safety zone, at a school function, or on a bus or other transportation furnished by a school a weapon which would otherwise be prohibited by this Code section. Such authorization shall specify the weapon or weapons which have been authorized and the time period during which the authorization is valid;

(7) A person who is licensed in accordance with Code Section 16-11-129 or issued a permit pursuant to Code Section 43-38-10, when such person carries or picks up a student within a school safety zone, at a school function, or on a bus or other transportation furnished by a school or a person who is licensed in accordance with Code Section 16-11-129 or issued a permit pursuant to Code Section 43-38-10 when he or she has any weapon legally kept within a vehicle when such vehicle is parked within a school safety zone or is in transit through a designated school safety zone;

(8) A weapon possessed by a license holder which is under the possessor's control in a motor vehicle or which is in a locked compartment of a motor vehicle or one which is in a locked container in or a locked firearms rack which is on a motor vehicle which is being used by an adult over 21 years of age to bring to or pick up a student within a school safety zone, at a school function, or on a bus or other transportation furnished by a school, or when such vehicle is used to transport someone to an activity being conducted within a school safety zone which has been authorized by a duly authorized official or local board of education as provided by paragraph (6) of this subsection; provided, however, that this exception shall not apply to a student attending a public or private elementary or secondary school;

(9) Persons employed in fulfilling defense contracts with the government of the United States or agencies thereof when possession of the weapon is necessary for manufacture, transport, installation, and testing under the requirements of such contract;

(10) Those employees of the State Board of Pardons and Paroles when specifically designated and authorized in writing by the members of the State Board of Pardons and Paroles to carry a weapon;

(11) The Attorney General and those members of his or her staff whom he or she specifically authorizes in writing to carry a weapon;

(12) Probation supervisors employed by and under the authority of the Department of Corrections pursuant to Article 2 of Chapter 8 of Title 42, known as the "State-wide Probation Act," when specifically designated and authorized in writing by the director of the Division of Probation;

(13) Public safety directors of municipal corporations;

(14) State and federal trial and appellate judges;

(15) United States attorneys and assistant United States attorneys;

(16) Clerks of the superior courts;

(17) Teachers and other personnel who are otherwise authorized to possess or carry weapons, provided that any such weapon is in a locked compartment of a motor vehicle or one which is in a locked container in or a locked firearms rack which is on a motor vehicle; or

(18) Constables of any county of this state.

(d)(1) This Code section shall not prohibit any person who resides or works in a business or is in the ordinary course transacting lawful business or any person who is a visitor of such resident located within a school safety zone from carrying, possessing, or having under such person's control a weapon within a school safety zone; provided, however, that it shall be unlawful for any such person to carry, possess, or have under such person's control while at a school building or school function or on school property or a bus or other transportation furnished by a school any weapon or explosive compound, other than fireworks the possession of which is regulated by Chapter 10 of Title 25.

(2) Any person who violates this subsection shall be subject to the penalties specified in subsection (b) of this Code section.

(e) It shall be no defense to a prosecution for a violation of this Code section that:

(1) School was or was not in session at the time of the offense;

(2) The real property was being used for other purposes besides school purposes at the time of the offense; or

(3) The offense took place on a bus or other transportation furnished by a school.

(g) A county school board may adopt regulations requiring the posting of signs designating the areas of school boards and private or public elementary and secondary schools as "Weapon-free and

Violence-free School Safety Zones."

§ 16-11-136. Possession, manufacture, sale, or transfer of knives

(a) As used in this Code section, the term:

(1) "Courthouse" shall have the same meaning as set forth in Code Section 16-11-127.

(2) "Government building" shall have the same meaning as set forth in Code Section 16-11-127.

(3) "Knife" means any cutting instrument with a blade and shall include, without limitation, a knife as such term is defined in Code Section 16-11-125.1.

(b) Except for restrictions in courthouses and government buildings, no county, municipality, or consolidated government shall, by rule or ordinance, constrain the possession, manufacture, sale, or transfer of a knife more restrictively than the provisions of this part.

§ 16-11-137 Weapons carry license possession; penalties

(a) Every license holder shall have his or her valid weapons carry license in his or her immediate possession at all times when carrying a weapon, or if such person is exempt from having a weapons carry license pursuant to Code Section 16-11-130 or subsection (c) of Code Section 16-11-127.1, he or she shall have proof of his or her exemption in his or her immediate possession at all times when carrying a weapon, and his or her failure to do so shall be prima-facie evidence of a violation of the applicable provision of Code Sections 16-11-126 through 16-11-127.2.

(b) A person carrying a weapon shall not be subject to detention for the sole purpose of investigating whether such person has a weapons carry license.

(c) A person convicted of a violation of this Code section shall be fined not more than $10.00 if he or she produces in court his or her weapons carry license, provided that it was valid at the time of his or her arrest, or produces proof of his or her exemption.

§ 16-11-138. Defense of self or others absolute defense

Defense of self or others, as contemplated by and provided for under Article 2 of Chapter 3 of this title, shall be an absolute defense to any violation under this part.

⚔ HAWAII ⚔
KNIFE RIGHTS MOVEMENT RATING
★ ★ ★ ☆ ☆

CUTTING TO THE CHASE

Hawaii bans switchblades and balisongs. It also bans concealed carry or carry in a vehicle of dirks, daggers or the vague "…other deadly or dangerous weapon…"

Quick Points Concerning Hawaii's Knife Law*

KNIFE TYPE	POSSESSION	(Open/Concealed) CARRY	SALE	MANUFACTURE
Assisted Opening	Legal	Legal/Legal	Legal	Legal
Automatic/Switchblade	Prohibited	Prohibited/Prohibited	Prohibited	Prohibited
Ballistic	Legal	Legal/ Prohibited	Legal	Legal
Bayonets	Legal	Legal/ Prohibited	Legal	Legal

KNIFE TYPE	POSSESSION	(Open/Concealed) CARRY	SALE	MANUFACTURE
Bowie	Legal	Legal/Gray	Legal	Legal
Butterfly/Balisong	Prohibited	Prohibited/Prohibited	Prohibited	Prohibited
Combat/Survival	Legal	Legal/ Prohibited	Legal	Legal
Dagger	Legal	Legal/Prohibited	Legal	Legal
Dirk	Legal	Legal/Prohibited	Legal	Legal
Disguised	Legal	Legal/Gray	Legal	Legal
Fixed	Legal	Legal/Gray	Legal	Legal
Folding	Legal	Legal/Gray	Legal	Legal
Gravity	Legal	Legal/Gray	Legal	Legal
Hunting/Fishing	Legal	Legal/Gray	Legal	Legal
Machete	Legal	Legal/Gray	Legal	Legal
Razor	Legal	Legal/Gray	Legal	Legal
Stiletto	Legal	Legal/Prohibited	Legal	Legal
Sword	Legal	Legal/Gray	Legal	Legal
Throwing	Legal	Legal/Gray	Legal	Legal
Undetectable	Legal	Legal/Gray	Legal	Legal

Pre-emption (Only State Law May Regulate, No Local Laws Permitted) – NO
*See all information above and below for more details.

SHARP TIPS ABOUT HAWAII'S KNIFE LAWS

Open carry of non-banned knives is permitted. No pre-emption, so watch out for local laws.

EDGE –U- CATIONAL --- HAWAII'S KNIFE LAWS
§ 134-52. Switchblade knives; prohibitions; penalty

(a) Whoever knowingly manufactures, sells, transfers, possesses, or transports in the State any switchblade knife, being any knife having a blade which opens automatically (1) by hand pressure applied to a button or other device in the handle of the knife, or (2) by operation of inertia, gravity, or both, shall be guilty of a misdemeanor.

(b) Whoever knowingly possesses or intentionally uses or threatens to use a switchblade knife while engaged in the commission of a crime shall be guilty of a class C felony.

§ 134-53. Butterfly knives; prohibitions; penalty

(a) Whoever knowingly manufactures, sells, transfers, possesses, or transports in the State any butterfly knife, being a knife having a blade encased in a split handle that manually unfolds with hand or wrist action with the assistance of inertia, gravity or both, shall be guilty of a misdemeanor.

(b) Whoever knowingly possesses or intentionally uses or threatens to use a butterfly knife while engaged in the commission of a crime shall be guilty of a class C felony.

§ 134-51. Deadly weapons; prohibitions; penalty

(a) Any person, not authorized by law, who carries concealed upon the person's self or within any vehicle used or occupied by the person or who is found armed with any dirk, dagger, blackjack, slug shot, billy, metal knuckles, pistol, or other deadly or dangerous weapon shall be guilty of a misdemeanor and may be immediately arrested without warrant by any sheriff, police officer, or other officer or person. Any weapon, above enumerated, upon conviction of the one carrying or possessing it under this section, shall be summarily destroyed by the chief of police or sheriff.

(b) Whoever knowingly possesses or intentionally uses or threatens to use a deadly or dangerous weapon while engaged in the commission of a crime shall be guilty of a class C felony.

⊹ IDAHO ⊹
KNIFE RIGHTS MOVEMENT RATING
★ ★ ★ ★ ☆

CUTTING TO THE CHASE
Idaho does not ban possession of any knife by feature or type. Concealed carry is regulated and having a carry license allows for the concealed carry of any knife.

Quick Points Concerning Idaho's Knife Law*

KNIFE TYPE	POSSESSION	(Open/Concealed) CARRY	SALE	MANUFACTURE
Assisted Opening	Legal	Legal/Gray	Legal	Legal
Automatic/Switchblade	Legal	Legal/Gray	Legal	Legal
Ballistic	Legal	Legal/Gray	Legal	Legal
Bayonets	Legal	Legal/Gray	Legal	Legal
Bowie	Legal	Legal/Gray	Legal	Legal
Butterfly/Balisong	Legal	Legal/Gray	Legal	Legal
Combat/Survival	Legal	Legal/Gray	Legal	Legal
Dagger	Legal	Legal/Gray	Legal	Legal
Dirk	Legal	Legal/Gray	Legal	Legal
Disguised	Legal	Legal/Gray	Legal	Legal
Fixed	Legal	Legal/Gray	Legal	Legal
Folding	Legal	Legal/Gray	Legal	Legal
Gravity	Legal	Legal/Gray	Legal	Legal
Hunting/Fishing	Legal	Legal/Gray	Legal	Legal
Machete	Legal	Legal/Gray	Legal	Legal
Razor	Legal	Legal/Gray	Legal	Legal
Stiletto	Legal	Legal/Gray	Legal	Legal
Sword	Legal	Legal/Gray	Legal	Legal
Throwing	Legal	Legal/Gray	Legal	Legal
Undetectable	Legal	Legal/Gray	Legal	Legal

Pre-emption (Only State Law May Regulate, No Local Laws Permitted) – NO
*See all information above and below for more details.

SHARP TIPS ABOUT IDAHO'S KNIFE LAWS
Possession of a knife by minors is regulated. Sales to minors are also controlled. No carrying of any concealed weapon when under the influence of alcohol or drugs. No pre-emption, so beware of local laws.

EDGE –U- CATIONAL --- IDAHO'S KNIFE LAWS
§ 18-3302. Issuance of licenses to carry concealed weapons
(7) Except in the person's place of abode or fixed place of business, or on property in which the person has any ownership or leasehold interest, a person shall not carry a concealed weapon without a license to carry a concealed weapon. For the purposes of this section, a concealed weapon means any dirk, dirk knife, bowie knife, dagger, pistol, revolver or any other deadly or dangerous weapon. The provisions of this section shall not apply to any lawfully possessed shotgun or rifle, any knife, cleaver or other instrument primarily used in the processing, preparation or eating of food, any knife with a blade four (4) inches or less or any lawfully possessed taser, stun gun or pepper spray.

(9) While in any motor vehicle, inside the limits or confines of any city, a person shall not carry a concealed weapon on or about his person without a license to carry a concealed weapon. This shall not apply to any firearm located in plain view whether it is loaded or unloaded. A firearm may be concealed legally in a motor vehicle so long as the weapon is disassembled or unloaded.

(14) A person carrying a concealed weapon in violation of the provisions of this section shall be guilty of a misdemeanor.

§ 18-3302A. Sale of weapons to minors
It shall be unlawful to directly or indirectly sell to any minor under the age of eighteen (18) years any weapon without the written consent of the parent or guardian of the minor. Any person violating the provisions of this section shall be guilty of a misdemeanor and shall be punished by a fine not in excess of one thousand dollars ($1,000), by imprisonment in the county jail for a term not in excess of six (6) months, or by both such fine and imprisonment. As used in this section, "weapon" shall mean any dirk, dirk knife, bowie knife, dagger, pistol, revolver or gun.

§ 18-3302B. Carrying concealed weapons under the influence of alcohol or drugs
(1) It shall be unlawful for any person to carry a concealed weapon on or about his person when intoxicated or under the influence of an intoxicating drink or drug. Any violation of the provisions of this section shall be a misdemeanor.

(2) In addition to any other penalty, any person who enters a plea of guilty, who is found guilty or who is convicted of a violation of subsection (1) of this section when such violation occurs on a college or university campus shall have any and all licenses issued pursuant to section 18-3302, 18-3302H or 18-3302K, Idaho Code, revoked for a period of three (3) years and such person shall be ineligible to obtain or renew any such license or use any other license recognized by this state for the same period.

§ 18-3302D. Possessing weapons or firearms on school property
(1)(a) It shall be unlawful and is a misdemeanor for any person to possess a firearm or other deadly or dangerous weapon while on the property of a school or in those portions of any building, stadium or other structure on school grounds which, at the time of the violation, were being used for an activity sponsored by or through a school in this state or while riding school provided transportation.

(b) The provisions of this section regarding the possession of a firearm or other deadly or dangerous weapon on school property shall also apply to students of schools while attending or participating in any school sponsored activity, program or event regardless of location.

(4) The provisions of this section shall not apply to the following persons:

(a) A peace officer;

(b) A person who lawfully possesses a firearm or deadly or dangerous weapon as an appropriate part of a program, an event, activity or other circumstance approved by the board of trustees or governing board;

(c) A person or persons complying with the provisions of section 19-202A, Idaho Code;

(d) Any adult over eighteen (18) years of age and not enrolled in a public or private elementary or secondary school who has lawful possession of a firearm or other deadly or dangerous weapon, secured and locked in his vehicle in an unobtrusive, nonthreatening manner;

(e) A person who lawfully possesses a firearm or other deadly or dangerous weapon in a private vehicle while delivering minor children, students or school employees to and from school or a school activity;

(f) Notwithstanding the provisions of section 18-3302C, Idaho Code, a person or an employee of the school or school district who is authorized to carry a firearm with the permission of the board of trustees of the school district or the governing board.

(5) Penalties. Persons who are found guilty of violating the provisions of this section may be sentenced to a jail term of not more than one (1) year or fined an amount not in excess of one thousand dollars ($1,000) or both. If a violator is a student and under the age of eighteen (18) years, the court may place the violator on probation and suspend the juvenile detention or fine or both as long as the violator is enrolled in a program of study recognized by the court that, upon successful completion, will grant the violator a general equivalency diploma (GED) or a high school diploma or other educational program authorized by the court. Upon successful completion of the terms imposed by the court, the court shall discharge the offender from serving the remainder of the sentence. If the violator does not complete, is suspended from, or otherwise withdraws from the program of study imposed by the court, the court, upon receiving such information, shall order the violator to commence serving the sentence provided for in this section.

§ 18-3302E. Possession of a weapon by a minor

(1) It shall be unlawful for any person under the age of eighteen (18) years to possess or have in possession any weapon, as defined in section 18-3302A, Idaho Code, unless he:

(a) Has the written permission of his parent or guardian to possess the weapon; or

(b) Is accompanied by his parent or guardian while he has the weapon in his possession.

(2) Any minor under the age of twelve (12) years in possession of a weapon shall be accompanied by an adult.

(3) Any person who violates the provisions of this section is guilty of a misdemeanor.

§ 18-3303. Exhibition or use of deadly weapon

Every person who, not in necessary self-defense, in the presence of two (2) or more persons, draws or exhibits any deadly weapon in a rude, angry and threatening manner, or who, in any manner, unlawfully uses the same, in any fight or quarrel, is guilty of a misdemeanor.

§ 18-7503. Weapons aboard aircraft--Penalty

(1) No person, while aboard an airplane being operated by a holder of a certificate issued by the federal government or the state of Idaho, shall carry on or about his person a deadly or dangerous weapon, either concealed or unconcealed; nor shall any person enter or attempt to enter any sterile area of an airport, which is a holder of a certificate issued by the federal government or the state of Idaho, while knowingly carrying on or about his person, or in a bag, case, pouch or other container, a deadly or dangerous weapon, either concealed or unconcealed. Any person who pleads guilty or is found guilty of this subsection shall be guilty of a misdemeanor. As used in this section "sterile area" shall mean that area of a certificated airport to which access is controlled as required by the federal aviation administration regulations.

(3) This section does not apply to:

(a) Law enforcement officials of a city, county or state, or of the United States, who are authorized to carry arms and who have fulfilled the requirements of federal aviation administration regulations 107 and 108 in effect on January 1, 2001, and as may be amended from time to time;

(b) Crew members and other persons authorized by the certificate holder to carry arms;

(c) Parties chartering an aircraft for the purpose of hunting when a weapon is properly stored and/or in the custody of the pilot in command of the aircraft; or

(d) An aircraft owner and his invited guests when the weapon is properly stored and/or in the custody of the pilot of the aircraft.

(4) Any person convicted of violating the provisions of subsection (2) of this section shall be guilty of a felony, punishable by imprisonment in the state prison not exceeding five (5) years or by fine not exceeding five thousand dollars ($5,000) or by both such fine and imprisonment.

⤙ ILLINOIS ⤙
KNIFE RIGHTS MOVEMENT RATING
★ ★ ★ ☆ ☆

CUTTING TO THE CHASE

Illinois bans certain knives by feature such as switchblades and ballistic knives. Possession of most other knives is permitted.

Quick Points Concerning Illinois's Knife Law*

KNIFE TYPE	POSSESSION	(Open/Concealed) CARRY	SALE	MANUFACTURE
Assisted Opening	Legal	Gray/Gray	Legal	Legal
Automatic/Switchblade	Prohibited	Prohibited/Prohibited	Prohibited	Prohibited
Ballistic	Prohibited	Prohibited/Prohibited	Prohibited	Prohibited
Bayonets	Legal	Gray/Gray	Legal	Legal
Bowie	Legal	Gray/Gray	Legal	Legal
Butterfly/Balisong	Legal	Gray/Gray	Legal	Legal
Combat/Survival	Legal	Gray/Gray	Legal	Legal
Dagger	Legal	Gray/Gray	Legal	Legal
Dirk	Legal	Gray/Gray	Legal	Legal
Disguised	Legal	Gray/Gray	Legal	Legal
Fixed	Legal	Gray/Gray	Legal	Legal
Folding	Legal	Gray/Gray	Legal	Legal
Gravity	Gray	Gray/Gray	Gray	Gray
Hunting/Fishing	Legal	Gray/Gray	Legal	Legal
Machete	Legal	Gray/Gray	Legal	Legal
Razor	Legal	Gray/Gray	Legal	Legal
Stiletto	Legal	Gray/Gray	Legal	Legal
Sword	Legal	Gray/Gray	Legal	Legal
Throwing	Gray	Gray/Gray	Gray	Gray
Undetectable	Legal	Gray/Gray	Legal	Legal

Pre-emption (Only State Law May Regulate, No Local Laws Permitted) – NO
*See all information above and below for more details.

SHARP TIPS ABOUT ILLINOIS'S KNIFE LAWS

Carry of "...a dagger, dirk, billy, dangerous knife, razor, stiletto, broken bottle or other piece of glass..." is unlawful if one is carrying it with the intent to use it unlawfully against another. The problem is that one's intent is not always easy to determine by a law enforcement officer. Illinois prohibits having knives in schools, bars, and courthouses. Illinois does not have pre-emption, so beware of local laws.

EDGE –U- CATIONAL --- ILLINOIS'S KNIFE LAWS
720 ILCS 5/33A-1. Legislative intent and definitions

(a) Legislative findings. The legislature finds and declares the following:

(1) The use of a dangerous weapon in the commission of a felony offense poses a much greater threat to the public health, safety, and general welfare, than when a weapon is not used in the commission of the offense.

(c) Definitions.

(1) "Armed with a dangerous weapon". A person is considered armed with a dangerous weapon for purposes of this Article, when he or she carries on or about his or her person or is otherwise armed with a Category I, Category II, or Category III weapon.

(2) A Category I weapon is a handgun, sawed-off shotgun, sawed-off rifle, any other firearm small enough to be concealed upon the person, semiautomatic firearm, or machine gun. A Category II weapon is any other rifle, shotgun, spring gun, other firearm, stun gun or taser as defined in paragraph (a) of Section 24-1 of this Code, knife with a blade of at least 3 inches in length, dagger, dirk, switch-blade knife, stiletto, axe, hatchet, or other deadly or dangerous weapon or instrument of like character. As used in this subsection (b) "semiautomatic firearm" means a repeating firearm that utilizes a portion of the energy of a firing cartridge to extract the fired cartridge case and chamber the next round and that requires a separate pull of the trigger to fire each cartridge.

(3) A Category III weapon is a bludgeon, black-jack, slungshot, sand-bag, sand-club, metal knuckles, billy, or other dangerous weapon of like character.

720 ILCS 5/24-1. Unlawful Use of Weapons

(a) A person commits the offense of unlawful use of weapons when he knowingly:

(1) Sells, manufactures, purchases, possesses or carries any bludgeon, black-jack, slung-shot, sand-club, sand-bag, metal knuckles or other knuckle weapon regardless of its composition, throwing star, or any knife, commonly referred to as a switchblade knife, which has a blade that opens automatically by hand pressure applied to a button, spring or other device in the handle of the knife, or a ballistic knife, which is a device that propels a knifelike blade as a projectile by means of a coil spring, elastic material or compressed gas; or

(2) Carries or possesses with intent to use the same unlawfully against another, a dagger, dirk, billy, dangerous knife, razor, stiletto, broken bottle or other piece of glass, stun gun or taser or any other dangerous or deadly weapon or instrument of like character; or

(8) Carries or possesses any firearm, stun gun or taser or other deadly weapon in any place which is licensed to sell intoxicating beverages, or at any public gathering held pursuant to a license issued by any governmental body or any public gathering at which an admission is charged, excluding a place where a showing, demonstration or lecture involving the exhibition of unloaded firearms is conducted.

This subsection (a)(8) does not apply to any auction or raffle of a firearm held pursuant to a license or permit issued by a governmental body, nor does it apply to persons engaged in firearm safety training courses; or

(9) Carries or possesses in a vehicle or on or about his person any pistol, revolver, stun gun or taser or firearm or ballistic knife, when he is hooded, robed or masked in such manner as to conceal his identity; or

(b) Sentence. A person convicted of a violation of subsection 24-1(a)(1) through (5), subsection 24-1(a)(10), subsection 24-1(a)(11), or subsection 24-1(a)(13) commits a Class A misdemeanor. A person convicted of a violation of subsection 24-1(a)(8) or 24-1(a)(9) commits a Class 4 felony; a person convicted of a violation of subsection 24-1(a)(6) or 24-1(a)(7)(ii) or (iii) commits a Class 3 felony. A person convicted of a violation of subsection 24-1(a)(7)(i) commits a Class 2 felony and shall be sentenced to a term of imprisonment of not less than 3 years and not more than 7 years, unless the weapon is possessed in the passenger compartment of a motor vehicle as defined in Section 1-146 of the Illinois Vehicle Code,1 or on the person, while the weapon is loaded, in which case it shall be a Class X felony. A person convicted of a second or subsequent violation of subsection 24-1(a)(4), 24-1(a)(8), 24-1(a)(9), or 24-1(a)(10) commits a Class 3 felony. The possession of each weapon in violation of this Section constitutes a single and separate violation.

(c) Violations in specific places.

(1) A person who violates subsection 24-1(a)(6) or 24-1(a)(7) in any school, regardless of the time of day or the time of year, in residential property owned, operated or managed by a public housing agency or leased by a public housing agency as part of a scattered site or mixed-income development, in a public park, in a courthouse, on the real property comprising any school, regardless of the time of day or the time of year, on residential property owned, operated or managed by a public housing agency or leased by a public housing agency as part of a scattered site or mixed-income development, on the real property comprising any public park, on the real property comprising any courthouse, in any conveyance owned, leased or contracted by a school to transport students to or from school or a school related activity, in any conveyance owned, leased, or contracted by a public transportation agency, or on any public way within 1,000 feet of the real property comprising any school, public park, courthouse, public transportation facility, or residential property owned, operated, or managed by a public housing agency or leased by a public housing agency as part of a scattered site or mixed-income development commits a Class 2 felony and shall be sentenced to a term of imprisonment of not less than 3 years and not more than 7 years.

(1.5) A person who violates subsection 24-1(a)(4), 24-1(a)(9), or 24-1(a)(10) in any school, regardless of the time of day or the time of year, in residential property owned, operated, or managed by a public housing agency or leased by a public housing agency as part of a scattered site or mixed-income development, in a public park, in a courthouse, on the real property comprising any school, regardless of the time of day or the time of year, on residential property owned, operated, or managed by a public housing agency or leased by a public housing agency as part of a scattered site or mixed-income development, on the real property comprising any public park, on the real property comprising any courthouse, in any conveyance owned, leased, or contracted by a school to transport students to or from school or a school related activity, in any conveyance owned, leased, or contracted by a public transportation agency, or on any public way within 1,000 feet of the real property comprising any school, public park, courthouse, public transportation facility, or residential property owned, operated, or managed by a public housing agency or leased by a public housing agency as part of a scattered site or mixed-income development commits a Class 3 felony.

(2) A person who violates subsection 24-1(a)(1), 24-1(a)(2), or 24-1(a)(3) in any school, regardless of the time of day or the time of year, in residential property owned, operated or managed by a public housing agency or leased by a public housing agency as part of a scattered site or mixed-income development, in a public park, in a courthouse, on the real property comprising any school, regardless of the time of day or the time of year, on residential property owned, operated or managed by a public housing agency or leased by a public housing agency as part of a scattered site or mixed-income development, on the real property comprising any public park, on the real property comprising any courthouse, in any conveyance owned, leased or contracted by a school to transport students to or from school or a school related activity, in any conveyance owned, leased, or contracted by a public transportation agency, or on any public way within 1,000 feet of the real property comprising any school, public park, courthouse, public transportation facility, or residential property owned, operated, or managed by a public housing agency or leased by a public housing agency as part of a scattered site or mixed-income development commits a Class 4 felony. "Courthouse" means any building that is used by the Circuit, Appellate, or Supreme Court of this State for the conduct of official business.

(3) Paragraphs (1), (1.5), and (2) of this subsection (c) shall not apply to law enforcement officers or security officers of such school, college, or university or to students carrying or possessing firearms for use in training courses, parades, hunting, target shooting on school ranges, or otherwise with the consent of school authorities and which firearms are transported unloaded enclosed in a suitable case, box, or transportation package.

(4) For the purposes of this subsection (c), "school" means any public or private elementary or secondary school, community college, college, or university.

(5) For the purposes of this subsection (c), "public transportation agency" means a public or private agency that provides for the transportation or conveyance of persons by means available to the general public, except for transportation by automobiles not used for conveyance of the general public as passengers; and "public transportation facility" means a terminal or other place where one may obtain public transportation.

(e) Exemptions. Crossbows, Common or Compound bows and Underwater Spearguns are exempted from the definition of ballistic knife as defined in paragraph (1) of subsection (a) of this Section.

§ 10-22.6. Suspension or expulsion of pupils; school searches.

(d) The board may expel a student for a definite period of time not to exceed 2 calendar years, as determined on a case by case basis. A student who is determined to have brought one of the following objects to school, any school-sponsored activity or event, or any activity or event that bears a reasonable relationship to school shall be expelled for a period of not less than one year:

(1) A firearm. For the purposes of this Section, "firearm" means any gun, rifle, shotgun, weapon as defined by Section 921 of Title 18 of the United States Code, firearm as defined in Section 1.1 of the Firearm Owners Identification Card Act, [FN1] or firearm as defined in Section 24-1 of the Criminal Code of 2012. [FN2] The expulsion period under this subdivision (1) may be modified by the superintendent, and the superintendent's determination may be modified by the board on a case-by-case basis.

(2) A knife, brass knuckles or other knuckle weapon regardless of its composition, a billy club, or any other object if used or attempted to be used to cause bodily harm, including "look alikes" of any firearm as defined in subdivision (1) of this subsection (d). The expulsion requirement under this subdivision (2) may be modified by the superintendent, and the superintendent's determination may be modified by the board on a case-by-case basis.

Expulsion or suspension shall be construed in a manner consistent with the Federal Individuals with Disabilities Education Act. [FN3] A student who is subject to suspension or expulsion as provided in this Section may be eligible for a transfer to an alternative school program in accordance with Article 13A of the School Code. [FN4] The provisions of this subsection (d) apply in all school districts, including special charter districts and districts organized under Article 34. [FN5]

720 ILCS 5/21-6. Unauthorized Possession or Storage of Weapons

(a) Whoever possesses or stores any weapon enumerated in Section 33A-1 in any building or on land supported in whole or in part with public funds or in any building on such land without prior written permission from the chief security officer for such land or building commits a Class A misdemeanor.

(b) The chief security officer must grant any reasonable request for permission under paragraph (a).

⊹ **INDIANA** ⊹
KNIFE RIGHTS MOVEMENT RATING
★ ★ ★ ★ ☆

CUTTING TO THE CHASE
Other than banning ballistic knives, throwing stars and not having pre-emption, Indiana respects knife rights. This State recently repealed its ban on switchblades.

Quick Points Concerning Indiana's Knife Law*

KNIFE TYPE	POSSESSION	*(Open/Concealed)* CARRY	SALE	MANUFACTURE
Assisted Opening	Legal	Legal / Legal	Legal	Legal
Automatic/Switchblade	Legal	Legal / Legal	Legal	Legal
Ballistic	Prohibited	Prohibited/Prohibited	Prohibited	Prohibited
Bayonets	Legal	Legal / Legal	Legal	Legal
Bowie	Legal	Legal / Legal	Legal	Legal
Butterfly/Balisong	Legal	Legal / Legal	Legal	Legal
Combat/Survival	Legal	Legal / Legal	Legal	Legal
Dagger	Legal	Legal / Legal	Legal	Legal
Dirk	Legal	Legal / Legal	Legal	Legal
Disguised	Legal	Legal / Legal	Legal	Legal
Fixed	Legal	Legal / Legal	Legal	Legal
Folding	Legal	Legal / Legal	Legal	Legal
Gravity	Legal	Legal / Legal	Legal	Legal
Hunting/Fishing	Legal	Legal / Legal	Legal	Legal
Machete	Legal	Legal / Legal	Legal	Legal
Razor	Legal	Legal / Legal	Legal	Legal
Stiletto	Legal	Legal / Legal	Legal	Legal
Sword	Legal	Legal / Legal	Legal	Legal
Throwing	Gray	Gray/Gray	Gray	Gray
Undetectable	Legal	Legal / Legal	Legal	Legal

Pre-emption (Only State Law May Regulate, No Local Laws Permitted) – NO
*See all information above and below for more details.

SHARP TIPS ABOUT INDIANA'S KNIFE LAWS
Do not give a knife to an intoxicated person. Throwing star ban includes certain throwing knives. No knives in schools. No pre-emption, so beware of local laws.

EDGE –U- CATIONAL --- INDIANA'S KNIFE LAWS
35-31.5-2-86 "Deadly weapon"
Sec. 86. (a) Except as provided in subsection (b), "deadly weapon" means the following:

(1) A loaded or unloaded firearm.

(2) A destructive device, weapon, device, taser (as defined in IC 35-47-8-3) or electronic stun weapon (as defined in IC 35-47-8-1), equipment, chemical substance, or other material that in the manner it:

(A) is used;

(B) could ordinarily be used; or

(C) is intended to be used;

is readily capable of causing serious bodily injury.

35-47-4-1 Delivery of deadly weapon to intoxicated person
Sec. 1. A person who sells, barters, gives, or delivers any deadly weapon to any person at the time in a state of intoxication, knowing him to be in a state of intoxication, or to any person who is in the habit of becoming intoxicated, and knowing him to be a person who is in the habit of becoming intoxicated, commits a Class B misdemeanor.

35-47-5-12 "Chinese throwing star" defined; related offenses
Sec. 12. (a) A person who:

(1) manufactures;

(2) causes to be manufactured;

(3) imports into Indiana;

(4) keeps for sale;

(5) offers or exposes for sale; or

(6) gives, lends, or possesses;

a Chinese throwing star commits a Class C misdemeanor.

(b) As used in this section, "Chinese throwing star" means a throwing-knife, throwing-iron, or other knife-like weapon with blades set at different angles.

35-47-5-2 Knife with blade that opens automatically or may be propelled
Sec. 2. It is a Class B misdemeanor for a person to manufacture, possess, display, offer, sell, lend, give away, or purchase any knife with a detachable blade that may be ejected from the handle as a projectile by means of gas, a spring, or any other device contained in the handle of the knife.

35-47-5-2.5 Possession of knife on school property; violations; exceptions
Sec. 2.5. (a) As used in this section, "knife" means an instrument that:

(1) consists of a sharp edged or sharp pointed blade capable of inflicting cutting, stabbing, or tearing wounds; and

(2) is intended to be used as a weapon.

(b) The term includes a dagger, dirk, poniard, stiletto, switchblade knife, or gravity knife.

(c) A person who recklessly, knowingly, or intentionally possesses a knife on:

(1) school property (as defined in IC 35-31.5-2-285);

(2) a school bus (as defined in IC 20-27-2-8); or

(3) a special purpose bus (as defined in IC 20-27-2-10); commits a Class B misdemeanor. However, the offense is a Class A misdemeanor if the person has a previous unrelated conviction under this section and a Level 6 felony if the offense results in bodily injury to another person.

(d) This section does not apply to a person who possesses a knife:

(1) if:

(A) the knife is provided to the person by the school corporation or possession of the knife is authorized by the school corporation; and

(B) the person uses the knife for a purpose authorized by the school corporation; or

(2) if the knife is secured in a motor vehicle.

35-31.5-2-180 "Knife"
Sec. 180. "Knife", for purposes of IC 35-47-5-2.5, has the meaning set forth in IC 35-47-5-2.5(a) and IC 35-47-5-2.5(b).

⊷ IOWA ⊷
KNIFE RIGHTS MOVEMENT RATING
★ ★ ★ ☆ ☆

CUTTING TO THE CHASE
Iowa bans ballistic knives. Open carry is allowed, but concealed carry is regulated. Iowa has blade length restrictions.

Quick Points Concerning Iowa's Knife Law*

KNIFE TYPE	POSSESSION	(Open/Concealed) CARRY	SALE	MANUFACTURE
Assisted Opening	Legal	Legal/Gray	Legal	Legal
Automatic/Switchblade	Legal	Legal/Prohibited	Legal	Legal
Ballistic	Prohibited	Prohibited /Prohibited	Prohibited	Prohibited
Bayonets	Legal	Legal/Gray	Legal	Legal
Bowie	Legal	Legal/Gray	Legal	Legal
Butterfly/Balisong	Legal	Legal/Gray	Legal	Legal
Combat/Survival	Legal	Legal/Gray	Legal	Legal
Dagger	Legal	Legal/Prohibited	Legal	Legal
Dirk	Legal	Legal/Gray	Legal	Legal
Disguised	Legal	Legal/Gray	Legal	Legal
Fixed	Legal	Legal/Gray	Legal	Legal
Folding	Legal	Legal/Gray	Legal	Legal
Gravity	Legal	Legal/Gray	Legal	Legal
Hunting/Fishing	Legal	Legal/Gray	Legal	Legal
Machete	Legal	Legal/Gray	Legal	Legal
Razor	Legal	Legal/Prohibited	Legal	Legal
Stiletto	Legal	Legal/Prohibited	Legal	Legal
Sword	Legal	Legal/Gray	Legal	Legal
Throwing	Legal	Legal/Gray	Legal	Legal
Undetectable	Legal	Legal/Gray	Legal	Legal

Pre-emption (Only State Law May Regulate, No Local Laws Permitted) – NO
*See all information above and below for more details.

SHARP TIPS ABOUT IOWA'S KNIFE LAWS
Do not carry a concealed knife with a blade over 5 inches. If the blade is over 8 inches, it's even more serious. Size matters in Iowa. No knives in schools. No pre-emption, so beware of local laws.

EDGE –U- CATIONAL --- IOWA'S KNIFE LAWS

§ 702.7. Dangerous weapon

A "dangerous weapon" is any instrument or device designed primarily for use in inflicting death or injury upon a human being or animal, and which is capable of inflicting death upon a human being when used in the manner for which it was designed, except a bow and arrow when possessed and used for hunting or any other lawful purpose. Additionally, any instrument or device of any sort whatsoever which is actually used in such a manner as to indicate that the defendant intends to inflict death or serious injury upon the other, and which, when so used, is capable of inflicting death upon a human being, is a dangerous weapon. Dangerous weapons include but are not limited to any offensive weapon, pistol, revolver, or other firearm, dagger, razor, stiletto, switchblade knife, knife having a blade exceeding five inches in length, or any portable device or weapon directing an electric current, impulse, wave, or beam that produces a high-voltage pulse designed to immobilize a person.

§ 724.1. Offensive weapons

1. An offensive weapon is any device or instrumentality of the following types:

e. A ballistic knife. A ballistic knife is a knife with a detachable blade which is propelled by a spring-operated mechanism, elastic material, or compressed gas.

f. Any part or combination of parts either designed or intended to be used to convert any device into an offensive weapon as described in paragraphs "a" through "e", or to assemble into such an offensive weapon, except magazines or other parts, ammunition, or ammunition components used in common with lawful sporting firearms or parts including but not limited to barrels suitable for refitting to sporting firearms.

§ 724.2. Authority to possess offensive weapons

1. Any of the following persons or entities is authorized to possess an offensive weapon when the person's or entity's duties or lawful activities require or permit such possession:

a. Any peace officer.

b. Any member of the armed forces of the United States or of the national guard.

c. Any person in the service of the United States.

d. A correctional officer, serving in an institution under the authority of the Iowa department of corrections.

e. Any person who under the laws of this state and the United States, is lawfully engaged in the business of supplying those authorized to possess such devices.

f. Any person, firm or corporation who under the laws of this state and the United States is lawfully engaged in the improvement, invention or manufacture of firearms.

g. Any museum or similar place which possesses, solely as relics, offensive weapons which are rendered permanently unfit for use.

2. Notwithstanding subsection 1, a person is not authorized to possess in this state a shotshell or cartridge intended to project a flame or fireball of the type described in section 724.1.

§ 724.3. Unauthorized possession of offensive weapons

Any person, other than a person authorized herein, who knowingly possesses an offensive weapon commits a class "D" felony.

§ 724.4. Carrying weapons

1. Except as otherwise provided in this section, a person who goes armed with a dangerous weapon concealed on or about the person, or who, within the limits of any city, goes armed with a pistol or revolver, or any loaded firearm of any kind, whether concealed or not, or who knowingly carries or transports in a vehicle a pistol or revolver, commits an aggravated misdemeanor.

2. A person who goes armed with a knife concealed on or about the person, if the person uses the knife in the commission of a crime, commits an aggravated misdemeanor.

3. A person who goes armed with a knife concealed on or about the person, if the person does not use the knife in the commission of a crime:

a. If the knife has a blade exceeding eight inches in length, commits an aggravated misdemeanor.

b. If the knife has a blade exceeding five inches but not exceeding eight inches in length, commits a serious misdemeanor.

4. Subsections 1 through 3 do not apply to any of the following:

a. A person who goes armed with a dangerous weapon in the person's own dwelling or place of business, or on land owned or possessed by the person.

b. A peace officer, when the officer's duties require the person to carry such weapons.

c. A member of the armed forces of the United States or of the national guard or person in the service of the United States, when the weapons are carried in connection with the person's duties as such.

d. A correctional officer, when the officer's duties require, serving under the authority of the Iowa department of corrections.

e. A person who for any lawful purpose carries an unloaded pistol, revolver, or other dangerous weapon inside a closed and fastened container or securely wrapped package which is too large to be concealed on the person.

f. A person who for any lawful purpose carries or transports an unloaded pistol or revolver in a vehicle inside a closed and fastened container or securely wrapped package which is too large to be concealed on the person or inside a cargo or luggage compartment where the pistol or revolver will not be readily accessible to any person riding in the vehicle or common carrier.

g. A person while the person is lawfully engaged in target practice on a range designed for that purpose or while actually engaged in lawful hunting.

h. A person who carries a knife used in hunting or fishing, while actually engaged in lawful hunting or fishing.

i. A person who has in the person's possession and who displays to a peace officer on demand a valid permit to carry weapons which has been issued to the person, and whose conduct is within the limits of that permit. A person shall not be convicted of a violation of this section if the person produces at the person's trial a permit to carry weapons which was valid at the time of the alleged offense and which would have brought the person's conduct within this exception if the permit had been produced at the time of the alleged offense.

j. A law enforcement officer from another state when the officer's duties require the officer to carry the weapon and the officer is in this state for any of the following reasons:

(1) The extradition or other lawful removal of a prisoner from this state.

(2) Pursuit of a suspect in compliance with chapter 806.

(3) Activities in the capacity of a law enforcement officer with the knowledge and consent of the chief of police of the city or the sheriff of the county in which the activities occur or of the commissioner of public safety.

k. A person engaged in the business of transporting prisoners under a contract with the Iowa department of corrections or a county sheriff, a similar agency from another state, or the federal government.

§ 724.4A. Weapons free zones--enhanced penalties
1. As used in this section, "weapons free zone" means the area in or on, or within one thousand feet

of, the real property comprising a public or private elementary or secondary school, or in or on the real property comprising a public park. A weapons free zone shall not include that portion of a public park designated as a hunting area under section 461A.42.

2. Notwithstanding sections 902.9 and 903.1, a person who commits a public offense involving a firearm or offensive weapon, within a weapons free zone, in violation of this or any other chapter shall be subject to a fine of twice the maximum amount which may otherwise be imposed for the public offense.

§ 724.4B. Carrying weapons on school grounds--penalty--exceptions

1. A person who goes armed with, carries, or transports a firearm of any kind, whether concealed or not, on the grounds of a school commits a class "D" felony. For the purposes of this section, "school" means a public or nonpublic school as defined in section 280.2.

2. Subsection 1 does not apply to the following:

a. A person listed under section 724.4, subsection 4, paragraphs "b" through "f" or "j".

b. A person who has been specifically authorized by the school to go armed with, carry, or transport a firearm on the school grounds, including for purposes of conducting an instructional program regarding firearms.

§ 724.26. Possession, receipt, transportation, or dominion and control of firearms, offensive weapons, and ammunition by felons and others

1. A person who is convicted of a felony in a state or federal court, or who is adjudicated delinquent on the basis of conduct that would constitute a felony if committed by an adult, and who knowingly has under the person's dominion and control or possession, receives, or transports or causes to be transported a firearm or offensive weapon is guilty of a class "D" felony.

2. a. Except as provided in paragraph "b", a person who is subject to a protective order under 18 U.S.C. § 922(g)(8) or who has been convicted of a misdemeanor crime of domestic violence under 18 U.S.C. § 922(g)(9) and who knowingly possesses, ships, transports, or receives a firearm, offensive weapon, or ammunition is guilty of a class "D" felony.

b. This subsection shall not apply to the possession, shipment, transportation, or receipt of a firearm, offensive weapon, or ammunition issued by a state department or agency or political subdivision for use in the performance of the official duties of the person who is the subject of a protective order under 18 U.S.C. § 922(g)(8).

c. For purposes of this section, "misdemeanor crime of domestic violence" means an assault under section 708.1, subsection 2, paragraph "a" or "c", committed by a current or former spouse, parent, or guardian of the victim, by a person with whom the victim shares a child in common, by a person who is cohabiting with or has cohabited with the victim as a spouse, parent, or guardian, or by a person similarly situated to a spouse, parent, or guardian of the victim.

3. Upon the issuance of a protective order or entry of a judgment of conviction described in subsection 2, the court shall inform the person who is the subject of such order or conviction that the person shall not possess, ship, transport, or receive a firearm, offensive weapon, or ammunition while such order is in effect or until such conviction is vacated or until the person's rights have been restored in accordance with section 724.27.

4. Except as provided in section 809A.17, subsection 5, paragraph "b", a court that issues an order or that enters a judgment of conviction described in subsection 2 and that finds the subject of the order or conviction to be in possession of any firearm, offensive weapon, or ammunition shall order that such firearm, offensive weapon, or ammunition be sold or transferred by a date certain to the custody of a qualified person in this state, as determined by the court. The qualified person must be able to lawfully possess such firearm, offensive weapon, or ammunition in this state. If the court is unable to identify a qualified person to receive such firearm, offensive weapon, or ammunition, the court shall order that the

firearm, offensive weapon, or ammunition be transferred by a date certain to the county sheriff or a local law enforcement agency designated by the court for safekeeping until a qualified person is identified to receive the firearm, offensive weapon, or ammunition, until such order is no longer in effect, until such conviction is vacated, or until the person's rights have been restored in accordance with section 724.27. If the firearm, offensive weapon, or ammunition is to be transferred to the sheriff's office or a local law enforcement agency, the court shall assess the person the reasonable cost of storing the firearm, offensive weapon, or ammunition, payable to the county sheriff or the local law enforcement agency.

6. If a firearm, offensive weapon, or ammunition has been transferred to a qualified person pursuant to subsection 4 and the protective order described in subsection 2 is no longer in effect, the firearm, offensive weapon, or ammunition shall be returned to the person who was subject to the protective order within five days of that person's request to have the firearm, offensive weapon, or ammunition returned.

⊷ KANSAS ⊶
KNIFE RIGHTS MOVEMENT RATING

★ ★ ★ ★ ★

CUTTING TO THE CHASE

Kansas is a great state for knife rights freedom. They passed major knife law reforms in 2012. The only knives banned are throwing stars. Some Kansas legislator must have watched way too much David Carradine in the television show Kung Fu.

Quick Points Concerning Kansas' Knife Law*

KNIFE TYPE	POSSESSION	(Open/Concealed) CARRY	SALE	MANUFACTURE
Assisted Opening	Legal	Legal/Legal	Legal	Legal
Automatic/Switchblade	Legal	Legal/Legal	Legal	Legal
Ballistic	Legal	Legal/Legal	Legal	Legal
Bayonets	Legal	Legal/Legal	Legal	Legal
Bowie	Legal	Legal/Legal	Legal	Legal
Butterfly/Balisong	Legal	Legal/Legal	Legal	Legal
Combat/Survival	Legal	Legal/Legal	Legal	Legal
Dagger	Legal	Legal/Legal	Legal	Legal
Dirk	Legal	Legal/Legal	Legal	Legal
Disguised	Legal	Legal/Legal	Legal	Legal
Fixed	Legal	Legal/Legal	Legal	Legal
Folding	Legal	Legal/Legal	Legal	Legal
Gravity	Legal	Legal/Legal	Legal	Legal
Hunting/Fishing	Legal	Legal/Legal	Legal	Legal
Machete	Legal	Legal/Legal	Legal	Legal
Razor	Legal	Legal/Legal	Legal	Legal
Stiletto	Legal	Legal/Legal	Legal	Legal
Sword	Legal	Legal/Legal	Legal	Legal
Throwing	Gray	Gray/Gray	Gray	Gray
Undetectable	Legal	Legal/Legal	Legal	Legal

Pre-emption (Only State Law May Regulate, No Local Laws Permitted) – YES
*See all information above and below for more details.

SHARP TIPS ABOUT KANSAS' KNIFE LAWS

Possession by convicted felons is generally prohibited. Schools and jails are off limits. Throwing stars are prohibited.

EDGE –U- CATIONAL --- KANSAS' KNIFE LAWS

21-6301. Criminal use of weapons

(a) Criminal use of weapons is knowingly:

(1) Selling, manufacturing, purchasing or possessing any bludgeon, sand club, metal knuckles or throwing star;

(2) possessing with intent to use the same unlawfully against another, a dagger, dirk, billy, blackjack, slungshot, dangerous knife, straight-edged razor, stiletto or any other dangerous or deadly weapon or instrument of like character;

(b) Criminal use of weapons as defined in:

(1) Subsection (a)(1), (a)(2), (a)(3), (a)(7), (a)(8), (a)(9) or (a)(12) is a class A nonperson misdemeanor;

(2) subsection (a)(4), (a)(5) or (a)(6) is a severity level 9, nonperson felony;

(3) subsection (a)(10) or (a)(11) is a class B nonperson select misdemeanor;

(4) subsection (a)(13) is a severity level 8, nonperson felony; and

(5) subsection (a)(14) is a:

(A) Class A nonperson misdemeanor except as provided in subsection (b)(5)(B);

(B) severity level 8, nonperson felony upon a second or subsequent conviction.

(c) Subsections (a)(1), (a)(2) and (a)(5) shall not apply to:

(1) Law enforcement officers, or any person summoned by any such officers to assist in making arrests or preserving the peace while actually engaged in assisting such officer;

(2) wardens, superintendents, directors, security personnel and keepers of prisons, penitentiaries, jails and other institutions for the detention of persons accused or convicted of crime, while acting within the scope of their authority;

(3) members of the armed services or reserve forces of the United States or the Kansas national guard while in the performance of their official duty; or

(4) the manufacture of, transportation to, or sale of weapons to a person authorized under subsections (c)(1), (c)(2) and (c)(3) to possess such weapons.

21-6302. Criminal carrying of a weapon

(a) Criminal carrying of a weapon is knowingly carrying:

(1) Any bludgeon, sandclub, metal knuckles or throwing star;

(2) concealed on one's person, a billy, blackjack, slungshot or any other dangerous or deadly weapon or instrument of like character;

(b) Criminal carrying of a weapon as defined in:

(1) Subsections (a)(1), (a)(2), (a)(3) or (a)(4) is a class A nonperson misdemeanor; and

(2) subsection (a)(5) is a severity level 9, nonperson felony.

(c) Subsection (a) shall not apply to:

(1) Law enforcement officers, or any person summoned by any such officers to assist in making arrests or preserving the peace while actually engaged in assisting such officer;

(2) wardens, superintendents, directors, security personnel and keepers of prisons, penitentiaries, jails and other institutions for the detention of persons accused or convicted of crime, while acting within the scope of their authority;

(3) members of the armed services or reserve forces of the United States or the Kansas national guard while in the performance of their official duty; or

(4) the manufacture of, transportation to, or sale of weapons to a person authorized under subsections (c)(1), (c)(2) and (c)(3) to possess such weapons.

(d) Subsection (a)(4) shall not apply to:

(1) Watchmen, while actually engaged in the performance of the duties of their employment;

(2) licensed hunters or fishermen, while engaged in hunting or fishing;

(3) private detectives licensed by the state to carry the firearm involved, while actually engaged in the duties of their employment;

(4) detectives or special agents regularly employed by railroad companies or other corporations to perform full-time security or investigative service, while actually engaged in the duties of their employment;

(5) the state fire marshal, the state fire marshal's deputies or any member of a fire department authorized to carry a firearm pursuant to K.S.A. 31-157, and amendments thereto, while engaged in an investigation in which such fire marshal, deputy or member is authorized to carry a firearm pursuant to K.S.A. 31-157, and amendments thereto;

(6) special deputy sheriffs described in K.S.A. 19-827, and amendments thereto, who have satisfactorily completed the basic course of instruction required for permanent appointment as a part-time law enforcement officer under K.S.A. 74-5607a, and amendments thereto;

(7) the United States attorney for the district of Kansas, the attorney general, any district attorney or county attorney, any assistant United States attorney if authorized by the United States attorney for the district of Kansas, any assistant attorney general if authorized by the attorney general, or any assistant district attorney or assistant county attorney if authorized by the district attorney or county attorney by whom such assistant is employed. The provisions of this paragraph shall not apply to any person not in compliance with K.S.A. 75-7c19, and amendments thereto;

(8) any law enforcement officer, as that term is defined in K.S.A. 75-7c22, and amendments thereto, who satisfies the requirements of either subsection (a) or (b) of K.S.A. 75-7c22, and amendments thereto; or

(9) any person carrying a concealed handgun as authorized by K.S.A. 75-7c01 et seq., and amendments thereto.

(g) As used in this section, "throwing star" means the same as prescribed by K.S.A. 21-6301, and amendments thereto.

12-16,134. Knives and knife making components; regulation by municipality, limitations

(a) A municipality shall not enact or enforce any ordinance, resolution, regulation or tax relating to the transportation, possession, carrying, sale, transfer, purchase, gift, devise, licensing, registration or use of a knife or knife making components.

(b) A municipality shall not enact or enforce any ordinance, resolution or regulation relating to the manufacture of a knife that is more restrictive than any such ordinance, resolution or regulation relating to the manufacture of any other commercial goods.

(c) Any ordinance, resolution or regulation prohibited by either subsection (a) or (b) that was adopted prior to July 1, 2014, shall be null and void.

(d) No action shall be commenced or prosecuted against any individual for a violation of any ordinance, resolution or regulation that is prohibited by either subsection (a) or (b) and which was adopted prior to July 1, 2014, if such violation occurred on or after July 1, 2013.

(e) As used in this section:

(1) "Knife" means a cutting instrument and includes a sharpened or pointed blade.

(2) "Municipality" has the same meaning as defined in K.S.A. 75-6102, and amendments thereto, but shall not include unified school districts, jails, as defined in K.S.A. 38-2302, and amendments thereto, or juvenile correctional facilities, as defined in K.S.A. 38-2302, and amendments thereto.

21-6319. Unlawful failure to report a wound

(a) Unlawful failure to report a wound is, with no requirement of a culpable mental state, the failure by an attending physician or other person to report such person's treatment of any of the following wounds, to the office of the chief of police of the city or the office of the sheriff of the county in which such treatment took place:

(1) Any bullet wound, gunshot wound, powder burn or other injury arising from or caused by the discharge of a firearm; or

(2) any wound which is likely to or may result in death and is apparently inflicted by a knife, ice pick or other sharp or pointed instrument.

(b) Unlawful failure to report a wound is a class C misdemeanor.

21-6304. Criminal possession of a firearm by a convicted felon

(a) Criminal possession of a weapon by a convicted felon is possession of any weapon by a person who:

(1) Has been convicted of a person felony or a violation of article 57 of chapter 21 of the Kansas Statutes Annotated, and amendments thereto, K.S.A. 21-36a01 through 21-36a17, prior to their transfer, or any violation of any provision of the uniform controlled substances act prior to July 1, 2009, or a crime under a law of another jurisdiction which is substantially the same as such felony or violation, or was adjudicated a juvenile offender because of the commission of an act which if done by an adult would constitute the commission of a person felony or a violation of article 57 of chapter 21 of the Kansas Statutes Annotated, and amendments thereto, K.S.A. 21-36a01 through 21-36a17, prior to their transfer, or any violation of any provision of the uniform controlled substances act prior to July 1, 2009, and was found to have been in possession of a firearm at the time of the commission of the crime;

(2) within the preceding five years has been convicted of a felony, other than those specified in subsection (a)(3)(A), under the laws of Kansas or a crime under a law of another jurisdiction which is substantially the same as such felony, has been released from imprisonment for a felony or was adjudicated as a juvenile offender because of the commission of an act which if done by an adult would constitute the commission of a felony, and was not found to have been in possession of a firearm at the time of the commission of the crime; or

(3) within the preceding 10 years, has been convicted of a:

(A) Felony under K.S.A. 21-5402, 21-5403, 21-5404, 21-5405, 21-5408, subsection (b) or (d) of 21-5412, subsection (b) or (d) of 21-5413, subsection (a) of 21-5415, subsection (b) of 21-5420, 21-5503, subsection (b) of 21-5504, subsection (b) of 21-5505, and subsection (b) of 21-5807, and amendments thereto; article 57 of chapter 21 of the Kansas Statutes Annotated, and amendments thereto; K.S.A. 21-3401, 21-3402, 21-3403, 21-3404, 21-3410, 21-3411, 21-3414, 21-3415, 21-3419, 21-3420,

21-3421, 21-3427, 21-3442, 21-3502, 21-3506, 21-3518, 21-3716, 65-4127a, 65-4127b, 65-4159 through 65-4165 or 65-7006, prior to their repeal; an attempt, conspiracy or criminal solicitation as defined in K.S.A. 21-3301, 21-3302 or 21-3303, prior to their repeal, or K.S.A. 21-5301, 21-5302 or 21-5303, and amendments thereto, of any such felony; or a crime under a law of another jurisdiction which is substantially the same as such felony, has been released from imprisonment for such felony, or was adjudicated as a juvenile offender because of the commission of an act which if done by an adult would constitute the commission of such felony, was not found to have been in possession of a firearm at the time of the commission of the crime, and has not had the conviction of such crime expunged or been pardoned for such crime. The provisions of subsection (j)(2) of K.S.A. 21-6614, and amendments thereto, shall not apply to an individual who has had a conviction under this paragraph expunged; or

(B) nonperson felony under the laws of Kansas or a crime under the laws of another jurisdiction which is substantially the same as such nonperson felony, has been released from imprisonment for such nonperson felony or was adjudicated as a juvenile offender because of the commission of an act which if done by an adult would constitute the commission of a nonperson felony, and was found to have been in possession of a firearm at the time of the commission of the crime.

(b) Criminal possession of a weapon by a convicted felon is a severity level 8, nonperson felony.

(c) As used in this section:

(1) "Knife" means a dagger, dirk, switchblade, stiletto, straight-edged razor or any other dangerous or deadly cutting instrument of like character; and

(2) "weapon" means a firearm or a knife.

⚔ KENTUCKY ⚔
KNIFE RIGHTS MOVEMENT RATING
★ ★ ★ ★ ☆

CUTTING TO THE CHASE
Kentucky bans no knives by type or feature. Concealed carry is heavily restricted to only allow concealed carry of the vaguely described "ordinary pocket knife or hunting knife".

Quick Points Concerning Kentucky's Knife Law*

KNIFE TYPE	POSSESSION	(Open/Concealed) CARRY	SALE	MANUFACTURE
Assisted Opening	Legal	Legal/Gray	Legal	Legal
Automatic/Switchblade	Legal	Legal/Gray	Legal	Legal
Ballistic	Legal	Legal/Gray	Legal	Legal
Bayonets	Legal	Legal/Gray	Legal	Legal
Bowie	Legal	Legal/Gray	Legal	Legal
Butterfly/Balisong	Legal	Legal/Gray	Legal	Legal
Combat/Survival	Legal	Legal/Gray	Legal	Legal
Dagger	Legal	Legal/Gray	Legal	Legal
Dirk	Legal	Legal/Gray	Legal	Legal
Disguised	Legal	Legal/Gray	Legal	Legal
Fixed	Legal	Legal/Gray	Legal	Legal

KNIFE TYPE	POSSESSION	(Open/Concealed) CARRY	SALE	MANUFACTURE
Folding	Legal	Legal/Gray	Legal	Legal
Gravity	Legal	Legal/Gray	Legal	Legal
Hunting/Fishing	Legal	Legal/Gray	Legal	Legal
Machete	Legal	Legal/Gray	Legal	Legal
Razor	Legal	Legal/Gray	Legal	Legal
Stiletto	Legal	Legal/Gray	Legal	Legal
Sword	Legal	Legal/Gray	Legal	Legal
Throwing	Legal	Legal/Gray	Legal	Legal
Undetectable	Legal	Legal/Gray	Legal	Legal

Pre-emption (Only State Law May Regulate, No Local Laws Permitted) – YES
*See all information above and below for more details.

SHARP TIPS ABOUT KENTUCKY'S KNIFE LAWS

Make sure your concealed carry knife is an "ordinary" pocket or hunting knife. Do not have knives in schools, jails or courts.

EDGE –U- CATIONAL --- KENTUCKY'S KNIFE LAWS

§ 500.080 Definitions for Kentucky Penal Code

As used in the Kentucky Penal Code, unless the context otherwise requires:

(3) "Dangerous instrument" means any instrument, including parts of the human body when a serious physical injury is a direct result of the use of that part of the human body, article, or substance which, under the circumstances in which it is used, attempted to be used, or threatened to be used, is readily capable of causing death or serious physical injury;

(4) "Deadly weapon" means any of the following:

(a) A weapon of mass destruction;

(b) Any weapon from which a shot, readily capable of producing death or other serious physical injury, may be discharged;

(c) Any knife other than an ordinary pocket knife or hunting knife;

(d) Billy, nightstick, or club;

(e) Blackjack or slapjack;

(f) Nunchaku karate sticks;

(g) Shuriken or death star; or

(h) Artificial knuckles made from metal, plastic, or other similar hard material;

§ 527.020 Carrying concealed deadly weapon

(1) A person is guilty of carrying a concealed weapon when he or she carries concealed a firearm or other deadly weapon on or about his or her person.

(2) Peace officers and certified court security officers, when necessary for their protection in the discharge of their official duties; United States mail carriers when actually engaged in their duties; and agents and messengers of express companies, when necessary for their protection in the discharge of their official duties, may carry concealed weapons on or about their person.

(3) The director of the Division of Law Enforcement in the Department of Fish and Wildlife Resources, conservation officers of the Department of Fish and Wildlife Resources, and policemen directly employed

by state, county, city, or urban-county governments may carry concealed deadly weapons on or about their person at all times within the Commonwealth of Kentucky, when expressly authorized to do so by law or by the government employing the officer.

(4) Persons, except those specified in subsection (5) of this section, licensed to carry a concealed deadly weapon pursuant to KRS 237.110 may carry a firearm or other concealed deadly weapon on or about their persons at all times within the Commonwealth of Kentucky, if the firearm or concealed deadly weapon is carried in conformity with the requirements of that section. Unless otherwise specifically provided by the Kentucky Revised Statutes or applicable federal law, no criminal penalty shall attach to carrying a concealed firearm or other deadly weapon with a permit at any location at which an unconcealed firearm or other deadly weapon may be constitutionally carried. No person or organization, public or private, shall prohibit a person licensed to carry a concealed deadly weapon from possessing a firearm, ammunition, or both, or other deadly weapon in his or her vehicle in compliance with the provisions of KRS 237.110 and 237.115. Any attempt by a person or organization, public or private, to violate the provisions of this subsection may be the subject of an action for appropriate relief or for damages in a Circuit Court or District Court of competent jurisdiction.

(5) (a) The following persons, if they hold a license to carry a concealed deadly weapon pursuant to KRS 237.110 or 237.138 to 237.142, may carry a firearm or other concealed deadly weapon on or about their persons at all times and at all locations within the Commonwealth of Kentucky, without any limitation other than as provided in this subsection:

1. A Commonwealth's attorney or assistant Commonwealth's attorney;

2. A retired Commonwealth's attorney or retired assistant Commonwealth's attorney;

3. A county attorney or assistant county attorney;

4. A retired county attorney or retired assistant county attorney;

5. A justice or judge of the Court of Justice;

6. A retired or senior status justice or judge of the Court of Justice; and

7. A retired peace officer who holds a concealed deadly weapon license issued pursuant to the federal Law Enforcement Officers Safety Act, 18 U.S.C. sec. 926C, and KRS 237.138 to 237.142.

(b) The provisions of this subsection shall not authorize a person specified in this subsection to carry a concealed deadly weapon in a detention facility as defined in KRS 520.010 or on the premises of a detention facility without the permission of the warden, jailer, or other person in charge of the facility, or the permission of a person authorized by the warden, jailer, or other person in charge of the detention facility to give such permission. As used in this section, "detention facility" does not include courtrooms, facilities, or other premises used by the Court of Justice or administered by the Administrative Office of the Courts.

(c) A person specified in this section who is issued a concealed deadly weapon license shall be issued a license which bears on its face the statement that it is valid at all locations within the Commonwealth of Kentucky and may have such other identifying characteristics as determined by the Department of Kentucky State Police.

(6) (a) Except provided in this subsection, the following persons may carry concealed deadly weapons on or about their person at all times and at all locations within the Commonwealth of Kentucky:

1. An elected sheriff and full-time and part-time deputy sheriffs certified pursuant to KRS 15.380 to 15.404 when expressly authorized to do so by the unit of government employing the officer;

2. An elected jailer and a deputy jailer who has successfully completed Department of Corrections basic training and maintains his or her current in-service training when expressly authorized to do so by the jailer; and

3. The department head or any employee of a corrections department in any jurisdiction where the office of elected jailer has been merged with the office of sheriff who has successfully completed Department of Corrections basic training and maintains his or her current in-service training when expressly authorized to do so by the unit of government by which he or she is employed.

(b) The provisions of this subsection shall not authorize a person specified in this subsection to carry a concealed deadly weapon in a detention facility as defined in KRS 520.010 or on the premises of a detention facility without the permission of the warden, jailer, or other person in charge of the facility, or the permission of a person authorized by the warden, jailer, or other person in charge of the detention facility to give such permission. As used in this section, "detention facility" does not include courtrooms, facilities, or other premises used by the Court of Justice or administered by the Administrative Office of the Courts.

(7) (a) A full-time paid peace officer of a government agency from another state or territory of the United States or an elected sheriff from another territory of the United States may carry a concealed deadly weapon in Kentucky, on or off duty, if the other state or territory accords a Kentucky full-time paid peace officer and a Kentucky elected sheriff the same rights by law. If the other state or territory limits a Kentucky full-time paid peace officer or elected sheriff to carrying a concealed deadly weapon while on duty, then that same restriction shall apply to a full-time paid peace officer or elected sheriff from that state or territory.

(b) The provisions of this subsection shall not authorize a person specified in this subsection to carry a concealed deadly weapon in a detention facility as defined in KRS 520.010 or on the premises of a detention facility without the permission of the warden, jailer, or other person in charge of the facility, or the permission of a person authorized by the warden, jailer, or other person in charge of the detention facility to give such permission. As used in this section, "detention facility" does not include courtrooms, facilities, or other premises used by the Court of Justice or administered by the Administrative Office of the Courts.

(8) A loaded or unloaded firearm or other deadly weapon shall not be deemed concealed on or about the person if it is located in any enclosed container, compartment, or storage space installed as original equipment in a motor vehicle by its manufacturer, including but not limited to a glove compartment, center console, or seat pocket, regardless of whether said enclosed container, storage space, or compartment is locked, unlocked, or does not have a locking mechanism. No person or organization, public or private, shall prohibit a person from keeping a loaded or unloaded firearm or ammunition, or both, or other deadly weapon in a vehicle in accordance with the provisions of this subsection. Any attempt by a person or organization, public or private, to violate the provisions of this subsection may be the subject of an action for appropriate relief or for damages in a Circuit Court or District Court of competent jurisdiction. This subsection shall not apply to any person prohibited from possessing a firearm pursuant to KRS 527.040.

(9) The provisions of this section shall not apply to a person who carries a concealed deadly weapon on or about his or her person without a license issued pursuant to KRS 237.110:

(a) If he or she is the owner of the property or has the permission of the owner of the property, on real property which he or she or his or her spouse, parent, grandparent, or child owns;

(b) If he or she is the lessee of the property or has the permission of the lessee of the property, on real property which he or she or his or her spouse, parent, grandparent, or child occupies pursuant to a lease; or

(c) If he or she is the sole proprietor of the business, on real property owned or leased by the business.

(10) Carrying a concealed weapon is a Class A misdemeanor, unless the defendant has been previously convicted of a felony in which a deadly weapon was possessed, used, or displayed, in which case it is a Class D felony.

§ 527.070 Unlawful possession of a weapon on school property; posting of sign; exemptions
(1) A person is guilty of unlawful possession of a weapon on school property when he knowingly deposits, possesses, or carries, whether openly or concealed, for purposes other than instructional or

school-sanctioned ceremonial purposes, or the purposes permitted in subsection (3) of this section, any firearm or other deadly weapon, destructive device, or booby trap device in any public or private school building or bus, on any public or private school campus, grounds, recreation area, athletic field, or any other property owned, used, or operated by any board of education, school, board of trustees, regents, or directors for the administration of any public or private educational institution. The provisions of this section shall not apply to institutions of postsecondary or higher education.

(2) Each chief administrator of a public or private school shall display about the school in prominent locations, including, but not limited to, sports arenas, gymnasiums, stadiums, and cafeterias, a sign at least six (6) inches high and fourteen (14) inches wide stating:

UNLAWFUL POSSESSION OF A WEAPON ON SCHOOL PROPERTY IN KENTUCKY IS A FELONY PUNISHABLE BY A MAXIMUM OF FIVE (5) YEARS IN PRISON AND A TEN THOUSAND DOLLAR ($10,000) FINE.

Failure to post the sign shall not relieve any person of liability under this section.

(3) The provisions of this section prohibiting the unlawful possession of a weapon on school property shall not apply to:

(a) An adult who possesses a firearm, if the firearm is contained within a vehicle operated by the adult and is not removed from the vehicle, except for a purpose permitted herein, or brandished by the adult, or by any other person acting with expressed or implied consent of the adult, while the vehicle is on school property;

(b) Any pupils who are members of the reserve officers training corps or pupils enrolled in a course of instruction or members of a school club or team, to the extent they are required to carry arms or weapons in the discharge of their official class or team duties;

(c) Any peace officer or police officer authorized to carry a concealed weapon pursuant to KRS 527.020;

(d) Persons employed by the Armed Forces of the United States or members of the National Guard or militia when required in the discharge of their official duties to carry arms or weapons;

(e) Civil officers of the United States in the discharge of their official duties. Nothing in this section shall be construed as to allow any person to carry a concealed weapon into a public or private elementary or secondary school building;

(f) Any other persons, including, but not limited to, exhibitors of historical displays, who have been authorized to carry a firearm by the board of education or board of trustees of the public or private institution;

(g) A person hunting during the lawful hunting season on lands owned by any public or private educational institution and designated as open to hunting by the board of education or board of trustees of the educational institution;

(h) A person possessing unloaded hunting weapons while traversing the grounds of any public or private educational institution for the purpose of gaining access to public or private lands open to hunting with the intent to hunt on the public or private lands, unless the lands of the educational institution are posted prohibiting the entry; or

(i) A person possessing guns or knives when conducting or attending a "gun and knife show" when the program has been approved by the board of education or board of trustees of the educational institution.

(4) Unlawful possession of a weapon on school property is a Class D felony.

§ 237.104 Rights to acquire, carry, and use deadly weapons not to be impaired during disaster or emergency; seizure of deadly weapons during disaster or emergency prohibited; application of section

(1) No person, unit of government, or governmental organization shall, during a period of disaster or

emergency as specified in KRS Chapter 39A or at any other time, have the right to revoke; suspend, limit the use of, or otherwise impair the validity of the right of any person to purchase, transfer, loan, own, possess, carry, or use a firearm, firearm part, ammunition, ammunition component, or any deadly weapon or dangerous instrument.

(2) No person, unit of government, or governmental organization shall, during a period of disaster or emergency as specified in KRS Chapter 39A or at any other time, take, seize, confiscate, or impound a firearm, firearm part, ammunition, ammunition component, or any deadly weapon or dangerous instrument from any person.

(3) The provisions of this section shall not apply to the taking of an item specified in subsection (1) or (2) of this section from a person who is:

(a) Forbidden to possess a firearm pursuant to KRS 527.040;

(b) Forbidden to possess a firearm pursuant to federal law;

(c) Violating KRS 527.020;

(d) In possession of a stolen firearm;

(e) Using a firearm in the commission of a separate criminal offense; or

(f) Using a firearm or other weapon in the commission of an offense under KRS Chapter 150.

§ 237.115 Construction of KRS 237.110; prohibition by local government units of carrying concealed deadly weapons in governmental buildings; restriction on criminal penalties

(1) Except as provided in KRS 527.020, nothing contained in KRS 237.110 shall be construed to limit, restrict, or prohibit in any manner the right of a college, university, or any postsecondary education facility, including technical schools and community colleges, to control the possession of deadly weapons on any property owned or controlled by them or the right of a unit of state, city, county, urban-county, or charter county government to prohibit the carrying of concealed deadly weapons by licensees in that portion of a building actually owned, leased, or occupied by that unit of government.

(2) Except as provided in KRS 527.020, the legislative body of a state, city, county, or urban-county government may, by statute, administrative regulation, or ordinance, prohibit or limit the carrying of concealed deadly weapons by licensees in that portion of a building owned, leased, or controlled by that unit of government. That portion of a building in which the carrying of concealed deadly weapons is prohibited or limited shall be clearly identified by signs posted at the entrance to the restricted area. The statute or ordinance shall exempt any building used for public housing by private persons, highway rest areas, firing ranges, and private dwellings owned, leased, or controlled by that unit of government from any restriction on the carrying or possession of deadly weapons. The statute, administrative regulation, or ordinance shall not specify any criminal penalty for its violation but may specify that persons violating the statute or ordinance may be denied entrance to the building, ordered to leave the building, and if employees of the unit of government, be subject to employee disciplinary measures for violation of the provisions of the statute or ordinance. The provisions of this section shall not be deemed to be a violation of KRS 65.870 if the requirements of this section are followed. The provisions of this section shall not apply to any other unit of government.

(3) Unless otherwise specifically provided by the Kentucky Revised Statutes or applicable federal law, no criminal penalty shall attach to carrying a concealed firearm or other deadly weapon with a permit at any location at which an unconcealed firearm or other deadly weapon may be constitutionally carried.

✦ LOUISIANA ✦
KNIFE RIGHTS MOVEMENT RATING
★ ★ ★ ★ ☆

CUTTING TO THE CHASE
Louisiana needs to repeal its switchblade ban and enact preemption. It would then earn a maximum five rating.

Quick Points Concerning Louisiana's Knife Law*

KNIFE TYPE	POSSESSION	(Open/Concealed) CARRY	SALE	MANUFACTURE
Assisted Opening	Legal	Legal/Legal	Legal	Legal
Automatic/Switchblade	Prohibited	Prohibited/Prohibited	Prohibited	Prohibited
Ballistic	Legal	Legal/Legal	Legal	Legal
Bayonets	Legal	Legal/Legal	Legal	Legal
Bowie	Legal	Legal/Legal	Legal	Legal
Butterfly/Balisong	Legal	Legal/Legal	Legal	Legal
Combat/Survival	Legal	Legal/Legal	Legal	Legal
Dagger	Legal	Legal/Legal	Legal	Legal
Dirk	Legal	Legal/Legal	Legal	Legal
Disguised	Legal	Legal/Legal	Legal	Legal
Fixed	Legal	Legal/Legal	Legal	Legal
Folding	Legal	Legal/Legal	Legal	Legal
Gravity	Legal	Legal/Legal	Legal	Legal
Hunting/Fishing	Legal	Legal/Legal	Legal	Legal
Machete	Legal	Legal/Legal	Legal	Legal
Razor	Legal	Legal/Legal	Legal	Legal
Stiletto	Legal	Legal/Legal	Legal	Legal
Sword	Legal	Legal/Legal	Legal	Legal
Throwing	Legal	Legal/Legal	Legal	Legal
Undetectable	Legal	Legal/Legal	Legal	Legal

Pre-emption (Only State Law May Regulate, No Local Laws Permitted) – NO
*See all information above and below for more details.

SHARP TIPS ABOUT LOUISIANA'S KNIFE LAWS
Possession of a knife in schools, jails and courthouses is restricted. Certain felons are prohibited from knife possession. No pre-emption, so beware of local laws.

EDGE –U- CATIONAL --- LOUISIANA'S KNIFE LAWS
14§ 2. Definitions
A. In this Code the terms enumerated shall have the designated meanings:

(3) "Dangerous weapon" includes any gas, liquid or other substance or instrumentality, which, in the manner used, is calculated or likely to produce death or great bodily harm.

14§ 95. Illegal carrying of weapons
A. Illegal carrying of weapons is:

(1) The intentional concealment of any firearm, or other instrumentality customarily used or intended

for probable use as a dangerous weapon, on one's person; or

(2) The ownership, possession, custody or use of any firearm, or other instrumentality customarily used as a dangerous weapon, at any time by an enemy alien; or

(4)(a) The manufacture, ownership, possession, custody or use of any switchblade knife, spring knife or other knife or similar instrument having a blade which may be automatically unfolded or extended from a handle by the manipulation of a button, switch, latch or similar contrivance located on the handle.

(b) The provisions of this Paragraph shall not apply to the following:

(i) Any knife that may be opened with one hand by manual pressure applied to the blade or any projection of the blade.

(ii) Any knife that may be opened by means of inertia produced by the hand, wrist, or other movement, provided the knife has either a detent or other structure that provides resistance that shall be overcome in opening or initiating the opening movement of the blade or a bias or spring load toward the closed position.

(5)(a) The intentional possession or use by any person of a dangerous weapon on a school campus during regular school hours or on a school bus. "School" means any elementary, secondary, high school, or vo-tech school in this state and "campus" means all facilities and property within the boundary of the school property. "School bus" means any motor bus being used to transport children to and from school or in connection with school activities.

(b) The provisions of this Paragraph shall not apply to:

(i) A peace officer as defined by R.S. 14:30(B) in the performance of his official duties.

(ii) A school official or employee acting during the normal course of his employment or a student acting under the direction of such school official or employee.

(iii) Any person having the written permission of the principal or school board and engaged in competition or in marksmanship or safety instruction.

B. (1) Whoever commits the crime of illegal carrying of weapons shall be fined not more than five hundred dollars, or imprisoned for not more than six months, or both.

(2) Whoever commits the crime of illegal carrying of weapons with any firearm used in the commission of a crime of violence as defined in R.S. 14:2(B), shall be fined not more than two thousand dollars, or imprisoned, with or without hard labor, for not less than one year nor more than two years, or both. Any sentence issued pursuant to the provisions of this Paragraph and any sentence issued pursuant to a violation of a crime of violence as defined in R.S. 14:2(B) shall be served consecutively.

C. On a second conviction, the offender shall be imprisoned with or without hard labor for not more than five years.

D. On third and subsequent convictions, the offender shall be imprisoned with or without hard labor for not more than ten years without benefit of parole, probation, or suspension of sentence.

E. If the offender uses, possesses, or has under his immediate control any firearm, or other instrumentality customarily used or intended for probable use as a dangerous weapon, while committing or attempting to commit a crime of violence or while in the possession of or during the sale or distribution of a controlled dangerous substance, the offender shall be fined not more than ten thousand dollars and imprisoned at hard labor for not less than five nor more than ten years without the benefit of probation, parole, or suspension of sentence. Upon a second or subsequent conviction, the offender shall be imprisoned at hard labor for not less than twenty years nor more than thirty years without the benefit of probation, parole, or suspension of sentence.

F. (1) For purposes of determining whether a defendant has a prior conviction for a violation of this Section, a conviction pursuant to this Section or a conviction pursuant to an ordinance of a local governmental subdivision of this state which contains the elements provided for in Subsection A of this Section shall constitute a prior conviction.

(2) The enhanced penalty upon second, third, and subsequent convictions shall not be applicable in cases where more than five years have elapsed since the expiration of the maximum sentence, or sentences, of the previous conviction or convictions, and the time of the commission of the last offense for which he has been convicted; the sentence to be imposed in such event shall be the same as may be imposed upon a first conviction.

(3) Any ordinance that prohibits the unlawful carrying of firearms enacted by a municipality, town, or similar political subdivision or governing authority of this state shall be subject to the provisions of R.S. 40:1796.

G. (1) The provisions of this Section except Paragraph (4) of Subsection A shall not apply to sheriffs and their deputies, state and city police, constables and town marshals, or persons vested with police power when in the actual discharge of official duties. These provisions shall not apply to sheriffs and their deputies and state and city police who are not actually discharging their official duties, provided that such persons are full time, active, and certified by the Council on Peace Officer Standards and Training and have on their persons valid identification as duly commissioned law enforcement officers.

(2) The provisions of this Section except Paragraph (4) of Subsection A shall not apply to any law enforcement officer who is retired from full-time active law enforcement service with at least twelve years service upon retirement, nor shall it apply to any enforcement officer of the office of state parks, in the Department of Culture, Recreation and Tourism who is retired from active duty as an enforcement officer, provided that such retired officers have on their persons valid identification as retired law enforcement officers, which identification shall be provided by the entity which employed the officer prior to his or her public retirement. The retired law enforcement officer must be qualified annually in the use of firearms by the Council on Peace Officer Standards and Training and have proof of such qualification. This exception shall not apply to such officers who are medically retired based upon any mental impairment.

(3)(a) The provisions of this Section except Paragraph (4) of Subsection A shall not apply to active or retired reserve or auxiliary law enforcement officers qualified annually by the Council on Peace Officer Standards and Training and who have on their person valid identification as active or retired reserve law or auxiliary municipal police officers. The active or retired reserve or auxiliary municipal police officer shall be qualified annually in the use of firearms by the Council on Peace Officer Standards and Training and have proof of such certification.

(b) For the purposes of this Paragraph, a reserve or auxiliary municipal police officer shall be defined as a volunteer, non-regular, sworn member of a law enforcement agency who serves with or without compensation and has regular police powers while functioning as such agency's representative, and who participates on a regular basis in agency activities including, but not limited to those pertaining to crime prevention or control, and the preservation of the peace and enforcement of the law.

H. (1) Except as provided in Paragraph (A)(5) of this Section and in Paragraph (2) of this Subsection, the provisions of this Section shall not prohibit active justices or judges of the supreme court, courts of appeal, district courts, parish courts, juvenile courts, family courts, city courts, federal courts domiciled in the state of Louisiana, and traffic courts, members of either house of the legislature, officers of either house of the legislature, constables, coroners, designated coroner investigators, district attorneys and designated assistant district attorneys, United States attorneys and assistant United States attorneys and investigators, and justices of the peace from possessing and concealing a handgun on their person when the justice or judge, legislator or officer of the legislature, constable, coroner, designated coroner investigators, district attorneys and designated assistant district attorneys, United States attorneys and assistant United States attorneys and investigators, or justices of the peace are certified by the Peace Officer Standards and Training Council.

(2) Nothing in this Subsection shall permit the carrying of a weapon in the state capitol building.

J. The provisions of this Section shall not prohibit the ownership of rescue knives by commissioned full-time law enforcement officers. The provisions of this Section shall not prohibit the carrying of rescue knives by commissioned full-time law enforcement officers who are in the actual discharge of their official duties. The provisions of this Section shall not prohibit the sale of rescue knives to commissioned full-time law enforcement officers. The provisions of this Section shall not prohibit the ownership or possession of rescue knives by merchants who own or possess the knives solely as inventory to be offered for sale to commissioned full-time law enforcement officers. As used in this Subsection, a "rescue knife" is a folding knife, which can be readily and easily opened with one hand and which has at least one blade which is designed to be used to free individuals who are trapped by automobile seat belts, or at least one blade which is designed for a similar purpose. No blade of a rescue knife shall exceed five inches in length.

K. (1) The provisions of this Section shall not prohibit a retired justice or judge of the supreme court, courts of appeal, district courts, parish courts, juvenile courts, family courts, and city courts from possessing and concealing a handgun on their person provided that such retired justice or judge is certified by the Council on Peace Officer Standards and Training and has on their person valid identification showing proof of their status as a retired justice or judge.

(2) The retired justice or judge shall be qualified annually in the use of firearms by the Council on Peace Officer Standards and Training and have proof of such certification. However, this Subsection shall not apply to a retired justice or judge who is medically retired based upon any mental impairment.

14§ 95.1. Possession of firearm or carrying concealed weapon by a person convicted of certain felonies

A. It is unlawful for any person who has been convicted of a crime of violence as defined in R.S. 14:2(B) which is a felony or simple burglary, burglary of a pharmacy, burglary of an inhabited dwelling, unauthorized entry of an inhabited dwelling, felony illegal use of weapons or dangerous instrumentalities, manufacture or possession of a delayed action incendiary device, manufacture or possession of a bomb, or possession of a firearm while in the possession of or during the sale or distribution of a controlled dangerous substance, or any violation of the Uniform Controlled Dangerous Substances Law1 which is a felony, or any crime which is defined as a sex offense in R.S. 15:541, or any crime defined as an attempt to commit one of the above-enumerated offenses under the laws of this state, or who has been convicted under the laws of any other state or of the United States or of any foreign government or country of a crime which, if committed in this state, would be one of the above-enumerated crimes, to possess a firearm or carry a concealed weapon.

B. Whoever is found guilty of violating the provisions of this Section shall be imprisoned at hard labor for not less than ten nor more than twenty years without the benefit of probation, parole, or suspension of sentence and be fined not less than one thousand dollars nor more than five thousand dollars. Notwithstanding the provisions of R.S. 14:27, whoever is found guilty of attempting to violate the provisions of this Section shall be imprisoned at hard labor for not more than seven and one-half years and fined not less than five hundred dollars nor more than two thousand five hundred dollars.

C. The provisions of this Section prohibiting the possession of firearms and carrying concealed weapons by persons who have been convicted of certain felonies shall not apply to any person who has not been convicted of any felony for a period of ten years from the date of completion of sentence, probation, parole, or suspension of sentence.

D. For the purposes of this Section, "firearm" means any pistol, revolver, rifle, shotgun, machine gun, submachine gun, black powder weapon, or assault rifle which is designed to fire or is capable of firing fixed cartridge ammunition or from which a shot or projectile is discharged by an explosive.

14§ 95.2. Carrying a firearm or dangerous weapon by a student or nonstudent on school property, at school-sponsored functions, or in a firearm-free zone

A. Carrying a firearm, or dangerous weapon as defined in R.S. 14:2, by a student or nonstudent on school property, at a school sponsored function, or in a firearm-free zone is unlawful and shall be defined as possession of any firearm or dangerous weapon, on one's person, at any time while on a school campus, on school transportation, or at any school sponsored function in a specific designated area including but not limited to athletic competitions, dances, parties, or any extracurricular activities, or within one thousand feet of any school campus.

B. For purposes of this Section, the following words have the following meanings:

(1) "Campus" means all facilities and property within the boundary of the school property.

(2) "Nonstudent" means any person not registered and enrolled in that school or a suspended student who does not have permission to be on the school campus.

(3) "School" means any elementary, secondary, high school, vocational-technical school, college, or university in this state.

(4) "School bus" means any motor bus being used to transport children to and from school or in connection with school activities.

C. The provisions of this Section shall not apply to:

(1) A federal law enforcement officer or a Louisiana-commissioned state or local Post Certified law enforcement officer who is authorized to carry a firearm.

(2) A school official or employee acting during the normal course of his employment or a student acting under the direction of such school official or employee.

(3) Any person having the written permission of the principal or as provided in R.S. 17:3361.1.

(4) The possession of a firearm occurring within one thousand feet of school property and entirely on private property, or entirely within a private residence, or in accordance with a concealed handgun permit issued pursuant to R.S. 40:1379.1 or 1379.3.

(5) Any constitutionally protected activity which cannot be regulated by the state, such as a firearm contained entirely within a motor vehicle.

(6) Any student carrying a firearm to or from a class, in which he is duly enrolled, that requires the use of the firearm in the class.

(7) A student enrolled or participating in an activity requiring the use of a firearm including but not limited to any ROTC function under the authorization of a university.

(8) A student who possesses a firearm in his dormitory room or while going to or from his vehicle or any other person with permission of the administration.

D. (1) Whoever commits the crime of carrying a firearm, or a dangerous weapon as defined in R.S. 14:2, by a student or nonstudent on school property, at a school-sponsored function, or in a firearm-free zone shall be imprisoned at hard labor for not more than five years.

(2) Whoever commits the crime of carrying a firearm, or a dangerous weapon as defined in R.S. 14:2, on school property or in a firearm-free zone with the firearm or dangerous weapon being used in the commission of a crime of violence as defined in R.S. 14:2(B) on school property or in a firearm-free zone, shall be fined not more than two thousand dollars, or imprisoned, with or without hard labor, for not less than one year nor more than five years, or both. Any sentence issued pursuant to the provisions of this Paragraph and any sentence issued pursuant to a violation of a crime of violence as defined in R.S. 14:2(B) shall be served consecutively. Upon commitment to the Department of Public Safety and Corrections after conviction for a crime committed on school property, at a school-sponsored function or in a firearm-free zone, the depart-

ment shall have the offender evaluated through appropriate examinations or tests conducted under the supervision of the department. Such evaluation shall be made within thirty days of the order of commitment.

E. Lack of knowledge that the prohibited act occurred on or within one thousand feet of school property shall not be a defense.

F. (1) School officials shall notify all students and parents of the impact of this legislation and shall post notices of the impact of this Section at each major point of entry to the school. These notices shall be maintained as permanent notices.

(2)(a) If a student is detained by the principal or other school official for violation of this Section or the school principal or other school official confiscates or seizes a firearm or concealed weapon from a student while upon school property, at a school function, or on a school bus, the principal or other school official in charge at the time of the detention or seizure shall immediately report the detention or seizure to the police department or sheriff's department where the school is located and shall deliver any firearm or weapon seized to that agency.

(b) The confiscated weapon shall be disposed of or destroyed as provided by law.

(3) If a student is detained pursuant to Paragraph (2) of this Subsection for carrying a concealed weapon on campus, the principal shall immediately notify the student's parents.

(4) If a person is arrested for carrying a concealed weapon on campus by a university or college police officer, the weapon shall be given to the sheriff, chief of police, or other officer to whom custody of the arrested person is transferred as provided by R.S. 17:1805(B).

G. Any principal or school official in charge who fails to report the detention of a student or the seizure of a firearm or concealed weapon to a law enforcement agency as required by Paragraph F(2) of this Section within seventy-two hours of notice of the detention or seizure may be issued a misdemeanor summons for a violation hereof and may be fined not more than five hundred dollars or sentenced to not more than forty hours of community service, or both. Upon successful completion of the community service or payment of the fine, or both, the arrest and conviction shall be set aside as provided for in Code of Criminal Procedure Article 894(B).

✦— MAINE —✦
KNIFE RIGHTS MOVEMENT RATING
★ ★ ★ ★ ☆

CUTTING TO THE CHASE
Maine has joined nine other states including New Hampshire, Missouri, Kansas, Alaska, Oklahoma, Indiana, Texas, Nevada, and Tennessee, which have repealed their state ban of switchblades. By way of a court decision, butterfly/balisong knives were considered switchblades under the repealed law. Now they are legal as well.

Quick Points Concerning Maine's Knife Law*

KNIFE TYPE	POSSESSION	(Open/Concealed) CARRY	SALE	MANUFACTURE
Assisted Opening	Legal	Legal/Gray	Legal	Legal
Automatic/Switchblade	Legal	Legal/Gray	Legal	Legal

KNIFE TYPE	POSSESSION	(Open/Concealed) CARRY	SALE	MANUFACTURE
Ballistic	Legal	Legal/Gray	Legal	Legal
Bayonets	Legal	Legal/Gray	Legal	Legal
Bowie	Legal	Legal/Prohibited	Legal	Legal
Butterfly/Balisong	Legal	Legal/Gray	Legal	Legal
Combat/Survival	Legal	Legal/Gray	Legal	Legal
Dagger	Legal	Legal/Gray	Legal	Legal
Dirk	Legal	Legal/Prohibited	Legal	Legal
Disguised	Legal	Legal/Gray	Legal	Legal
Fixed	Legal	Legal/Gray	Legal	Legal
Folding	Legal	Legal/Gray	Legal	Legal
Gravity	Legal	Legal/Gray	Legal	Legal
Hunting/Fishing	Legal	Legal/Gray	Legal	Legal
Machete	Legal	Legal/Gray	Legal	Legal
Razor	Legal	Legal/Gray	Legal	Legal
Stiletto	Legal	Legal/Prohibited	Legal	Legal
Sword	Legal	Legal/Gray	Legal	Legal
Throwing	Legal	Legal/Gray	Legal	Legal
Undetectable	Legal	Legal/Gray	Legal	Legal

Pre-emption (Only State Law May Regulate, No Local Laws Permitted) – NO
*See all information above and below for more details.

SHARP TIPS ABOUT MAINE'S KNIFE LAWS

Concealed carry of a bowie knife, dirk, stiletto or other "dangerous or deadly weapon usually employed in the attack on or defense of a person" is prohibited. Open carry is not prohibited. Whether a knife falls under the prohibition requires a fact-specific inquiry to determine "whether the knife is designed for use against human beings or whether its primary function is to attack or defend a person." Knives used to hunt, fish or trap are allowed to be carried concealed. Do not bring knives to courthouses as they are apparently prohibited by court order. Maine does not have pre-emption, so localities may still have their own prohibitions.

EDGE –U- CATIONAL --- MAINE'S KNIFE LAWS

25 M.R.S. § 2001-A. Threatening display of or carrying concealed weapon

1. Display or carrying prohibited. A person may not, unless excepted by a provision of law:

A. Display in a threatening manner a firearm, slungshot, knuckles, bowie knife, dirk, stiletto or other dangerous or deadly weapon usually employed in the attack on or defense of a person; or

B. Wear under the person's clothes or conceal about the person's person a firearm, slungshot, knuckles, bowie knife, dirk, stiletto or other dangerous or deadly weapon usually employed in the attack on or defense of a person.

2. Exceptions. The provisions of this section concerning the carrying of concealed weapons do not apply to:

C. Knives used to hunt, fish or trap as defined in Title 12, section 10001;

12 M.R.S. § 10001. Definitions

As used in this Part, unless the context otherwise indicates, the following terms have the following meanings.

23. Fish, the verb. To "fish" means to take, catch, kill, molest or destroy fish or to attempt to take, catch, kill, molest or destroy fish.

31. Hunt. To "hunt" means to pursue, catch, take, kill or harvest wild animals or wild birds or to attempt to catch, take, kill or harvest wild animals or wild birds.

64. Trap, the verb. To "trap" means to set, place or tend a trap within the fields, forests or waters of the State, to kill an animal that is caught in a trap or to aid or assist another person in setting or placing a trap, tending a trap or killing an animal that is caught in a trap.

ORDER JB-05-9 (A. 5-11). CONCERNING THE BRINGING OF FIREARMS AND WEAPONS INTO SUPREME JUDICIAL, SUPERIOR, AND DISTRICT COURTS, AND RELATED AREAS

All persons are prohibited from entering or remaining in any Supreme Judicial, Superior, or District Court facility which shall include any courtroom, judicial chambers, clerk's office, conference room, mediation room, law library, lobby, or any other area or building within the control or supervision of the Maine Judicial Branch, if armed with a firearm, electronic control device, other dangerous weapon or in possession of a disabling chemical. As used herein, the term "firearm" has the same meaning as set forth in Title 17-A, section 2, subsection 12-A of the Maine Revised Statutes; "armed with a dangerous weapon" has the same meaning as set forth in Title 17-A, section 2, subsection 9(B) of the Maine Revised Statutes; "electronic control device" includes, but is not limited to, devices commonly called tasers and "disabling chemical" means chemical mace or any similar substance composed of a mixture of gas and chemicals (including organic agents) which has or is designed to have a disabling effect upon human beings. The determination of the dangers of any item shall be at the discretion of the Office of Judicial Marshals and the judicial deputy marshals1 assigned to any courthouse or other Judicial Branch facility. Judicial deputy marshals are authorized to take and hold for the purpose of safekeeping, those items that violate this Order, at least for the duration of the individual's time in the courthouse.

This Order applies to people who possess a valid permit to carry a concealed firearm issued under Title 25, sections 2001-A to 2006, of the Maine Revised Statutes. It is immaterial that the carrying of a firearm or other concealed weapon by a person would not constitute a violation of Title 25, section 2001-A, of the Maine Revised Statutes.

This Order does not apply to judicial deputy marshals, other law enforcement officers, or corrections officers who are armed as part of their duty attire unless the presiding judge or justice, by order, prohibits such officers from possessing firearms, dangerous weapons, or disabling chemicals in a designated area of a court facility. All law enforcement officers and corrections officers in civilian dress shall keep their weapon concealed and discreetly advise the judicial deputy marshal that he/she is armed with a concealed service or duty weapon. All judicial deputy marshals, law enforcement officers, and corrections officers shall keep their weapons in secure holsters.

Any law enforcement officer, corrections officer, or judicial deputy marshal, or who is a litigant or witness in an unofficial capacity in a court proceeding is prohibited from entering or remaining in any Supreme Judicial, Superior, or District Court facility which shall include any courtroom, judicial chambers, clerk's office, conference room, mediation room, law library, lobby, or any other area or building within the control or supervision of the Maine Judicial Branch, if armed with a firearm, other dangerous weapon or in possession of a disabling chemical.

This Order does not apply to people possessing a firearm, dangerous weapon, or disabling chemical if the purpose for such possession is to offer the item as evidence in a proceeding. Prior approval of the presiding judge or justice is required before any firearm, dangerous weapon, or disabling chemical shall be brought into any court facility for this purpose. All firearms, dangerous weapons, or disabling chemical presented as evidence shall be inspected by the judicial deputy marshal to assure that the items are rendered safe for handling in the facility.

The clerk of the court or facility supervisor shall post a copy of this order in locations where it is likely to come to the attention of all who enter the premises under the control and supervision of the Judicial Branch.

✦ MARYLAND ✦
KNIFE RIGHTS MOVEMENT RATING
★ ★ ★ ☆ ☆

CUTTING TO THE CHASE

Maryland does not ban possession of any knife, but it does ban concealed carry by knife feature and also by general characteristics. Pen knives that are not switchblades are lawful to carry concealed.

Quick Points Concerning Maryland's Knife Law*

KNIFE TYPE	POSSESSION	(Open/Concealed) CARRY	SALE	MANUFACTURE
Assisted Opening	Legal	Legal/Gray	Legal	Legal
Automatic/Switchblade	Legal	Legal/Prohibited	Prohibited	Gray
Ballistic	Legal	Legal/Gray	Prohibited	Gray
Bayonets	Legal	Legal/Gray	Legal	Legal
Bowie	Legal	Legal/Prohibited	Legal	Legal
Butterfly/Balisong	Legal	Legal/Gray	Legal	Legal
Combat/Survival	Legal	Legal/Gray	Legal	Legal
Dagger	Legal	Legal/Gray	Legal	Legal
Dirk	Legal	Legal/Prohibited	Legal	Legal
Disguised	Legal	Legal/Gray	Legal	Legal
Fixed	Legal	Legal/Gray	Legal	Legal
Folding	Legal	Legal/Gray	Legal	Legal
Gravity	Legal	Legal/Gray	Legal	Legal
Hunting/Fishing	Legal	Legal/Gray	Legal	Legal
Machete	Legal	Legal/Gray	Legal	Legal
Razor	Legal	Legal/ Prohibited	Legal	Legal
Stiletto	Legal	Legal/Gray	Legal	Legal
Sword	Legal	Legal/Gray	Legal	Legal
Throwing	Legal	Legal/ Prohibited	Legal	Legal
Undetectable	Legal	Legal/Gray	Legal	Legal

Pre-emption (Only State Law May Regulate, No Local Laws Permitted) – NO
*See all information above and below for more details.

SHARP TIPS ABOUT MARYLAND'S KNIFE LAWS

Sale of switchblades and ballistic knives are prohibited. Possession of a knife in a school is prohibited. No pre-emption, so watch out for local laws.

EDGE –U- CATIONAL ⋯ MARYLAND'S KNIFE LAWS
§ 4-101. Dangerous weapons Definitions

(a)(1) In this section the following words have the meanings indicated.

(4) "Star knife" means a device used as a throwing weapon, consisting of several sharp or pointed blades arrayed as radially disposed arms about a central disk.

(5)(i) "Weapon" includes a dirk knife, bowie knife, switchblade knife, star knife, sandclub, metal knuckles, razor, and nunchaku.

(ii) "Weapon" does not include:

1. a handgun; or

2. a penknife without a switchblade.

Exceptions for certain individuals

(b) This section does not prohibit the following individuals from carrying a weapon:

(1) an officer of the State, or of any county or municipal corporation of the State, who is entitled or required to carry the weapon as part of the officer's official equipment, or by any conservator of the peace, who is entitled or required to carry the weapon as part of the conservator's official equipment, or by any officer or conservator of the peace of another state who is temporarily in this State;

(2) a special agent of a railroad;

(3) a holder of a permit to carry a handgun issued under Title 5, Subtitle 3 of the Public Safety Article; or

(4) an individual who carries the weapon as a reasonable precaution against apprehended danger, subject to the right of the court in an action arising under this section to judge the reasonableness of the carrying of the weapon, and the proper occasion for carrying it, under the evidence in the case.

(c)(1) A person may not wear or carry a dangerous weapon of any kind concealed on or about the person.

(3)(i) This paragraph applies in Anne Arundel County, Baltimore County, Caroline County, Cecil County, Harford County, Kent County, Montgomery County, Prince George's County, St. Mary's County, Talbot County, Washington County, and Worcester County.

(ii) A minor may not carry a dangerous weapon between 1 hour after sunset and 1 hour before sunrise, whether concealed or not, except while:

1. on a bona fide hunting trip; or

2. engaged in or on the way to or returning from a bona fide trap shoot, sport shooting event, or any organized civic or military activity.

(d)(1) A person who violates this section is guilty of a misdemeanor and on conviction is subject to imprisonment not exceeding 3 years or a fine not exceeding $1,000 or both.

(2) For a person convicted under subsection (c)(1) or (2) of this section, if it appears from the evidence that the weapon was carried, concealed or openly, with the deliberate purpose of injuring or killing another, the court shall impose the highest sentence of imprisonment prescribed.

§ 4-105. Transfer of switchblade or shooting knife Prohibited

(a) A person may not sell, barter, display, or offer to sell or barter:

(1) a knife or a penknife having a blade that opens automatically by hand pressure applied to a button, spring, or other device in the handle of the knife, commonly called a switchblade knife or a switchblade penknife; or

(2) a device that is designed to propel a knife from a metal sheath by means of a high-compression ejector spring, commonly called a shooting knife.

(b) A person who violates this section is guilty of a misdemeanor and on conviction is subject to imprisonment not exceeding 12 months or a fine of not less than $50 and not exceeding $500 or both.

§ 4-102

(a) This section does not apply to:

(1) a law enforcement officer in the regular course of the officer's duty;

(2) an off-duty law enforcement officer who is a parent, guardian, or visitor of a student attending a school located on the public school property, provided that:

(i) the officer is displaying the officer's badge or credential; and

(ii) the weapon carried or possessed by the officer is concealed;

(3) a person hired by a county board of education specifically for the purpose of guarding public school property;

(4) a person engaged in organized shooting activity for educational purposes; or

(5) a person who, with a written invitation from the school principal, displays or engages in a historical demonstration using a weapon or a replica of a weapon for educational purposes.

(b) A person may not carry or possess a firearm, knife, or deadly weapon of any kind on public school property.

(c)(1) Except as provided in paragraph (2) of this subsection, a person who violates this section is guilty of a misdemeanor and on conviction is subject to imprisonment not exceeding 3 years or a fine not exceeding $1,000 or both.

(2) A person who is convicted of carrying or possessing a handgun in violation of this section shall be sentenced under Subtitle 2 of this title.

✦ **MASSACHUSETTS** ✦
KNIFE RIGHTS MOVEMENT RATING
★ ★ ☆ ☆ ☆

CUTTING TO THE CHASE
Massachusetts does not ban possession of any knife, but it does ban carry, sale and manufacturing by knife feature and also by general characteristics. This state's law creates a lot of "Gray" when it comes to knives, which is always problematic for folks who don't want to get in trouble, yet want to enjoy knife freedom.

Quick Points Concerning Massachusetts' Knife Law*

KNIFE TYPE	POSSESSION	(Open/Concealed) CARRY	SALE	MANUFACTURE
Assisted Opening	Legal	Gray/Gray	Gray	Gray
Automatic/Switchblade	Legal	Prohibited/Prohibited	Prohibited	Prohibited
Ballistic	Legal	Prohibited/Prohibited	Prohibited	Prohibited
Bayonets	Legal	Gray/Gray	Gray	Gray
Bowie	Legal	Gray/Gray	Gray	Gray
Butterfly/Balisong	Legal	Gray/Gray	Gray	Gray
Combat/Survival	Legal	Gray/Gray	Gray	Gray
Dagger	Legal	Prohibited/Prohibited	Gray	Gray
Dirk	Legal	Prohibited/Prohibited	Prohibited	Prohibited
Disguised	Legal	Gray/Gray	Gray	Gray
Fixed	Legal	Gray/Gray	Gray	Gray
Folding	Legal	Gray/Gray	Gray	Gray

KNIFE TYPE	POSSESSION	(Open/Concealed) CARRY	SALE	MANUFACTURE
Gravity	Legal	Gray/Gray	Gray	Gray
Hunting/Fishing	Legal	Gray/Gray	Gray	Gray
Machete	Legal	Gray/Gray	Gray	Gray
Razor	Legal	Gray/Gray	Gray	Gray
Stiletto	Legal	Prohibited/Prohibited	Prohibited	Prohibited
Sword	Legal	Gray/Gray	Gray	Gray
Throwing	Legal	Prohibited/Prohibited	Prohibited	Prohibited
Undetectable	Legal	Gray/Gray	Gray	Gray

Pre-emption (Only State Law May Regulate, No Local Laws Permitted) – NO
*See all information above and below for more details.

SHARP TIPS ABOUT MASSACHUSETTS' KNIFE LAWS

Knives in schools are restricted. Carrying, selling, or making knives is highly regulated. Dirks, switch-blades, throwing stars and ballistic knives are banned from manufacture. There is no pre-emption in Massachusetts so watch out for local laws.

EDGE –U· CATIONAL --- MASSACHUSETTS' KNIFE LAWS

269 § 10. Carrying dangerous weapons; possession of machine gun or sawed-off shotguns; posses-sion of large capacity weapon or large capacity feeding device; punishment

(b) Whoever, except as provided by law, carries on his person, or carries on his person or under his control in a vehicle, any stiletto, dagger or a device or case which enables a knife with a locking blade to be drawn at a locked position, any ballistic knife, or any knife with a detachable blade capable of being propelled by any mechanism, dirk knife, any knife having a double-edged blade, or a switch knife, or any knife having an automatic spring release device by which the blade is released from the handle, having a blade of over one and one-half inches, or a slung shot, blowgun, blackjack, metallic knuckles or knuckles of any substance which could be put to the same use with the same or similar effect as metallic knuckles, nunchaku, zoobow, also known as klackers or kung fu sticks, or any similar weapon consisting of two sticks of wood, plastic or metal connected at one end by a length of rope, chain, wire or leather, a shuriken or any similar pointed starlike object intended to injure a person when thrown, or any armband, made with leather which has metallic spikes, points or studs or any similar device made from any other substance or a cestus or similar material weighted with metal or other substance and worn on the hand, or a manrikigusari or similar length of chain having weighted ends; or whoever, when arrested upon a warrant for an alleged crime, or when arrested while committing a breach or disturbance of the public peace, is armed with or has on his person, or has on his person or under his control in a vehicle, a billy or other dangerous weapon other than those herein mentioned and those mentioned in paragraph (a), shall be punished by imprisonment for not less than two and one-half years nor more than five years in the state prison, or for not less than six months nor more than two and one-half years in a jail or house of correction, except that, if the court finds that the defendant has not been previously convicted of a felony, he may be punished by a fine of not more than fifty dollars or by imprisonment for not more than two and one-half years in a jail or house of correction.

269 § 12. Manufacturing and selling knives, slung shots, swords, bludgeons and similar weapons

Whoever manufactures or causes to be manufactured, or sells or exposes for sale, an instrument or weapon of the kind usually known as a dirk knife, a switch knife or any knife having an automatic spring release device by which the blade is released from the handle, having a blade of over one and one-half inches or a device or case which enables a knife with a locking blade to be drawn at a locked position, any ballistic knife, or any knife with a detachable blade capable of being propelled by any mechanism, slung shot, sling shot, bean blower, sword cane, pistol cane, bludgeon, blackjack, nunchaku, zoobow, also known as klackers or kung fu sticks, or any similar weapon consisting of two sticks of wood, plastic or metal connected at one end by a length of rope, chain, wire or leather, a shuriken or any similar pointed starlike object intended to injure a person when thrown, or a manrikigusari or similar length of chain having weighted ends; or metallic knuckles or knuckles of any other substance which could be put to the same use and with the same or similar effect as metallic knuckles, shall be punished by a fine of not less than fifty nor more than one thousand dollars or by imprisonment for not more than six months; provided, however, that sling shots may be manufactured and sold to clubs or associations conducting sporting events where such sling shots are used.

71 § 37H. Policies relative to conduct of teachers or students; student handbooks

Notwithstanding any general or special law to the contrary, all student handbooks shall contain the following provisions:

(a) Any student who is found on school premises or at school-sponsored or school-related events, including athletic games, in possession of a dangerous weapon, including, but not limited to, a gun or a knife; or a controlled substance as defined in chapter ninety-four C, including, but not limited to, marijuana, cocaine, and heroin, may be subject to expulsion from the school or school district by the principal.

✦— MICHIGAN —✦
KNIFE RIGHTS MOVEMENT RATING

★ ★ ★ ☆ ☆

CUTTING TO THE CHASE

Michigan bans switchblades and gravity knives. Concealed carry is regulated.

Quick Points Concerning Michigan's Knife Law*

KNIFE TYPE	POSSESSION	(Open/Concealed) CARRY	SALE	MANUFACTURE
Assisted Opening	Legal	Legal/Gray	Gray	Gray
Automatic/Switchblade	Prohibited	Prohibited/Prohibited	Prohibited	Prohibited
Ballistic	Legal	Legal/Gray	Legal	Legal
Bayonets	Legal	Legal/Gray	Legal	Legal
Bowie	Legal	Legal/Gray	Legal	Legal
Butterfly/Balisong	Legal	Legal/Gray	Gray	Gray
Combat/Survival	Legal	Legal/Gray	Legal	Legal
Dagger	Legal	Legal/ Prohibited	Legal	Legal
Dirk	Legal	Legal/ Prohibited	Legal	Legal
Disguised	Legal	Legal/Gray	Gray	Gray
Fixed	Legal	Legal/Gray	Legal	Legal
Folding	Legal	Legal/Gray	Gray	Gray
Gravity	Prohibited	Prohibited/Prohibited	Prohibited	Prohibited
Hunting/Fishing	Legal	Legal/Gray	Legal	Gray
Machete	Legal	Legal/Gray	Legal	Legal
Razor	Legal	Legal/Gray	Legal	Gray
Stiletto	Legal	Legal/ Prohibited	Gray	Legal
Sword	Legal	Legal/Gray	Legal	Legal
Throwing	Legal	Legal/Gray	Legal	Legal
Undetectable	Legal	Gray/Gray	Gray	Legal

Pre-emption (Only State Law May Regulate, No Local Laws Permitted) – NO

*See all information above and below for more details.

SHARP TIPS ABOUT MICHIGAN'S KNIFE LAWS

Knives are banned in schools and airports. Knife wounds get reported to the authorities. Carrying a knife with a blade under 3" that is not otherwise prohibited, is one's safest bet. No pre-emption, so beware of local laws.

EDGE –U- CATIONAL --- MICHIGAN'S KNIFE LAWS

750.222a. Doubled-edged, nonfolding stabbing instruments

Sec. 222a. (1) As used in this chapter, "doubled-edged, nonfolding stabbing instrument" does not include a knife, tool, implement, arrowhead, or artifact manufactured from stone by means of conchoidal fracturing.

(2) Subsection (1) does not apply to an item being transported in a vehicle, unless the item is in a container and inaccessible to the driver.

750.226. Firearm or dangerous weapon, carrying with unlawful intent

Sec. 226. Carrying firearm or dangerous weapon with unlawful intent--Any person who, with intent to use the same unlawfully against the person of another, goes armed with a pistol or other firearm or dagger, dirk, razor, stiletto, or knife having a blade over 3 inches in length, or any other dangerous or deadly weapon or instrument, shall be guilty of a felony, punishable by imprisonment in the state prison for not more than 5 years or by a fine of not more than 2,500 dollars.

750.226a. Pocket knife opened by mechanical device, unlawful sale or possession; persons exempted

Sec. 226a. Any person who shall sell or offer to sell, or any person who shall have in his possession any knife having the appearance of a pocket knife, the blade or blades of which can be opened by the flick of a button, pressure on a handle or other mechanical contrivance shall be guilty of a misdemeanor, punishable by imprisonment in the county jail for not to exceed 1 year or by a fine of not to exceed $300.00, or both.

The provisions of this section shall not apply to any one-armed person carrying a knife on his person in connection with his living requirements.

750.227. Concealed weapons, carrying

Sec. 227. (1) A person shall not carry a dagger, dirk, stiletto, a double-edged nonfolding stabbing instrument of any length, or any other dangerous weapon, except a hunting knife adapted and carried as such, concealed on or about his or her person, or whether concealed or otherwise in any vehicle operated or occupied by the person, except in his or her dwelling house, place of business or on other land possessed by the person.

(3) A person who violates this section is guilty of a felony, punishable by imprisonment for not more than 5 years, or by a fine of not more than $2,500.00.

750.237a. Weapon free school zone, engagement in certain proscribed conduct; possession of weapon in weapon free school zone

(4) Except as provided in subsection (5), an individual who possesses a weapon in a weapon free school zone is guilty of a misdemeanor punishable by 1 or more of the following:

(a) Imprisonment for not more than 93 days.

(b) Community service for not more than 100 hours.

(c) A fine of not more than $2,000.00.

(5) Subsection (4) does not apply to any of the following:

(a) An individual employed by or contracted by a school if the possession of that weapon is to provide security services for the school.

(b) A peace officer.

(c) An individual licensed by this state or another state to carry a concealed weapon.

(d) An individual who possesses a weapon provided by a school or a school's instructor on school property for purposes of providing or receiving instruction in the use of that weapon.

(6) As used in this section:

(d) "Weapon free school zone" means school property and a vehicle used by a school to transport students to or from school property.

259.80f. Possession, carrying, or attempted possession or carrying of particular objects in sterile area of commercial airport

Sec. 80f. (1) An individual shall not possess, carry, or attempt to possess or carry any of the following in a sterile area of a commercial airport:

(a) Firearm.

(b) Explosive.

(c) Knife with a blade of any length.

(d) Razor, box cutter, or item with a similar blade.

(e) Dangerous weapon.

(2) Except as provided in subsection (3), an individual who violates subsection (1) is guilty of a misdemeanor punishable by imprisonment for not more than 1 year or a fine of not more than $1,000.00, or both.

(4) This section does not apply to any of the following:

(a) A peace officer of a duly authorized police agency of this state, a political subdivision of this state, another state, a political subdivision of another state, or the United States.

(b) An individual regularly employed by the department of corrections and authorized in writing by the director of the department of corrections to possess or carry an item listed in subsection (1) during the performance of his or her duties or while going to or returning from his or her duties.

(c) A member of the United States army, air force, navy, marine corps, or coast guard while possessing or carrying an item listed in subsection (1) in the line of duty.

(d) A member of the national guard, armed forces reserves, or other duly authorized military organization while on duty or drill or while possessing or carrying an item listed in subsection (1) for purposes of that military organization.

(e) Security personnel employed to enforce federal regulations for access to a sterile area.

(f) A court officer while engaged in his or her duties as a court officer as authorized by a court.

(g) An airline or airport employee as authorized by his or her employer.

380.1313. Reporting and disposition of dangerous weapons found in possession of pupils

Sec. 1313. (1) If a dangerous weapon is found in the possession of a pupil while the pupil is in attendance at school or a school activity or while the pupil is enroute to or from school on a school bus, the superintendent of the school district or intermediate school district, or his or her designee, immediately shall report that finding to the pupil's parent or legal guardian and the local law enforcement agency.

(2) If a school official finds that a dangerous weapon is in the possession of a pupil as described in subsection (1), the school official may confiscate the dangerous weapon or shall request a law enforcement agency to respond as soon as possible and to confiscate the dangerous weapon. If a

school official confiscates a dangerous weapon under this subsection, the school official shall give the dangerous weapon to a law enforcement agency and shall not release the dangerous weapon to any other person, including the legal owner of the dangerous weapon. A school official who complies in good faith with this section is not civilly or criminally liable for that compliance.

(3) A law enforcement agency that takes possession of a dangerous weapon under subsection (2) shall check all available local and state stolen weapon and stolen property files and the national crime information center stolen gun and property files to determine the legal owner of the dangerous weapon. If the dangerous weapon is a pistol, the law enforcement agency also shall check the state pistol registration records to determine the legal owner. If the law enforcement agency is able to determine the legal owner of the dangerous weapon, and if the legal owner did not knowingly provide the dangerous weapon to the pupil or lawfully provided the dangerous weapon to the pupil but did not know or have reason to know that the pupil would possess the dangerous weapon while in attendance at school or a school activity or while en route to or from school on a school bus, the law enforcement agency shall send by certified mail to the legal owner a notice that the agency is in possession of the dangerous weapon and that the legal owner has 90 days from receipt of the notice to claim the dangerous weapon.

(4) As used in this section, "dangerous weapon" means a firearm, dagger, dirk, stiletto, knife with a blade over 3 inches in length, pocket knife opened by a mechanical device, iron bar, or brass knuckles.

750.411. Injuries by means of deadly weapons; duty to report; violation, misdemeanor; immunity

Sec. 411. (1) A person, firm, or corporation conducting a hospital or pharmacy in this state, the person managing or in charge of a hospital or pharmacy, or the person in charge of a ward or part of a hospital to which 1 or more persons come or are brought suffering from a wound or other injury inflicted by means of a knife, gun, pistol, or other deadly weapon, or by other means of violence, has a duty to report that fact immediately, both by telephone and in writing, to the chief of police or other head of the police force of the village or city in which the hospital or pharmacy is located, or to the county sheriff if the hospital or pharmacy is located outside the incorporated limits of a village or city. The report shall state the name and residence of the person, if known, his or her whereabouts, and the cause, character, and extent of the injuries and may state the identification of the perpetrator, if known.

(2) A physician or surgeon who has under his or her charge or care a person suffering from a wound or injury inflicted in the manner described in subsection (1) has a duty to report that fact in the same manner and to the same officer as required by subsection (1).

(3) A person, firm, or corporation that violates this section is guilty of a misdemeanor.

(5) The immunity from civil and criminal liability granted under subsection (4) extends only to the actions described in subsection (4) and does not extend to another act or omission that is negligent or that amounts to professional malpractice, or both, and that causes personal injury or death.

(6) The physician-patient privilege created under section 2157 of the revised judicature act of 1961, 1961 PA 236, MCL 600.2157, a health professional-patient privilege created under article 15 of the public health code, 1978 PA 368, MCL 333.16101 to 333.18838, and any other health professional-patient privilege created or recognized by law do not apply to a report made under subsection (1) or (2), are not valid reasons for a failure to comply with subsection (1) or (2), and are not a defense to a misdemeanor charge filed under this section.

✦ MINNESOTA ✦
KNIFE RIGHTS MOVEMENT RATING
★ ★ ☆ ☆ ☆

CUTTING TO THE CHASE
Minnesota bans switchblades in a way that wins the prize as the most poorly described switchblade ban in the US, for example, "…switch blade knife opening automatically." The phrase is nonsensical. Its archaic prohibition on carry is almost as badly written as its ban on switchblades.

Quick Points Concerning Minnesota's Knife Law*

KNIFE TYPE	POSSESSION	(Open/Concealed) CARRY	SALE	MANUFACTURE
Assisted Opening	Gray	Gray/Gray	Gray	Gray
Automatic/Switchblade	Prohibited	Prohibited/Prohibited	Prohibited	Prohibited
Ballistic	Legal	Gray/Gray	Legal	Legal
Bayonets	Legal	Gray/Gray	Legal	Legal
Bowie	Legal	Gray/Gray	Legal	Legal
Butterfly/Balisong	Legal	Gray/Gray	Legal	Legal
Combat/Survival	Legal	Gray/Gray	Legal	Legal
Dagger	Legal	Prohibited/Prohibited	Legal	Legal
Dirk	Legal	Prohibited/Prohibited	Legal	Legal
Disguised	Legal	Gray/Gray	Legal	Legal
Fixed	Legal	Gray/Gray	Legal	Legal
Folding	Legal	Gray/Gray	Legal	Legal
Gravity	Gray	Gray/Gray	Gray	Gray
Hunting/Fishing	Legal	Gray/Gray	Legal	Legal
Machete	Legal	Gray/Gray	Legal	Legal
Razor	Legal	Gray/Gray	Legal	Legal
Stiletto	Legal	Gray/Gray	Legal	Legal
Sword	Legal	Prohibited/Prohibited	Legal	Legal
Throwing	Legal	Gray/Gray	Legal	Legal
Undetectable	Legal	Gray/Gray	Legal	Legal

Pre-emption (Only State Law May Regulate, No Local Laws Permitted) – NO
*See all information above and below for more details.

SHARP TIPS ABOUT MINNESOTA'S KNIFE LAWS
No knives in schools or courthouses. No pre-emption, so beware of local laws.

EDGE –U- CATIONAL --- MINNESOTA'S KNIFE LAWS
§ 609.02. Definitions
Subd. 6. Dangerous weapon. "Dangerous weapon" means any firearm, whether loaded or unloaded, or any device designed as a weapon and capable of producing death or great bodily harm, any combustible or flammable liquid or other device or instrumentality that, in the manner it is used or intended to be used, is calculated or likely to produce death or great bodily harm, or any fire that is used to produce death or great bodily harm.

§ 609.66. Dangerous weapons
Subdivision 1. Misdemeanor and gross misdemeanor crimes. (a) Whoever does any of the following is

guilty of a crime and may be sentenced as provided in paragraph (b):

(1) recklessly handles or uses a gun or other dangerous weapon or explosive so as to endanger the safety of another; or

(4) manufactures, transfers, or possesses metal knuckles or a switch blade knife opening automatically; or

(5) possesses any other dangerous article or substance for the purpose of being used unlawfully as a weapon against another; or

Subd. 1c. Felony; furnishing dangerous weapon. Whoever recklessly furnishes a person with a dangerous weapon in conscious disregard of a known substantial risk that the object will be possessed or used in furtherance of a felony crime of violence is guilty of a felony and may be sentenced to imprisonment for not more than ten years or to payment of a fine of not more than $20,000, or both.

Subd. 1d. Possession on school property; penalty. (a) Except as provided under paragraphs (d) and (f), whoever possesses, stores, or keeps a dangerous weapon while knowingly on school property is guilty of a felony and may be sentenced to imprisonment for not more than five years or to payment of a fine of not more than $10,000, or both.

(2) "dangerous weapon" has the meaning given it in section 609.02, subdivision 6;

(4) "school property" means:

(i) a public or private elementary, middle, or secondary school building and its improved grounds, whether leased or owned by the school;

(ii) a child care center licensed under chapter 245A during the period children are present and participating in a child care program;

(iii) the area within a school bus when that bus is being used by a school to transport one or more elementary, middle, or secondary school students to and from school-related activities, including curricular, cocurricular, noncurricular, extracurricular, and supplementary activities; and

(iv) that portion of a building or facility under the temporary, exclusive control of a public or private school, a school district, or an association of such entities where conspicuous signs are prominently posted at each entrance that give actual notice to persons of the school-related use.

(f) This subdivision does not apply to:

(1) active licensed peace officers;

(2) military personnel or students participating in military training, who are on-duty, performing official duties;

(3) persons authorized to carry a pistol under section 624.714 while in a motor vehicle or outside of a motor vehicle to directly place a firearm in, or retrieve it from, the trunk or rear area of the vehicle;

(4) persons who keep or store in a motor vehicle pistols in accordance with section 624.714 or 624.715 or other firearms in accordance with section 97B.045;

(5) firearm safety or marksmanship courses or activities conducted on school property;

(6) possession of dangerous weapons, BB guns, or replica firearms by a ceremonial color guard;

(7) a gun or knife show held on school property;

(8) possession of dangerous weapons, BB guns, or replica firearms with written permission of the principal or other person having general control and supervision of the school or the director of a child care center; or

(9) persons who are on unimproved property owned or leased by a child care center, school, or school

district unless the person knows that a student is currently present on the land for a school-related act

(g) Notwithstanding section 471.634, a school district or other entity composed exclusively of school districts may not regulate firearms, ammunition, or their respective components, when possessed or carried by nonstudents or nonemployees, in a manner that is inconsistent with this subdivision.

Subd. 1g. Felony; possession in courthouse or certain state buildings. (a) A person who commits either of the following acts is guilty of a felony and may be sentenced to imprisonment for not more than five years or to payment of a fine of not more than $10,000, or both:

(1) possesses a dangerous weapon, ammunition, or explosives within any courthouse complex; or

(2) possesses a dangerous weapon, ammunition, or explosives in any state building within the Capitol Area described in chapter 15B, other than the National Guard Armory.

(b) Unless a person is otherwise prohibited or restricted by other law to possess a dangerous weapon, this subdivision does not apply to:

(1) licensed peace officers or military personnel who are performing official duties;

(2) persons who carry pistols according to the terms of a permit issued under section 624.714 and who so notify the sheriff or the commissioner of public safety, as appropriate;

(3) persons who possess dangerous weapons for the purpose of display as demonstrative evidence during testimony at a trial or hearing or exhibition in compliance with advance notice and safety guidelines set by the sheriff or the commissioner of public safety; or

(4) persons who possess dangerous weapons in a courthouse complex with the express consent of the county sheriff or who possess dangerous weapons in a state building with the express consent of the commissioner of public safety.

Subd. 2. Exceptions. Nothing in this section prohibits the possession of the articles mentioned by museums or collectors of art or for other lawful purposes of public exhibition.

§ 625.16. Carrying dangerous weapons
Whoever shall go armed with a dirk, dagger, sword, pistol, or other offensive and dangerous weapon, without reasonable cause to fear an assault or other injury or violence to person, family, or property, may, on complaint of any other person having reasonable cause to fear an injury or breach of the peace, be required to find sureties for keeping the peace, for a term not exceeding six months, with the right of appealing as before provided.

✦ MISSISSIPPI ✦
KNIFE RIGHTS MOVEMENT RATING
★ ★ ★ ★ ☆

CUTTING TO THE CHASE

Mississippi does not ban possession of any knife. Concealed carry is restricted for knives with certain features which includes "bowie knife, dirk knife, butcher knife, switchblade knife." These terms are undefined.

Quick Points Concerning Mississippi's Knife Law*

KNIFE TYPE	POSSESSION	(Open/Concealed) CARRY	SALE	MANUFACTURE
Assisted Opening	Legal	Legal/Gray	Legal	Legal
Automatic/Switchblade	Legal	Legal/Prohibited	Legal	Legal
Ballistic	Legal	Legal/Legal	Legal	Legal
Bayonets	Legal	Legal/Legal	Legal	Legal
Bowie	Legal	Legal/Prohibited	Legal	Legal
Butterfly/Balisong	Legal	Legal/Legal	Legal	Legal
Combat/Survival	Legal	Legal/Gray	Legal	Legal
Dagger	Legal	Legal/Gray	Legal	Legal
Dirk	Legal	Legal/Prohibited	Legal	Legal
Disguised	Legal	Legal/Gray	Legal	Legal
Fixed	Legal	Legal/Gray	Legal	Legal
Folding	Legal	Legal/Legal	Legal	Legal
Gravity	Legal	Legal/Legal	Legal	Legal
Hunting/Fishing	Legal	Legal/Legal	Legal	Legal
Machete	Legal	Legal/Legal	Legal	Legal
Razor	Legal	Legal/Legal	Legal	Legal
Stiletto	Legal	Legal/Gray	Legal	Legal
Sword	Legal	Legal/Legal	Legal	Legal
Throwing	Legal	Legal/Gray	Legal	Legal
Undetectable	Legal	Legal/Gray	Legal	Legal

Pre-emption (Only State Law May Regulate, No Local Laws Permitted) – NO
*See all information above and below for more details.

SHARP TIPS ABOUT MISSISSIPPI'S KNIFE LAWS

Possession by convicted felons is generally prohibited. Pawnbrokers are taxed for receiving a dirk, knife or sword-cane. Knives in schools are restricted. Mississippi has some archaic laws on knife fighting in public and brandishing certain knives. No pre-emption, so watch out for local laws.

EDGE –U- CATIONAL --- MISSISSIPPI'S KNIFE LAWS

§ 27-17-299. Tax upon pawnbrokers

Upon each pawn broker who receives in pawn any dirk, knife, sword-cane, brass or metal knucks or pistol, (additional tax) $250.00

§ 27-17-415. Dealers of deadly weapons

Upon each person selling pistols, dirk knives, sword canes, brass or metallic knuckles, or other deadly weapons (excepting hunting knives, shot guns and rifles) $100.00

§ 97-37-1. Concealment of deadly weapon

(1) Except as otherwise provided in Section 45-9-101, any person who carries, concealed on or about one's person, any bowie knife, dirk knife, butcher knife, switchblade knife, metallic knuckles, blackjack, slingshot, pistol, revolver, or any rifle with a barrel of less than sixteen (16) inches in length, or any shotgun with a barrel of less than eighteen (18) inches in length, machine gun or any fully automatic firearm or deadly weapon, or any muffler or silencer for any firearm, whether or not it is accompanied by a firearm, or uses or attempts to use against another person any imitation firearm, shall, upon conviction, be punished as follows:

(a) By a fine of not less than One Hundred Dollars ($100.00) nor more than Five Hundred Dollars ($500.00), or by imprisonment in the county jail for not more than six (6) months, or both, in the discretion of the court, for the first conviction under this section.

(b) By a fine of not less than One Hundred Dollars ($100.00) nor more than Five Hundred Dollars ($500.00), and imprisonment in the county jail for not less than thirty (30) days nor more than six (6) months, for the second conviction under this section.

(c) By confinement in the custody of the Department of Corrections for not less than one (1) year nor more than five (5) years, for the third or subsequent conviction under this section.

(d) By confinement in the custody of the Department of Corrections for not less than one (1) year nor more than ten (10) years for any person previously convicted of any felony who is convicted under this section.

(2) It shall not be a violation of this section for any person over the age of eighteen (18) years to carry a firearm or deadly weapon concealed within the confines of his own home or his place of business, or any real property associated with his home or business or within any motor vehicle.

(3) It shall not be a violation of this section for any person to carry a firearm or deadly weapon concealed if the possessor of the weapon is then engaged in a legitimate weapon-related sports activity or is going to or returning from such activity. For purposes of this subsection, "legitimate weapon-related sports activity" means hunting, fishing, target shooting or any other legal activity which normally involves the use of a firearm or other weapon.

(4) For the purposes of this section, "concealed" means hidden or obscured from common observation and shall not include any weapon listed in subsection (1) of this section, including, but not limited to, a loaded or unloaded pistol carried upon the person in a sheath, belt holster or shoulder holster that is wholly or partially visible, or carried upon the person in a scabbard or case for carrying the weapon that is wholly or partially visible.

§ 97-37-5. Possession by felon

(1) It shall be unlawful for any person who has been convicted of a felony under the laws of this state, any other state, or of the United States to possess any firearm or any bowie knife, dirk knife, butcher knife, switchblade knife, metallic knuckles, blackjack, or any muffler or silencer for any firearm unless such person has received a pardon for such felony, has received a relief from disability pursuant to Section 925(c) of Title 18 of the United States Code, or has received a certificate of rehabilitation pursuant to subsection (3) of this section.

(2) Any person violating this section shall be guilty of a felony and, upon conviction thereof, shall be fined not more than Five Thousand Dollars ($5,000.00), or committed to the custody of the State Department of Corrections for not less than one (1) year nor more than ten (10) years, or both.

§ 97-39-11. Fighting in public with deadly weapon

If any person shall be guilty of fighting in any city, town, village, or other public place, and shall in such fight use any rifle, shotgun, sword, sword-cane, pistol, dirk, bowie-knife, dirk-knife, or any other deadly weapon, or if any person shall be second or aid in such fight, the person so offending shall be fined not less than three hundred dollars, and shall be imprisoned not less than three months; and if any person shall be killed in such fight, the person so killing the other may be prosecuted and convicted as in other cases of murder.

§ 97-37-17. Weapons possession on educational property

(1) The following definitions apply to this section:

(a) "Educational property" shall mean any public or private school building or bus, public or private school campus, grounds, recreational area, athletic field, or other property owned, used or operated by any local school board, school, college or university board of trustees, or directors for the administration of any public or private educational institution or during a school-related activity, and shall include the facility and property of the Oakley Youth Development Center, operated by the Department of Human Services; provided, however, that the term "educational property" shall not include any sixteenth section school land or lieu land on which is not located a school building, school campus, recreational area or athletic field.

(b) "Student" shall mean a person enrolled in a public or private school, college or university, or a person who has been suspended or expelled within the last five (5) years from a public or private school, college or university, or a person in the custody of the Oakley Youth Development Center, operated by the Department of Human Services, whether the person is an adult or a minor.

(c) "Switchblade knife" shall mean a knife containing a blade or blades which open automatically by the release of a spring or a similar contrivance.

(d) "Weapon" shall mean any device enumerated in subsection (2) or (4) of this section.

(4) It shall be a misdemeanor for any person to possess or carry, whether openly or concealed, any BB gun, air rifle, air pistol, bowie knife, dirk, dagger, slingshot, leaded cane, switchblade knife, blackjack, metallic knuckles, razors and razor blades (except solely for personal shaving), and any sharp-pointed or edged instrument except instructional supplies, unaltered nail files and clips and tools used solely for preparation of food, instruction and maintenance on educational property. Any person violating this subsection shall be guilty of a misdemeanor and, upon conviction thereof, shall be fined not more than One Thousand Dollars ($1,000.00), or be imprisoned not exceeding six (6) months, or both.

(5) It shall be a misdemeanor for any person to cause, encourage or aid a minor who is less than eighteen (18) years old to possess or carry, whether openly or concealed, any BB gun, air rifle, air pistol, bowie knife, dirk, dagger, slingshot, leaded cane, switchblade, knife, blackjack, metallic knuckles, razors and razor blades (except solely for personal shaving) and any sharp-pointed or edged instrument except instructional supplies, unaltered nail files and clips and tools used solely for preparation of food, instruction and maintenance on educational property. Any person violating this subsection shall be guilty of a misdemeanor and, upon conviction thereof, shall be fined not more than One Thousand Dollars ($1,000.00), or be imprisoned not exceeding six (6) months, or both.

(7) This section shall not apply to:

(a) A weapon used solely for educational or school-sanctioned ceremonial purposes, or used in a school-approved program conducted under the supervision of an adult whose supervision has been approved by the school authority;

(b) Armed Forces personnel of the United States, officers and soldiers of the militia and National Guard, law enforcement personnel, any private police employed by an educational institution, State Militia or Emergency Management Corps and any guard or patrolman in a state or municipal institution, and any law enforcement personnel or guard at a state juvenile training school, when acting in the discharge of their official duties;

(c) Home schools as defined in the compulsory school attendance law, Section 37-13-91;

(d) Competitors while participating in organized shooting events;

(e) Any person as authorized in Section 97-37-7 while in the performance of his official duties;

(f) Any mail carrier while in the performance of his official duties; or

(g) Any weapon not prescribed by Section 97-37-1 which is in a motor vehicle under the control of a parent, guardian or custodian, as defined in Section 43-21-105, which is used to bring or pick up a student at a school building, school property or school function.

(8) All schools shall post in public view a copy of the provisions of this section.

§ 97-37-19. Threatening exhibition of weapons

If any person, having or carrying any dirk, dirk-knife, sword, sword-cane, or any deadly weapon, or other weapon the carrying of which concealed is prohibited by Section 97-37-1, shall, in the presence of another person, brandish or wield the same in a threatening manner, not in necessary self-defense, or shall in any manner unlawfully use the same in any fight or quarrel, the person so offending, upon conviction thereof, shall be fined in a sum not exceeding Five Hundred Dollars ($500.00) or be imprisoned in the county jail not exceeding three (3) months, or both. In prosecutions under this section it shall not be necessary for the affidavit or indictment to aver, nor for the state to prove on the trial, that any gun, pistol, or other firearm was charged, loaded, or in condition to be discharged.

⫯ MISSOURI ⫯
KNIFE RIGHTS MOVEMENT RATING
★ ★ ★ ★ ☆

CUTTING TO THE CHASE

In 2012 Missouri repealed its ban on possession, sale and manufacture of switchblade knives as long as it is not "in violation of federal law." An "ordinary" pocket knife with a blade less than 4" may be carried concealed.

Quick Points Concerning Missouri's Knife Law*

KNIFE TYPE	POSSESSION	(Open/Concealed) CARRY	SALE	MANUFACTURE
Assisted Opening	Legal	Legal/Prohibited	Legal	Legal
Automatic/Switchblade	Legal	Legal/Prohibited	Legal	Legal
Ballistic	Legal	Legal/Prohibited	Legal	Legal
Bayonets	Legal	Legal/Prohibited	Legal	Legal
Bowie	Legal	Legal/Prohibited	Legal	Legal
Butterfly/Balisong	Legal	Legal/Prohibited	Legal	Legal
Combat/Survival	Legal	Legal/Prohibited	Legal	Legal
Dagger	Legal	Legal/Prohibited	Legal	Legal
Dirk	Legal	Legal/Prohibited	Legal	Legal
Disguised	Legal	Legal/Prohibited	Legal	Legal
Fixed	Legal	Legal/Prohibited	Legal	Legal
Folding	Legal	Legal/Prohibited	Legal	Legal
Gravity	Legal	Legal/Prohibited	Legal	Legal
Hunting/Fishing	Legal	Legal/Prohibited	Legal	Legal
Machete	Legal	Legal/Prohibited	Legal	Legal
Razor	Legal	Legal/Prohibited	Legal	Legal

KNIFE TYPE	POSSESSION	(Open/Concealed) CARRY	SALE	MANUFACTURE
Stiletto	Legal	Legal/Prohibited	Legal	Legal
Sword	Legal	Legal/Prohibited	Legal	Legal
Throwing	Legal	Legal/Prohibited	Legal	Legal
Undetectable	Legal	Legal/Prohibited	Legal	Legal

Pre-emption (Only State Law May Regulate, No Local Laws Permitted) – NO
*See all information above and below for more details.

SHARP TIPS ABOUT MISSOURI'S KNIFE LAWS

Do not conceal carry any knife on your person or in a vehicle, except an "ordinary" pocket knife with a blade less than 4". Gravity knives appear to fit the definition of a "projectile weapon", which includes a "weapon that is not a firearm, which is capable of expelling a projectile that could inflict serious physical injury or death by striking or piercing a person" Do not possess one while drunk or recklessly or negligently use one. No pre-emption so beware of local laws.

EDGE –U- CATIONAL --- MISSOURI'S KNIFE LAWS
M.S. 571.010. Definitions

As used in this chapter, the following terms shall mean:

(12) "Knife", any dagger, dirk, stiletto, or bladed hand instrument that is readily capable of inflicting serious physical injury or death by cutting or stabbing a person. For purposes of this chapter, "knife" does not include any ordinary pocketknife with no blade more than four inches in length;

(15) "Projectile weapon", any bow, crossbow, pellet gun, slingshot or other weapon that is not a firearm, which is capable of expelling a projectile that could inflict serious physical injury or death by striking or piercing a person;

(20) "Switchblade knife", any knife which has a blade that folds or closes into the handle or sheath, and:

(a) That opens automatically by pressure applied to a button or other device located on the handle; or

(b) That opens or releases from the handle or sheath by the force of gravity or by the application of centrifugal force.

M.S. 571.020. Possession--manufacture--transport--repair--sale of certain weapons a crime--exceptions--penalties

1. A person commits a crime if such person knowingly possesses, manufactures, transports, repairs, or sells:

(5) Knuckles; or

(6) Any of the following in violation of federal law:

(d) A switchblade knife.

2. A person does not commit a crime pursuant to this section if his conduct involved any of the items in subdivisions (1) to (5) of subsection 1, the item was possessed in conformity with any applicable federal law, and the conduct:

(1) Was incident to the performance of official duty by the Armed Forces, National Guard, a governmental law enforcement agency, or a penal institution; or

(2) Was incident to engaging in a lawful commercial or business transaction with an organization enumerated in subdivision (1) of this section; or

(4) Was incident to displaying the weapon in a public museum or exhibition; or

(5) Was incident to using the weapon in a manner reasonably related to a lawful dramatic performance.

3. A crime pursuant to subdivision (1), (2), (3) or (6) of subsection 1 of this section is a class C felony; a crime pursuant to subdivision (4) or (5) of subsection 1 of this section is a class A misdemeanor.

M.S. 571.030. Unlawful use of weapons--exceptions--penalties

1. A person commits the crime of unlawful use of weapons if he or she knowingly:

(1) Carries concealed upon or about his or her person a knife, a firearm, a blackjack or any other weapon readily capable of lethal use; or

(4) Exhibits, in the presence of one or more persons, any weapon readily capable of lethal use in an angry or threatening manner; or

(5) Has a firearm or projectile weapon readily capable of lethal use on his or her person, while he or she is intoxicated, and handles or otherwise uses such firearm or projectile weapon in either a negligent or unlawful manner or discharges such firearm or projectile weapon unless acting in self-defense; or

(8) Carries a firearm or any other weapon readily capable of lethal use into any church or place where people have assembled for worship, or into any election precinct on any election day, or into any building owned or occupied by any agency of the federal government, state government, or political subdivision thereof; or

(10) Carries a firearm, whether loaded or unloaded, or any other weapon readily capable of lethal use into any school, onto any school bus, or onto the premises of any function or activity sponsored or sanctioned by school officials or the district school board; or

2. Subdivisions (1), (8), and (10) of subsection 1 of this section shall not apply to the persons described in this subsection, regardless of whether such uses are reasonably associated with or are necessary to the fulfillment of such person's official duties except as otherwise provided in this subsection. Subdivisions (3), (4), (6), (7), and (9) of subsection 1 of this section shall not apply to or affect any of the following persons, when such uses are reasonably associated with or are necessary to the fulfillment of such person's official duties, except as otherwise provided in this subsection:

(1) All state, county and municipal peace officers who have completed the training required by the police officer standards and training commission pursuant to sections 590.030 to 590.050 and who possess the duty and power of arrest for violation of the general criminal laws of the state or for violation of ordinances of counties or municipalities of the state, whether such officers are on or off duty, and whether such officers are within or outside of the law enforcement agency's jurisdiction, or all qualified retired peace officers, as defined in subsection 122 of this section, and who carry the identification defined in subsection 132 of this section, or any person summoned by such officers to assist in making arrests or preserving the peace while actually engaged in assisting such officer;

(2) Wardens, superintendents and keepers of prisons, penitentiaries, jails and other institutions for the detention of persons accused or convicted of crime;

(3) Members of the Armed Forces or National Guard while performing their official duty;

(4) Those persons vested by article V, section 1 of the Constitution of Missouri with the judicial power of the state and those persons vested by Article III of the Constitution of the United States with the judicial power of the United States, the members of the federal judiciary;

(5) Any person whose bona fide duty is to execute process, civil or criminal;

(6) Any federal probation officer or federal flight deck officer as defined under the federal flight deck officer program, 49 U.S.C. Section 44921 regardless of whether such officers are on duty, or within the law enforcement agency's jurisdiction;

(7) Any state probation or parole officer, including supervisors and members of the board of probation and parole;

(8) Any corporate security advisor meeting the definition and fulfilling the requirements of the regulations established by the department of public safety under section 590.750;

(9) Any coroner, deputy coroner, medical examiner, or assistant medical examiner;

(10) Any prosecuting attorney or assistant prosecuting attorney, circuit attorney or assistant circuit attorney, or any person appointed by a court to be a special prosecutor who has completed the firearms safety training course required under subsection 2 of section 571.111;

(11) Any member of a fire department or fire protection district who is employed on a full-time basis as a fire investigator and who has a valid concealed carry endorsement issued prior to August 28, 2013, or a valid concealed carry permit under section 571.111 when such uses are reasonably associated with or are necessary to the fulfillment of such person's official duties; and

(12) Upon the written approval of the governing body of a fire department or fire protection district, any paid fire department or fire protection district chief who is employed on a full-time basis and who has a valid concealed carry endorsement issued prior to August 28, 2013, or a valid concealed carry permit1, when such uses are reasonably associated with or are necessary to the fulfillment of such person's official duties.

3. Subdivisions (1), (5), (8), and (10) of subsection 1 of this section do not apply when the actor is transporting such weapons in a nonfunctioning state or in an unloaded state when ammunition is not readily accessible or when such weapons are not readily accessible. Subdivision (1) of subsection 1 of this section does not apply to any person nineteen1 years of age or older or eighteen years of age or older and a member of the United States Armed Forces, or honorably discharged from the United States Armed Forces, transporting a concealable firearm in the passenger compartment of a motor vehicle, so long as such concealable firearm is otherwise lawfully possessed, nor when the actor is also in possession of an exposed firearm or projectile weapon for the lawful pursuit of game, or is in his or her dwelling unit or upon premises over which the actor has possession, authority or control, or is traveling in a continuous journey peaceably through this state. Subdivision (10) of subsection 1 of this section does not apply if the firearm is otherwise lawfully possessed by a person while traversing school premises for the purposes of transporting a student to or from school, or possessed by an adult for the purposes of facilitation of a school-sanctioned firearm-related event or club event.

4. Subdivisions (1), (8), and (10) of subsection 1 of this section shall not apply to any person who has a valid concealed carry permit issued pursuant to sections 571.101 to 571.121, a valid concealed carry endorsement issued before August 28, 2013, or a valid permit or endorsement to carry concealed firearms issued by another state or political subdivision of another state.

5. Subdivisions (3), (4), (5), (6), (7), (8), (9), and (10) of subsection 1 of this section shall not apply to persons who are engaged in a lawful act of defense pursuant to section 563.031.

7. Nothing in this section shall make it unlawful for a student to actually participate in school-sanctioned gun safety courses, student military or ROTC courses, or other school-sponsored or club-sponsored firearm-related events, provided the student does not carry a firearm or other weapon readily capable of lethal use into any school, onto any school bus, or onto the premises of any other function or activity sponsored or sanctioned by school officials or the district school board.

11. Notwithstanding any other provision of law, no person who pleads guilty to or is found guilty of a felony violation of subsection 1 of this section shall receive a suspended imposition of sentence if such person has previously received a suspended imposition of sentence for any other firearms- or weapons-related felony offense.

-+- MONTANA -+-
KNIFE RIGHTS MOVEMENT RATING
★ ★ ★ ★ ☆

CUTTING TO THE CHASE

Montana gets a rating of four, but it could almost be a three. Montana has no pre-emption and it bans switchblades with some exceptions. Concealed carry is regulated, but with a permit to carry a concealed weapon one is covered for all knives except switchblades. Montana is normally pro Second Amendment. They should be doing better with regard to knives.

Quick Points Concerning Montana's Knife Law*

KNIFE TYPE	POSSESSION	(Open/Concealed) CARRY	SALE	MANUFACTURE
Assisted Opening	Legal	Legal/Gray	Legal	Legal
Automatic/Switchblade	Legal	Prohibited/Prohibited	Prohibited	Gray
Ballistic	Legal	Legal/Gray	Legal	Legal
Bayonets	Legal	Legal/Gray	Legal	Legal
Bowie	Legal	Legal/Gray	Legal	Legal
Butterfly/Balisong	Legal	Legal/Gray	Legal	Legal
Combat/Survival	Legal	Legal/Gray	Legal	Legal
Dagger	Legal	Legal/Gray	Legal	Legal
Dirk	Legal	Legal/Gray	Legal	Legal
Disguised	Legal	Legal/Gray	Legal	Legal
Fixed	Legal	Legal/Gray	Legal	Legal
Folding	Legal	Legal/Gray	Legal	Legal
Gravity	Legal	Legal/Gray	Legal	Legal
Hunting/Fishing	Legal	Legal/Gray	Legal	Legal
Machete	Legal	Legal/Gray	Legal	Legal
Razor	Legal	Legal/Gray	Legal	Legal
Stiletto	Legal	Legal/Gray	Legal	Legal
Sword	Legal	Legal/Gray	Legal	Legal
Throwing	Legal	Legal/Gray	Legal	Legal
Undetectable	Legal	Legal/Gray	Legal	Legal

Pre-emption (Only State Law May Regulate, No Local Laws Permitted) — NO
*See all information above and below for more details.

SHARP TIPS ABOUT MONTANA'S KNIFE LAWS

Open carry of any knife is permitted except for switchblades. With no pre-emption, watch out for local laws. Do not carry concealed weapons while drunk, in a bar or liquor store, government buildings, or in schools even with a carry permit.

EDGE –U- CATIONAL --- MONTANA'S KNIFE LAWS

45-2-101. General definitions

(79) "Weapon" means an instrument, article, or substance that, regardless of its primary function, is readily capable of being used to produce death or serious bodily injury.

45-3-111. Openly carrying weapon--display--exemption

(1) Any person who is not otherwise prohibited from doing so by federal or state law may openly carry

a weapon and may communicate to another person the fact that the person has a weapon.

(2) If a person reasonably believes that the person or another person is threatened with bodily harm, the person may warn or threaten the use of force, including deadly force, against the aggressor, including drawing or presenting a weapon.

(3) This section does not limit the authority of the board of regents or other postsecondary institutions to regulate the carrying of weapons, as defined in 45-8-361(5)(b), on their campuses.

45-8-315. Definition

"Concealed weapon" means any weapon mentioned in 45-8-316 through 45-8-318 and 45-8-321 through 45-8-328 that is wholly or partially covered by the clothing or wearing apparel of the person carrying or bearing the weapon, except that for purposes of 45-8-321 through 45-8-328, concealed weapon means a handgun or a knife with a blade 4 or more inches in length that is wholly or partially covered by the clothing or wearing apparel of the person carrying or bearing the weapon.

45-8-316. Carrying concealed weapons

(1) A person who carries or bears concealed upon the individual's person a dirk, dagger, pistol, revolver, slingshot, sword cane, billy, knuckles made of any metal or hard substance, knife having a blade 4 inches long or longer, razor, not including a safety razor, or other deadly weapon shall be punished by a fine not exceeding $500 or by imprisonment in the county jail for a period not exceeding 6 months, or both.

(2) A person who has previously been convicted of an offense, committed on a different occasion than the offense under this section, in this state or any other jurisdiction for which a sentence to a term of imprisonment in excess of 1 year could have been imposed and who carries or bears concealed upon the individual's person any of the weapons described in subsection (1) shall be punished by a fine not exceeding $1,000 or be imprisoned in the state prison for a period not exceeding 5 years, or both.

45-8-317. Exceptions

(1) Section 45-8-316 does not apply to:

(a) any peace officer of the state of Montana or of another state who has the power to make arrests;

(b) any officer of the United States government authorized to carry a concealed weapon;

(c) a person in actual service as a member of the national guard;

(d) a person summoned to the aid of any of the persons named in subsections (1)(a) through (1)(c);

(e) a civil officer or the officer's deputy engaged in the discharge of official business;

(f) a probation and parole officer authorized to carry a firearm under 46-23-1002;

(g) a person issued a permit under 45-8-321 or a person with a permit recognized under 45-8-329;

(h) an agent of the department of justice or a criminal investigator in a county attorney's office;

(i) a person who is outside the official boundaries of a city or town or the confines of a logging, lumbering, mining, or railroad camp or who is lawfully engaged in hunting, fishing, trapping, camping, hiking, backpacking, farming, ranching, or other outdoor activity in which weapons are often carried for recreation or protection;

(j) the carrying of arms on one's own premises or at one's home or place of business; or

(k) the carrying of a concealed weapon in the state capitol by a legislative security officer who has been issued a permit under 45-8-321 or with a permit recognized under 45-8-329.

(2) With regard to a person issued a permit under 45-8-321, the provisions of 45-8-328 do not apply to this section.

45-8-321. Permit to carry concealed weapon

(1) A county sheriff shall, within 60 days after the filing of an application, issue a permit to carry a concealed weapon to the applicant. The permit is valid for 4 years from the date of issuance. An applicant must be a United States citizen who is 18 years of age or older and who holds a valid Montana driver's license or other form of identification issued by the state that has a picture of the person identified. An applicant must have been a resident of the state for at least 6 months. Except as provided in subsection (2), this privilege may not be denied an applicant unless the applicant:

(a) is ineligible under Montana or federal law to own, possess, or receive a firearm;

(b) has been charged and is awaiting judgment in any state of a state or federal crime that is punishable by incarceration for 1 year or more;

(c) subject to the provisions of subsection (6), has been convicted in any state or federal court of:

(i) a crime punishable by more than 1 year of incarceration; or

(ii) regardless of the sentence that may be imposed, a crime that includes as an element of the crime an act, attempted act, or threat of intentional homicide, serious bodily harm, unlawful restraint, sexual abuse, or sexual intercourse or contact without consent;

(d) has been convicted under 45-8-327 or 45-8-328, unless the applicant has been pardoned or 5 years have elapsed since the date of the conviction;

(e) has a warrant of any state or the federal government out for the applicant's arrest;

(f) has been adjudicated in a criminal or civil proceeding in any state or federal court to be an unlawful user of an intoxicating substance and is under a court order of imprisonment or other incarceration, probation, suspended or deferred imposition of sentence, treatment or education, or other conditions of release or is otherwise under state supervision;

(g) has been adjudicated in a criminal or civil proceeding in any state or federal court to be mentally ill, mentally defective, or mentally disabled and is still subject to a disposition order of that court; or

(h) was dishonorably discharged from the United States armed forces.

(2) The sheriff may deny an applicant a permit to carry a concealed weapon if the sheriff has reasonable cause to believe that the applicant is mentally ill, mentally defective, or mentally disabled or otherwise may be a threat to the peace and good order of the community to the extent that the applicant should not be allowed to carry a concealed weapon. At the time an application is denied, the sheriff shall, unless the applicant is the subject of an active criminal investigation, give the applicant a written statement of the reasonable cause upon which the denial is based.

(3) An applicant for a permit under this section must, as a condition to issuance of the permit, be required by the sheriff to demonstrate familiarity with a firearm by:

(a) completion of a hunter education or safety course approved or conducted by the department of fish, wildlife, and parks or a similar agency of another state;

(b) completion of a firearms safety or training course approved or conducted by the department of fish, wildlife, and parks, a similar agency of another state, a national firearms association, a law enforcement agency, an institution of higher education, or an organization that uses instructors certified by a national firearms association;

(c) completion of a law enforcement firearms safety or training course offered to or required of public or private law enforcement personnel and conducted or approved by a law enforcement agency;

(d) possession of a license from another state to carry a firearm, concealed or otherwise, that is granted by that state upon completion of a course described in subsections (3)(a) through (3)(c); or

(e) evidence that the applicant, during military service, was found to be qualified to operate firearms, including handguns.

(4) A photocopy of a certificate of completion of a course described in subsection (3), an affidavit from the entity or instructor that conducted the course attesting to completion of the course, or a copy of any other document that attests to completion of the course and can be verified through contact with the entity or instructor that conducted the course creates a presumption that the applicant has completed a course described in subsection (3).

(5) If the sheriff and applicant agree, the requirement in subsection (3) of demonstrating familiarity with a firearm may be satisfied by the applicant's passing, to the satisfaction of the sheriff or of any person or entity to which the sheriff delegates authority to give the test, a physical test in which the applicant demonstrates the applicant's familiarity with a firearm.

(6) A person, except a person referred to in subsection (1)(c)(ii), who has been convicted of a felony and whose rights have been restored pursuant to Article II, section 28, of the Montana constitution is entitled to issuance of a concealed weapons permit if otherwise eligible.

45-8-327. Carrying concealed weapon while under influence

A person commits the offense of carrying a concealed weapon while under the influence if the person purposely or knowingly carries a concealed weapon while under the influence of an intoxicating substance. It is not a defense that the person had a valid permit to carry a concealed weapon. A person convicted of the offense shall be imprisoned in the county jail for a term not to exceed 6 months or be fined an amount not to exceed $500, or both.

45-8-328. Carrying concealed weapon in prohibited place--penalty

(1) Except for legislative security officers authorized to carry a concealed weapon in the state capitol as provided in 45-8-317(1)(k), a person commits the offense of carrying a concealed weapon in a prohibited place if the person purposely or knowingly carries a concealed weapon in:

(a) portions of a building used for state or local government offices and related areas in the building that have been restricted;

(b) a bank, credit union, savings and loan institution, or similar institution during the institution's normal business hours. It is not an offense under this section to carry a concealed weapon while:

(i) using an institution's drive-up window, automatic teller machine, or unstaffed night depository; or

(ii) at or near a branch office of an institution in a mall, grocery store, or other place unless the person is inside the enclosure used for the institution's financial services or is using the institution's financial services.

(c) a room in which alcoholic beverages are sold, dispensed, and consumed under a license issued under Title 16 for the sale of alcoholic beverages for consumption on the premises.

(2) It is not a defense that the person had a valid permit to carry a concealed weapon. A person convicted of the offense shall be imprisoned in the county jail for a term not to exceed 6 months or fined an amount not to exceed $500, or both.

45-8-331. Switchblade knives

(1) A person who carries or bears upon the individual's person, who carries or bears within or on any motor vehicle or other means of conveyance owned or operated by the person, or who owns, possesses, uses, stores, gives away, sells, or offers for sale a switchblade knife shall be punished by a fine not exceeding $500 or by imprisonment in the county jail for a period not exceeding 6 months, or both.

(2) A bona fide collector whose collection is registered with the sheriff of the county in which the collection is located is exempted from the provisions of this section.

(3) For the purpose of this section, a switchblade knife is defined as any knife that has a blade 1 ½ inches long or longer that opens automatically by hand pressure applied to a button, spring, or other device in the handle of the knife.

45-8-361. Possession or allowing possession of weapon in school building--exceptions--penalties--seizure and forfeiture or return authorized--definitions

(1) A person commits the offense of possession of a weapon in a school building if the person purposely and knowingly possesses, carries, or stores a weapon in a school building.

(2) A parent or guardian of a minor commits the offense of allowing possession of a weapon in a school building if the parent or guardian purposely and knowingly permits the minor to possess, carry, or store a weapon in a school building.

(3)(a) Subsection (1) does not apply to law enforcement personnel.

(b) The trustees of a district may grant persons and entities advance permission to possess, carry, or store a weapon in a school building.

(4)(a) A person convicted under this section shall be fined an amount not to exceed $500, imprisoned in the county jail for a term not to exceed 6 months, or both. The court shall consider alternatives to incarceration that are available in the community.

(b)(i) A weapon in violation of this section may be seized and, upon conviction of the person possessing or permitting possession of the weapon, may be forfeited to the state or returned to the lawful owner.

(ii) If a weapon seized under the provisions of this section is subsequently determined to have been stolen or otherwise taken from the owner's possession without permission, the weapon must be returned to the lawful owner.

(5) As used in this section:

(a) "school building" means all buildings owned or leased by a local school district that are used for instruction or for student activities. The term does not include a home school provided for in 20-5-109.

(b) "weapon" means any type of firearm, a knife with a blade 4 or more inches in length, a sword, a straight razor, a throwing star, nun-chucks, or brass or other metal knuckles. The term also includes any other article or instrument possessed with the purpose to commit a criminal offense.

CHAPTER 14
STATE KNIFE LAW GUIDE N-O

HOW TO USE THIS GUIDE

The "Quick Points" chart for each jurisdiction contains 100 legal questions answered by either "Legal", "Prohibited", or "Gray".

"Legal" means that it is generally lawful.

"Prohibited" means that it is generally unlawful.

"Gray" means that it is neither generally lawful nor unlawful and that there are ambiguities, conflicting law, exceptions, requirements or special considerations that may determine legality.

The laws provided have been selected because of their relevance to knives. Sections of the law may have been edited. It is also possible that some laws may have been inadvertently omitted due to legal research not revealing same. In other words, your author tried his best, but he is not perfect.

KNIFE RIGHTS MOVEMENT RATING SYSTEM

The Knife Rights Movement rating system grades the States, the District of Columbia, and the United States of America on a scale from one to five.

The highest rating is a five, which means that jurisdiction stands out for knife liberty. A rating of one means that jurisdiction has a disdain for knives and individual rights, and has arbitrary laws that treat honest citizens like criminals. Ratings of two, three, or four show where that jurisdiction is in regards to its respect for knife rights freedom. If a place has a rating lower than five, then there is work to be done there restoring knife liberty and continuing the Knife Rights Movement.

⊹ NEBRASKA ⊹
KNIFE RIGHTS MOVEMENT RATING
★ ★ ★ ★ ☆

CUTTING TO THE CHASE

Nebraska does not ban possession of any knives. Concealed carry of all knives with a blade over 3.5 inches is prohibited. Unfortunately, knives with a blade under 3.5 inches can still fall under the concealed carry ban if it is a "dangerous instrument capable of inflicting cutting, stabbing, or tearing wounds." Open carry of any knife is allowed.

Quick Points Concerning Nebraska's Knife Law*

KNIFE TYPE	POSSESSION	(Open/Concealed) CARRY	SALE	MANUFACTURE
Assisted Opening	Legal	Legal/Gray	Legal	Legal
Automatic/Switchblade	Legal	Legal/Gray	Legal	Legal
Ballistic	Legal	Legal/Gray	Legal	Legal
Bayonets	Legal	Legal/Gray	Legal	Legal
Bowie	Legal	Legal/Gray	Legal	Legal
Butterfly/Balisong	Legal	Legal/Gray	Legal	Legal
Combat/Survival	Legal	Legal/Gray	Legal	Legal
Dagger	Legal	Legal/Gray	Legal	Legal
Dirk	Legal	Legal/Gray	Legal	Legal
Disguised	Legal	Legal/Gray	Legal	Legal
Fixed	Legal	Legal/Gray	Legal	Legal
Folding	Legal	Legal/Gray	Legal	Legal
Gravity	Legal	Legal/Gray	Legal	Legal
Hunting/Fishing	Legal	Legal/Gray	Legal	Legal
Machete	Legal	Legal/Gray	Legal	Legal
Razor	Legal	Legal/Gray	Legal	Legal
Stiletto	Legal	Legal/Gray	Legal	Legal
Sword	Legal	Legal/Gray	Legal	Legal
Throwing	Legal	Legal/Gray	Legal	Legal
Undetectable	Legal	Legal/Gray	Legal	Legal

<u>Pre-emption</u> (Only State Law May Regulate, No Local Laws Permitted) – NO
*See all information above and below for more details.

SHARP TIPS ABOUT NEBRASKA'S KNIFE LAWS

Felons, fugitives, and domestic abusers are prohibited from possessing knives. No pre-emption, so beware of local laws.

EDGE –U– CATIONAL --- NEBRASKA'S KNIFE LAWS

§ 28-1201. Terms, defined

For purposes of sections 28-1201 to 28-1212.04, unless the context otherwise requires:

(5) Knife means any dagger, dirk, knife, or stiletto with a blade over three and one-half inches in length or any other dangerous instrument capable of inflicting cutting, stabbing, or tearing wounds;

(6) Knuckles and brass or iron knuckles means any instrument that consists of finger rings or guards

made of a hard substance and that is designed, made, or adapted for the purpose of inflicting serious bodily injury or death by striking a person with a fist enclosed in the knuckles;

§ 28-1202. Carrying concealed weapon; penalty; affirmative defense
(1)(a) Except as otherwise provided in this section, any person who carries a weapon or weapons concealed on or about his or her person, such as a handgun, a knife, brass or iron knuckles, or any other deadly weapon, commits the offense of carrying a concealed weapon.

(b) It is an affirmative defense that the defendant was engaged in any lawful business, calling, or employment at the time he or she was carrying any weapon or weapons and the circumstances in which such person was placed at the time were such as to justify a prudent person in carrying the weapon or weapons for the defense of his or her person, property, or family.

(3) Carrying a concealed weapon is a Class I misdemeanor.

(4) In the case of a second or subsequent conviction under this section, carrying a concealed weapon is a Class IV felony.

§ 28-1206. Possession of a deadly weapon by a prohibited person; penalty
(1)(a) Any person who possesses a firearm, a knife, or brass or iron knuckles and who has previously been convicted of a felony, who is a fugitive from justice, or who is the subject of a current and validly issued domestic violence protection order and is knowingly violating such order, or (b) any person who possesses a firearm or brass or iron knuckles and who has been convicted within the past seven years of a misdemeanor crime of domestic violence, commits the offense of possession of a deadly weapon by a prohibited person.

(2) The felony conviction may have been had in any court in the United States, the several states, territories, or possessions, or the District of Columbia.

⟶ NEVADA ⟵
KNIFE RIGHTS MOVEMENT RATING
★ ★ ★ ★ ☆

CUTTING TO THE CHASE
Nevada repealed its ban on possession of switchblades and belt buckle knives. Concealed carry of daggers, dirks and machetes is specifically prohibited. Any other knife that is an "other dangerous or deadly weapon" is also banned from concealed carry. Open carry of any knife that is legal to have is allowed.

Quick Points Concerning Nevada's Knife Law*

KNIFE TYPE	POSSESSION	(Open/Concealed) CARRY	SALE	MANUFACTURE
Assisted Opening	Legal	Legal/Gray	Legal	Legal
Automatic/Switchblade	Legal	Legal/Gray	Legal	Legal
Ballistic	Legal	Legal/Gray	Legal	Legal
Bayonets	Legal	Legal/Gray	Legal	Legal
Bowie	Legal	Legal/Gray	Legal	Legal
Butterfly/Balisong	Legal	Legal/Gray	Legal	Legal
Combat/Survival	Legal	Legal/Gray	Legal	Legal

KNIFE TYPE	POSSESSION	(Open/Concealed) CARRY	SALE	MANUFACTURE
Dagger	Legal	Legal/Prohibited	Legal	Legal
Dirk	Legal	Legal/Prohibited	Legal	Legal
Disguised	Legal	Legal/Gray	Legal	Legal
Fixed	Legal	Legal/Gray	Legal	Legal
Folding	Legal	Legal/Gray	Legal	Legal
Gravity	Legal	Legal/Gray	Legal	Legal
Hunting/Fishing	Legal	Legal/Gray	Legal	Legal
Machete	Legal	Legal/Prohibited	Legal	Legal
Razor	Legal	Legal/Gray	Legal	Legal
Stiletto	Legal	Legal/Gray	Legal	Legal
Sword	Legal	Legal/Gray	Legal	Legal
Throwing	Legal	Legal/Gray	Legal	Legal
Undetectable	Legal	Legal/Gray	Legal	Legal

Pre-emption (Only State Law May Regulate, No Local Laws Permitted) – NO
*See all information above and below for more details.

SHARP TIPS ABOUT NEVADA'S KNIFE LAWS

No dirks, daggers or switchblades in schools. No pre-emption, so beware of local laws.

EDGE –U- CATIONAL --- NEVADA'S KNIFE LAWS

N.R.S. 202.265. Possession of dangerous weapon on property or in vehicle of school or child care facility; penalty; exceptions

1. Except as otherwise provided in this section, a person shall not carry or possess while on the property of the Nevada System of Higher Education, a private or public school or child care facility, or while in a vehicle of a private or public school or child care facility:

(b) A dirk, dagger or switchblade knife;

(d) A blackjack or billy club or metal knuckles;

2. Any person who violates subsection 1 is guilty of a gross misdemeanor.

3. This section does not prohibit the possession of a weapon listed in subsection 1 on the property of:

(a) A private or public school or child care facility by a:

(1) Peace officer;

(2) School security guard; or

(3) Person having written permission from the president of a branch or facility of the Nevada System of Higher Education or the principal of the school or the person designated by a child care facility to give permission to carry or possess the weapon.

(b) A child care facility which is located at or in the home of a natural person by the person who owns or operates the facility so long as the person resides in the home and the person complies with any laws governing the possession of such a weapon.

4. The provisions of this section apply to a child care facility located at or in the home of a natural person only during the normal hours of business of the facility.

5. For the purposes of this section:

(d) "Switchblade knife" has the meaning ascribed to it in NRS 202.350. means a spring-blade knife, snap-blade knife or any other knife having the appearance of a pocketknife, any blade of which is

2 or more inches long and which can be released automatically by a flick of a button, pressure on the handle or other mecanical device, or is released by any type of mechanism. The term does not include a knife which has a blade that is held in place by a spring if the blade does not have any type of automatic release.

(e) "Trefoil" has the meaning ascribed to it in NRS 202.350.

N.R.S. 202.320. Drawing deadly weapon in threatening manner

1. Unless a greater penalty is provided in NRS 202.287, a person having, carrying or procuring from another person any dirk, dirk-knife, sword, sword cane, pistol, gun or other deadly weapon, who, in the presence of two or more persons, draws or exhibits any of such deadly weapons in a rude, angry or threatening manner not in necessary self-defense, or who in any manner unlawfully uses that weapon in any fight or quarrel, is guilty of a misdemeanor.

2. A sheriff, deputy sheriff, marshal, constable or other peace officer shall not be held to answer, under the provisions of subsection 1, for drawing or exhibiting any of the weapons mentioned therein while in the lawful discharge of his or her duties.

N.R.S. 202.350. Manufacture, importation, possession or use of dangerous weapon or silencer; carrying concealed weapon without permit; penalties; issuance of permit to carry concealed weapon; exceptions

1. Except as otherwise provided in this section and NRS 202.355 and 202.3653 to 202.369, inclusive, a person within this State shall not:

(a) Manufacture or cause to be manufactured, or import into the State, or keep, offer or expose for sale, or give, lend or possess any knife which is made an integral part of a belt buckle or any instrument or weapon of the kind commonly known as a switchblade knife, blackjack, slungshot, billy, sandclub, sandbag or metal knuckles;

(c) With the intent to inflict harm upon the person of another, possess or use a nunchaku or trefoil; or

(d) Carry concealed upon his or her person any:

(1) Explosive substance, other than ammunition or any components thereof;

(2) Machete;

(3) Pistol, revolver or other firearm, or other dangerous or deadly weapon; or

3. Except as otherwise provided in this subsection, the sheriff of any county may, upon written application by a resident of that county showing the reason or the purpose for which a concealed weapon is to be carried, issue a permit authorizing the applicant to carry in this State the concealed weapon described in the permit. This subsection does not authorize the sheriff to issue a permit to a person to carry a pistol, revolver or other firearm.

4. Except as otherwise provided in subsection 5, this section does not apply to:

(a) Sheriffs, constables, marshals, peace officers, correctional officers employed by the Department of Corrections, special police officers, police officers of this State, whether active or honorably retired, or other appointed officers.

(b) Any person summoned by any peace officer to assist in making arrests or preserving the peace while the person so summoned is actually engaged in assisting such an officer.

(c) Any full-time paid peace officer of an agency of the United States or another state or political subdivision thereof when carrying out official duties in the State of Nevada.

(d) Members of the Armed Forces of the United States when on duty.

5. The exemptions provided in subsection 4 do not include a former peace officer who is retired for disability unless his or her former employer has approved his or her fitness to carry a concealed weapon.

7. This section shall not be construed to prohibit a qualified law enforcement officer or a qualified retired law enforcement officer from carrying a concealed weapon in this State if he or she is authorized to do so pursuant to 18 U.S.C. § 926B or 926C.

8. As used in this section:

(a) "Concealed weapon" means a weapon described in this section that is carried upon a person in such a manner as not to be discernible by ordinary observation.

(i) "Trefoil" means an instrument consisting of a metal plate having three or more radiating points with sharp edges, designed in the shape of a star, cross or other geometric figure and used as a weapon for throwing.

⚜ NEW HAMPSHIRE ⚜
KNIFE RIGHTS MOVEMENT RATING
★ ★ ★ ★ ★

CUTTING TO THE CHASE

New Hampshire lives up to its state motto, "Live free or die." It has the most knife freedom of any state. ANY knife (regardless of blade length, design or operation) may be freely bought and sold (even no sales tax), owned, possessed, carried open or concealed, transported, displayed, collected, made, manufactured, produced, given, loaned, acquired, transferred, bequeathed, or inherited under state law. The only exception is possession in a courthouse and by felons. All localities are prohibited from passing or enforcing any of their own knife laws. In 2010 New Hampshire was the first state to repeal its knife bans. Since then nine more states including Missouri, Oklahoma, Kansas, Alaska, Indiana, Texas, Tennessee, Nevada, and Maine have also enacted repeals.

Quick Points Concerning New Hampshire's Knife Law*

KNIFE TYPE	POSSESSION	(Open/Concealed) CARRY	SALE	MANUFACTURE
Assisted Opening	Legal	Legal/Legal	Legal	Legal
Automatic/Switchblade	Legal	Legal/Legal	Legal	Legal
Ballistic	Legal	Legal/Legal	Legal	Legal
Bayonets	Legal	Legal/Legal	Legal	Legal
Bowie	Legal	Legal/Legal	Legal	Legal
Butterfly/Balisong	Legal	Legal/Legal	Legal	Legal
Combat/Survival	Legal	Legal/Legal	Legal	Legal
Dagger	Legal	Legal/Legal	Legal	Legal
Dirk	Legal	Legal/Legal	Legal	Legal
Disguised	Legal	Legal/Legal	Legal	Legal
Fixed	Legal	Legal/Legal	Legal	Legal
Folding	Legal	Legal/Legal	Legal	Legal
Gravity	Legal	Legal/Legal	Legal	Legal
Hunting/Fishing	Legal	Legal/Legal	Legal	Legal
Machete	Legal	Legal/Legal	Legal	Legal
Razor	Legal	Legal/Legal	Legal	Legal
Stiletto	Legal	Legal/Legal	Legal	Legal
Sword	Legal	Legal/Legal	Legal	Legal
Throwing	Legal	Legal/Legal	Legal	Legal
Undetectable	Legal	Legal/Legal	Legal	Legal

Pre-emption (Only State Law May Regulate, No Local Laws Permitted) – YES
*See all information above and below for more details.

SHARP TIPS ABOUT NEW HAMPSHIRE'S KNIFE LAWS

Possession of a knife in a courthouse is prohibited. Possession by convicted felons is generally prohibited. Sale of a sword, knife, spear, throwing star, throwing dart, or any other martial arts weapon to those under 18 without written consent of the parent or guardian is prohibited.

EDGE –U- CATIONAL --- NEW HAMPSHIRE'S KNIFE LAWS

625:11 General Definitions. – The following definitions apply to this code.

V. "Deadly weapon" means any firearm, knife or other substance or thing which, in the manner it is used, intended to be used, or threatened to be used, is known to be capable of producing death or serious bodily injury.

159:3 Convicted Felons. –
I. A person is guilty of a class B felony if he:

(a) Owns or has in his possession or under his control, a pistol, revolver, or other firearm, or slungshot, metallic knuckles, billies, stiletto, switchblade knife, sword cane, pistol cane, blackjack, dagger, dirk-knife, or other deadly weapon as defined in RSA 625:11, V; and

(b) Has been convicted in either a state or federal court in this or any other state, the District of Columbia, the Commonwealth of Puerto Rico, or any territory or possession of the United States of:

(1) A felony against the person or property of another; or

(2) A felony under RSA 318-B; or

(3) A felony violation of the laws of any other state, the District of Columbia, the United States, the Commonwealth of Puerto Rico or any territory or possession of the United States relating to controlled drugs as defined in RSA 318-B.

I-a. A person is guilty of a class B felony if such person completes and signs an application for purchase of a firearm and the person is a convicted felon under the provisions of paragraph I.

II. The state shall confiscate to the use of the state the weapon or weapons of persons convicted under this section.

III. It is an affirmative defense to a charge under this section that a felony of which a defendant has been convicted in another jurisdiction would not have constituted a felony in the state of New Hampshire at the time such felony was committed.

159:19 Courthouse Security. –
I. No person shall knowingly carry a loaded or unloaded pistol, revolver, or firearm or any other deadly weapon as defined in RSA 625:11, V, whether open or concealed or whether licensed or unlicensed, upon the person or within any of the person's possessions owned or within the person's control in a courtroom or area used by a court. Whoever violates the provisions of this paragraph shall be guilty of a class B felony.

III. For purposes of paragraph I, "area used by a court" means:

(a) In a building dedicated exclusively to court use, the entire building exclusive of the area between the entrance and the courthouse security.

(b) In any other building which includes a court facility, courtrooms, jury assembly rooms, deliberation rooms, conference and interview rooms, the judge's chambers, other court staff facilities, holding facilities, and corridors, stairways, waiting areas, and elevators directly connecting these rooms and facilities.

IV. The provisions of this section shall not apply to marshals, sheriffs, deputy sheriffs, police or other duly appointed or elected law enforcement officers, bailiffs and court security officers, or persons with prior authorization of the court for the purpose of introducing weapons into evidence and as otherwise provided for in RSA 159:5.

V. It shall be an affirmative defense to any prosecution under paragraph I that there was no notice of the provisions of paragraph I posted in a conspicuous place at each public entrance to the court building.

159:24 Sale of Martial Arts Weapons. –
I. "Martial arts weapon" means any kind of sword, knife, spear, throwing star, throwing dart, or nunchaku or any other object designed for use in the martial arts which is capable of being used as a lethal or dangerous weapon.

II. Any person who shall sell, deliver, or otherwise transfer any martial arts weapon to a person under the age of 18 without first obtaining the written consent of such person's parent or guardian shall be guilty of a misdemeanor.

III. Paragraph II shall not apply to fathers, mothers, guardians, administrators or executors who give a martial arts weapon to their children or wards or to heirs to an estate.

✢ NEW JERSEY ✢
KNIFE RIGHTS MOVEMENT RATING
★ ★ ☆ ☆ ☆

CUTTING TO THE CHASE

All knife offenses in New Jersey are felonies. New Jersey basically hates anything that cuts or shoots. There is some ability to legally carry a knife as long as it's not a "per se" prohibited knife, which includes switchblade, gravity, dagger, dirk, stiletto and ballistic knives. A knife which is not a "per se" prohibited knife may be carried/possessed as long as it is not "under circumstances not manifestly appropriate for such lawful uses as it may have." Additionally, statutory exemptions exist for possession in the home and while hunting and fishing.

Quick Points Concerning New Jersey's Knife Law*

KNIFE TYPE	POSSESSION	(Open/Concealed) CARRY	SALE	MANUFACTURE
Assisted Opening	Legal	Gray/Gray	Legal	Legal
Automatic/Switchblade	Gray	Gray/Gray	Prohibited	Prohibited
Ballistic	Gray	Gray/Gray	Prohibited	Prohibited
Bayonets	Legal	Gray/Gray	Legal	Legal
Bowie	Legal	Gray/Gray	Legal	Legal
Butterfly/Balisong	Gray	Gray/Gray	Gray	Gray
Combat/Survival	Legal	Gray/Gray	Legal	Legal
Dagger	Gray	Gray/Gray	Prohibited	Prohibited
Dirk	Gray	Gray/Gray	Prohibited	Prohibited
Disguised	Legal	Gray/Gray	Legal	Legal
Fixed	Legal	Gray/Gray	Legal	Legal
Folding	Legal	Gray/Gray	Legal	Legal
Gravity	Gray	Gray/Gray	Prohibited	Prohibited
Hunting/Fishing	Legal	Gray/Gray	Legal	Legal
Machete	Legal	Gray/Gray	Legal	Legal
Razor	Legal	Gray/Gray	Legal	Legal
Stiletto	Gray	Gray/Gray	Prohibited	Prohibited
Sword	Legal	Gray/Gray	Legal	Legal
Throwing	Legal	Gray/Gray	Legal	Legal
Undetectable	Legal	Gray/Gray	Legal	Legal

Pre-emption (Only State Law May Regulate, No Local Laws Permitted) – YES
*See below for more details

SHARP TIPS ABOUT NEW JERSEY'S KNIFE LAWS

Knife possession is prohibited under two New Jersey laws: N.J.S. 2C:39-5d. and/or N.J.S. 2C:39-3e.

Gravity knife, switchblade, dagger, dirk, stiletto or ballistic knife, are considered a "per se" weapon and prohibited under N.J.S. 2C:39-3e. N.J.S. 2C:39-5d. prohibits possession of any other weapon "…under circumstances not manifestly appropriate for such lawful uses as it may have…" Possession under N.J.S. 2C:39-5d is exempted in one's home or pursuant to hunting or fishing.

N.J.S. 2C:39-3e. specifically prohibits gravity knives, switchblade knives, daggers, dirks, stilettos, razor blades imbedded in wood and ballistic knives "…without any explainable lawful purpose…"

A knife generally (other than a gravity knife, switchblade, dagger, dirk, stiletto or ballistic knife) may be legally possessed/carried in New Jersey if it is not "…under circumstances not manifestly appropriate for such lawful uses as it may have…" This phrase is actually an element of the offense under N.J.S. 2C:39-5d. which the State has the burden of proving.

Contrast this with possessing a "per se" weapon such as a gravity knife, switchblade, dagger, dirk, stiletto or ballistic knife under N.J.S. 2C:39-3e, which is, prohibited "…without any explainable lawful purpose…" This element in the statute is known as an affirmative defense, and the burden of proof is on you, the defendant, to prove you are within this exception.

A person cannot manufacture, transport, ship, sell or dispose of a gravity knife, switchblade, dagger, dirk, stiletto or ballistic knife. No exceptions. New Jersey does not have blade length restrictions other than on sales to minors.

EDGE –U- CATIONAL --- NEW JERSEY'S KNIFE LAWS
2C:39-1. Definitions. The following definitions apply to this chapter and to chapter 58:
h. "Gravity knife" means any knife which has a blade which is released from the handle or sheath thereof by the force of gravity or the application of centrifugal force.

p. "Switchblade knife" means any knife or similar device which has a blade which opens automatically by hand pressure applied to a button, spring or other device in the handle of the knife.

r. "Weapon" means anything readily capable of lethal use or of inflicting serious bodily injury. The term includes, but is not limited to, all (1) firearms, even though not loaded or lacking a clip or other component to render them immediately operable; (2) components which can be readily assembled into a weapon; (3) gravity knives, switchblade knives, daggers, dirks, stilettos, or other dangerous knives, billies, blackjacks, bludgeons, metal knuckles, sandclubs, slingshots, cesti or similar leather bands studded with metal filings or razor blades imbedded in wood; and (4) stun guns; and any weapon or other device which projects, releases, or emits tear gas or any other substance intended to produce temporary physical discomfort or permanent injury through being vaporized or otherwise dispensed in the air.

u. "Ballistic knife" means any weapon or other device capable of lethal use and which can propel a knife blade.

2C:39-3. Prohibited Weapons and Devices.
e. Certain weapons. Any person who knowingly has in his possession any gravity knife, switchblade knife, dagger, dirk, stiletto, billy, blackjack, metal knuckle, sandclub, slingshot, cestus or similar leather band studded with metal filings or razor blades imbedded in wood, ballistic knife, without any explainable lawful purpose, is guilty of a crime of the fourth degree.

g. Exceptions. (1) Nothing in subsection a., b., c., d., e., f., j. or k. of this section shall apply to any member of the Armed Forces of the United States or the National Guard, or except as otherwise provided, to any law enforcement officer while actually on duty or traveling to or from an authorized place of duty, provided that his possession of the prohibited weapon or device has been duly authorized under the applicable laws, regulations or military or law enforcement orders. Nothing in subsection h. of this section shall apply to any law enforcement officer who is exempted from the provisions of that subsection by the Attorney General. Nothing in this section shall apply to the possession of any weapon or device by a law enforcement officer who has confiscated, seized or otherwise taken possession of said weapon or device as evidence of the commission of a crime or because he believed it to be possessed illegally by the person from whom it was taken, provided that said law enforcement officer promptly notifies his superiors of his possession of such prohibited weapon or device.

2C:39-5 Unlawful possession of weapons.

d. Other weapons. Any person who knowingly has in his possession any other weapon under circumstances not manifestly appropriate for such lawful uses as it may have is guilty of a crime of the fourth degree.

2C:39-6 Exemptions.

a. Provided a person complies with the requirements of subsection j. of this section, N.J.S.2C:39-5 does not apply to:

(1) Members of the Armed Forces of the United States or of the National Guard while actually on duty, or while traveling between places of duty and carrying authorized weapons in the manner prescribed by the appropriate military authorities;

(2) Federal law enforcement officers, and any other federal officers and employees required to carry firearms in the performance of their official duties;

(3) Members of the State Police and, under conditions prescribed by the superintendent, members of the Marine Law Enforcement Bureau of the Division of State Police;

(4) A sheriff, undersheriff, sheriff's officer, county prosecutor, assistant prosecutor, prosecutor's detective or investigator, deputy attorney general or State investigator employed by the Division of Criminal Justice of the Department of Law and Public Safety, investigator employed by the State Commission of Investigation, inspector of the Alcoholic Beverage Control Enforcement Bureau of the Division of State Police in the Department of Law and Public Safety authorized to carry such weapons by the Superintendent of State Police, State park police officer, or State conservation officer;

(5) Except as hereinafter provided, a prison or jail warden of any penal institution in this State or his deputies, or an employee of the Department of Corrections engaged in the interstate transportation of convicted offenders, while in the performance of his duties, and when required to possess the weapon by his superior officer, or a corrections officer or keeper of a penal institution in this State at all times while in the State of New Jersey, provided he annually passes an examination approved by the superintendent testing his proficiency in the handling of firearms;

(6) A civilian employee of the United States Government under the supervision of the commanding officer of any post, camp, station, base or other military or naval installation located in this State who is required, in the performance of his official duties, to carry firearms, and who is authorized to carry such firearms by said commanding officer, while in the actual performance of his official duties;

(7) (a) A regularly employed member, including a detective, of the police department of any county or municipality, or of any State, interstate, municipal or county park police force or boulevard police force, at all times while in the State of New Jersey;

(b) A special law enforcement officer authorized to carry a weapon as provided in subsection b. of section 7 of P.L.1985, c.439 (C.40A:14-146.14);

(c) An airport security officer or a special law enforcement officer appointed by the governing body of any county or municipality, except as provided in subsection (b) of this section, or by the commission, board or other body having control of a county park or airport or boulevard police force, while engaged in the actual performance of his official duties and when specifically authorized by the governing body to carry weapons;

(8) A full-time, paid member of a paid or part-paid fire department or force of any municipality who

is assigned full-time or part-time to an arson investigation unit created pursuant to section 1 of P.L.1981, c.409 (C.40A:14-7.1) or to the county arson investigation unit in the county prosecutor's office, while either engaged in the actual performance of arson investigation duties or while actually on call to perform arson investigation duties and when specifically authorized by the governing body or the county prosecutor, as the case may be, to carry weapons. Prior to being permitted to carry a firearm, such a member shall take and successfully complete a firearms training course administered by the Police Training Commission pursuant to P.L.1961, c.56 (C.52:17B-66 et seq.), and shall annually qualify in the use of a revolver or similar weapon prior to being permitted to carry a firearm;

(9) A juvenile corrections officer in the employment of the Juvenile Justice Commission established pursuant to section 2 of P.L.1995, c.284 (C.52:17B-170) subject to the regulations promulgated by the commission;

(10) A designated employee or designated licensed agent for a nuclear power plant under license of the Nuclear Regulatory Commission, while in the actual performance of his official duties, if the federal licensee certifies that the designated employee or designated licensed agent is assigned to perform site protection, guard, armed response or armed escort duties and is appropriately trained and qualified, as prescribed by federal regulation, to perform those duties. Any firearm utilized by an employee or agent for a nuclear power plant pursuant to this paragraph shall be returned each day at the end of the employee's or agent's authorized official duties to the employee's or agent's supervisor. All firearms returned each day pursuant to this paragraph shall be stored in locked containers located in a secure area;

(11) A county corrections officer at all times while in the State of New Jersey, provided he annually passes an examination approved by the superintendent testing his proficiency in the handling of firearms.

f. Nothing in subsections b., c. and d. of N.J.S.2C:39-5 shall be construed to prevent:

(2) A person carrying a firearm or knife in the woods or fields or upon the waters of this State for the purpose of hunting, target practice or fishing, provided that the firearm or knife is legal and appropriate for hunting or fishing purposes in this State and he has in his possession a valid hunting license, or, with respect to fresh water fishing, a valid fishing license;

(3) A person transporting any firearm or knife while traveling:

(a) Directly to or from any place for the purpose of hunting or fishing, provided the person has in his possession a valid hunting or fishing license;

g. All weapons being transported under paragraph (2) of subsection b., subsection e., or paragraph (1) or (3) of subsection f. of this section shall be carried unloaded and contained in a closed and fastened case, gunbox, securely tied package, or locked in the trunk of the automobile in which it is being transported, and in the course of travel shall include only such deviations as are reasonably necessary under the circumstances.

2C:39-7 Certain persons not to have weapons.

a. Except as provided in subsection b. of this section, any person, having been convicted in this State or elsewhere of the crime of aggravated assault, arson, burglary, escape, extortion, homicide, kidnapping, robbery, aggravated sexual assault, sexual assault, bias intimidation in violation of N.J.S.2C:16-1 or endangering the welfare of a child pursuant to N.J.S.2C:24-4, whether or not armed with or having in his possession any weapon enumerated in subsection r. of N.J.S.2C:39-1, or any person convicted of a crime pursuant to the provisions of N.J.S.2C:39-3, N.J.S.2C:39-4 or N.J.S.2C:39-9, or any person who has ever been committed for a mental disorder to any hospital, mental institution or sanitarium unless he possesses a certificate of a medical doctor or psychiatrist licensed to practice in New Jersey or other satisfactory proof that he is no longer suffering from a mental disorder which interferes with or handicaps him in the handling of a firearm, or any person who has been convicted of other than a disorderly persons or petty disorderly persons offense for the unlawful use, possession or sale of a controlled dangerous substance as defined in N.J.S.2C:35-2 who purchases, owns, possesses or controls any of the said weapons is guilty of a crime of the fourth degree.

c. Whenever any person shall have been convicted in another state, territory, commonwealth or other jurisdiction of the United States, or any country in the world, in a court of competent jurisdiction, of a crime which in said other jurisdiction or country is comparable to one of the crimes enumerated in subsection a. or b. of this section, then that person shall be subject to the provisions of this section.

2C:39-9 Manufacture, transport, disposition and defacement of weapons and danger instruments and appliances.

d. Weapons. Any person who manufactures, causes to be manufactured, transports, ships, sells or disposes of any weapon, including gravity knives, switchblade knives, ballistic knives, daggers, dirks, stilettos, billies, blackjacks, metal knuckles, sandclubs, slingshots, cesti or similar leather bands studded with metal filings, or, except as otherwise provided in subsection i. of this section, in the case of firearms if he is not licensed or registered to do so as provided in chapter 58, is guilty of a crime of the fourth degree. Any person who manufactures, causes to be manufactured, transports, ships, sells or disposes of any weapon or other device which projects, releases or emits tear gas or other substances intended to produce temporary physical discomfort or permanent injury through being vaporized or otherwise dispensed in the air, which is intended to be used for any purpose other than for authorized military or law enforcement purposes by duly authorized military or law enforcement personnel or the device is for the purpose of personal self-defense, is pocket-sized and contains not more than three-quarters of an ounce of chemical substance not ordinarily capable of lethal use or of inflicting serious bodily injury, or other than to be used by any person permitted to possess such weapon or device under the provisions of subsection d. of N.J.S.2C:39-5, which is intended for use by financial and other business institutions as part of an integrated security system, placed at fixed locations, for the protection of money and property, by the duly authorized personnel of those institutions, is guilty of a crime of the fourth degree.

2C:39-9.1. Sale of knives to minors; crime of the fourth degree; exceptions

A person who sells any hunting, fishing, combat or survival knife having a blade length of five inches or more or an overall length of 10 inches or more to a person under 18 years of age commits a crime of the fourth degree; except that the establishment by a preponderance of the evidence of all of the following facts by a person making the sale shall constitute an affirmative defense to any prosecution therefor: a. that the purchaser falsely represented his age by producing a driver's license bearing a photograph of the licensee, or by producing a photographic identification card issued pursuant to section 2 of P.L.1980, c. 47 (C.39:3-29.3), or by producing a similar card purporting to be a valid identification card indicating that he was 18 years of age or older, and b. that the appearance of the purchaser was such that an ordinary prudent person would believe him to be 18 years of age or older, and c. that the sale was made in good faith relying upon the indicators of age listed in a. and b. above.

⚔ NEW MEXICO ⚔
KNIFE RIGHTS MOVEMENT RATING
★ ★ ☆ ☆ ☆

CUTTING TO THE CHASE

New Mexico bans switchblades, gravity, and balisong knives with a broad definition that may ensnare other knives. The state also prohibits carrying concealed, any knife, with another very broad definition that includes: "daggers, brass knuckles, switchblade knives, bowie knives, poniards, butcher knives, dirk knives and all such weapons with which dangerous cuts can be given, or with which dangerous thrusts can be inflicted, including swordcanes, and any kind of sharp pointed canes...or any other weapons with which dangerous wounds can be inflicted..."

Quick Points Concerning New Mexico's Knife Law*

KNIFE TYPE	POSSESSION	(Open/Concealed) CARRY	SALE	MANUFACTURE
Assisted Opening	Gray	Gray/Prohibited	Gray	Gray
Automatic/Switchblade	Prohibited	Prohibited/Prohibited	Prohibited	Prohibited
Ballistic	Legal	Legal/Prohibited	Legal	Legal
Bayonets	Legal	Legal/Prohibited	Legal	Legal
Bowie	Legal	Legal/Prohibited	Legal	Legal
Butterfly/Balisong	Prohibited	Prohibited/Prohibited	Legal	Legal
Combat/Survival	Legal	Legal/Prohibited	Legal	Legal
Dagger	Legal	Legal/Prohibited	Legal	Legal
Dirk	Legal	Legal/Prohibited	Legal	Legal
Disguised	Legal	Legal/Prohibited	Legal	Legal
Fixed	Legal	Legal/Prohibited	Legal	Legal
Folding	Legal	Legal/Gray	Legal	Legal
Gravity	Prohibited	Prohibited/Prohibited	Prohibited	Prohibited
Hunting/Fishing	Legal	Legal/Prohibited	Legal	Legal
Machete	Legal	Legal/Prohibited	Legal	Legal
Razor	Legal	Legal/Prohibited	Legal	Legal
Stiletto	Legal	Legal/Prohibited	Legal	Legal
Sword	Legal	Legal/Prohibited	Legal	Legal
Throwing	Legal	Legal/Prohibited	Legal	Legal
Undetectable	Legal	Legal/Prohibited	Legal	Legal

Pre-emption (Only State Law May Regulate, No Local Laws Permitted) – YES
*See all information above and below for more details.

SHARP TIPS ABOUT NEW MEXICO'S KNIFE LAWS

An ordinary pocket knife may be carried, but the citizen is left at risk of hoping his or her knife qualifies as such. If not, it becomes the burden of the state to prove the bad intent of the knife carrier. Open carry of a knife that is not per se banned (switchblades, gravity, and balisongs) is lawful. No carrying "deadly weapons" in schools or on buses.

EDGE –U- CATIONAL --- NEW MEXICO'S KNIFE LAWS
N. M. S. 1978, § 30-1-12. Definitions

As used in the Criminal Code:

A. "great bodily harm" means an injury to the person which creates a high probability of death; or which causes serious disfigurement; or which results in permanent or protracted loss or impairment of the function of any member or organ of the body;

B. "deadly weapon" means any firearm, whether loaded or unloaded; or any weapon which is capable of producing death or great bodily harm, including but not restricted to any types of daggers, brass knuckles, switchblade knives, bowie knives, poniards, butcher knives, dirk knives and all such weapons with which dangerous cuts can be given, or with which dangerous thrusts can be inflicted, including swordcanes, and any kind of sharp pointed canes, also slingshots, slung shots, bludgeons; or any other weapons with which dangerous wounds can be inflicted;

N. M. S. 1978, § 30-7-1. "Carrying a deadly weapon"
"Carrying a deadly weapon" means being armed with a deadly weapon by having it on the person, or in close proximity thereto, so that the weapon is readily accessible for use.

N. M. S. 1978, § 30-7-2. Unlawful carrying of a deadly weapon
A. Unlawful carrying of a deadly weapon consists of carrying a concealed loaded firearm or any other type of deadly weapon anywhere, except in the following cases:

(1) in the person's residence or on real property belonging to him as owner, lessee, tenant or licensee;

(2) in a private automobile or other private means of conveyance, for lawful protection of the person's or another's person or property;

(3) by a peace officer in accordance with the policies of his law enforcement agency who is certified pursuant to the Law Enforcement Training Act;

(4) by a peace officer in accordance with the policies of his law enforcement agency who is employed on a temporary basis by that agency and who has successfully completed a course of firearms instruction prescribed by the New Mexico law enforcement academy or provided by a certified firearms instructor who is employed on a permanent basis by a law enforcement agency; or

(5) by a person in possession of a valid concealed handgun license issued to him by the department of public safety pursuant to the provisions of the Concealed Handgun Carry Act.

C. Whoever commits unlawful carrying of a deadly weapon is guilty of a petty misdemeanor.

N. M. S. 1978, § 30-7-2.1. Unlawful carrying of a deadly weapon on school premises
A. Unlawful carrying of a deadly weapon on school premises consists of carrying a deadly weapon on school premises except by:

(1) a peace officer;

(2) school security personnel;

(3) a student, instructor or other school-authorized personnel engaged in army, navy, marine corps or air force reserve officer training corps programs or state-authorized hunter safety training instruction;

(4) a person conducting or participating in a school-approved program, class or other activity involving the carrying of a deadly weapon; or

(5) a person older than nineteen years of age on school premises in a private automobile or other private means of conveyance, for lawful protection of the person's or another's person or property.

B. As used in this section, "school premises" means:

(1) the buildings and grounds, including playgrounds, playing fields and parking areas and any school bus of any public elementary, secondary, junior high or high school in or on which school or school-related activities are being operated under the supervision of a local school board; or

(2) any other public buildings or grounds, including playing fields and parking areas that are not [school property, in or on which public school-related and sanctioned activities are being perforn

C. Whoever commits unlawful carrying of a deadly weapon on school premises is guilty of a fourth degree felony.

N. M. S. 1978, § 30-7-8. Unlawful possession of switchblades

Unlawful possession of switchblades consists of any person, either manufacturing, causing to be manufactured, possessing, displaying, offering, selling, lending, giving away or purchasing any knife which has a blade which opens automatically by hand pressure applied to a button, spring or other device in the handle of the knife, or any knife having a blade which opens or falls or is ejected into position by the force of gravity or by any outward or centrifugal thrust or movement.

Whoever commits unlawful possession of switchblades is guilty of a petty misdemeanor.

N. M. S. 1978, § 30-7-13. Carrying weapons prohibited

A. It is unlawful for any person without prior approval from the company to board or attempt to board a bus while in possession of a firearm or other deadly weapon upon his person or effects and readily accessible to him while on the bus. Any person who violates the provisions of this subsection is guilty of a misdemeanor.

B. Subsection A of this section does not apply to duly elected or appointed law enforcement officers or commercial security personnel in the lawful discharge of their duties.

N. M. S. 1978, § 30-7-15. Weapons; transporting

Any person wishing to transport a firearm or other deadly weapon on a bus may do so only in accordance with regulations established by the company; provided that any firearm or deadly weapon must be transported in a compartment which is not accessible to passengers while the bus is moving.

⁺⵻ NEW YORK ⵻⁺
KNIFE RIGHTS MOVEMENT RATING
★ ☆ ☆ ☆ ☆

CUTTING TO THE CHASE

New York bans gravity, switchblade, ballistic, and knuckle knives, throwing stars, and swordcanes. New York also prohibits "any dagger, dangerous knife, dirk, razor, stiletto ... or any other dangerous or deadly instrument or weapon with intent to use the same unlawfully against another." Mere possession creates a presumption of unlawful intent to use. Such knives are considered prohibited knives until one can establish otherwise.

Quick Points Concerning New York's Knife Law*

KNIFE TYPE	POSSESSION	(Open/Concealed) CARRY	SALE	MANUFACTURE
Assisted Opening	Gray	Gray/Gray	Gray	Gray
Automatic/Switchblade	Prohibited	Prohibited /Prohibited	Prohibited	Prohibited
Ballistic	Prohibited	Prohibited /Prohibited	Prohibited	Prohibited
Bayonets	Gray	Gray/Gray	Legal	Legal
Bowie	Gray	Gray/Gray	Legal	Legal
Butterfly/Balisong	Gray	Gray/Gray	Gray	Gray

KNIFE TYPE	POSSESSION	(Open/Concealed) CARRY	SALE	MANUFACTURE
Combat/Survival	Gray	Gray/Gray	Legal	Legal
Dagger	Gray	Gray/Gray	Prohibited	Prohibited
Dirk	Gray	Gray/Gray	Prohibited	Prohibited
Disguised	Gray	Gray/Gray	Legal	Legal
Fixed	Gray	Gray/Gray	Legal	Legal
Folding	Gray	Gray/Gray	Legal	Legal
Gravity	Prohibited	Prohibited /Prohibited	Prohibited	Prohibited
Hunting/Fishing	Gray	Gray/Gray	Legal	Legal
Machete	Gray	Gray/Gray	Legal	Legal
Razor	Gray	Gray/Gray	Legal	Legal
Stiletto	Gray	Gray/Gray	Legal	Legal
Sword	Gray	Gray/Gray	Legal	Legal
Throwing	Gray	Gray/Gray	Gray	Gray
Undetectable	Gray	Gray/Gray	Legal	Legal

<u>Pre-emption</u> (Only State Law May Regulate, No Local Laws Permitted) – NO
*See all information above and below for more details.

SHARP TIPS ABOUT NEW YORK'S KNIFE LAWS

New York does allow for the possession of a switchblade or gravity knife for use while hunting, trapping or fishing by a person carrying a valid license. Juveniles cannot possess a "dangerous knife." Having a knife in New York appears to perpetually make the knife owner live under vague laws that have a presumption of illegality. Beware of New York City, which has even more restrictive knife laws and aggressively prosecutes knife possessors. Law enforcement officers in New York City particularly look for exposed pocket clips to initiate stop, search and arrest.

EDGE –U- CATIONAL --- NEW YORK'S KNIFE LAWS
§ 265.00 Definitions.
As used in this article and in article four hundred, the following terms shall mean and include:

4. "Switchblade knife" means any knife which has a blade which opens automatically by hand pressure applied to a button, spring or other device in the handle of the knife.

5. "Gravity knife" means any knife which has a blade which is released from the handle or sheath thereof by the force of gravity or the application of centrifugal force which, when released, is locked in place by means of a button, spring, lever or other device.

5-a. "Pilum ballistic knife" means any knife which has a blade which can be projected from the handle by hand pressure applied to a button, lever, spring or other device in the handle of the knife.

5-b. "Metal knuckle knife" means a weapon that, when closed, cannot function as a set of plastic knuckles or metal knuckles, nor as a knife and when open, can function as both a set of plastic knuckles or metal knuckles as well as a knife.

5-c. "Automatic knife" includes a stiletto, a switchblade knife, a gravity knife, a cane sword, a pilum ballistic knife, and a metal knuckle knife.

13. "Cane Sword" means a cane or swagger stick having concealed within it a blade that may be used as a sword or stilletto.

§ 265.01 Criminal possession of a weapon in the fourth degree.
A person is guilty of criminal possession of a weapon in the fourth degree when:

(1) He or she possesses any firearm, electronic dart gun, electronic stun gun, gravity knife, switch-

blade knife, pilum ballistic knife, metal knuckle knife, cane sword, billy, blackjack, bludgeon, pla [illegible] knuckles, metal knuckles, chuka stick, sand bag, sandclub, wrist-brace type slingshot or slungsho [illegible] shirken or "Kung Fu star"; or

(2) He possesses any dagger, dangerous knife, dirk, razor, stiletto, imitation pistol, or any other dangerous or deadly instrument or weapon with intent to use the same unlawfully against another; or

(5) He possesses any dangerous or deadly weapon and is not a citizen of the United States; or

Criminal possession of a weapon in the fourth degree is a class A misdemeanor.

§ 265.05 Unlawful possession of weapons by persons under sixteen.

It shall be unlawful for any person under the age of sixteen to possess any air-gun, spring-gun or other instrument or weapon in which the propelling force is a spring or air, or any gun or any instrument or weapon in or upon which any loaded or blank cartridges may be used, or any loaded or blank cartridges or ammunition therefor, or any dangerous knife; provided that the possession of rifle or shotgun or ammunition therefor by the holder of a hunting license or permit issued pursuant to article eleven of the environmental conservation law and used in accordance with said law shall not be governed by this section.

A person who violates the provisions of this section shall be adjudged a juvenile delinquent.

§ 265.10 Manufacture, transport, disposition and defacement of weapons and dangerous instruments and appliances

1. Any person who manufactures or causes to be manufactured any machine-gun, assault weapon, large capacity ammunition feeding device or disguised gun is guilty of a class D felony. Any person who manufactures or causes to be manufactured any switchblade knife, gravity knife, pilum ballistic knife, metal knuckle knife, billy, blackjack, bludgeon, plastic knuckles, metal knuckles, Kung Fu star, chuka stick, sandbag, sandclub or slungshot is guilty of a class A misdemeanor.

2. Any person who transports or ships any machine-gun, firearm silencer, assault weapon or large capacity ammunition feeding device or disguised gun, or who transports or ships as merchandise five or more firearms, is guilty of a class D felony. Any person who transports or ships as merchandise any firearm, other than an assault weapon, switchblade knife, gravity knife, pilum ballistic knife, billy, blackjack, bludgeon, plastic knuckles, metal knuckles, Kung Fu star, chuka stick, sandbag or slungshot is guilty of a class A misdemeanor.

4. Any person who disposes of any of the weapons, instruments or appliances specified in subdivision one of section 265.01, except a firearm, is guilty of a class A misdemeanor, and he is guilty of a class D felony if he has previously been convicted of any crime.

5. Any person who disposes of any of the weapons, instruments, appliances or substances specified in section 265.05 to any other person under the age of sixteen years is guilty of a class A misdemeanor.

§ 265.15 Presumptions of possession, unlawful intent and defacement.

2. The presence in any stolen vehicle of any weapon, instrument,

appliance or substance specified in sections 265.01, 265.02, 265.03, 265.04 and 265.05 is presumptive evidence of its possession by all persons occupying such vehicle at the time such weapon, instrument, appliance or substance is found.

3. The presence in an automobile, other than a stolen one or a public omnibus, of any firearm, large capacity ammunition feeding device, defaced firearm, defaced rifle or shotgun, defaced large capacity ammunition feeding device, firearm silencer, explosive or incendiary bomb, bombshell, gravity knife, switchblade knife, pilum ballistic knife, metal knuckle knife, dagger, dirk, stiletto, billy, blackjack, plastic knuckles, metal knuckles, chuka stick, sandbag, sandclub or slungshot is presumptive evidence of its

persons occupying such automobile at the time such weapon, instrument or appli-
~~ept~~ under the following circumstances: (a) if such weapon, instrument or appliance
~~~~person of one of the occupants therein; (b) if such weapon, instrument or appliance
~~~~mobile which is being operated for hire by a duly licensed driver in the due, lawful
~~~~of his or her trade, then such presumption shall not apply to the driver; or (c) if the
~~~~~~s a pistol or revolver and one of the occupants, not present under duress, has in his
or her possession a valid license to have and carry concealed the same.

4. The possession by any person of the substance as specified in section 265.04 is presumptive evidence of possessing such substance with intent to use the same unlawfully against the person or property of another if such person is not licensed or otherwise authorized to possess such substance. The possession by any person of any dagger, dirk, stiletto, dangerous knife or any other weapon, instrument, appliance or substance designed, made or adapted for use primarily as a weapon, is presumptive evidence of intent to use the same unlawfully against another.

§ 265.20 Exemptions
1. Possession of a switchblade or gravity knife for use while hunting, trapping or fishing by a person carrying a valid license issued to him pursuant to section 11-0713 of the environmental conservation law.

✦ NORTH CAROLINA ✦
KNIFE RIGHTS MOVEMENT RATING
★ ★ ★ ☆ ☆

CUTTING TO THE CHASE
North Carolina bans ballistic knives. Carrying a concealed bowie, dirk, dagger, razor, throwing star or "…other deadly weapon of like kind…" is prohibited. The "like kind" language is vague. An ordinary pocket knife may be carried in a closed position. "Ordinary pocket knife" means a "…small knife, designed for carrying in a pocket or purse, that has its cutting edge and point entirely enclosed by its handle, and that may not be opened by a throwing, explosive, or spring action."

Quick Points Concerning North Carolina's Knife Law*

KNIFE TYPE	POSSESSION	(Open/Concealed) CARRY	SALE	MANUFACTURE
Assisted Opening	Legal	Gray/Gray	Legal	Legal
Automatic/Switchblade	Legal	Gray/Gray	Legal	Legal
Ballistic	Prohibited	Prohibited/Prohibited	Prohibited	Prohibited
Bayonets	Legal	Gray/Gray	Legal	Legal
Bowie	Legal	Gray/Prohibited	Legal	Legal
Butterfly/Balisong	Legal	Gray/Gray	Legal	Legal
Combat/Survival	Legal	Gray/Gray	Legal	Legal
Dagger	Legal	Gray/Prohibited	Legal	Legal
Dirk	Legal	Gray/Prohibited	Legal	Legal
Disguised	Legal	Gray/Gray	Legal	Legal
Fixed	Legal	Gray/Gray	Legal	Legal
Folding	Legal	Gray/Gray	Legal	Legal
Gravity	Legal	Gray/Gray	Legal	Legal
Hunting/Fishing	Legal	Gray/Gray	Legal	Legal

KNIFE TYPE	POSSESSION	(Open/Concealed) CARRY	SALE	MANUFACTURE
Machete	Legal	Gray/Gray	Legal	Legal
Razor	Legal	Gray/Prohibited	Legal	Legal
Stiletto	Legal	Gray/Gray	Legal	Legal
Sword	Legal	Gray/Gray	Legal	Legal
Throwing	Legal	Gray/Gray	Legal	Legal
Undetectable	Legal	Gray/Gray	Legal	Legal

Pre-emption (Only State Law May Regulate, No Local Laws Permitted) – NO
*See all information above and below for more details.

SHARP TIPS ABOUT NORTH CAROLINA'S KNIFE LAWS

Open carry of any knife, except a ballistic knife, is not prohibited by statute, but old case law from 1843 says that even a legal knife carried openly to terrorize or alarm the public is a common law crime that one can be prosecuted for violating. Carrying a knife on school grounds, state property, or in a courthouse is prohibited. Carrying any "dangerous weapon" at "any parade, funeral procession, picket line, or demonstration upon any private health care facility or upon any public place owned or under the control of the State…" is unlawful. No pre-emption, so beware of local laws.

EDGE –U- CATIONAL --- NORTH CAROLINA'S KNIFE LAWS

§ 14-269. Carrying concealed weapons

(a) It shall be unlawful for any person willfully and intentionally to carry concealed about his person any bowie knife, dirk, dagger, slung shot, loaded cane, metallic knuckles, razor, shurikin, stun gun, or other deadly weapon of like kind, except when the person is on the person's own premises.

(b) This prohibition shall not apply to the following persons:

(1) Officers and enlisted personnel of the Armed Forces of the United States when in discharge of their official duties as such and acting under orders requiring them to carry arms and weapons;

(2) Civil and law enforcement officers of the United States;

(3) Officers and soldiers of the militia and the National Guard when called into actual service;

(4) Officers of the State, or of any county, city, town, or company police agency charged with the execution of the laws of the State, when acting in the discharge of their official duties;

(4a) Any person who is a district attorney, an assistant district attorney, or an investigator employed by the office of a district attorney and who has a concealed handgun permit issued in accordance with Article 54B of this Chapter or considered valid under G.S. 14-415.24; provided that the person shall not carry a concealed weapon at any time while in a courtroom or while consuming alcohol or an unlawful controlled substance or while alcohol or an unlawful controlled substance remains in the person's body. The district attorney, assistant district attorney, or investigator shall secure the weapon in a locked compartment when the weapon is not on the person of the district attorney, assistant district attorney, or investigator;

(4b) Any person who is a qualified retired law enforcement officer as defined in G.S. 14-415.10 and meets any one of the following conditions:

a. Is the holder of a concealed handgun permit in accordance with Article 54B of this Chapter.

b. Is exempt from obtaining a permit pursuant to G.S. 14-415.25.

c. Is certified by the North Carolina Criminal Justice Education and Training Standards Commission pursuant to G.S. 14-415.26;

(4c) Detention personnel or correctional officers employed by the State or a unit of local government who park a vehicle in a space that is authorized for their use in the course of their duties may transport a firearm to the parking space and store that firearm in the vehicle parked in the parking space, provided that: (i) the firearm is in a closed compartment or container within the locked vehicle, or (ii) the firearm is in a locked container securely affixed to the vehicle;

(4d) Any person who is a North Carolina district court judge, North Carolina superior court judge, or a North Carolina magistrate and who has a concealed handgun permit issued in accordance with Article 54B of this Chapter or considered valid under G.S. 14-415.24; provided that the person shall not carry a concealed weapon at any time while consuming alcohol or an unlawful controlled substance or while alcohol or an unlawful controlled substance remains in the person's body. The judge or magistrate shall secure the weapon in a locked compartment when the weapon is not on the person of the judge or magistrate;

(4e) Any person who is serving as a clerk of court or as a register of deeds and who has a concealed handgun permit issued in accordance with Article 54B of this Chapter or considered valid under G.S. 14-415.24; provided that the person shall not carry a concealed weapon at any time while consuming alcohol or an unlawful controlled substance or while alcohol or an unlawful controlled substance remains in the person's body. The clerk of court or register of deeds shall secure the weapon in a locked compartment when the weapon is not on the person of the clerk of court or register of deeds. This subdivision does not apply to assistants, deputies, or other employees of the clerk of court or register of deeds;

(5) Sworn law-enforcement officers, when off-duty, provided that an officer does not carry a concealed weapon while consuming alcohol or an unlawful controlled substance or while alcohol or an unlawful controlled substance remains in the officer's body;

(6) State probation or parole certified officers, when off-duty, provided that an officer does not carry a concealed weapon while consuming alcohol or an unlawful controlled substance or while alcohol or an unlawful controlled substance remains in the officer's body.

(b1) It is a defense to a prosecution under this section that:

(1) The weapon was not a firearm;

(2) The defendant was engaged in, or on the way to or from, an activity in which he legitimately used the weapon;

(3) The defendant possessed the weapon for that legitimate use; and

(4) The defendant did not use or attempt to use the weapon for an illegal purpose.

The burden of proving this defense is on the defendant.

(b2) It is a defense to a prosecution under this section that:

(1) The deadly weapon is a handgun;

(2) The defendant is a military permittee as defined under G.S. 14-415.10(2a); and

(3) The defendant provides to the court proof of deployment as defined under G.S. 14-415.10(3a).

(c) Any person violating the provisions of subsection (a) of this section shall be guilty of a Class 2 misdemeanor. Any person violating the provisions of subsection (a1) of this section shall be guilty of a Class 2 misdemeanor for the first offense and a Class H felony for a second or subsequent offense. A violation of subsection (a1) of this section punishable under G.S. 14-415.21(a) is not punishable under this section.

(d) This section does not apply to an ordinary pocket knife carried in a closed position. As used in this section, "ordinary pocket knife" means a small knife, designed for carrying in a pocket or purse, that has its cutting edge and point entirely enclosed by its handle, and that may not be opened by a throwing, explosive, or spring action.

§ 14-269.2. Weapons on campus or other educational property

(a) The following definitions apply to this section:

(3) Switchblade knife. -- A knife containing a blade that opens automatically by the release of a spring or a similar contrivance.

(3a) Volunteer school safety resource officer.--A person who volunteers as a school safety resource officer as provided by G.S. 162-26 or G.S. 160A-288.4.

(4) Weapon. -- Any device enumerated in subsection (b), (b1), or (d) of this section.

(d) It shall be a Class 1 misdemeanor for any person to possess or carry, whether openly or concealed, any BB gun, stun gun, air rifle, air pistol, bowie knife, dirk, dagger, slungshot, leaded cane, switchblade knife, blackjack, metallic knuckles, razors and razor blades (except solely for personal shaving), firework, or any sharp-pointed or edged instrument except instructional supplies, unaltered nail files and clips and tools used solely for preparation of food, instruction, and maintenance, on educational property.

(e) It shall be a Class 1 misdemeanor for any person to cause, encourage, or aid a minor who is less than 18 years old to possess or carry, whether openly or concealed, any BB gun, stun gun, air rifle, air pistol, bowie knife, dirk, dagger, slungshot, leaded cane, switchblade knife, blackjack, metallic knuckles, razors and razor blades (except solely for personal shaving), firework, or any sharp-pointed or edged instrument except instructional supplies, unaltered nail files and clips and tools used solely for preparation of food, instruction, and maintenance, on educational property.

(g) This section shall not apply to any of the following:

(1) A weapon used solely for educational or school-sanctioned ceremonial purposes, or used in a school-approved program conducted under the supervision of an adult whose supervision has been approved by the school authority.

(1a) A person exempted by the provisions of G.S. 14-269(b).

(2) Firefighters, emergency service personnel, North Carolina Forest Service personnel, detention officers employed by and authorized by the sheriff to carry firearms, and any private police employed by a school, when acting in the discharge of their official duties.

(3) Home schools as defined in G.S. 115C-563(a).

(4) Weapons used for hunting purposes on the Howell Woods Nature Center property in Johnston County owned by Johnston Community College when used with the written permission of Johnston Community College or for hunting purposes on other educational property when used with the written permission of the governing body of the school that controls the educational property.

(5) A person registered under Chapter 74C of the General Statutes as an armed armored car service guard or an armed courier service guard when acting in the discharge of the guard's duties and with the permission of the college or university.

(6) A person registered under Chapter 74C of the General Statutes as an armed security guard while on the premises of a hospital or health care facility located on educational property when acting in the discharge of the guard's duties with the permission of the college or university.

(7) A volunteer school safety resource officer providing security at a school pursuant to an agreement as provided in G.S. 115C-47(61) and either G.S. 162-26 or G.S. 160A-288.4, provided that the volunteer school safety resource officer is acting in the discharge of the person's official duties and is on the educational property of the school that the officer was assigned to by the head of the appropriate local law enforcement agency.

(h) No person shall be guilty of a criminal violation of this section with regard to the possession or carrying of a weapon so long as both of the following apply:

(1) The person comes into possession of a weapon by taking or receiving the weapon from another person or by finding the weapon.

(2) The person delivers the weapon, directly or indirectly, as soon as practical to law enforcement authorities.

§ 14-269.6. Possession and sale of spring-loaded projectile knives prohibited

(a) On and after October 1, 1986, it shall be unlawful for any person including law-enforcement officers of the State, or of any county, city, or town to possess, offer for sale, hold for sale, sell, give, loan, deliver, transport, manufacture or go armed with any spring-loaded projectile knife, a ballistic knife, or any weapon of similar character. Except that it shall be lawful for a law-enforcement agency to possess such weapons solely for evidentiary, education or training purposes.

(b) Any person violating the provisions of this section shall be guilty of a Class 1 misdemeanor.

§ 14-277.2. Weapons at parades, etc., prohibited

(a) It shall be unlawful for any person participating in, affiliated with, or present as a spectator at any parade, funeral procession, picket line, or demonstration upon any private health care facility or upon any public place owned or under the control of the State or any of its political subdivisions to willfully or intentionally possess or have immediate access to any dangerous weapon. Violation of this subsection shall be a Class 1 misdemeanor. It shall be presumed that any rifle or gun carried on a rack in a pickup truck at a holiday parade or in a funeral procession does not violate the terms of this act.

(b) For the purposes of this section the term "dangerous weapon" shall include those weapons specified in G.S. 14-269, 14-269.2, 14-284.1, or 14-288.8 or any other object capable of inflicting serious bodily injury or death when used as a weapon.

(c) The provisions of this section shall not apply to a person exempted by the provisions of G.S. 14-269(b) or to persons authorized by State or federal law to carry dangerous weapons in the performance of their duties or to any person who obtains a permit to carry a dangerous weapon at a parade, funeral procession, picket line, or demonstration from the sheriff or police chief, whichever is appropriate, of the locality where such parade, funeral procession, picket line, or demonstration is to take place.

(d) The provisions of this section shall not apply to concealed carry of a handgun at a parade or funeral procession by a person with a valid permit issued in accordance with Article 54B of this Chapter, with a permit considered valid under G.S. 14-415.24, or who is exempt from obtaining a permit pursuant to G.S. 14-415.25. This subsection shall not be construed to permit a person to carry a concealed handgun on any premises where the person in legal possession or control of the premises has posted a conspicuous notice prohibiting the carrying of a concealed handgun on the premises in accordance with G.S. 14-415.11(c).

§ 14-402. Sale of certain weapons without permit forbidden

(a) It is unlawful for any person, firm, or corporation in this State to sell, give away, or transfer, or to purchase or receive, at any place within this State from any other place within or without the State any pistol unless: (i) a license or permit is first obtained under this Article by the purchaser or receiver from the sheriff of the county in which the purchaser or receiver resides; or (ii) a valid North Carolina concealed handgun permit is held under Article 54B of this Chapter by the purchaser or receiver who must be a resident of the State at the time of the purchase.

It is unlawful for any person or persons to receive from any postmaster, postal clerk, employee in the parcel post department, rural mail carrier, express agent or employee, railroad agent or employee within the State of North Carolina any pistol without having in his or their possession and without exhibiting at the time of the delivery of the same and to the person delivering the same the permit from the sheriff as provided in G.S. 14-403. Any person violating the provisions of this section is guilty of a Class 2 misdemeanor.

(b) This section does not apply to an antique firearm or an historic edged weapon.

(c) The following definitions apply in this Article:

(1) Antique firearm.--Defined in G.S. 14-409.11.

(2), (3) Repealed by S.L. 2011-56, § 1, eff. April 28, 2011.

(4) Historic edged weapon.--Defined in G.S. 14-409.12.

(5) to (7) Repealed by S.L. 2011-56, § 1, eff. April 28, 2011.

§ 14-409.12. "Historic edged weapons" defined
The term "historic edged weapon" means any bayonet, trench knife, sword or dagger manufactured during or prior to World War II but in no event later than January 1, 1946.

§ 14-315. Selling or giving weapons to minors
(a) Sale of Weapons Other Than Handguns. If a person sells, offers for sale, gives, or in any way transfers to a minor any pistol cartridge, brass knucks, bowie knife, dirk, shurikin, leaded cane, or slungshot, the person is guilty of a Class 1 misdemeanor and, in addition, shall forfeit the proceeds of any sale made in violation of this section.

⚔ NORTH DAKOTA ⚔
KNIFE RIGHTS MOVEMENT RATING
★ ★ ★ ★ ☆

CUTTING TO THE CHASE
North Dakota does not ban possession of any knife by feature or type. The state does prohibit concealed carry of a "dangerous weapon" which includes "any switchblade or gravity knife, machete, scimitar, stiletto, sword, dagger, or knife with a blade of five inches [12.7 centimeters] or more; any throwing star … or other martial arts weapon; … or spear" One may obtain a license to carry a "dangerous weapon."

Quick Points Concerning North Dakota's Knife Law*

KNIFE TYPE	POSSESSION	(Open/Concealed) CARRY	SALE	MANUFACTURE
Assisted Opening	Legal	Legal/Gray	Legal	Legal
Automatic/Switchblade	Legal	Legal/Prohibited	Legal	Legal
Ballistic	Legal	Legal/ Gray	Legal	Legal
Bayonets	Legal	Legal/ Gray	Legal	Legal
Bowie	Legal	Legal/ Gray	Legal	Legal
Butterfly/Balisong	Legal	Legal/ Gray	Legal	Legal
Combat/Survival	Legal	Legal/ Gray	Legal	Legal
Dagger	Legal	Legal/ Prohibited	Legal	Legal
Dirk	Legal	Legal/ Gray	Legal	Legal
Disguised	Legal	Legal/ Gray	Legal	Legal

KNIFE TYPE	POSSESSION	(Open/Concealed) CARRY	SALE	MANUFACTURE
Fixed	Legal	Legal/ Gray	Legal	Legal
Folding	Legal	Legal/ Gray	Legal	Legal
Gravity	Legal	Legal/ Prohibited	Legal	Legal
Hunting/Fishing	Legal	Legal/ Gray	Legal	Legal
Machete	Legal	Legal/ Prohibited	Legal	Legal
Razor	Legal	Legal/ Gray	Legal	Legal
Stiletto	Legal	Legal/ Prohibited	Legal	Legal
Sword	Legal	Legal/ Prohibited	Legal	Legal
Throwing	Legal	Legal/ Gray	Legal	Legal
Undetectable	Legal	Legal/ Gray	Legal	Legal

Pre-emption (Only State Law May Regulate, No Local Laws Permitted) – NO
*See all information above and below for more details.

SHARP TIPS ABOUT NORTH DAKOTA'S KNIFE LAWS

If one's knife is not a per se named knife and has a blade shorter than five inches, it may be carried concealed. Open carry of any knife is permitted. Do not carry dangerous weapons where alcohol is sold, or at athletic or sporting events, schools or school functions, churches or church functions, political rallies or functions, musical concerts, or at publicly owned parks where hunting is not allowed, or at publicly owned or operated buildings. No weapons in schools or school property. North Dakota does not have pre-emption, so beware of local laws.

EDGE –U- CATIONAL --- NORTH DAKOTA'S KNIFE LAWS
§ 62.1-01-01. General definitions

As used in this title, unless the context otherwise requires:

1. "Dangerous weapon" includes any switchblade or gravity knife, machete, scimitar, stiletto, sword, dagger, or knife with a blade of five inches [12.7 centimeters] or more; any throwing star, nunchaku, or other martial arts weapon; any billy, blackjack, sap, bludgeon, cudgel, metal knuckles, or sand club; any slungshot; any bow and arrow, crossbow, or spear; any weapon that will expel, or is readily capable of expelling, a projectile by the action of a spring, compressed air, or compressed gas, including any such weapon, loaded or unloaded, commonly referred to as a BB gun, air rifle, or CO2 gun; and any projector of a bomb or any object containing or capable of producing and emitting any noxious liquid, gas, or substance. "Dangerous weapon" does not include a spray or aerosol containing CS, also known as ortho-chlorobenzamalonitrile; CN, also known as alpha-chloroacetophenone; or other irritating agent intended for use in the defense of an individual, nor does the term include a device that uses direct contact to deliver voltage for the defense of an individual.

2. "Direct supervision of an adult" means that an adult is present in such close proximity so as to be capable of observing and directing the actions of the individual supervised.

§ 62.1-04-01. Definition of concealed

A firearm or dangerous weapon is concealed if it is carried in such a manner as to not be discernible by the ordinary observation of a passerby. There is no requirement that there be absolute invisibility of the firearm or dangerous weapon, merely that it not be ordinarily discernible. A firearm or dangerous weapon is considered concealed if it is not secured, and is worn under clothing or carried in a bundle that is held or carried by the individual, or transported in a vehicle under the individual's control or direction and available to the individual, including beneath the seat or in a glove compartment. A firearm or dangerous weapon is not considered concealed if it is:

1. Carried in a belt holster which is wholly or substantially visible or carried in a case designed for carrying a firearm or dangerous weapon and which is wholly or substantially visible;

2. Locked in a closed trunk or luggage compartment of a motor vehicle;

3. Carried in the field while lawfully engaged in hunting, trapping, or target shooting, whether visible or not; or

4. Carried by any person permitted by law to possess a handgun unloaded and in a secure wrapper from the place of purchase to that person's home or place of business, or to a place of repair, or back from those locations.

§ 62.1-04-02. Carrying concealed firearms or dangerous weapons prohibited

An individual, other than a law enforcement officer, may not carry any firearm or dangerous weapon concealed unless the individual is licensed to do so or exempted under this chapter. For purposes of this chapter, the term "dangerous weapon" does not include a spray or aerosol containing CS (ortho-chlorobenzamalonitrile), CN (alpha-chloroacetophenone) or other irritating agent intended for use in the defense of an individual, nor does the term include any stun gun or device that uses direct contact to deliver voltage for the defense of an individual.

§ 62.1-02-04. Possession of firearm or dangerous weapon in liquor establishment prohibited--Penalty--Exceptions

1. An individual who enters or remains in that part of the establishment that is set aside for the retail sale of alcoholic beverages or used as a gaming site at which bingo is the primary gaming activity while in the possession of a firearm or dangerous weapon is guilty of a class A misdemeanor.

2. This section does not apply to:

a. A law enforcement officer.

b. The proprietor.

c. The proprietor's employee.

d. A designee of the proprietor when the designee is displaying an unloaded firearm or dangerous weapon as a prize or sale item in a raffle or auction.

e. Private security personnel while on duty for the purpose of delivering or receiving moneys used at the liquor establishment or at the gaming site at which bingo is the primary gaming activity.

f. The restaurant part of an establishment if an individual under twenty-one years of age is not prohibited in that part of the establishment.

§ 62.1-02-05. Possession of a firearm or dangerous weapon at a public gathering--Penalty--Application

1. An individual who possesses a firearm or dangerous weapon at a public gathering is guilty of a class B misdemeanor. For the purpose of this section, "public gathering" includes athletic or sporting events, schools or school functions, churches or church functions, political rallies or functions, musical concerts, and individuals in publicly owned parks where hunting is not allowed by proclamation and publicly owned or operated buildings.

2. This section does not apply to:

a. A law enforcement officer;

b. A member of the armed forces of the United States or national guard, organized reserves, state defense forces, or state guard organizations, when on duty;

c. A competitor participating in an organized sport shooting event;

d. A gun or antique show;

e. A participant using a blank cartridge firearm at a sporting or theatrical event;

f. A firearm or dangerous weapon carried in a temporary residence or motor vehicle;

g. A student and an instructor at a hunter safety class;

h. Private security personnel while on duty;

i. A state or federal park;

j. An instructor, a test administrator, an official, or a participant in educational, training, cultural, or competitive events involving the authorized use of a dangerous weapon if the event occurs with permission of the person or entity with authority over the function or premises in question;

k. An individual possessing a valid class 1 concealed weapons license from this state or who has reciprocity under section 62.1-04-03.1 authorizing the individual to carry a dangerous weapon concealed if the individual is in a church building or other place of worship and has the approval to carry in the church building or other place of worship by a primary religious leader of the church or other place of worship or the governing body of the church or other place of worship. If a church or other place of worship authorizes an individual to carry a concealed weapon, local law enforcement must be informed of the name of the authorized individual; and

l. A municipal court judge, a district court judge, a staff member of the office of attorney general, and a retired North Dakota law enforcement officer, if the individual maintains the same level of firearms proficiency as is required by the peace officer standards and training board for law enforcement officers. A local law enforcement agency shall issue a certificate of compliance under this section to an individual who is proficient.

3. This section does not prevent any political subdivision from enacting an ordinance that is less restrictive than this section relating to the possession of firearms or dangerous weapons at a public gathering. An enacted ordinance supersedes this section within the jurisdiction of the political subdivision.

§ 15.1-19-10. Possession of a weapon--Policy--Expulsion from school

1. The board of each school district shall adopt a policy governing the possession of weapons and firearms on school property or at a school function and provide for the punishment of any student found to be in violation of the policy.

2. The policy must prohibit the possession of a weapon or a firearm by a student on school property and at school functions and provide for the punishment of any student found to be in violation. Punishment must include immediate suspension from school and expulsion. A student who possesses a firearm in violation of this section must be expelled for at least one year. The school district firearms policy must authorize the school district superintendent or the school principal, if the school district does not have a superintendent, to modify an expulsion for firearms possession under this section on a case-by-case basis in accordance with criteria established by the board. Before expelling a student, a school board or its designated hearing officer, within ten days of the student's suspension, shall provide the student with a hearing at which time the school board or its designated hearing officer shall take testimony and consider evidence, including the existence of mitigating circumstances. If a designated hearing officer orders that a student be expelled, the student may seek a review of the decision by the school board, based on the record of the expulsion hearing.

3. If a school district expels a student under this section, the district may authorize the provision of educational services to the student in an alternative setting.

4. Actions under this section may not conflict with state special education laws or with the Individuals With Disabilities Education Act [Pub. L. 91-230; 84 Stat. 121; 20 U.S.C. 1400 et seq.].

5. This section does not apply to any student participating in a school-sponsored shooting sport, pro-

vided the student informs the school principal of the student's participation and the student complies with all requirements set by the principal regarding the safe handling and storage of the firearm.

6. For purposes of this section:

b. "School property" includes all land within the perimeter of the school site and all school buildings, structures, facilities, and school vehicles, whether owned or leased by a school district, and the site of any school-sponsored event or activity.

⊰– OHIO –⊱
KNIFE RIGHTS MOVEMENT RATING
★ ★ ★ ☆ ☆

CUTTING TO THE CHASE

Ohio defines a ballistic knife as "dangerous ordnance". Concealed carry of dangerous ordnance and deadly weapons is banned. A "deadly weapon" means any instrument, device, or thing capable of inflicting death, and designed or specially adapted for use as a weapon, or possessed, carried, or used as a weapon. This is so vague that honest citizens cannot know for sure what is legal. Possession and open carry of any knife is not prohibited.

Quick Points Concerning Ohio's Knife Law*

KNIFE TYPE	POSSESSION	(Open/Concealed) CARRY	SALE	MANUFACTURE
Assisted Opening	Legal	Legal/Gray	Gray	Gray
Automatic/Switchblade	Legal	Legal/Gray	Prohibited	Prohibited
Ballistic	Legal	Legal/ Prohibited	Prohibited	Prohibited
Bayonets	Legal	Legal/ Gray	Legal	Legal
Bowie	Legal	Legal/ Gray	Legal	Legal
Butterfly/Balisong	Legal	Legal/ Gray	Legal	Legal
Combat/Survival	Legal	Legal/ Gray	Legal	Legal
Dagger	Legal	Legal/ Gray	Legal	Legal
Dirk	Legal	Legal/ Gray	Legal	Legal
Disguised	Legal	Legal/ Gray	Legal	Legal
Fixed	Legal	Legal/ Gray	Legal	Legal
Folding	Legal	Legal/ Gray	Legal	Legal
Gravity	Legal	Legal/ Gray	Prohibited	Prohibited
Hunting/Fishing	Legal	Legal/ Gray	Legal	Legal
Machete	Legal	Legal/ Gray	Legal	Legal
Razor	Legal	Legal/ Gray	Legal	Legal
Stiletto	Legal	Legal/ Gray	Legal	Legal
Sword	Legal	Legal/ Gray	Legal	Legal
Throwing	Legal	Legal/ Gray	Legal	Legal
Undetectable	Legal	Legal/ Gray	Legal	Legal

Pre-emption (Only State Law May Regulate, No Local Laws Permitted) – NO
*See all information above and below for more details.

SHARP TIPS ABOUT OHIO'S KNIFE LAWS

No knives in school zones or courthouses. Carrying any knife concealed "as a weapon" is prohibited. No pre-emption, so watch out for local laws.

EDGE –U- CATIONAL --- OHIO'S KNIFE LAWS

§ 2923.11 Definitions

As used in sections 2923.11 to 2923.24 of the Revised Code:

(A) "Deadly weapon" means any instrument, device, or thing capable of inflicting death, and designed or specially adapted for use as a weapon, or possessed, carried, or used as a weapon.

(J) "Ballistic knife" means a knife with a detachable blade that is propelled by a spring-operated mechanism.

(K) "Dangerous ordnance" means any of the following, except as provided in division (L) of this section:

(1) Any automatic or sawed-off firearm, zip-gun, or ballistic knife;

§ 2923.12 Carrying concealed weapons; affirmative defenses

(A) No person shall knowingly carry or have, concealed on the person's person or concealed ready at hand, any of the following:

(1) A deadly weapon other than a handgun;

(2) A handgun other than a dangerous ordnance;

(3) A dangerous ordnance.

(C)(1) This section does not apply to any of the following:

(a) An officer, agent, or employee of this or any other state or the United States, or to a law enforcement officer, who is authorized to carry concealed weapons or dangerous ordnance or is authorized to carry handguns and is acting within the scope of the officer's, agent's, or employee's duties;

(b) Any person who is employed in this state, who is authorized to carry concealed weapons or dangerous ordnance or is authorized to carry handguns, and who is subject to and in compliance with the requirements of section 109. 801 of the Revised Code, unless the appointing authority of the person has expressly specified that the exemption provided in division (C)(1)(b) of this section does not apply to the person;

(D) It is an affirmative defense to a charge under division (A)(1) of this section of carrying or having control of a weapon other than a handgun and other than a dangerous ordnance that the actor was not otherwise prohibited by law from having the weapon and that any of the following applies:

(1) The weapon was carried or kept ready at hand by the actor for defensive purposes while the actor was engaged in or was going to or from the actor's lawful business or occupation, which business or occupation was of a character or was necessarily carried on in a manner or at a time or place as to render the actor particularly susceptible to criminal attack, such as would justify a prudent person in going armed.

(2) The weapon was carried or kept ready at hand by the actor for defensive purposes while the actor was engaged in a lawful activity and had reasonable cause to fear a criminal attack upon the actor, a member of the actor's family, or the actor's home, such as would justify a prudent person in going armed.

(3) The weapon was carried or kept ready at hand by the actor for any lawful purpose and while in the actor's own home.

§ 2923.122 Conveyance or possession of deadly weapons or dangerous ordnance in school safety zone

(A) No person shall knowingly convey, or attempt to convey, a deadly weapon or dangerous ordnance into a school safety zone.

(B) No person shall knowingly possess a deadly weapon or dangerous ordnance in a school safety zone.

(C) No person shall knowingly possess an object in a school safety zone if both of the following apply:

(1) The object is indistinguishable from a firearm, whether or not the object is capable of being fired.

(2) The person indicates that the person possesses the object and that it is a firearm, or the person knowingly displays or brandishes the object and indicates that it is a firearm.

(D)(1) This section does not apply to any of the following:

(a) An officer, agent, or employee of this or any other state or the United States, or a law enforcement officer, who is authorized to carry deadly weapons or dangerous ordnance and is acting within the scope of the officer's, agent's, or employee's duties, a security officer employed by a board of education or governing body of a school during the time that the security officer is on duty pursuant to that contract of employment, or any other person who has written authorization from the board of education or governing body of a school to convey deadly weapons or dangerous ordnance into a school safety zone or to possess a deadly weapon or dangerous ordnance in a school safety zone and who conveys or possesses the deadly weapon or dangerous ordnance in accordance with that authorization;

(b) Any person who is employed in this state, who is authorized to carry deadly weapons or dangerous ordnance, and who is subject to and in compliance with the requirements of section 109.801 of the Revised Code, unless the appointing authority of the person has expressly specified that the exemption provided in division (D)(1)(b) of this section does not apply to the person.

(2) Division (C) of this section does not apply to premises upon which home schooling is conducted. Division (C) of this section also does not apply to a school administrator, teacher, or employee who possesses an object that is indistinguishable from a firearm for legitimate school purposes during the course of employment, a student who uses an object that is indistinguishable from a firearm under the direction of a school administrator, teacher, or employee, or any other person who with the express prior approval of a school administrator possesses an object that is indistinguishable from a firearm for a legitimate purpose, including the use of the object in a ceremonial activity, a play, reenactment, or other dramatic presentation, or a ROTC activity or another similar use of the object.

(3) This section does not apply to a person who conveys or attempts to convey a handgun into, or possesses a handgun in, a school safety zone if, at the time of that conveyance, attempted conveyance, or possession of the handgun, all of the following apply:

(a) The person does not enter into a school building or onto school premises and is not at a school activity.

(b) The person is carrying a valid concealed handgun license.

(c) The person is in the school safety zone in accordance with 18 U.S.C. 922(q)(2)(B).

(d) The person is not knowingly in a place described in division (B)(1) or (B)(3) to (10) of section 2923.126 of the Revised Code.

(4) This section does not apply to a person who conveys or attempts to convey a handgun into, or possesses a handgun in, a school safety zone if at the time of that conveyance, attempted conveyance, or possession of the handgun all of the following apply:

(a) The person is carrying a valid concealed handgun license.

(b) The person is the driver or passenger in a motor vehicle and is in the school safety zone while immediately in the process of picking up or dropping off a child.

(c) The person is not in violation of section 2923.16 of the Revised Code.

(E)(1) Whoever violates division (A) or (B) of this section is guilty of illegal conveyance or possession of a deadly weapon or dangerous ordnance in a school safety zone. Except as otherwise provided in this division, illegal conveyance or possession of a deadly weapon or dangerous ordnance in a school safety zone is a felony of the fifth degree. If the offender previously has been convicted of a violation of this section, illegal conveyance or possession of a deadly weapon or dangerous ordnance in a school safety zone is a felony of the fourth degree.

(2) Whoever violates division (C) of this section is guilty of illegal possession of an object indistinguishable from a firearm in a school safety zone. Except as otherwise provided in this division, illegal possession of an object indistinguishable from a firearm in a school safety zone is a misdemeanor of the first degree. If the offender previously has been convicted of a violation of this section, illegal possession of an object indistinguishable from a firearm in a school safety zone is a felony of the fifth degree.

§ 2923.123 Illegal conveyance, possession or control of a deadly weapon or dangerous ordnance in a courthouse

(A) No person shall knowingly convey or attempt to convey a deadly weapon or dangerous ordnance into a courthouse or into another building or structure in which a courtroom is located.

(B) No person shall knowingly possess or have under the person's control a deadly weapon or dangerous ordnance in a courthouse or in another building or structure in which a courtroom is located.

(C) This section does not apply to any of the following:

(1) Except as provided in division (E) of this section, a judge of a court of record of this state or a magistrate;

(2) A peace officer, officer of a law enforcement agency, or person who is in either of the following categories:

(a) Except as provided in division (E) of this section, a peace officer, or an officer of a law enforcement agency of another state, a political subdivision of another state, or the United States, who is authorized to carry a deadly weapon or dangerous ordnance, who possesses or has under that individual's control a deadly weapon or dangerous ordnance as a requirement of that individual's duties, and who is acting within the scope of that individual's duties at the time of that possession or control;

(b) Except as provided in division (E) of this section, a person who is employed in this state, who is authorized to carry a deadly weapon or dangerous ordnance, who possesses or has under that individual's control a deadly weapon or dangerous ordnance as a requirement of that person's duties, and who is subject to and in compliance with the requirements of section 109.801 of the Revised Code, unless the appointing authority of the person has expressly specified that the exemption provided in division (C)(2)(b) of this section does not apply to the person.

(3) A person who conveys, attempts to convey, possesses, or has under the person's control a deadly weapon or dangerous ordnance that is to be used as evidence in a pending criminal or civil action or proceeding;

(4) Except as provided in division (E) of this section, a bailiff or deputy bailiff of a court of record of this state who is authorized to carry a firearm pursuant to section 109.77 of the Revised Code, who possesses or has under that individual's control a firearm as a requirement of that individual's duties, and who is acting within the scope of that individual's duties at the time of that possession or control;

(5) Except as provided in division (E) of this section, a prosecutor, or a secret service officer appointed by a county prosecuting attorney, who is authorized to carry a deadly weapon or dangerous ordnance in the performance of the individual's duties, who possesses or has under that individual's control a

deadly weapon or dangerous ordnance as a requirement of that individual's duties, and who is acting within the scope of that individual's duties at the time of that possession or control;

(6) Except as provided in division (E) of this section, a person who conveys or attempts to convey a handgun into a courthouse or into another building or structure in which a courtroom is located, who, at the time of the conveyance or attempt, is carrying a valid concealed handgun license, and who transfers possession of the handgun to the officer or officer's designee who has charge of the courthouse or building. The officer shall secure the handgun until the licensee is prepared to leave the premises. The exemption described in this division applies only if the officer who has charge of the courthouse or building provides services of the nature described in this division. An officer who has charge of the courthouse or building is not required to offer services of the nature described in this division.

(D)(1) Whoever violates division (A) of this section is guilty of illegal conveyance of a deadly weapon or dangerous ordnance into a courthouse. Except as otherwise provided in this division, illegal conveyance of a deadly weapon or dangerous ordnance into a courthouse is a felony of the fifth degree. If the offender previously has been convicted of a violation of division (A) or (B) of this section, illegal conveyance of a deadly weapon or dangerous ordnance into a courthouse is a felony of the fourth degree.

(2) Whoever violates division (B) of this section is guilty of illegal possession or control of a deadly weapon or dangerous ordnance in a courthouse. Except as otherwise provided in this division, illegal possession or control of a deadly weapon or dangerous ordnance in a courthouse is a felony of the fifth degree. If the offender previously has been convicted of a violation of division (A) or (B) of this section, illegal possession or control of a deadly weapon or dangerous ordnance in a courthouse is a felony of the fourth degree.

(E) The exemptions described in divisions (C)(1), (2)(a), (2)(b), (4), (5), and (6) of this section do not apply to any judge, magistrate, peace officer, officer of a law enforcement agency, bailiff, deputy bailiff, prosecutor, secret service officer, or other person described in any of those divisions if a rule of superintendence or another type of rule adopted by the supreme court pursuant to Article IV, Ohio Constitution, or an applicable local rule of court prohibits all persons from conveying or attempting to convey a deadly weapon or dangerous ordnance into a courthouse or into another building or structure in which a courtroom is located or from possessing or having under one's control a deadly weapon or dangerous ordnance in a courthouse or in another building or structure in which a courtroom is located.

(F) As used in this section:

(1) "Magistrate" means an individual who is appointed by a court of record of this state and who has the powers and may perform the functions specified in Civil Rule 53, Criminal Rule 19, or Juvenile Rule 40.

(2) "Peace officer" and "prosecutor" have the same meanings as in section 2935.01 of the Revised Code.

§ 2923.20 Unlawful transactions in weapons
(A) No person shall:

(1) Recklessly sell, lend, give, or furnish any firearm to any person prohibited by section 2923.13 or 2923.15 of the Revised Code from acquiring or using any firearm, or recklessly sell, lend, give, or furnish any dangerous ordnance to any person prohibited by section 2923.13, 2923.15, or 2923.17 of the Revised Code from acquiring or using any dangerous ordnance;

(2) Possess any firearm or dangerous ordnance with purpose to dispose of it in violation of division (A) of this section;

(3) Manufacture, possess for sale, sell, or furnish to any person other than a law enforcement agency for authorized use in police work, any brass knuckles, cestus, billy, blackjack, sandbag, switchblade knife, springblade knife, gravity knife, or similar weapon;

(4) When transferring any dangerous ordnance to another, negligently fail to require the transferee

to exhibit such identification, license, or permit showing him to be authorized to acquire dangerous ordnance pursuant to section 2923.17 of the Revised Code, or negligently fail to take a complete record of the transaction and forthwith forward a copy of that record to the sheriff of the county or safety director or police chief of the municipality where the transaction takes place;

(5) Knowingly fail to report to law enforcement authorities forthwith the loss or theft of any firearm or dangerous ordnance in the person's possession or under the person's control.

✦ OKLAHOMA ✦
KNIFE RIGHTS MOVEMENT RATING
★ ★ ★ ★ ☆

CUTTING TO THE CHASE

Oklahoma does not ban possession of any knife by feature or type. The State recently passed pre-emption and removed switchblade from the list of per se type knives that cannot be carried. However, the state still prohibits both open and concealed carry of "…any dagger, bowie knife, dirk knife, sword cane … or any other offensive weapon." "Offensive weapon" is vague and not statutorily defined.

Quick Points Concerning Oklahoma's Knife Law*

KNIFE TYPE	POSSESSION	(Open/Concealed) CARRY	SALE	MANUFACTURE
Assisted Opening	Legal	Gray/Gray	Legal	Legal
Automatic/Switchblade	Legal	Gray/Gray	Legal	Legal
Ballistic	Legal	Gray/Gray	Legal	Legal
Bayonets	Legal	Gray/Gray	Legal	Legal
Bowie	Legal	Prohibited/Prohibited	Legal	Legal
Butterfly/Balisong	Legal	Gray/Gray	Legal	Legal
Combat/Survival	Legal	Gray/Gray	Legal	Legal
Dagger	Legal	Prohibited/Prohibited	Legal	Legal
Dirk	Legal	Prohibited/Prohibited	Legal	Legal
Disguised	Legal	Gray/Gray	Legal	Legal
Fixed	Legal	Gray/Gray	Legal	Legal
Folding	Legal	Gray/Gray	Legal	Legal
Gravity	Legal	Gray/Gray	Legal	Legal
Hunting/Fishing	Legal	Gray/Gray	Legal	Legal
Machete	Legal	Gray/Gray	Legal	Legal
Razor	Legal	Gray/Gray	Legal	Legal
Stiletto	Legal	Gray/Gray	Legal	Legal
Sword	Legal	Gray/Gray	Legal	Legal
Throwing	Legal	Gray/Gray	Legal	Legal
Undetectable	Legal	Gray/Gray	Legal	Legal

Pre-emption (Only State Law May Regulate, No Local Laws Permitted) – YES
*See all information above and below for more details.

SHARP TIPS ABOUT OKLAHOMA'S KNIFE LAWS

Carrying of knives is permitted if properly being used for "hunting, fishing, educational or recreational purposes", or for living history reenactment. No knives on school property.

EDGE –U- CATIONAL --- OKLAHOMA'S KNIFE LAWS

21 O.S. § 1272. Unlawful carry

A. It shall be unlawful for any person to carry upon or about his or her person, or in a purse or other container belonging to the person, any pistol, revolver, shotgun or rifle whether loaded or unloaded or any dagger, bowie knife, dirk knife, sword cane, blackjack, loaded cane, billy, hand chain, metal knuckles, or any other offensive weapon, whether such weapon be concealed or unconcealed, except this section shall not prohibit:

1. The proper use of guns and knives for hunting, fishing, educational or recreational purposes;

2. The carrying or use of weapons in a manner otherwise permitted by statute or authorized by the Oklahoma Self-Defense Act;1

3. The carrying, possession and use of any weapon by a peace officer or other person authorized by law to carry a weapon in the performance of official duties and in compliance with the rules of the employing agency;

4. The carrying or use of weapons in a courthouse by a district judge, associate district judge or special district judge within this state, who is in possession of a valid handgun license issued pursuant to the provisions of the Oklahoma Self-Defense Act and whose name appears on a list maintained by the Administrative Director of the Courts; or

5. The carrying and use of firearms and other weapons provided in this subsection when used for the purpose of living history reenactment. For purposes of this paragraph, "living history reenactment" means depiction of historical characters, scenes, historical life or events for entertainment, education, or historical documentation through the wearing or use of period, historical, antique or vintage clothing, accessories, firearms, weapons, and other implements of the historical period.

B. Any person convicted of violating the foregoing provision shall be guilty of a misdemeanor punishable as provided in Section 1276 of this title.

21 O.S. § 1276. Penalty for 1272 and 1273

Any person violating the provisions of Section 1272 or 1273 of this title shall, upon a first conviction, be adjudged guilty of a misdemeanor and the party offending shall be punished by a fine of not less than One Hundred Dollars ($100.00) nor more than Two Hundred Fifty Dollars ($250.00), or by imprisonment in the county jail for a period not to exceed thirty (30) days or both such fine and imprisonment. On the second and every subsequent violation, the party offending shall, upon conviction, be punished by a fine of not less than Two Hundred Fifty Dollars ($250.00) nor more than Five Hundred Dollars ($500.00), or by imprisonment in the county jail for a period not less than thirty (30) days nor more than three (3) months, or by both such fine and imprisonment.

Any person convicted of violating the provisions of Section 1272 or 1273 of this title after having been issued a handgun license pursuant to the provisions of the Oklahoma Self-Defense Act1 shall have the license suspended for a period of six (6) months and shall be liable for an administrative fine of Fifty Dollars ($50.00) upon a hearing and determination by the Oklahoma State Bureau of Investigation that the person is in violation of the provisions of this section.

21 O.S. § 1280.1. Possession of firearm on school property

A. It shall be unlawful for any person to have in his or her possession on any public or private school property or while in any school bus or vehicle used by any school for transportation of students or teachers any firearm or weapon designated in Section 1272 of this title, except as provided in subsection C of this section or as otherwise authorized by law.

B. For purposes of this section:

1. "School property" means any publicly owned property held for purposes of elementary, secondary or vocational-technical education, and shall not include property owned by public school districts or

where such property is leased or rented to an individual or corporation and used for purposes other than educational;

2. "Private school" means a school that offers a course of instruction for students in one or more grades from prekindergarten through grade twelve and is not operated by a governmental entity; and

3. "Motor vehicle" means any automobile, truck, minivan or sports utility vehicle.

C. Firearms and weapons are allowed on school property and deemed not in violation of subsection A of this section as follows:

1. A gun or knife designed for hunting or fishing purposes kept in a privately owned vehicle and properly displayed or stored as required by law, provided such vehicle containing said gun or knife is driven onto school property only to transport a student to and from school and such vehicle does not remain unattended on school property;

2. A gun or knife used for the purposes of participating in the Oklahoma Department of Wildlife Conservation certified hunter training education course or any other hunting, fishing, safety or firearms training courses, or a recognized firearms sports event, team shooting program or competition, or living history reenactment, provided the course or event is approved by the principal or chief administrator of the school where the course or event is offered, and provided the weapon is properly displayed or stored as required by law pending participation in the course, event, program or competition;

3. Weapons in the possession of any peace officer or other person authorized by law to possess a weapon in the performance of his or her duties and responsibilities;

4. A concealed or unconcealed weapon carried onto private school property or in any school bus or vehicle used by any private school for transportation of students or teachers by a person who is licensed pursuant to the Oklahoma Self-Defense Act,1 provided a policy has been adopted by the governing entity of the private school that authorizes the possession of a weapon on private school property or in any school bus or vehicle used by a private school. Except for acts of gross negligence or willful or wanton misconduct, a governing entity of a private school that adopts a policy which authorizes the possession of a weapon on private school property, a school bus or vehicle used by the private school shall be immune from liability for any injuries arising from the adoption of the policy. The provisions of this paragraph shall not apply to claims pursuant to the Workers' Compensation Code;

5. A gun, knife, bayonet or other weapon in the possession of a member of a veterans group, the national guard, active military, the Reserve Officers' Training Corps (ROTC) or Junior ROTC, in order to participate in a ceremony, assembly or educational program approved by the principal or chief administrator of a school or school district where the ceremony, assembly or educational program is being held; provided, however, the gun or other weapon that uses projectiles is not loaded and is inoperable at all times while on school property; and

D. Any person violating the provisions of this section shall, upon conviction, be guilty of a misdemeanor punishable by a fine of not to exceed Two Hundred Fifty Dollars ($250.00).

21 O.S. § 1289.24 State Preemption

A. 1. The State Legislature hereby occupies and preempts the entire field of legislation in this state touching in any way firearms, knives, components, ammunition, and supplies to the complete exclusion of any order, ordinance, or regulation by any municipality or other political subdivision of this state. Any existing or future orders, ordinances, or regulations in this field, except as provided for in paragraph 2 of this subsection and subsection C of this section, are null and void.

2. A municipality may adopt any ordinance:

4. A public or private school may create a policy regulating the possession of knives on school prop-

erty or in any school bus or vehicle used by the school for purposes of transportation.

B. No municipality or other political subdivision of this state shall adopt any order, ordinance, or regulation concerning in any way the sale, purchase, purchase delay, transfer, ownership, use, keeping, possession, carrying, bearing, transportation, licensing, permit, registration, taxation other than sales and compensating use taxes, or other controls on firearms, knives, components, ammunition, and supplies.

C. Except as hereinafter provided, this section shall not prohibit any order, ordinance, or regulation by any municipality concerning the confiscation of property used in violation of the ordinances of the municipality as provided for in Section 28–121 of Title 11 of the Oklahoma Statutes. Provided, however, no municipal ordinance relating to transporting a firearm or knife improperly may include a provision for confiscation of property.

D. When a person's rights pursuant to the protection of the preemption provisions of this section have been violated, the person shall have the right to bring a civil action against the persons, municipality, and political subdivision jointly and severally for injunctive relief or monetary damages or both.

SECTION 2. This act shall become effective November 1, 2015.

⊶ OREGON ⊷
KNIFE RIGHTS MOVEMENT RATING
★ ★ ★ ☆ ☆

CUTTING TO THE CHASE
Oregon was a pioneer state in recognizing the right to keep and bear arms and its application to knives. Quotes from Oregon case law are in the U.S. Supreme Court's landmark Heller decision, which found that the Second Amendment protects an individual right to keep and bear arms. Oregon does not ban any knife by feature or type. Open carry of any knife is lawful as long as there is no bad intent. Concealed carry of any knife, except a pocket knife, is problematic.

Quick Points Concerning Oregon's Knife Law*

KNIFE TYPE	POSSESSION	(Open/Concealed) CARRY	SALE	MANUFACTURE
Assisted Opening	Legal	Legal/Gray	Legal	Legal
Automatic/Switchblade	Legal	Legal/Gray	Legal	Legal
Ballistic	Legal	Legal/Gray	Legal	Legal
Bayonets	Legal	Legal/Gray	Legal	Legal
Bowie	Legal	Legal/Gray	Legal	Legal
Butterfly/Balisong	Legal	Legal/Gray	Legal	Legal
Combat/Survival	Legal	Legal/Gray	Legal	Legal
Dagger	Legal	Legal/Prohibited	Legal	Legal
Dirk	Legal	Legal/Prohibited	Legal	Legal
Disguised	Legal	Legal/Gray	Legal	Legal
Fixed	Legal	Legal/Gray	Legal	Legal
Folding	Legal	Legal/Gray	Legal	Legal
Gravity	Legal	Legal/Gray	Legal	Legal
Hunting/Fishing	Legal	Legal/Gray	Legal	Legal
Machete	Legal	Legal/Gray	Legal	Legal

KNIFE TYPE	POSSESSION	(Open/Concealed) CARRY	SALE	MANUFACTURE
Razor	Legal	Legal/Gray	Legal	Legal
Stiletto	Legal	Legal/Gray	Legal	Legal
Sword	Legal	Legal/Gray	Legal	Legal
Throwing	Legal	Legal/Gray	Legal	Legal
Undetectable	Legal	Legal/Gray	Legal	Legal

Pre-emption (Only State Law May Regulate, No Local Laws Permitted) – NO
*See all information above and below for more details.

SHARP TIPS ABOUT OREGON'S KNIFE LAWS

Do not conceal carry any "knife having a blade that projects or swings into position by force of a spring or by centrifugal force, any dirk, dagger, ice pick, or any similar instrument by the use of which injury could be inflicted upon the person or property of any other person." Case law may allow one to have a switchblade or other "pocket knife," but case law can be very fact sensitive. The safest course of action is to only conceal carry an ordinary pocket knife. Do not carry knives in courthouses, public buildings or schools. Certain felons are prohibited from knife possession. No pre-emption, so beware of local laws.

EDGE –U- CATIONAL --- OREGON'S KNIFE LAWS
O.R.S. § 166.220. Unlawful use of weapon

(1) A person commits the crime of unlawful use of a weapon if the person:

(a) Attempts to use unlawfully against another, or carries or possesses with intent to use unlawfully against another, any dangerous or deadly weapon as defined in ORS 161.015;

(2) This section does not apply to:

(a) Police officers or military personnel in the lawful performance of their official duties;

(b) Persons lawfully defending life or property as provided in ORS 161.219;

(d) Persons lawfully engaged in hunting in compliance with rules and regulations adopted by the State Department of Fish and Wildlife; or

(e) An employee of the United States Department of Agriculture, acting within the scope of employment, discharging a firearm in the course of the lawful taking of wildlife.

(3) Unlawful use of a weapon is a Class C felony.

O.R.S. § 166.240. Carrying of concealed weapons

(1) Except as provided in subsection (2) of this section, any person who carries concealed upon the person any knife having a blade that projects or swings into position by force of a spring or by centrifugal force, any dirk, dagger, ice pick, slungshot, metal knuckles, or any similar instrument by the use of which injury could be inflicted upon the person or property of any other person, commits a Class B misdemeanor.

(2) Nothing in subsection (1) of this section applies to any peace officer as defined in ORS 133.005, whose duty it is to serve process or make arrests. Justice courts have concurrent jurisdiction to try any person charged with violating any of the provisions of subsection (1) of this section.

O.R.S. § 166.270. Possession of weapons by felons

(2) Any person who has been convicted of a felony under the law of this state or any other state, or who has been convicted of a felony under the laws of the Government of the United States, who owns or has in the person's possession or under the person's custody or control any instrument or weapon having a blade that projects or swings into position by force of a spring or by centrifugal force or any blackjack, slungshot, sandclub, sandbag, sap glove, metal knuckles or an Electro-Muscular Disruption

Technology device as defined in ORS 165.540, or who carries a dirk, dagger or stiletto, commits the crime of felon in possession of a restricted weapon.

(3) For the purposes of this section, a person "has been convicted of a felony" if, at the time of conviction for an offense, that offense was a felony under the law of the jurisdiction in which it was committed. Such conviction shall not be deemed a conviction of a felony if:

(a) The court declared the conviction to be a misdemeanor at the time of judgment; or

(b) The offense was possession of marijuana and the conviction was prior to January 1, 1972.

(4) Subsection (1) of this section does not apply to any person who has been:

(a) Convicted of only one felony under the law of this state or any other state, or who has been convicted of only one felony under the laws of the United States, which felony did not involve criminal homicide, as defined in ORS 163.005, or the possession or use of a firearm or a weapon having a blade that projects or swings into position by force of a spring or by centrifugal force, and who has been discharged from imprisonment, parole or probation for said offense for a period of 15 years prior to the date of alleged violation of subsection (1) of this section; or

(b) Granted relief from the disability under 18 U.S.C. 925(c) or ORS 166.274 or has had the person's record expunged under the laws of this state or equivalent laws of another jurisdiction.

(5) Felon in possession of a firearm is a Class C felony. Felon in possession of a restricted weapon is a Class A misdemeanor.

O.R.S. § 166.360. Definitions
As used in ORS 166.360 to 166.380, unless the context requires otherwise:

(1) "Capitol building" means the Capitol, the State Office Building, the State Library Building, the Labor and Industries Building, the State Transportation Building, the Agriculture Building or the Public Service Building and includes any new buildings which may be constructed on the same grounds as an addition to the group of buildings listed in this subsection.

(2) "Court facility" means a courthouse or that portion of any other building occupied by a circuit court, the Court of Appeals, the Supreme Court or the Oregon Tax Court or occupied by personnel related to the operations of those courts, or in which activities related to the operations of those courts take place.

(4) "Public building" means a hospital, a capitol building, a public or private school, as defined in ORS 339.315, a college or university, a city hall or the residence of any state official elected by the state at large, and the grounds adjacent to each such building. The term also includes that portion of any other building occupied by an agency of the state or a municipal corporation, as defined in ORS 297.405, other than a court facility.

(5) "Weapon" means:

(b) Any dirk, dagger, ice pick, slingshot, metal knuckles or any similar instrument or a knife other than an ordinary pocket knife, the use of which could inflict injury upon a person or property;

(g) A dangerous or deadly weapon as those terms are defined in ORS 161.015.

O.R.S. § 166.370. Possession of firearm or dangerous weapon in public building or court facility; exceptions
(1) Any person who intentionally possesses a loaded or unloaded firearm or any other instrument used as a dangerous weapon, while in or on a public building, shall upon conviction be guilty of a Class C felony.

(2)(a) Except as otherwise provided in paragraph (b) of this subsection, a person who intentionally possesses:

(B) A weapon, other than a firearm, in a court facility may be required to surrender the weapon to a law enforcement officer or to immediately remove it from the court facility. A person who fails to comply with this subparagraph is guilty, upon conviction, of a Class C felony.

(b) The presiding judge of a judicial district may enter an order permitting the possession of specified weapons in a court facility.

(3) Subsection (1) of this section does not apply to:

(a) A sheriff, police officer, other duly appointed peace officers or a corrections officer while acting within the scope of employment.

(b) A person summoned by a peace officer to assist in making an arrest or preserving the peace, while the summoned person is engaged in assisting the officer.

(c) An active or reserve member of the military forces of this state or the United States, when engaged in the performance of duty.

(d) A person who is licensed under ORS 166.291 and 166.292 to carry a concealed handgun.

(e) A person who is authorized by the officer or agency that controls the public building to possess a firearm or dangerous weapon in that public building.

(f) An employee of the United States Department of Agriculture, acting within the scope of employment, who possesses a firearm in the course of the lawful taking of wildlife.

(g) Possession of a firearm on school property if the firearm:

(A) Is possessed by a person who is not otherwise prohibited from possessing the firearm; and

(B) Is unloaded and locked in a motor vehicle.

(4) The exceptions listed in subsection (3)(b) to (g) of this section constitute affirmative defenses to a charge of violating subsection (1) of this section.

(5)(a) Any person who knowingly, or with reckless disregard for the safety of another, discharges or attempts to discharge a firearm at a place that the person knows is a school shall upon conviction be guilty of a Class C felony.

(b) Paragraph (a) of this subsection does not apply to the discharge of a firearm:

(A) As part of a program approved by a school in the school by an individual who is participating in the program;

(B) By a law enforcement officer acting in the officer's official capacity; or

(C) By an employee of the United States Department of Agriculture, acting within the scope of employment, in the course of the lawful taking of wildlife.

(6) Any weapon carried in violation of this section is subject to the forfeiture provisions of ORS 166.279.

(7) Notwithstanding the fact that a person's conduct in a single criminal episode constitutes a violation of both subsections (1) and (5) of this section, the district attorney may charge the person with only one of the offenses.

(8) As used in this section, "dangerous weapon" means a dangerous weapon as that term is defined in ORS 161.015.

Uniform Trial Court Rules, UTCR 6.180 Weapons and hazardous substances in the court facilities

Unless otherwise ordered by the court, no person except a law enforcement officer shall possess in a court facility a firearm, knife, device, or hazardous substance capable of inflicting death or physical injury.

✦ CHAPTER 15 ✦
STATE KNIFE LAW GUIDE P-W

HOW TO USE THIS GUIDE

The "Quick Points" chart for each jurisdiction contains 100 legal questions answered by either "Legal", "Prohibited," or "Gray".

"Legal" means that it is generally lawful.

"Prohibited" means that it is generally unlawful.

"Gray" means that it is neither generally lawful nor unlawful and that there are ambiguities, conflicting law, exceptions, requirements or special considerations that may determine legality.

The laws provided have been selected because of their relevance to knives. Sections of the law may have been edited. It is also possible that some laws may have been inadvertently omitted due to legal research not revealing same. In other words, your author tried his best, but he is not perfect.

KNIFE RIGHTS MOVEMENT RATING SYSTEM

The Knife Rights Movement rating system grades the States, the District of Columbia, and the United States of America on a scale from one to five.

The highest rating is a five, which means that jurisdiction stands out for knife liberty. A rating of one means that jurisdiction has a disdain for knives and individual rights, and has arbitrary laws that treat honest citizens like criminals. Ratings of two, three, or four show where that jurisdiction is in regards to its respect for knife rights freedom. If a place has a rating lower than five, then there is work to be done there restoring knife liberty and continuing the Knife Rights Movement.

✦ PENNSYLVANIA ✦
KNIFE RIGHTS MOVEMENT RATING
★ ★ ☆ ☆ ☆

CUTTING TO THE CHASE

Aside from switchblade knives, there are no per se prohibited knives under the state statutes. However, the state prohibits anyone who "makes repairs, sells, or otherwise deals in, uses, or possesses" a "dagger, knife, razor or cutting instrument, the blade of which is exposed in an automatic way by switch, push-button, spring mechanism, or otherwise, …or other implement for the infliction of serious bodily injury which serves no common lawful purpose." The definition of "implement for the infliction of serious bodily injury" and "common lawful purpose" is vague and continues to be defined by often contradictory and fact sensitive case law.

Quick Points Concerning Pennsylvania's Knife Law*

KNIFE TYPE	POSSESSION	(Open/Concealed) CARRY	SALE	MANUFACTURE
Automatic/Switchblade	Prohibited	Prohibited / Prohibited	Prohibited	Prohibited
Ballistic	Gray	Gray /Gray	Gray	Gray
Bayonets	Gray	Gray /Gray	Gray	Gray
Bowie	Gray	Gray /Gray	Gray	Gray
Butterfly/Balisong	Gray	Gray /Gray	Gray	Gray
Combat/Survival	Gray	Gray /Gray	Gray	Gray
Dagger	Gray	Gray /Gray	Gray	Gray
Dirk	Gray	Gray /Gray	Gray	Gray
Disguised	Gray	Gray /Gray	Gray	Gray
Fixed	Gray	Gray /Gray	Gray	Gray
Folding	Gray	Gray /Gray	Gray	Gray
Gravity	Gray	Gray /Gray	Gray	Gray
Hunting/Fishing	Gray	Gray /Gray	Gray	Gray
Machete	Gray	Gray /Gray	Gray	Gray
Razor	Gray	Gray /Gray	Gray	Gray
Stiletto	Gray	Gray /Gray	Gray	Gray
Sword	Gray	Gray /Gray	Gray	Gray
Throwing	Gray	Gray /Gray	Gray	Gray
Undetectable	Gray	Gray /Gray	Gray	Gray

Pre-emption (Only State Law May Regulate, No Local Laws Permitted) – NO
*See all information above and below for more details.

SHARP TIPS ABOUT PENNSYLVANIA'S KNIFE LAWS

A statutory defense exists for switchblades and other banned knives, if one can show that he or she "possessed or dealt with the weapon solely as a curio or in a dramatic performance." Interestingly, law enforcement and military are not exempted. No knives on school grounds including buildings and school buses.

There is no pre-emption in Pennsylvania. Counties can have their own statutes prohibiting the carrying of knives in different areas or circumstances, most notably is Philadelphia's § 10-820 "Cutting Weapons in Public Places" which essentially prohibits the possession or use of anything with a cutting edge in the public unless being used in active exercise of a job which requires such tool, with penalties of "a fine of not less than three hundred (300) dollars and imprisonment of not less than ninety days."

EDGE –U- CATIONAL --- PENNSYLVANIA'S KNIFE LAWS

18 P.S. § 908. Prohibited offensive weapons.

(a) Offense defined.--A person commits a misdemeanor of the first degree if, except as authorized by law, he makes repairs, sells, or otherwise deals in, uses, or possesses any offensive weapon. (b) Exceptions.– (1) It is a defense under this section for the defendant to prove by a preponderance of evidence that he possessed or dealt with the weapon solely as a curio or in a dramatic performance, or that, with the exception of a bomb, grenade or incendiary device, he complied with the National Firearms Act (26 U.S.C. § 5801 et seq.), or that he possessed it briefly in consequence of having found it or taken it from an aggressor, or under circumstances similarly negativing any intent or likelihood that the weapon would be used unlawfully. (2) This section does not apply to police forensic firearms experts or police forensic firearms laboratories. Also exempt from this section are forensic firearms experts or forensic firearms laboratories operating in the ordinary course of business and engaged in lawful operation who notify in writing, on an annual basis, the chief or head of any police force or police department of a city, and, elsewhere, the sheriff of a county in which they are located, of the possession, type and use of offensive weapons. (3) This section shall not apply to any person who makes, repairs, sells or otherwise deals in, uses or possesses any firearm for purposes not prohibited by the laws of this Commonwealth. (c) Definitions.--As used in this section, the following words and phrases shall have the meanings given to them in this subsection: "Firearm." Any weapon which is designed to or may readily be converted to expel any projectile by the action of an explosive or the frame or receiver of any such weapon. "Offensive weapons." Any bomb, grenade, machine gun, sawed-off shotgun with a barrel less than 18 inches, firearm specially made or specially adapted for concealment or silent discharge, any blackjack, sandbag, metal knuckles, dagger, knife, razor or cutting instrument, the blade of which is exposed in an automatic way by switch, push-button, spring mechanism, or otherwise, any stun gun, stun baton, taser or other electronic or electric weapon or other implement for the infliction of serious bodily injury which serves no common lawful purpose. (d) Exemptions.--The use and possession of blackjacks by the following persons in the course of their duties are exempt from this section:

(1) Police officers, as defined by and who meet the requirements of the act of June 18, 1974 (P.L.359, No.120), referred to as the Municipal Police Education and Training Law.

(2) Police officers of first class cities who have successfully completed training which is substantially equivalent to the program under the Municipal Police Education and Training Law.

(3) Pennsylvania State Police officers.

(4) Sheriffs and deputy sheriffs of the various counties who have satisfactorily met the requirements of the Municipal Police Education and Training Law.

(5) Police officers employed by the Commonwealth who have satisfactorily met the requirements of the Municipal Police Education and Training Law.

(6) Deputy sheriffs with adequate training as determined by the Pennsylvania Commission on Crime and Delinquency.

(7) Liquor Control Board agents who have satisfactorily met the requirements of the Municipal Police Education and Training Law.

18 P.S. § 912. Possession of weapon on school property.

(a) Definition.--Notwithstanding the definition of "weapon" in section 907 (relating to possessing instruments of crime), "weapon" for purposes of this section shall include but not be limited to any knife, cutting instrument, cutting tool, nun-chuck stick, firearm, shotgun, rifle and any other tool, instrument or implement capable of inflicting serious bodily injury. (b) Offense defined.--A person commits a misdemeanor of the first degree if he possesses a weapon in the buildings of, on the grounds of, or in any conveyance providing transportation to or from any elementary or secondary publicly-funded educational institution, any elementary or secondary private school licensed by the Department of Education or any elementary or secondary parochial school. (c) Defense.--It shall be a defense that the weapon is possessed and used in conjunction with a lawful supervised school activity or course or is possessed for other lawful purpose.

18 P.S. § 4416. Carrying deadly weapons

(a) Whoever carries any firearm, slungshot, handy-billy, dirk-knife, razor or any other deadly weapon, concealed upon his person, or any knife, razor or cutting instrument, the blade of which can be exposed in an automatic way by switch, push-button, spring mechanism, or otherwise, with the intent therewith unlawfully and maliciously to do injury to any other person, is guilty of a misdemeanor, and upon conviction thereof, shall be sentenced to pay a fine not exceeding five hundred dollars ($500), or undergo imprisonment not exceeding one (1) year, or both. The jury trying the case may infer such intent from the fact the defendant carried such weapon.(b) Whoever is convicted of committing a crime of violence, which for the purposes of this section means murder, rape, robbery, burglary, entering a building with intent to commit a crime therein, kidnapping or participation in riot and during the commission thereof had in his possession a firearm shall, in addition to the penalties prescribed by law, be sentenced to undergo imprisonment for not less than five (5) years and not more than ten (10) years.

⁍ RHODE ISLAND ⁌
KNIFE RIGHTS MOVEMENT RATING
★ ★ ★ ☆ ☆

CUTTING TO THE CHASE

Rhode Island does not ban possession of any knife by feature or type. Concealed carry is restricted. One may not conceal carry a "dagger, dirk, stiletto, sword-in-cane, bowie knife, or other similar weapon designed to cut and stab another" or a razor, or any knife with a blade over three inches long. Open carry of any knife is allowed as long as one is not committing or attempting to commit a crime.

Quick Points Concerning Rhode Island's Knife Law*

KNIFE TYPE	POSSESSION	(Open/Concealed) CARRY	SALE	MANUFACTURE
Assisted Opening	Legal	Legal/Gray	Legal	Legal
Automatic/Switchblade	Legal	Legal/Gray	Legal	Legal
Ballistic	Legal	Legal/Gray	Legal	Legal
Bayonets	Legal	Legal/Gray	Legal	Legal
Bowie	Legal	Legal/Prohibited	Legal	Legal
Butterfly/Balisong	Legal	Legal/Gray	Legal	Legal
Combat/Survival	Legal	Legal/Gray	Legal	Legal
Dagger	Legal	Legal/Prohibited	Legal	Legal
Dirk	Legal	Legal/Prohibited	Legal	Legal
Disguised	Legal	Legal/Gray	Legal	Legal
Fixed	Legal	Legal/Gray	Legal	Legal
Folding	Legal	Legal/Gray	Legal	Legal
Gravity	Legal	Legal/Gray	Legal	Legal
Hunting/Fishing	Legal	Legal/Gray	Legal	Legal

KNIFE TYPE	POSSESSION	(Open/Concealed) CARRY	SALE	MANUFACTU
Machete	Legal	Legal/Gray	Legal	Legal
Razor	Legal	Legal/Prohibited	Legal	Legal
Stiletto	Legal	Legal/Prohibited	Legal	Legal
Sword	Legal	Legal/Gray	Legal	Legal
Throwing	Legal	Legal/Gray	Legal	Legal
Undetectable	Legal	Legal/Gray	Legal	Legal

Pre-emption (Only State Law May Regulate, No Local Laws Permitted) – NO
*See all information above and below for more details.

SHARP TIPS ABOUT RHODE ISLAND'S KNIFE LAWS

Knife sales to persons under 18 are regulated. Store window displays of a dagger, dirk, bowie knife, or stiletto is prohibited. No pre-emption, watch out for local laws.

EDGE –U- CATIONAL --- RHODE ISLAND'S KNIFE LAWS

§ 11-47-42. Weapons other than firearms prohibited

(a)(1) No person shall carry or possess or attempt to use against another any instrument or weapon of the kind commonly known as a blackjack, slingshot, billy, sandclub, sandbag, metal knuckles, slap glove, bludgeon, stun-gun, or the so called "Kung-Fu" weapons.

(2) No person shall with intent to use unlawfully against another, carry or possess a crossbow, dagger, dirk, stiletto, sword-in-cane, bowie knife, or other similar weapon designed to cut and stab another.

(3) No person shall wear or carry concealed upon his person, any of the above-mentioned instruments or weapons, or any razor, or knife of any description having a blade of more than three (3) inches in length measuring from the end of the handle where the blade is attached to the end of the blade, or other weapon of like kind or description.

Any person violating the provisions of these subsections shall be punished by a fine of not more than one thousand dollars ($1,000) or by imprisonment for not more than one year, or both, and the weapon so found shall be confiscated. Any person violating the provisions of these subsections while he or she is incarcerated within the confines of the adult correctional institutions shall be punished by a fine of not less than one thousand dollars ($1,000) nor more than three thousand dollars ($3,000), or by imprisonment for not less than one year nor more than five (5) years, or both, and the weapon so found shall be confiscated.

(b) No person shall sell to a person under eighteen (18) years of age, without the written authorization of the minor's parent or legal guardian, any stink bomb, blackjack, slingshot, bill, sandclub, sandbag, metal knuckles, slap glove, bludgeon, stungun, paint ball gun, so called "kung-fu" weapons, dagger, dirk, stiletto, sword-in-cane, bowie knife, razor, or knife of any description having a blade of more than three inches (3) in length as described in subsection (a) of this section, or any multi-pronged star with sharpened edges designed to be used as a weapon and commonly known as a Chinese throwing star, except that an individual who is actually engaged in the instruction of martial arts and licensed under § 5-43-1 may carry and possess any multi-pronged star with sharpened edges for the sole purpose of instructional use. Any person violating the provisions of this subsection shall be punished by a fine of not less than one thousand dollars ($1,000) nor more than three thousand dollars ($3,000), or by imprisonment for not less than one year nor more than five (5) years, or both, and the weapons so found shall be confiscated.

§ 11-47-47. Display of weapons

No person, firm, or corporation shall display in a place of business by means of a window display any pistol, revolver, or other firearm, as defined in § 11-47-2, or any dagger, dirk, bowie knife, stiletto, metal knuckles, or blackjack; provided, that dealers in sporting goods may include in a window display pistols or revolvers upon a permit issued by the chief of police or town sergeant of any city or town.

corporation violating the provisions of this section shall be punished by a fine not
~~~~ dollars ($25.00) for the first offense and one hundred dollars ($100) for every

~~~~sion of knife during commission of crime
~~~~t or attempt to commit any crime of violence while having in his or her possession
~~~~re than three (3) inches long. Every person violating the provisions of this section
~~~~~~~~, be sentenced for a term not less than one year nor more than five (5) years and/or
fined not exceeding three thousand dollars ($3,000).

⫟ SOUTH CAROLINA ⫟
KNIFE RIGHTS MOVEMENT RATING
★ ★ ★ ★ ☆

CUTTING TO THE CHASE

South Carolina prohibits a "person carrying a deadly weapon usually used for the infliction of personal in-jury concealed about his person." A "weapon" includes "…any other type of device, or object which may be used to inflict bodily injury or death." However, the prohibition does not apply to "… dirks, knives, or razors unless they are used with the intent to commit a crime or in furtherance of a crime." If South Carolina had pre-emption, it would get a five rating.

Quick Points Concerning South Carolina's Knife Law*

KNIFE TYPE	POSSESSION	(Open/Concealed) CARRY	SALE	MANUFACTURE
Assisted Opening	Legal	Legal/Legal	Legal	Legal
Automatic/Switchblade	Legal	Legal/Legal	Legal	Legal
Ballistic	Legal	Legal/Legal	Legal	Legal
Bayonets	Legal	Legal/Legal	Legal	Legal
Bowie	Legal	Legal/Legal	Legal	Legal
Butterfly/Balisong	Legal	Legal/Legal	Legal	Legal
Combat/Survival	Legal	Legal/Legal	Legal	Legal
Dagger	Legal	Legal/Legal	Legal	Legal
Dirk	Legal	Legal/Legal	Legal	Legal
Disguised	Legal	Legal/Legal	Legal	Legal
Fixed	Legal	Legal/Legal	Legal	Legal
Folding	Legal	Legal/Legal	Legal	Legal
Gravity	Legal	Legal/Legal	Legal	Legal
Hunting/Fishing	Legal	Legal/Legal	Legal	Legal
Machete	Legal	Legal/Legal	Legal	Legal
Razor	Legal	Legal/Legal	Legal	Legal
Stiletto	Legal	Legal/Legal	Legal	Legal
Sword	Legal	Legal/Legal	Legal	Legal
Throwing	Legal	Legal/Legal	Legal	Legal
Undetectable	Legal	Legal/Legal	Legal	Legal

Pre-emption (Only State Law May Regulate, No Local Laws Permitted) – NO
*See all information above and below for more details.

SHARP TIPS ABOUT SOUTH CAROLINA'S KNIFE LAWS

South Carolina prohibits a person carrying a knife on school property. South Carolina does not have pre-emption so beware of local laws.

EDGE –U- CATIONAL --- SOUTH CAROLINA'S KNIFE LAWS

§ 16-23-405. Definition of "weapon"; confiscation and disposition of weapons used in commission or in furtherance of crime.

(A) Except for the provisions relating to rifles and shotguns in Section 16-23-460, as used in this chapter, "weapon" means firearm (rifle, shotgun, pistol, or similar device that propels a projectile through the energy of an explosive), a blackjack, a metal pipe or pole, or any other type of device, or object which may be used to inflict bodily injury or death.

(B) A person convicted of a crime, in addition to a penalty, shall have a weapon used in the commission or in furtherance of the crime confiscated. Each weapon must be delivered to the chief of police of the municipality or to the sheriff of the county if the violation occurred outside the corporate limits of a municipality. The law enforcement agency that receives the confiscated weapon may use it within the agency, transfer it to another law enforcement agency for the lawful use of that agency, trade it with a retail dealer licensed to sell pistols in this State for a pistol or other equipment approved by the agency, or destroy it. A weapon may not be disposed of until the results of all legal proceedings in which it may be involved are finally determined. A firearm seized by the State Law Enforcement Division may be kept by the division for use by its forensic laboratory.

§ 16-23-430. Carrying weapon on school property; concealed weapons.

(A) It shall be unlawful for any person, except state, county, or municipal law enforcement officers or personnel authorized by school officials, to carry on his person, while on any elementary or secondary school property, a knife, with a blade over two inches long, a blackjack, a metal pipe or pole, firearms, or any other type of weapon, device, or object which may be used to inflict bodily injury or death.

(B) This section does not apply to a person who is authorized to carry a concealed weapon pursuant to Article 4, Chapter 31, Title 23 when the weapon remains inside an attended or locked motor vehicle and is secured in a closed glove compartment, closed console, closed trunk, or in a closed container secured by an integral fastener and transported in the luggage compartment of the vehicle.

(C) A person who violates the provisions of this section is guilty of a felony and, upon conviction, must be fined not more than one thousand dollars or imprisoned not more than five years, or both. Any weapon or object used in violation of this section may be confiscated by the law enforcement division making the arrest.

§ 16-23-460. Carrying concealed weapons; forfeiture of weapons.

(A) A person carrying a deadly weapon usually used for the infliction of personal injury concealed about his person is guilty of a misdemeanor, must forfeit to the county, or, if convicted in a municipal court, to the municipality, the concealed weapon, and must be fined not less than two hundred dollars nor more than five hundred dollars or imprisoned not less than thirty days nor more than ninety days.

(B) The provisions of this section do not apply to:

(1) A person carrying a concealed weapon upon his own premises or pursuant to and in compliance with Article 4, Chapter 31 of Title 23; or

(2) peace officers in the actual discharge of their duties.

(C) The provisions of this section also do not apply to rifles, shotguns, dirks, slingshots, metal knuckles, knives, or razors unless they are used with the intent to commit a crime or in furtherance of a crime.

§ 23-31-225. Carrying concealed weapons into residences or dwellings.

No person who holds a permit issued pursuant to Article 4, Chapter 31, Title 23 may carry a concealable weapon into the residence or dwelling place of another person without the express permission of the owner or person in legal control or possession, as appropriate. A person who violates this provision is guilty of a misdemeanor and, upon conviction, must be fined not less than one thousand dollars or imprisoned for not more than one year, or both, at the discretion of the court and have his permit revoked for five years.

§ 23-31-230. Carrying concealed weapons between automobile and accommodation.

Notwithstanding any provision of law, any person may carry a concealable weapon from an automobile or other motorized conveyance to a room or other accommodation he has rented and upon which an accommodations tax has been paid.

⊹– SOUTH DAKOTA –⊹
KNIFE RIGHTS MOVEMENT RATING
★ ★ ★ ★ ☆

CUTTING TO THE CHASE

If South Dakota had pre-emption it would get a five rating. South Dakota bans possession of no knife by feature or type. It does prohibit a "…person who conceals on or about his or her person a controlled or dangerous weapon with intent to commit a felony." (emphasis added) "Dangerous weapon" includes any "…knife, or device, instrument, material, or substance, whether animate or inanimate, which is calculated or designed to inflict death or serious bodily harm, or by the manner in which it is used is likely to inflict death or serious bodily harm."

Quick Points Concerning South Dakota's Knife Law*

KNIFE TYPE	POSSESSION	(Open/Concealed) CARRY	SALE	MANUFACTURE
Assisted Opening	Legal	Legal/Legal	Legal	Legal
Automatic/Switchblade	Legal	Legal/Legal	Legal	Legal
Ballistic	Legal	Legal/Legal	Legal	Legal
Bayonets	Legal	Legal/Legal	Legal	Legal
Bowie	Legal	Legal/Legal	Legal	Legal
Butterfly/Balisong	Legal	Legal/Legal	Legal	Legal
Combat/Survival	Legal	Legal/Legal	Legal	Legal
Dagger	Legal	Legal/Legal	Legal	Legal
Dirk	Legal	Legal/Legal	Legal	Legal
Disguised	Legal	Legal/Legal	Legal	Legal
Fixed	Legal	Legal/Legal	Legal	Legal
Folding	Legal	Legal/Legal	Legal	Legal
Gravity	Legal	Legal/Legal	Legal	Legal
Hunting/Fishing	Legal	Legal/Legal	Legal	Legal
Machete	Legal	Legal/Legal	Legal	Legal
Razor	Legal	Legal/Legal	Legal	Legal
Stiletto	Legal	Legal/Legal	Legal	Legal
Sword	Legal	Legal/Legal	Legal	Legal
Throwing	Legal	Legal/Legal	Legal	Legal
Undetectable	Legal	Legal/Legal	Legal	Legal

Pre-emption (Only State Law May Regulate, No Local Laws Permitted) – NO
*See all information above and below for more details.

SHARP TIPS ABOUT SOUTH DAKOTA'S KNIFE LAWS

South Dakota prohibits "dangerous weapons" in courthouses. South Dakota does not have pre-emption, so beware of local laws.

EDGE –U- CATIONAL --- SOUTH DAKOTA'S KNIFE LAWS

§ 22-1-2. Definition of terms

Terms used in this title mean:

(10) "Dangerous weapon" or "deadly weapon," any firearm, stun gun, knife, or device, instrument, material, or substance, whether animate or inanimate, which is calculated or designed to inflict death or serious bodily harm, or by the manner in which it is used is likely to inflict death or serious bodily harm;

§ 22-14-8. Concealment of weapon with intent to commit felony--Felony

Any person who conceals on or about his or her person a controlled or dangerous weapon with intent to commit a felony is guilty of a Class 5 felony.

§ 22-14-23. Possession in county courthouse--Misdemeanor

Except as provided in § 22-14-24, any person who knowingly possesses or causes to be present any firearm or other dangerous weapon, in any county courthouse, or attempts to do so, is guilty of a Class 1 misdemeanor.

§ 22-14-24. Exceptions to penalty for possession in a county courthouse

The provisions of § 22-14-23 do not apply to:

(1) The lawful performance of official duties by an officer, agent, or employee of the United States, the state, political subdivision thereof, or a municipality, who is authorized by law to engage in or supervise the prevention, detection, investigation, or prosecution of any violation of law or an officer of the court;

(2) Possession by a judge or magistrate;

(3) The possession of a firearm or other dangerous weapon by a federal or state official or member of the armed services if such possession is authorized by law; or

(4) The lawful carrying of firearms, or other dangerous weapons in a county courthouse incident to hunting, or gun safety course or to other lawful purposes.

⭲– TENNESSEE –⭰
KNIFE RIGHTS MOVEMENT RATING
★ ★ ★ ★ ★

CUTTING TO THE CHASE

Tennessee has recently become one of the states that stand tall for knife liberty. It repealed its antiquated knife laws and passed pre-emption as well.

Quick Points Concerning Tennessee's Knife Law*

KNIFE TYPE	POSSESSION	(Open/Concealed) CARRY	SALE	MANUFACTURE
Assisted Opening	Legal	Legal/Legal	Legal	Legal
Automatic/Switchblade	Legal	Legal/Legal	Legal	Legal
Ballistic	Legal	Legal/Legal	Legal	Legal

KNIFE TYPE	POSSESSION	(Open/Concealed) CARRY	SALE	MANUFACTURE
Bayonets	Legal	Legal/Legal	Legal	Legal
Bowie	Legal	Legal/Legal	Legal	Legal
Butterfly/Balisong	Legal	Legal/Legal	Legal	Legal
Combat/Survival	Legal	Legal/Legal	Legal	Legal
Dagger	Legal	Legal/Legal	Legal	Legal
Dirk	Legal	Legal/Legal	Legal	Legal
Disguised	Legal	Legal/Legal	Legal	Legal
Fixed	Legal	Legal/Legal	Legal	Legal
Folding	Legal	Legal/Legal	Legal	Legal
Gravity	Legal	Legal/Legal	Legal	Legal
Hunting/Fishing	Legal	Legal/Legal	Legal	Legal
Machete	Legal	Legal/Legal	Legal	Legal
Razor	Legal	Legal/Legal	Legal	Legal
Stiletto	Legal	Legal/Legal	Legal	Legal
Sword	Legal	Legal/Legal	Legal	Legal
Throwing	Legal	Legal/Legal	Legal	Legal
Undetectable	Legal	Legal/Legal	Legal	Legal

Pre-emption (Only State Law May Regulate, No Local Laws Permitted) – YES
*See all information above and below for more details.

SHARP TIPS ABOUT TENNESSEE'S KNIFE LAWS

Do not carry knives on school grounds or in school buildings. No knives in courthouses.

EDGE –U- CATIONAL --- TENNESSEE'S KNIFE LAWS
§ 39-17-1301. Definitions

As used in this part, unless the context otherwise requires:

(9) "Knife" means any bladed hand instrument that is capable of inflicting serious bodily injury or death by cutting or stabbing a person with the instrument;

(17) "Switchblade knife" means any knife that has a blade which opens automatically by:

(A) Hand pressure applied to a button or other device in the handle; or

(B) Operation of gravity or inertia; and

§ 39-17-1302. Prohibited weapons

(a) A person commits an offense who intentionally or knowingly possesses, manufactures, transports, repairs or sells:

(8) Any other implement for infliction of serious bodily injury or death that has no common lawful purpose.

(b) It is a defense to prosecution under this section that the person's conduct:

(1) Was incident to the performance of official duty and pursuant to military regulations in the army, navy, air force, coast guard or marine service of the United States or the Tennessee national guard, or was incident to the performance of official duty in a governmental law enforcement agency or a penal institution;

(2) Was incident to engaging in a lawful commercial or business transaction with an organization identified in subdivision (b)(1);

(4) Was incident to using the weapon in a manner reasonably related to a lawful dramatic performance or scientific research;

(5) Was incident to displaying the weapon in a public museum or exhibition;

(6) Was licensed by the state of Tennessee as a manufacturer, importer or dealer in weapons; provided, that the manufacture, import, purchase, possession, sale or disposition of weapons is authorized and incident to carrying on the business for which licensed and is for scientific or research purposes or sale or disposition to an organization designated in subdivision (b)(1); or

(c) It is an affirmative defense to prosecution under this section that the person must prove by a preponderance of the evidence that:

(1) The person's conduct was relative to dealing with the weapon solely as a curio, ornament or keepsake, and if the weapon is a type described in subdivisions (a)(1)-(5), that it was in a nonfunctioning condition and could not readily be made operable; or

(2) The possession was brief and occurred as a consequence of having found the weapon or taken it from an aggressor.

(d)(1) An offense under subdivision (a)(1) is a Class B felony.

(2) An offense under subdivisions (a)(2)-(5) is a Class E felony.

(3) An offense under subdivision (a)(6) is a Class C felony.

(4) An offense under subdivisions (a)(7)-(8) is a Class A misdemeanor

§ 39-17-1306. Judicial proceedings; carrying weapons
(a) No person shall intentionally, knowingly, or recklessly carry on or about the person while inside any room in which judicial proceedings are in progress any weapon prohibited by § 39-17-1302(a), for the purpose of going armed; provided, that if the weapon carried is a firearm, the person is in violation of this section regardless of whether the weapon is carried for the purpose of going armed.

(b) Any person violating subsection (a) commits a Class E felony.

(c) Subsection (a) shall not apply to any person who:

(1) Is in the actual discharge of official duties as a law enforcement officer, or is employed in the army, air force, navy, coast guard or marine service of the United States or any member of the Tennessee national guard in the line of duty and pursuant to military regulations, or is in the actual discharge of official duties as a guard employed by a penal institution, or as a bailiff, marshal or other court officer who has responsibility for protecting persons or property or providing security;

(3) Is in the actual discharge of official duties as a judge, and:

§ 39-17-1307. Carrying or possession of weapons
(d)(1) A person commits an offense who possesses a deadly weapon other than a firearm with the intent to employ it during the commission of, attempt to commit, or escape from a dangerous offense as defined in § 39-17-1324.

(2) A person commits an offense who possesses any deadly weapon with the intent to employ it during the commission of, attempt to commit, or escape from any offense not defined as a dangerous offense by § 39-17-1324.

(3)(A) Except as provided in subdivision (d)(3)(B), a violation of this subsection (d) is a Class E felony.

(B) A violation of this subsection (d) is a Class E felony with a maximum fine of six thousand dollars ($6,000), if the deadly weapon is a switchblade knife.

§ 39-17-1309. Carrying or possession of weapons; school buildings and grounds
(a) As used in this section, "weapon of like kind" includes razors and razor blades, except those used

solely for personal shaving, and any sharp pointed or edged instrument, except unaltered nail files and clips and tools used solely for preparation of food, instruction and maintenance.

(b)(1) It is an offense for any person to possess or carry, whether openly or concealed, with the intent to go armed, any firearm, explosive, explosive weapon, bowie knife, hawk bill knife, ice pick, dagger, slingshot, leaded cane, switchblade knife, blackjack, knuckles or any other weapon of like kind, not used solely for instructional or school-sanctioned ceremonial purposes, in any public or private school building or bus, on any public or private school campus, grounds, recreation area, athletic field or any other property owned, used or operated by any board of education, school, college or university board of trustees, regents or directors for the administration of any public or private educational institution.

(2) A violation of this subsection (b) is a Class E felony.

(2) As used in this subsection (d), "prominent locations about a school" includes, but is not limited to, sports arenas, gymnasiums, stadiums and cafeterias.

(e) Subsections (b) and (c) do not apply to the following persons:

(1) Persons employed in the army, air force, navy, coast guard or marine service of the United States or any member of the Tennessee national guard when in discharge of their official duties and acting under orders requiring them to carry arms or weapons;

(2) Civil officers of the United States in the discharge of their official duties;

(3) Officers and soldiers of the militia and the national guard when called into actual service;

(4) Officers of the state, or of any county, city or town, charged with the enforcement of the laws of the state, when in the discharge of their official duties;

(5) Any pupils who are members of the reserve officers training corps or pupils enrolled in a course of instruction or members of a club or team, and who are required to carry arms or weapons in the discharge of their official class or team duties;

(6) Any private police employed by the administration or board of trustees of any public or private institution of higher education in the discharge of their duties; and

(7) Any registered security guard/officer who meets the requirements of title 62, chapter 35, and who is discharging the officer's official duties.

§ 39-17-1310. Carrying or possession of weapons; school buildings and grounds; affirmative defenses

It is an affirmative defense to prosecution under § 39-17-1309(a)-(d) that the person's behavior was in strict compliance with the requirements of one (1) of the following classifications:

(1) A person hunting during the lawful hunting season on lands owned by any public or private educational institution and designated as open to hunting by the administrator of the educational institution;

(2) A person possessing unloaded hunting weapons while transversing the grounds of any public or private educational institution for the purpose of gaining access to public or private lands open to hunting with the intent to hunt on the public or private lands unless the lands of the educational institution are posted prohibiting entry;

(3) A person possessing guns or knives when conducting or attending "gun and knife shows" and the program has been approved by the administrator of the educational institution; or

(4) A person entering the property for the sole purpose of delivering or picking up passengers and who does not remove, utilize or allow to be removed or utilized any weapon from the vehicle.

§ 39-17-1364. Purchase and shipment of weapons to residence

Notwithstanding § 39-17-1307, or any other law, it is lawful in this state for a person to purchase, and have shipped directly to such person's residence, the following:

(2) A knife, even if the blade is in excess of four inches (4); or

(3) A sword or bayonet, whether for ornamental, ceremonial, historical, theatrical or collecting purposes, or otherwise.

⸻ TEXAS ⸻
KNIFE RIGHTS MOVEMENT RATING
★ ★ ★ ☆ ☆

CUTTING TO THE CHASE

One would expect better of Texas, a state that is generally believed to be very supportive of the Second Amendment. When it comes to firearms maybe so, but with knives, not so much. Texas bans both open and concealed carry of a knife with a blade over five and one-half inches, tomahawks, throwing knives, throwing stars, daggers, dirks, stilettos, poniards, bowie knives, swords and spears. There is exception for a person's premises, motor vehicle or watercraft.

Quick Points Concerning Texas' Knife Law*

KNIFE TYPE	POSSESSION	(Open/Concealed) CARRY	SALE	MANUFACTURE
Assisted Opening	Legal	Gray/Gray	Legal	Legal
Automatic/Switchblade	Legal	Gray/Gray	Legal	Legal
Ballistic	Legal	Gray/Gray	Legal	Legal
Bayonets	Legal	Gray/Gray	Legal	Legal
Bowie	Legal	Prohibited/Prohibited	Legal	Legal
Butterfly/Balisong	Legal	Gray/Gray	Legal	Legal
Combat/Survival	Legal	Gray/Gray	Legal	Legal
Dagger	Legal	Prohibited/Prohibited	Legal	Legal
Dirk	Legal	Prohibited/Prohibited	Legal	Legal
Disguised	Legal	Gray/Gray	Legal	Legal
Fixed	Legal	Legal/Gray	Legal	Legal
Folding	Legal	Gray/Gray	Legal	Legal
Gravity	Legal	Gray/Gray	Legal	Legal
Hunting/Fishing	Legal	Gray/Gray	Legal	Legal
Machete	Legal	Gray/Gray	Legal	Legal
Razor	Legal	Gray/Gray	Legal	Legal
Stiletto	Legal	Prohibited/Prohibited	Legal	Legal
Sword	Legal	Prohibited/Prohibited	Legal	Legal
Throwing	Legal	Prohibited/Prohibited	Legal	Legal
Undetectable	Legal	Gray/Gray	Legal	Legal

Pre-emption (Only State Law May Regulate, No Local Laws Permitted) – YES
*See all information above and below for more details.

SHARP TIPS ABOUT TEXAS' KNIFE LAWS

Texas did repeal its ban on possessing switchblades and gravity knives. Possession is prohibited of a knife with a blade over five and one-half inches, tomahawks, throwing knives, throwing stars, daggers, dirks, stilettos, poniards, bowie knives, swords and spears in a school building, on school grounds, in school bus, at polling place, courthouse, government building, racetrack, airport, within 1000 feet of a place of execution, and being within 1000 feet of any of these prohibited places.

EDGE –U-CATIONAL --- TEXAS' KNIFE LAWS
§ 46.01. Definitions

In this chapter:

(1) "Club" means an instrument that is specially designed, made, or adapted for the purpose of inflicting serious bodily injury or death by striking a person with the instrument, and includes but is not limited to the following:

(D) tomahawk.

(6) "Illegal knife" means a:

(A) knife with a blade over five and one-half inches;

(B) hand instrument designed to cut or stab another by being thrown;

(C) dagger, including but not limited to a dirk, stiletto, and poniard;

(D) bowie knife;

(E) sword; or

(F) spear.

(7) "Knife" means any bladed hand instrument that is capable of inflicting serious bodily injury or death by cutting or stabbing a person with the instrument.

(11) "Switchblade knife" means any knife that has a blade that folds, closes, or retracts into the handle or sheath and that opens automatically by pressure applied to a button or other device located on the handle or opens or releases a blade from the handle or sheath by the force of gravity or by the application of centrifugal force. The term does not include a knife that has a spring, detent, or other mechanism designed to create a bias toward closure and that requires exertion applied to the blade by hand, wrist, or arm to overcome the bias toward closure and open the knife.

§ 46.02. Unlawful Carrying Weapons

(a) A person commits an offense if the person intentionally, knowingly, or recklessly carries on or about his or her person a handgun, illegal knife, or club if the person is not:

(1) on the person's own premises or premises under the person's control; or

(2) inside of or directly en route to a motor vehicle or watercraft that is owned by the person or under the person's control.

(a-2) For purposes of this section, "premises" includes real property and a recreational vehicle that is being used as living quarters, regardless of whether that use is temporary or permanent. In this subsection, "recreational vehicle" means a motor vehicle primarily designed as temporary living quarters or a vehicle that contains temporary living quarters and is designed to be towed by a motor vehicle. The term includes a travel trailer, camping trailer, truck camper, motor home, and horse trailer with living quarters.

(a-3) For purposes of this section, "watercraft" means any boat, motorboat, vessel, or personal watercraft, other than a seaplane on water, used or capable of being used for transportation on water.

(b) Except as provided by Subsection (c), an offense under this section is a Class A misdemeanor.

(c) An offense under this section is a felony of the third degree if the offense is committed on any premises licensed or issued a permit by this state for the sale of alcoholic beverages.

§ 46.03. Places Weapons Prohibited

(a) A person commits an offense if the person intentionally, knowingly, or recklessly possesses or goes with a firearm, illegal knife, club, or prohibited weapon listed in Section 46.05(a):

(1) on the physical premises of a school or educational institution, any grounds or building on which an activity sponsored by a school or educational institution is being conducted, or a passenger transportation vehicle of a school or educational institution, whether the school or educational institution is public or private, unless pursuant to written regulations or written authorization of the institution;

(2) on the premises of a polling place on the day of an election or while early voting is in progress;

(3) on the premises of any government court or offices utilized by the court, unless pursuant to written regulations or written authorization of the court;

(4) on the premises of a racetrack;

(5) in or into a secured area of an airport; or

(6) within 1,000 feet of premises the location of which is designated by the Texas Department of Criminal Justice as a place of execution under Article 43.19, Code of Criminal Procedure, on a day that a sentence of death is set to be imposed on the designated premises and the person received notice that:

(A) going within 1,000 feet of the premises with a weapon listed under this subsection was prohibited; or

(B) possessing a weapon listed under this subsection within 1,000 feet of the premises was prohibited.

(c) In this section:

(1) "Premises" has the meaning assigned by Section 46.035.

(2) "Secured area" means an area of an airport terminal building to which access is controlled by the inspection of persons and property under federal law.

§ 46.06. Unlawful Transfer of Certain Weapons

(a) A person commits an offense if the person:

(2) intentionally or knowingly sells, rents, leases, or gives or offers to sell, rent, lease, or give to any child younger than 18 years any firearm, club, or illegal knife;

(c) It is an affirmative defense to prosecution under Subsection (a)(2) that the transfer was to a minor whose parent or the person having legal custody of the minor had given written permission for the sale or, if the transfer was other than a sale, the parent or person having legal custody had given effective consent.

(d) An offense under this section is a Class A misdemeanor, except that an offense under Subsection (a)(2) is a state jail felony if the weapon that is the subject of the offense is a handgun.

§ 46.11. Penalty If Offense Committed Within Weapon-Free School Zone

(a) Except as provided by Subsection (b), the punishment prescribed for an offense under this chapter is increased to the punishment prescribed for the next highest category of offense if it is shown beyond a reasonable doubt on the trial of the offense that the actor committed the offense in a place that the actor knew was:

(1) within 300 feet of the premises of a school; or

(2) on premises where:

(A) an official school function is taking place; or

(B) an event sponsored or sanctioned by the University Interscholastic League is taking place.

(b) This section does not apply to an offense under Section 46.03(a)(1).

(c) In this section:

(1) "Premises" has the meaning assigned by Section 481.134, Health and Safety Code.

(2) "School" means a private or public elementary or secondary school.

⊹ UTAH ⊹
KNIFE RIGHTS MOVEMENT RATING
★ ★ ★ ★ ★

CUTTING TO THE CHASE

Utah has excellent knife freedom. No knives are banned by feature. Utah was one of the nine states including Arizona, New Hampshire, Oklahoma, Nevada, Texas, Georgia, Kansas, Alaska & Tennessee to recently enact pre-emption.

Quick Points Concerning Utah's Knife Law*

KNIFE TYPE	POSSESSION	(Open/Concealed) CARRY	SALE	MANUFACTURE
Assisted Opening	Legal	Legal/Legal	Legal	Legal
Automatic/Switchblade	Legal	Legal/Legal	Legal	Legal
Ballistic	Legal	Legal/Legal	Legal	Legal
Bayonets	Legal	Legal/Legal	Legal	Legal
Bowie	Legal	Legal/Legal	Legal	Legal
Butterfly/Balisong	Legal	Legal/Legal	Legal	Legal
Combat/Survival	Legal	Legal/Legal	Legal	Legal
Dagger	Legal	Legal/Legal	Legal	Legal
Dirk	Legal	Legal/Legal	Legal	Legal
Disguised	Legal	Legal/Legal	Legal	Legal
Fixed	Legal	Legal/Legal	Legal	Legal
Folding	Legal	Legal/Legal	Legal	Legal
Gravity	Legal	Legal/Legal	Legal	Legal
Hunting/Fishing	Legal	Legal/Legal	Legal	Legal
Machete	Legal	Legal/Legal	Legal	Legal
Razor	Legal	Legal/Legal	Legal	Legal
Stiletto	Legal	Legal/Legal	Legal	Legal
Sword	Legal	Legal/Legal	Legal	Legal
Throwing	Legal	Legal/Legal	Legal	Legal
Undetectable	Legal	Legal/Legal	Legal	Legal

Pre-emption (Only State Law May Regulate, No Local Laws Permitted) – YES
*See all information above and below for more details.

SHARP TIPS ABOUT UTAH'S KNIFE LAWS

Possession of a knife in a courthouse is prohibited. Possession by convicted felons and other prohibited person is generally prohibited. Sale of a sword, knife, spear, throwing star, throwing dart, or any other martial arts weapon to those under 18 without written consent of the parent or guardian is prohibited. Do not possess a knife while intoxicated, at school premises, jails, police stations, mental health facilities, "secure areas," or at an airport.

EDGE –U- CATIONAL --- UTAH'S KNIFE LAWS
U.C. 1953 § 10-8-47.5. Knives regulated by state

(1) As used in this section, "knife" means a cutting instrument that includes a sharpened or pointed blade.

(2) The authority to regulate a knife is reserved to the state except where the Legislature specifically delegates responsibility to a municipality.

(3)(a) Unless specifically authorized by the Legislature or, subject to Subsection (3)(b), a municipal ordinance with a criminal penalty, a municipality may not enact or enforce an ordinance or a regulation pertaining to a knife.

(b) A municipality may not enact an ordinance with a criminal penalty pertaining to a knife that is:

(i) more restrictive than a state criminal penalty pertaining to a knife; or

(ii) has a greater criminal penalty than a state penalty pertaining to a knife.

U.C. 1953 § 76-8-311.1. Secure areas--Items prohibited--Penalty

(1) In addition to the definitions in Section 76-10-501, as used in this section:

(a) "Correctional facility" has the same meaning as defined in Section 76-8-311.3.

(c) "Law enforcement facility" means a facility which is owned, leased, or operated by a law enforcement agency.

(d) "Mental health facility" has the same meaning as defined in Section 62A-15-602.

(e)(i) "Secure area" means any area into which certain persons are restricted from transporting any firearm, ammunition, dangerous weapon, or explosive.

(ii) A "secure area" may not include any area normally accessible to the public.

(2)(a) A person in charge of a correctional, law enforcement, or mental health facility may establish secure areas within the facility and may prohibit or control by rule any firearm, ammunition, dangerous weapon, or explosive.

(b) Subsections (2)(a), (3), (4), (5), and (6) apply to higher education secure area hearing rooms referred to in Subsections 53B-3-103(2)(a)(ii) and (b).

(3) At least one notice shall be prominently displayed at each entrance to an area in which a firearm, ammunition, dangerous weapon, or explosive is restricted.

(4)(a) Provisions shall be made to provide a secure weapons storage area so that persons entering the secure area may store their weapons prior to entering the secure area.

(b) The entity operating the facility shall be responsible for weapons while they are stored in the storage area.

(5) It is a defense to any prosecution under this section that the accused, in committing the act made criminal by this section, acted in conformity with the facility's rule or policy established pursuant to this section.

(6)(a) Any person who knowingly or intentionally transports into a secure area of a facility any firearm, ammunition, or dangerous weapon is guilty of a third degree felony.

(b) Any person violates Section 76-10-306 who knowingly or intentionally transports, possesses, distributes, or sells any explosive in a secure area of a facility.

§ 76–10–501 Definitions

As used in this part:

(3)(a) "Concealed dangerous weapon" firearm" means a dangerous weapon firearm that is:

(i) covered, hidden, or secreted in a manner that the public would not be aware of its presence; and

(ii) readily accessible for immediate use.

(b) A dangerous weapon is not a concealed dangerous weapon if it is a firearm which is unloaded and is securely encased.

(b) A firearm that is unloaded and securely encased is not a concealed firearm for the purposes of this part.

(6)(a) "Dangerous weapon" means:

(ii) an object that in the manner of its use or intended use is capable of causing death or serious bodily injury.

(b) The following factors are used in determining whether any object, other than a firearm, is a dangerous weapon:

(i) the location and circumstances in which the object was used or possessed;

(ii) the primary purpose for which the object was made;

(iii) the character of the wound, if any, produced by the object's unlawful use;

(iv) the manner in which the object was unlawfully used;

(v) whether the manner in which the object is used or possessed constitutes a potential imminent threat to public safety; and

(vi) the lawful purposes for which the object may be used.

(7) "Dealer" means a person who is:

(a) licensed under 18 U.S.C. Sec. 923; and

(b) engaged in the business of selling, leasing, or otherwise transferring a handgun, whether the person is a retail or wholesale dealer, pawnbroker, or otherwise.

(16) "Readily accessible for immediate use" means that a firearm or other dangerous weapon is carried on the person or within such close proximity and in such a manner that it can be retrieved and used as readily as if carried on the person.

(17) "Residence" means an improvement to real property used or occupied as a primary or secondary residence.

(20) "State entity" means a department, commission, board, council, agency, institution, officer, corporation, fund, division, office, committee, authority, laboratory, library, unit, bureau, panel, or other administrative unit of the state.

(21) "Violent felony" has the same meaning as defined in Section 76–3–203.5.

U.C. 1953 § 76-10-503. Restrictions on possession, purchase, transfer, and ownership of dangerous weapons by certain persons--Exceptions

(1) For purposes of this section:

(a) A Category I restricted person is a person who:

(i) has been convicted of any violent felony as defined in Section 76-3-203.5;

(ii) is on probation or parole for any felony;

(iii) is on parole from a secure facility as defined in Section 62A-7-101;

(iv) within the last 10 years has been adjudicated delinquent for an offense which if committed by an adult would have been a violent felony as defined in Section 76-3-203.5; or

(v) is an alien who is illegally or unlawfully in the United States.

(b) A Category II restricted person is a person who:

(i) has been convicted of any felony;

(ii) within the last seven years has been adjudicated delinquent for an offense which if committed by an adult would have been a felony;

(iii) is an unlawful user of a controlled substance as defined in Section 58-37-2;

(iv) is in possession of a dangerous weapon and is knowingly and intentionally in unlawful possession of a Schedule I or II controlled substance as defined in Section 58-37-2;

(v) has been found not guilty by reason of insanity for a felony offense;

(vi) has been found mentally incompetent to stand trial for a felony offense;

(vii) has been adjudicated as mentally defective as provided in the Brady Handgun Violence Prevention Act, Pub. L. No. 103-159, 107 Stat. 1536 (1993),1 or has been committed to a mental institution;

(viii) has been dishonorably discharged from the armed forces; or

(ix) has renounced his citizenship after having been a citizen of the United States.

(c) As used in this section, a conviction of a felony or adjudication of delinquency for an offense which would be a felony if committed by an adult does not include:

(i) a conviction or adjudication of delinquency for an offense pertaining to antitrust violations, unfair trade practices, restraint of trade, or other similar offenses relating to the regulation of business practices not involving theft or fraud; or

(ii) a conviction or adjudication of delinquency which, according to the law of the jurisdiction in which it occurred, has been expunged, set aside, reduced to a misdemeanor by court order, pardoned or regarding which the person's civil rights have been restored unless the pardon, reduction, expungement, or restoration of civil rights expressly provides that the person may not ship, transport, possess, or receive firearms.

(d) It is the burden of the defendant in a criminal case to provide evidence that a conviction or adjudication of delinquency is subject to an exception provided in Subsection (1)(c), after which it is the burden of the state to prove beyond a reasonable doubt that the conviction or adjudication of delinquency is not subject to that exception.

(2) A Category I restricted person who intentionally or knowingly agrees, consents, offers, or arranges to purchase, transfer, possess, use, or have under the person's custody or control, or who intentionally or knowingly purchases, transfers, possesses, uses, or has under the person's custody or control:

(b) any dangerous weapon other than a firearm is guilty of a third degree felony.

(3) A Category II restricted person who intentionally or knowingly purchases, transfers, possesses, uses, or has under the person's custody or control:

(b) any dangerous weapon other than a firearm is guilty of a class A misdemeanor.

(5) If a higher penalty than is prescribed in this section is provided in another section for one who purchases, transfers, possesses, uses, or has under this custody or control any dangerous weapon, the penalties of that section control.

(7)(a) It is an affirmative defense to transferring a firearm or other dangerous weapon by a person restricted under Subsection (2) or (3) that the firearm or dangerous weapon:

(i) was possessed by the person or was under the person's custody or control before the person became a restricted person;

(ii) was not used in or possessed during the commission of a crime or subject to disposition under Section 24-3-103;

(iii) is not being held as evidence by a court or law enforcement agency;

(iv) was transferred to a person not legally prohibited from possessing the weapon; and

(v) unless a different time is ordered by the court, was transferred within 10 days of the person becoming a restricted person.

(b) Subsection (7)(a) is not a defense to the use, purchase, or possession on the person of a firearm or other dangerous weapon by a restricted person.

(8)(a) A person may not sell, transfer, or otherwise dispose of any firearm or dangerous weapon to any person, knowing that the recipient is a person described in Subsection (1)(a) or (b).

(b) A person who violates Subsection (8)(a) when the recipient is:

(i) a person described in Subsection (1)(a) and the transaction involves a firearm, is guilty of a second degree felony;

(ii) a person described in Subsection (1)(a) and the transaction involves any dangerous weapon other than a firearm, and the transferor has knowledge that the recipient intends to use the weapon for any unlawful purpose, is guilty of a third degree felony;

(iii) a person described in Subsection (1)(b) and the transaction involves a firearm, is guilty of a third degree felony; or

(iv) a person described in Subsection (1)(b) and the transaction involves any dangerous weapon other than a firearm, and the transferor has knowledge that the recipient intends to use the weapon for any unlawful purpose, is guilty of a class A misdemeanor.

(9)(a) A person may not knowingly solicit, persuade, encourage or entice a dealer or other person to sell, transfer or otherwise dispose of a firearm or dangerous weapon under circumstances which the person knows would be a violation of the law.

(b) A person may not provide to a dealer or other person any information that the person knows to be materially false information with intent to deceive the dealer or other person about the legality of a sale, transfer or other disposition of a firearm or dangerous weapon.

(c) "Materially false information" means information that portrays an illegal transaction as legal or a legal transaction as illegal.

(d) A person who violates this Subsection (9) is guilty of:

(i) a third degree felony if the transaction involved a firearm; or

(ii) a class A misdemeanor if the transaction involved a dangerous weapon other than a firearm.

U.C. 1953 § 76-10-505.5. Possession of a dangerous weapon, firearm, or short barreled shotgun on or about school premises--Penalties

(1) As used in this section, "on or about school premises" means:

(a)(i) in a public or private elementary or secondary school; or

(ii) on the grounds of any of those schools;

(b)(i) in a public or private institution of higher education; or

(ii) on the grounds of a public or private institution of higher education; and

(iii)(A) inside the building where a preschool or child care is being held, if the entire building is being used for the operation of the preschool or child care; or

(B) if only a portion of a building is being used to operate a preschool or child care, in that room or rooms where the preschool or child care operation is being held.

(2) A person may not possess any dangerous weapon, firearm, or short barreled shotgun, as those terms are defined in Section 76-10-501, at a place that the person knows, or has reasonable cause to believe, is on or about school premises as defined in this section.

(3)(a) Possession of a dangerous weapon on or about school premises is a class B misdemeanor.

(4) This section does not apply if:

(a) the person is authorized to possess a firearm as provided under Section 53-5-704, 53-5-705, 76-10-511, or 76-10-523, or as otherwise authorized by law;

(b) the possession is approved by the responsible school administrator;

(c) the item is present or to be used in connection with a lawful, approved activity and is in the possession or under the control of the person responsible for its possession or use; or

(d) the possession is:

(i) at the person's place of residence or on the person's property; or

(ii) in any vehicle lawfully under the person's control, other than a vehicle owned by the school or used by the school to transport students.

(5) This section does not prohibit prosecution of a more serious weapons offense that may occur on or about school premises.

U.C. 1953 § 76-10-509. Possession of dangerous weapon by minor

(1) A minor under 18 years of age may not possess a dangerous weapon unless he:

(a) has the permission of his parent or guardian to have the weapon; or

(b) is accompanied by a parent or guardian while he has the weapon in his possession.

(2) Any minor under 14 years of age in possession of a dangerous weapon shall be accompanied by a responsible adult.

(3) Any person who violates this section is guilty of:

(a) a class B misdemeanor upon the first offense; and

(b) a class A misdemeanor for each subsequent offense.

U.C. 1953 § 76-10-528. Carrying a dangerous weapon while under influence of alcohol or drugs unlawful

(1) Any person who carries a dangerous weapon while under the influence of alcohol or a controlled substance as defined in Section 58-37-2 is guilty of a class B misdemeanor. Under the influence means the same level of influence or blood or breath alcohol concentration as provided in Subsections 41-6a-502(1)(a) through (c).

(2) It is not a defense to prosecution under this section that the person:

(a) is licensed in the pursuit of wildlife of any kind; or

(b) has a valid permit to carry a concealed firearm.

U.C. 1953 § 76-10-529. Possession of dangerous weapons, firearms, or explosives in airport secure areas prohibited--Penalty

(1) As used in this section:

(a) "Airport authority" has the same meaning as defined in Section 72-10-102.

(b) "Dangerous weapon" is the same as defined in Section 76-10-501

(c) "Explosive" is the same as defined for "explosive, chemical, or incendiary device" in Section 76-10-306

(d) "Firearm" is the same as defined in Section 76-10-501.

(2)(a) Within a secure area of an airport established pursuant to this section, a person, including a person licensed to carry a concealed firearm under Title 53, Chapter 5, Part 7, Concealed Firearm Act, is guilty of:

(i) a class A misdemeanor if the person knowingly or intentionally possesses any dangerous weapon or firearm;

(ii) an infraction if the person recklessly or with criminal negligence possesses any dangerous weapon or firearm; or

(iii) a violation of Section 76-10-306 if the person transports, possesses, distributes, or sells any explosive, chemical, or incendiary device.

(b) Subsection (2)(a) does not apply to:

(i) persons exempted under Section 76-10-523; and

(ii) members of the state or federal military forces while engaged in the performance of their official duties.

(3) An airport authority, county, or municipality regulating the airport may:

(a) establish any secure area located beyond the main area where the public generally buys tickets, checks and retrieves luggage; and

(b) use reasonable means, including mechanical, electronic, x-ray, or any other device, to detect dangerous weapons, firearms, or explosives concealed in baggage or upon the person of any individual attempting to enter the secure area.

(4) At least one notice shall be prominently displayed at each entrance to a secure area in which a dangerous weapon, firearm, or explosive is restricted.

(5) Upon the discovery of any dangerous weapon, firearm, or explosive, the airport authority, county, or municipality, the employees, or other personnel administering the secure area may:

(a) require the individual to deliver the item to the air freight office or airline ticket counter;

(b) require the individual to exit the secure area; or

(c) obtain possession or retain custody of the item until it is transferred to law enforcement officers.

⫷ **VERMONT** ⫸
KNIFE RIGHTS MOVEMENT RATING
★ ★ ★ ★ ☆

CUTTING TO THE CHASE
Vermont bans switchblades with blades three inches or longer and does not have pre-emption. Other than those issues, Vermont is very knife friendly.

Quick Points Concerning Vermont's Knife Law*

KNIFE TYPE	POSSESSION	(Open/Concealed) CARRY	SALE	MANUFACTURE
Assisted Opening	Legal	Legal/Legal	Legal	Legal
Automatic/Switchblade	Prohibited	Prohibited/Prohibited	Prohibited	Prohibited
Ballistic	Legal	Legal/Legal	Legal	Legal
Bayonets	Legal	Legal/Legal	Legal	Legal
Bowie	Legal	Legal/Legal	Legal	Legal
Butterfly/Balisong	Legal	Legal/Legal	Legal	Legal
Combat/Survival	Legal	Legal/Legal	Legal	Legal
Dagger	Legal	Legal/Legal	Legal	Legal
Dirk	Legal	Legal/Legal	Legal	Legal
Disguised	Legal	Legal/Legal	Legal	Legal
Fixed	Legal	Legal/Legal	Legal	Legal
Folding	Legal	Legal/Legal	Legal	Legal
Gravity	Legal	Legal/Legal	Legal	Legal
Hunting/Fishing	Legal	Legal/Legal	Legal	Legal
Machete	Legal	Legal/Legal	Legal	Legal
Razor	Legal	Legal/Legal	Legal	Legal
Stiletto	Legal	Legal/Legal	Legal	Legal
Sword	Legal	Legal/Legal	Legal	Legal
Throwing	Legal	Legal/Legal	Legal	Legal
Undetectable	Legal	Legal/Legal	Legal	Legal

<u>Pre-emption</u> (Only State Law May Regulate, No Local Laws Permitted) – NO
*See all information above and below for more details.

SHARP TIPS ABOUT VERMONT'S KNIFE LAWS
Do not carry a knife "with the intent or avowed purpose of injuring a fellow man," or at state institutions, on school property or buildings, or in courthouses. There is no pre-emption, so beware of local laws.

EDGE -U- CATIONAL --- VERMONT'S KNIFE LAWS

13 V.S. § 1021. Definitions

For the purpose of this chapter:

(1) "Bodily injury" means physical pain, illness or any impairment of physical condition.

(2) "Serious bodily injury" means:

(A) bodily injury which creates any of the following:

(i) a substantial risk of death;

(ii) a substantial loss or impairment of the function of any bodily member or organ;

(iii) a substantial impairment of health; or

(iv) substantial disfigurement; or

(3) "Deadly weapon" means any firearm, or other weapon, device, instrument, material or substance, whether animate or inanimate which in the manner it is used or is intended to be used is known to be capable of producing death or serious bodily injury.

(4) "Course of conduct" means a pattern of conduct composed of two or more acts over a period of time, however short, evidencing a continuity of purpose. Constitutionally protected activity is not included within the meaning of "course of conduct."

13 V.S.§ 4003. Carrying dangerous weapons

A person who carries a dangerous or deadly weapon, openly or concealed, with the intent or avowed purpose of injuring a fellow man, or who carries a dangerous or deadly weapon within any state institution or upon the grounds or lands owned or leased for the use of such institution, without the approval of the warden or superintendent of the institution, shall be imprisoned not more than two years or fined not more than $200.00, or both.

13 V.S.§ 4004. Possession of dangerous or deadly weapon in a school bus or school building or on school property

(a) No person shall knowingly possess a firearm or a dangerous or deadly weapon while within a school building or on a school bus. A person who violates this section shall, for the first offense, be imprisoned not more than one year or fined not more than $1,000.00, or both, and for a second or subsequent offense shall be imprisoned not more than three years or fined not more than $5,000.00, or both.

(b) No person shall knowingly possess a firearm or a dangerous or deadly weapon on any school property with the intent to injure another person. A person who violates this section shall, for the first offense, be imprisoned not more than two years or fined not more than $1,000.00, or both, and for a second or subsequent offense shall be imprisoned not more than three years or fined not more than $5,000.00, or both.

(c) This section shall not apply to:

(1) A law enforcement officer while engaged in law enforcement duties.

(2) Possession and use of firearms or dangerous or deadly weapons if the board of school directors, or the superintendent or principal if delegated authority to do so by the board, authorizes possession or use for specific occasions or for instructional or other specific purposes.

(d) As used in this section:

(1) "School property" means any property owned by a school, including motor vehicles.

(2) "Owned by the school" means owned, leased, controlled or subcontracted by the school.

(3) "Dangerous or deadly weapon" has the meaning defined in section 4016 of this title.

(4) "Firearm" has the meaning defined in section 4016 of this title.

(5) "Law enforcement officer" has the meaning defined in section 4016 of this title.

(e) The provisions of this section shall not limit or restrict any prosecution for any other offense, including simple assault or aggravated assault.

13 V.S. § 4013. Zip guns; switchblade knives

A person who possesses, sells or offers for sale a weapon commonly known as a "zip" gun, or a weapon commonly known as a switchblade knife, the blade of which is three inches or more in length, shall be imprisoned not more than 90 days or fined not more than $100.00, or both.

13 V.S.§ 4016. Weapons in court

(a) As used in this section:

(1) "Courthouse" means a building or any portion of a building designated by the supreme court of Vermont as a courthouse.

(2) "Dangerous or deadly weapon" means any firearm, or other weapon, device, instrument, material or substance, whether animate or inanimate, which in the manner it is used or is intended to be used is known to be capable of producing death or serious bodily injury.

(4) "Law enforcement officer" means a person certified by the Vermont criminal justice training council as having satisfactorily completed the approved training programs required to meet the minimum training standards applicable to that person pursuant to 20 V.S.A. § 2358.

(5) "Secured building" means a building with controlled points of public access, metal screening devices at each point of public access, and locked compartments, accessible only to security personnel, for storage of checked firearms.

(c) Notice of the provisions of subsection (b) of this section shall be posted conspicuously at each public entrance to each courthouse.

(d) No dangerous or deadly weapon shall be allowed in a courthouse that has been certified by the court administrator to be a secured building.

✦ VIRGINIA ✦
KNIFE RIGHTS MOVEMENT RATING
★ ★ ★ ☆ ☆

CUTTING TO THE CHASE
In Virginia it is unlawful to conceal carry a dirk, bowie knife, switchblade knife, ballistic knife, machete, razor, throwing star, oriental dart, or "any weapon of like kind." No selling or giving a throwing star, oriental dart, switchblade knife, ballistic knife or like weapons to any person.

Quick Points Concerning Virginia's Knife Law*

KNIFE TYPE	POSSESSION	(Open/Concealed) CARRY	SALE	MANUFACTURE
Assisted Opening	Legal	Legal/Gray	Gray	Gray
Automatic/Switchblade	Legal	Legal/Prohibited	Prohibited	Prohibited
Ballistic	Legal	Legal/Prohibited	Prohibited	Prohibited
Bayonets	Legal	Legal/Gray	Legal	Legal
Bowie	Legal	Legal/Prohibited	Legal	Legal
Butterfly/Balisong	Legal	Legal/Gray	Gray	Gray
Combat/Survival	Legal	Legal/Gray	Legal	Legal
Dagger	Legal	Legal/Gray	Legal	Legal
Dirk	Legal	Legal/Prohibited	Legal	Legal
Disguised	Legal	Legal/Gray	Legal	Legal
Fixed	Legal	Legal/Gray	Legal	Legal
Folding	Legal	Legal/Gray	Legal	Legal
Gravity	Legal	Legal/Gray	Gray	Gray
Hunting/Fishing	Legal	Legal/Gray	Legal	Legal
Machete	Legal	Legal/Prohibited	Legal	Legal
Razor	Legal	Legal/Prohibited	Legal	Legal
Stiletto	Legal	Legal/Gray	Legal	Legal
Sword	Legal	Legal/Gray	Legal	Legal
Throwing	Legal	Legal/Gray	Gray	Gray
Undetectable	Legal	Legal/Gray	Legal	Legal

<u>Pre-emption</u> (Only State Law May Regulate, No Local Laws Permitted) – NO
*See all information above and below for more details.

SHARP TIPS ABOUT VIRGINIA'S KNIFE LAWS
Do not carry a "bowie knife, dagger or other dangerous weapon, without good and sufficient reason" in a place of religious worship. No dangerous weapons in courthouses or airports. No dangerous weapon or "…knife, except a pocket knife having a folding metal blade of less than three inches…" is allowed on school property or in school buses. Certain convicted persons are prohibited from weapon possession. No sales of a dirk, switchblade knife or bowie knife to a minor. No pre-emption, so beware of local laws.

EDGE –U- CATIONAL --- VIRGINIA'S KNIFE LAWS
§ 18.2-283. Carrying dangerous weapon to place of religious worship
If any person carry any gun, pistol, bowie knife, dagger or other dangerous weapon, without good and sufficient reason, to a place of worship while a meeting for religious purposes is being held at such place he shall be guilty of a Class 4 misdemeanor.

§ 18.2-283.1. Carrying weapon into courthouse

It shall be unlawful for any person to possess in or transport into any courthouse in this Commonwealth any (iii) any other dangerous weapon, including explosives, stun weapons as defined in § 18.2-308.1, and those weapons specified in subsection A of § 18.2-308. Any such weapon shall be subject to seizure by a law-enforcement officer. A violation of this section is punishable as a Class 1 misdemeanor.

The provisions of this section shall not apply to any police officer, sheriff, law-enforcement agent or official, conservation police officer, conservator of the peace, magistrate, court officer, judge, or city or county treasurer while in the conduct of such person's official duties.

§ 18.2-287.01. Carrying weapon in air carrier airport terminal

It shall be unlawful for any person to possess or transport into any air carrier airport terminal in the Commonwealth any (i) gun or other weapon designed or intended to propel a missile or projectile of any kind, (ii) frame, receiver, muffler, silencer, missile, projectile or ammunition designed for use with a dangerous weapon, and (iii) any other dangerous weapon, including explosives, stun weapons as defined in § 18.2-308.1, and those weapons specified in subsection A of § 18.2-308. Any such weapon shall be subject to seizure by a law-enforcement officer. A violation of this section is punishable as a Class 1 misdemeanor. Any weapon possessed or transported in violation of this section shall be forfeited to the Commonwealth and disposed of as provided in § 19.2-386.28.

The provisions of this section shall not apply to any police officer, sheriff, law-enforcement agent or official, or conservation police officer, or conservator of the peace employed by the air carrier airport, nor shall the provisions of this section apply to any passenger of an airline who, to the extent otherwise permitted by law, transports a lawful firearm, weapon, or ammunition into or out of an air carrier airport terminal for the sole purposes, respectively, of (i) presenting such firearm, weapon, or ammunition to U.S. Customs agents in advance of an international flight, in order to comply with federal law, (ii) checking such firearm, weapon, or ammunition with his luggage, or (iii) retrieving such firearm, weapon, or ammunition from the baggage claim area.

Any other statute, rule, regulation, or ordinance specifically addressing the possession or transportation of weapons in any airport in the Commonwealth shall be invalid, and this section shall control.

§ 18.2-307.1. Definitions

As used in this article, unless the context requires a different meaning:

"Ballistic knife" means any knife with a detachable blade that is propelled by a spring-operated mechanism.

"Law-enforcement officer" means those individuals defined as a law-enforcement officer in § 9.1-101, law-enforcement agents of the armed forces of the United States and the Naval Criminal Investigative Service, and federal agents who are otherwise authorized to carry weapons by federal law. "Law-enforcement officer" also means any sworn full-time law-enforcement officer employed by a law-enforcement agency of the United States or any state or political subdivision thereof, whose duties are substantially similar to those set forth in § 9.1-101.

"Lawfully admitted for permanent residence" means the status of having been lawfully accorded the privilege of residing permanently in the United States as an immigrant in accordance with the immigration laws, such status not having changed.

§ 18.2-308. Carrying concealed weapons; exceptions; penalty

A. If any person carries about his person, hidden from common observation, (ii) any dirk, bowie knife, switchblade knife, ballistic knife, machete, razor, slingshot, spring stick, metal knucks, or blackjack; (iii) any flailing instrument consisting of two or more rigid parts connected in such a manner as to allow them to swing freely, which may be known as a nun chahka, nun chuck, nunchaku, shuriken, or fighting chain; (iv) any disc, of whatever configuration, having at least two points or pointed blades which is designed to be thrown or propelled and which may be known as a throwing star or oriental dart; or (v) any weapon of like kind as those enumerated in this subsection, he is guilty of a Class 1 misdemeanor. A second violation of this section or a conviction under this section subsequent to any conviction under any substantially similar ordinance of any county, city, or town shall be punishable as a Class 6 felony, and a third or subsequent such violation shall be punishable as a Class 5 felony. For the purpose of this section, a weapon shall be deemed to be hidden from common observation when it is observable but is of such deceptive appearance as to disguise the weapon's true nature. It shall be an affirmative defense to a violation of clause (i) regarding a handgun, that a person had been issued, at the time of the offense, a valid concealed handgun permit.

B. This section shall not apply to any person while in his own place of abode or the curtilage thereof.

C. Except as provided in subsection A of § 18.2-308.012, this section shall not apply to:

1. Any person while in his own place of business;

2. Any law-enforcement officer, wherever such law-enforcement officer may travel in the Commonwealth;

3. Any person who is at, or going to or from, an established shooting range, provided that the weapons are unloaded and securely wrapped while being transported;

4. Any regularly enrolled member of a weapons collecting organization who is at, or going to or from, a bona fide weapons exhibition, provided that the weapons are unloaded and securely wrapped while being transported;

5. Any person carrying such weapons between his place of abode and a place of purchase or repair, provided the weapons are unloaded and securely wrapped while being transported;

9. Any attorney for the Commonwealth or assistant attorney for the Commonwealth, wherever such attorney may travel in the Commonwealth;

D. This section shall also not apply to any of the following individuals while in the discharge of their official duties, or while in transit to or from such duties:

1. Carriers of the United States mail;

2. Officers or guards of any state correctional institution;

3. Conservators of the peace, except that an attorney for the Commonwealth or assistant attorney for the Commonwealth may carry a concealed handgun pursuant to subdivision C 9. However, the following conservators of the peace shall not be permitted to carry a concealed handgun without obtaining a permit as provided in this article: (i) notaries public; (ii) registrars; (iii) drivers, operators or other persons in charge of any motor vehicle carrier of passengers for hire; or (iv) commissioners in chancery;

4. Noncustodial employees of the Department of Corrections designated to carry weapons by the Director of the Department of Corrections pursuant to § 53.1-29; and

5. Harbormaster of the City of Hopewell.

§ 18.2-308.1. Possession of firearm, stun weapon, or other weapon on school property prohibited

A. If any person possesses any (i) stun weapon as defined in this section; (ii) knife, except a pocket knife having a folding metal blade of less than three inches; or (iii) weapon, including a weapon of like kind, designated in subsection A of § 18.2-308, other than a firearm; upon (a) the property of any public, private or religious elementary, middle or high school, including buildings and grounds; (b) that portion of any property open to the public and then exclusively used for school-sponsored functions or extracurricular activities while such functions or activities are taking place; or (c) any school bus owned or operated by any such school, he shall be guilty of a Class 1 misdemeanor.

The exemptions set out in § 18.2-308 shall apply, mutatis mutandis, to the provisions of this section.

The provisions of this section shall not apply to (i) persons who possess such weapon or weapons as a part of the school's curriculum or activities; (ii) a person possessing a knife customarily used for food preparation or service and using it for such purpose; (iii) persons who possess such weapon or weapons as a part of any program sponsored or facilitated by either the school or any organization authorized by the school to conduct its programs either on or off the school premises; (iv) any law-enforcement officer; (v) any person who possesses a knife or blade which he uses customarily in his trade; (vi) a person who possesses an unloaded firearm that is in a closed container, or a knife having a metal blade, in or upon a motor vehicle, or an unloaded shotgun or rifle in a firearms rack in or upon a motor vehicle; (vii) a person who has a valid concealed handgun permit and possesses a concealed handgun while in a motor vehicle in a parking lot, traffic circle, or other means of vehicular ingress or egress to the school; or (viii) an armed security officer, licensed pursuant to Article 4 (§ 9.1-138 et seq.) of Chapter 1 of Title 9.1, hired by a private or religious school for the protection of students and employees as authorized by such school. For the purposes of this paragraph, "weapon" includes a knife having a metal blade of three inches or longer and "closed container" includes a locked vehicle trunk.

§ 18.2-308.2. Possession or transportation of firearms, firearms ammunition, stun weapons, explosives or concealed weapons by convicted felons; penalties; petition for permit; when issued

A. It shall be unlawful for (i) any person who has been convicted of a felony; (ii) any person adjudicated delinquent as a juvenile 14 years of age or older at the time of the offense of murder in violation of § 18.2-31 or 18.2-32, kidnapping in violation of § 18.2-47, robbery by the threat or presentation of firearms in violation of § 18.2-58, or rape in violation of § 18.2-61; or (iii) any person under the age of 29 who was adjudicated delinquent as a juvenile 14 years of age or older at the time of the offense of a delinquent act which would be a felony if committed by an adult, other than those felonies set forth in clause (ii), whether such conviction or adjudication occurred under the laws of the Commonwealth, or any other state, the District of Columbia, the United States or any territory thereof, to knowingly and intentionally possess or transport any firearm or ammunition for a firearm, any stun weapon as defined by § 18.2-308.1, or any explosive material, or to knowingly and intentionally carry about his person, hidden from common observation, any weapon described in subsection A of § 18.2-308. However, such person may possess in his residence or the curtilage thereof a stun weapon as defined by § 18.2-308.1. Any person who violates this section shall be guilty of a Class 6 felony. However, any person who violates this section by knowingly and intentionally possessing or transporting any firearm and who was previously convicted of a violent felony as defined in § 17.1-805 shall be sentenced to a mandatory minimum term of imprisonment of five years. Any person who violates this section by knowingly and intentionally possessing or transporting any firearm and who was previously convicted of any other felony within the prior 10 years shall be sentenced to a mandatory minimum term of imprisonment of two years. The mandatory minimum terms of imprisonment prescribed for violations of this section shall be served consecutively with any other sentence.

B. The prohibitions of subsection A shall not apply to (i) any person who possesses a firearm, ammunition for a firearm, explosive material or other weapon while carrying out his duties as a member of the Armed Forces of the United States or of the National Guard of Virginia or of any other state, (ii) any law-enforcement officer in the performance of his duties, or (iii) any person who has been pardoned or whose political disabilities have been removed pursuant to Article V, Section 12 of the Constitution of Virginia provided the Governor, in the document granting the pardon or removing the person's political disabilities, may expressly place conditions upon the reinstatement of the person's right to ship, transport, possess or receive firearms.

§ 18.2-309. Furnishing certain weapons to minors; penalty

A. If any person sells, barters, gives or furnishes, or causes to be sold, bartered, given or furnished, to any minor a dirk, switchblade knife or bowie knife, having good cause to believe him to be a minor, such person shall be guilty of a Class 1 misdemeanor.

§ 18.2-311. Prohibiting the selling or having in possession blackjacks, etc.

If any person sells or barters, or exhibits for sale or for barter, or gives or furnishes, or causes to be sold, bartered, given or furnished, or has in his possession, or under his control, with the intent of selling, bartering, giving or furnishing, any blackjack, brass or metal knucks, any disc of whatever configuration having at least two points or pointed blades which is designed to be thrown or propelled and which may be known as a throwing star or oriental dart, switchblade knife, ballistic knife as defined in § 18.2-307.1, or like weapons, such person is guilty of a Class 4 misdemeanor. The having in one's possession of any such weapon shall be prima facie evidence, except in the case of a conservator of the peace, of his intent to sell, barter, give or furnish the same.

✦ WASHINGTON ✦
KNIFE RIGHTS MOVEMENT RATING
★ ★ ★ ☆ ☆

CUTTING TO THE CHASE

One may not conceal carry any dagger, dirk, or other "dangerous weapon." Dangerous weapon is defined as "under the circumstances in which it is used, attempted to be used, or threatened to be used, is readily capable of causing death or substantial bodily harm." Additionally, "one may not carry, exhibit, display, or draw any … dagger, sword, knife or other cutting or stabbing instrument, club, or any other weapon apparently capable of producing bodily harm, in a manner, under circumstances, and at a time and place that either manifests an intent to intimidate another or that warrants alarm for the safety of other persons." Washington's vague laws make lawful carry difficult and risky for an honest citizen.

Quick Points Concerning Washington's Knife Law*

KNIFE TYPE	POSSESSION	(Open/Concealed) CARRY	SALE	MANUFACTURE
Assisted Opening	Legal	Legal/Gray	Legal	Legal
Automatic/Switchblade	Prohibited	Prohibited/Prohibited	Gray	Gray
Ballistic	Gray	Gray/Gray	Gray	Gray
Bayonets	Legal	Legal/Gray	Legal	Legal
Bowie	Legal	Legal/Gray	Legal	Legal
Butterfly/Balisong	Gray	Gray/Gray	Gray	Gray
Combat/Survival	Legal	Legal/Gray	Legal	Legal
Dagger	Legal	Legal/Prohibited	Legal	Legal
Dirk	Legal	Legal/Prohibited	Legal	Legal
Disguised	Legal	Legal/Gray	Legal	Legal
Fixed	Legal	Legal/Gray	Legal	Legal
Folding	Legal	Legal/Gray	Legal	Legal
Gravity	Prohibited	Prohibited/Prohibited	Gray	Gray
Hunting/Fishing	Legal	Legal/Gray	Legal	Legal
Machete	Legal	Legal/Gray	Legal	Legal
Razor	Legal	Legal/Gray	Legal	Legal
Stiletto	Legal	Legal/Gray	Legal	Legal
Sword	Legal	Legal/Gray	Legal	Legal
Throwing	Legal	Legal/Gray	Legal	Legal
Undetectable	Legal	Legal/Gray	Legal	Legal

Pre-emption (Only State Law May Regulate, No Local Laws Permitted) – NO

*See all information above and below for more details.

SHARP TIPS ABOUT WASHINGTON'S KNIFE LAWS

Washington bans possession of switchblades and gravity knives. In 2012 Washington reformed their switchblade and gravity knife ban. It now allows the manufacture, sale, transportation, transfer, distribution, or possession of switchblades and gravity knives pursuant to a contract with a law enforcement agency, fire or rescue agency, or military, with another manufacturer or a commercial distributor of knives for use, sale, or other disposition by the manufacturer or commercial distributor, or solely for trial, test, or evaluation. Knives are generally not allowed in jails, school premises, law enforcement facilities, airports, mental health facilities, or an "establishment classified by the state liquor control board as off-limits to persons under twenty-one years of age." There is no pre-emption, so beware of local laws.

EDGE –U- CATIONAL --- WASHINGTON'S KNIFE LAWS

9A.04.110. Definitions

In this title unless a different meaning plainly is required:

(6) "Deadly weapon" means any explosive or loaded or unloaded firearm, and shall include any other weapon, device, instrument, article, or substance, including a "vehicle" as defined in this section, which, under the circumstances in which it is used, attempted to be used, or threatened to be used, is readily capable of causing death or substantial bodily harm;

9.41.250. Dangerous weapons--Penalty

(1) Every person who:

(a) Manufactures, sells, or disposes of or possesses any instrument or weapon of the kind usually known as slung shot, sand club, or metal knuckles, or spring blade knife;

(b) Furtively carries with intent to conceal any dagger, dirk, pistol, or other dangerous weapon; or

is guilty of a gross misdemeanor punishable under chapter 9A.20 RCW.

(2) "Spring blade knife" means any knife, including a prototype, model, or other sample, with a blade that is automatically released by a spring mechanism or other mechanical device, or any knife having a blade which opens, or falls, or is ejected into position by the force of gravity, or by an outward, downward, or centrifugal thrust or movement. A knife that contains a spring, detent, or other mechanism designed to create a bias toward closure of the blade and that requires physical exertion applied to the blade by hand, wrist, or arm to overcome the bias toward closure to assist in opening the knife is not a spring blade knife.

9.41.251. Dangerous weapons--Application of restrictions to law enforcement, firefighting, rescue, and military personnel

(1) RCW 9.41.250 does not apply to:

(a) The possession or use of a spring blade knife by a general authority law enforcement officer, firefighter or rescue member, Washington state patrol officer, or military member, while the officer or member:

(i) Is on official duty; or

(ii) Is transporting a spring blade knife to or from the place where the knife is stored when the officer or member is not on official duty; or

(iii) Is storing a spring blade knife;

(b) The manufacture, sale, transportation, transfer, distribution, or possession of spring blade knives pursuant to contract with a general authority law enforcement agency, fire or rescue agency, Washington state patrol, or military service, or pursuant to a contract with another manufacturer or a commercial distributor of knives for use, sale, or other disposition by the manufacturer or commercial distributor;

(c) The manufacture, transportation, transfer, distribution, or possession of spring blade knives, with or without compensation and with or without a contract, solely for trial, test, or other provisional use for evaluation and assessment purposes, by a general authority law enforcement agency, fire or rescue agency, Washington state patrol, military service, or a manufacturer or commercial distributor of knives.

(2) For the purposes of this section:

(a) "Military member" means an active member of the United States military or naval forces, or a Washington national guard member called to active duty or during training.

(b) "General law enforcement agency" means any agency, department, or division of a municipal corporation, political subdivision, or other unit of local government of this state or any other state, and any agency, department, or division of any state government, having as its primary function the detection and apprehension of persons committing infractions or violating the traffic or criminal laws in general.

(c) "General law enforcement officer" means any person who is commissioned and employed by an employer on a full-time, fully compensated basis to enforce the criminal laws of the state of Washington generally. No person who is serving in a position that is basically clerical or secretarial in nature, or who is not commissioned shall be considered a law enforcement officer.

(d) "Fire or rescue agency" means any agency, department, or division of a municipal corporation, political subdivision, or other unit of local government of this state or any other state, and any agency, department, or division of any state government, having as its primary function the prevention, control, or extinguishment of fire or provision of emergency medical services or rescue actions for persons.

(e) "Firefighter or rescue member" means any person who is serving on a full-time, fully compensated basis as a member of a fire or rescue agency to prevent, control, or extinguish fire or provide emergency medical services or rescue actions for persons. No person who is serving in a position that is basically clerical or secretarial in nature shall be considered a firefighter or rescue member.

(f) "Military service" means the active, reserve, or national guard components of the United States military, including the army, navy, air force, marines, and coast guard.

9.41.270. Weapons apparently capable of producing bodily harm--Unlawful carrying or handling--Penalty--Exceptions

(1) It shall be unlawful for any person to carry, exhibit, display, or draw any firearm, dagger, sword, knife or other cutting or stabbing instrument, club, or any other weapon apparently capable of producing bodily harm, in a manner, under circumstances, and at a time and place that either manifests an intent to intimidate another or that warrants alarm for the safety of other persons.

(2) Any person violating the provisions of subsection (1) above shall be guilty of a gross misdemeanor. If any person is convicted of a violation of subsection (1) of this section, the person shall lose his or her concealed pistol license, if any. The court shall send notice of the revocation to the department of licensing, and the city, town, or county which issued the license.

(3) Subsection (1) of this section shall not apply to or affect the following:

(a) Any act committed by a person while in his or her place of abode or fixed place of business;

(b) Any person who by virtue of his or her office or public employment is vested by law with a duty to preserve public safety, maintain public order, or to make arrests for offenses, while in the performance of such duty;

(c) Any person acting for the purpose of protecting himself or herself against the use of presently threatened unlawful force by another, or for the purpose of protecting another against the use of such unlawful force by a third person;

(d) Any person making or assisting in making a lawful arrest for the commission of a felony; or

(e) Any person engaged in military activities sponsored by the federal or state governments.

9.41.280. Possessing dangerous weapons on school facilities--Penalty--Exceptions (Effective April 1, 2016)

(1) It is unlawful for a person to carry onto, or to possess on, public or private elementary or secondary school premises, school-provided transportation, or areas of facilities while being used exclusively by public or private schools:

(b) Any other dangerous weapon as defined in RCW 9.41.250;

(d) Any device, commonly known as "throwing stars," which are multipointed, metal objects designed to embed upon impact from any aspect;

(2) Any such person violating subsection (1) of this section is guilty of a gross misdemeanor. If any person is convicted of a violation of subsection (1)(a) of this section, the person shall have his or her concealed pistol license, if any revoked for a period of three years. Anyone convicted under this subsection is prohibited from applying for a concealed pistol license for a period of three years. The court shall send notice of the revocation to the department of licensing, and the city, town, or county which issued the license.

Any violation of subsection (1) of this section by elementary or secondary school students constitutes grounds for expulsion from the state's public schools in accordance with RCW 28A.600.010. An appropriate school authority shall promptly notify law enforcement and the student's parent or guardian regarding any allegation or indication of such violation.

Upon the arrest of a person at least twelve years of age and not more than twenty-one years of age for violating subsection (1)(a) of this section, the person shall be detained or confined in a juvenile or adult facility for up to seventy-two hours. The person shall not be released within the seventy-two hours until after the person has been examined and evaluated by the designated mental health professional unless the court in its discretion releases the person sooner after a determination regarding probable cause or on probation bond or bail.

Within twenty-four hours of the arrest, the arresting law enforcement agency shall refer the person to the designated mental health professional for examination and evaluation under chapter 71.05 or 71.34 RCW and inform a parent or guardian of the person of the arrest, detention, and examination. The designated mental health professional shall examine and evaluate the person subject to the provisions of chapter 71.05 or 71.34 RCW. The examination shall occur at the facility in which the person is detained or confined. If the person has been released on probation, bond, or bail, the examination shall occur wherever is appropriate.

The designated mental health professional may determine whether to refer the person to the county-designated chemical dependency specialist for examination and evaluation in accordance with chapter 70.96A RCW. The county-designated chemical dependency specialist shall examine the person subject to the provisions of chapter 70.96A RCW. The examination shall occur at the facility in which the person is detained or confined. If the person has been released on probation, bond, or bail, the examination shall occur wherever is appropriate.

Upon completion of any examination by the designated mental health professional or the county-designated chemical dependency specialist, the results of the examination shall be sent to the court, and the court shall consider those results in making any determination about the person.

The designated mental health professional and county-designated chemical dependency specialist shall, to the extent permitted by law, notify a parent or guardian of the person that an examination and evaluation has taken place and the results of the examination. Nothing in this subsection prohibits the delivery of additional, appropriate mental health examinations to the person while the person is detained or confined.

If the designated mental health professional determines it is appropriate, the designated mental health professional may refer the person to the local behavioral health organization for follow-up services or the department of social and health services or other community providers for other services to the family and individual.

(3) Subsection (1) of this section does not apply to:

(a) Any student or employee of a private military academy when on the property of the academy;

(b) Any person engaged in military, law enforcement, or school district security activities. However, a person who is not a commissioned law enforcement officer and who provides school security services under the direction of a school administrator may not possess a device listed in subsection (1)(f) of this section unless he or she has successfully completed training in the use of such devices that is equivalent to the training received by commissioned law enforcement officers;

(c) Any person who is involved in a convention, showing, demonstration, lecture, or firearms safety course authorized by school authorities in which the firearms of collectors or instructors are handled or displayed;

(f) Any nonstudent at least eighteen years of age legally in possession of a firearm or dangerous weapon that is secured within an attended vehicle or concealed from view within a locked unattended vehicle while conducting legitimate business at the school;

(h) Any law enforcement officer of the federal, state, or local government agency.

(4) Subsections (1)(c) and (d) of this section do not apply to any person who possesses nun-chu-ka sticks, throwing stars, or other dangerous weapons to be used in martial arts classes authorized to be conducted on the school premises.

(5) Subsection (1)(f)(i) of this section does not apply to any person who possesses a device listed in subsection (1)(f)(i) of this section, if the device is possessed and used solely for the purpose approved by a school for use in a school authorized event, lecture, or activity conducted on the school premises.

9.41.300. Weapons prohibited in certain places--Local laws and ordinances--Exceptions--Penalty

(1) It is unlawful for any person to enter the following places when he or she knowingly possesses or knowingly has under his or her control a weapon:

(a) The restricted access areas of a jail, or of a law enforcement facility, or any place used for the confinement of a person (i) arrested for, charged with, or convicted of an offense, (ii) held for extradition or as a material witness, or (iii) otherwise confined pursuant to an order of a court, except an order under chapter 13.32A or 13.34 RCW. Restricted access areas do not include common areas of egress or ingress open to the general public;

(b) Those areas in any building which are used in connection with court proceedings, including courtrooms, jury rooms, judge's chambers, offices and areas used to conduct court business, waiting areas, and corridors adjacent to areas used in connection with court proceedings. The restricted areas do not include common areas of ingress and egress to the building that is used in connection with court proceedings, when it is possible to protect court areas without restricting ingress and egress to the building. The restricted areas shall be the minimum necessary to fulfill the objective of this subsection (1)(b).

For purposes of this subsection (1)(b), "weapon" means any firearm, explosive as defined in RCW 70.74.010, or any weapon of the kind usually known as slung shot, sand club, or metal knuckles, or any knife, dagger, dirk, or other similar weapon that is capable of causing death or bodily injury and is commonly used with the intent to cause death or bodily injury.

In addition, the local legislative authority shall provide either a stationary locked box sufficient in size for pistols and key to a weapon owner for weapon storage, or shall designate an official to receive weapons for safekeeping, during the owner's visit to restricted areas of the building. The locked box or designated official shall be located within the same building used in connection with court proceedings. The local legislative authority shall be liable for any negligence causing damage to or loss of a weapon either placed in a locked box or left with an official during the owner's visit to restricted areas of the building.

The local judicial authority shall designate and clearly mark those areas where weapons are prohibited, and shall post notices at each entrance to the building of the prohibition against weapons in the restricted areas;

(c) The restricted access areas of a public mental health facility certified by the department of social and health services for inpatient hospital care and state institutions for the care of the mentally ill, excluding those facilities solely for evaluation and treatment. Restricted access areas do not include common areas of egress and ingress open to the general public;

(d) That portion of an establishment classified by the state liquor control board as off-limits to persons under twenty-one years of age; or

(e) The restricted access areas of a commercial service airport designated in the airport security plan approved by the federal transportation security administration, including passenger screening checkpoints at or beyond the point at which a passenger initiates the screening process. These areas do not include airport drives, general parking areas and walkways, and shops and areas of the terminal that are outside the screening checkpoints and that are normally open to unscreened passengers or visitors to the airport. Any restricted access area shall be clearly indicated by prominent signs indicating that firearms and other weapons are prohibited in the area.

(5) The perimeter of the premises of any specific location covered by subsection (1) of this section shall be posted at reasonable intervals to alert the public as to the existence of any law restricting the possession of firearms on the premises.

(6) Subsection (1) of this section does not apply to:

(a) A person engaged in military activities sponsored by the federal or state governments, while engaged in official duties;

(b) Law enforcement personnel, except that subsection (1)(b) of this section does apply to a law enforcement officer who is present at a courthouse building as a party to an action under chapter 10.14, 10.99, or 26.50 RCW, or an action under Title 26 RCW where any party has alleged the existence of domestic violence as defined in RCW 26.50.010; or

(c) Security personnel while engaged in official duties.

(7) Subsection (1)(a), (b), (c), and (e) of this section does not apply to correctional personnel or community corrections officers, as long as they are employed as such, who have completed government-sponsored law enforcement firearms training, except that subsection (1)(b) of this section does apply to a correctional employee or community corrections officer who is present at a courthouse building as a party to an action under chapter 10. 14, 10.99, or 26.50 RCW, or an action under Title 26 RCW where any party has alleged the existence of domestic violence as defined in RCW 26.50.010.

(10) Subsection (1)(d) of this section does not apply to the proprietor of the premises or his or her employees while engaged in their employment.

(11) Government-sponsored law enforcement firearms training must be training that correctional personnel and community corrections officers receive as part of their job requirement and reference to such training does not constitute a mandate that it be provided by the correctional facility.

(12) Any person violating subsection (1) of this section is guilty of a gross misdemeanor.

(13) "Weapon" as used in this section means any firearm, explosive as defined in RCW 70.74.010, or instrument or weapon listed in RCW 9.41.250.

WEST VIRGINIA
KNIFE RIGHTS MOVEMENT RATING
★ ★ ★ ★ ☆

CUTTING TO THE CHASE

West Virginia does not ban possession of any knife. Concealed carry of "deadly weapons" is prohibited. "Deadly weapons" include, any knife which is "an instrument, intended to be used or readily adaptable to be used as a weapon, consisting of a sharp-edged or sharp-pointed blade, usually made of steel, attached to a handle which is capable of inflicting cutting, stabbing or tearing wounds. The term "knife" shall include, but not be limited to, any dagger, dirk, poniard or stiletto, with a blade over three and one-half inches in length, any switchblade knife or gravity knife and any other instrument capable of inflicting cutting, stabbing or tearing wounds."

Quick Points Concerning West Virginia's Knife Law*

KNIFE TYPE	POSSESSION	(Open/Concealed) CARRY	SALE	MANUFACTURE
Assisted Opening	Legal	Legal/Gray	Legal	Legal
Automatic/Switchblade	Legal	Legal/Prohibited	Legal	Legal
Ballistic	Legal	Legal/Gray	Legal	Legal
Bayonets	Legal	Legal/Gray	Legal	Legal
Bowie	Legal	Legal/Gray	Legal	Legal
Butterfly/Balisong	Legal	Legal/Prohibited	Legal	Legal
Combat/Survival	Legal	Legal/Gray	Legal	Legal
Dagger	Legal	Legal/Prohibited	Legal	Legal
Dirk	Legal	Legal/Prohibited	Legal	Legal
Disguised	Legal	Legal/Gray	Legal	Legal
Fixed	Legal	Legal/Gray	Legal	Legal
Folding	Legal	Legal/Gray	Legal	Legal
Gravity	Legal	Legal/Prohibited	Legal	Legal
Hunting/Fishing	Legal	Legal/Gray	Legal	Legal
Machete	Legal	Legal/Gray	Legal	Legal
Razor	Legal	Legal/Gray	Legal	Legal
Stiletto	Legal	Legal/Prohibited	Legal	Legal
Sword	Legal	Legal/Gray	Legal	Legal
Throwing	Legal	Legal/Gray	Legal	Legal
Undetectable	Legal	Legal/Gray	Legal	Legal

Pre-emption (Only State Law May Regulate, No Local Laws Permitted) – NO
*See all information above and below for more details.

SHARP TIPS ABOUT WEST VIRGINIA'S KNIFE LAWS

A pocket knife "with a blade 3.5 inches or less in length, a hunting or fishing knife carried for hunting, fishing, sports or other recreational uses or a knife designed for use as a tool or household implement" is exempted from term "knife" unless it is "knowingly used or intended to be used to produce serious bodily injury or death." Generally, no knives for minors, or in schools, on school buses, or on school grounds. No pre-emption, so beware of local laws.

EDGE –U- CATIONAL --- WEST VIRGINIA'S KNIFE LAWS

§ 61-7-2. Definitions

As used in this article, unless the context otherwise requires:

(2) "Gravity knife" means any knife that has a blade released from the handle by the force of gravity or the application of centrifugal force and when so released is locked in place by means of a button, spring, lever or other locking or catching device.

(3) "Knife" means an instrument, intended to be used or readily adaptable to be used as a weapon, consisting of a sharp-edged or sharp-pointed blade, usually made of steel, attached to a handle which is capable of inflicting cutting, stabbing or tearing wounds. The term "knife" shall include, but not be limited to, any dagger, dirk, poniard or stiletto, with a blade over three and one-half inches in length, any switchblade knife or gravity knife and any other instrument capable of inflicting cutting, stabbing or tearing wounds. A pocket knife with a blade three and one-half inches or less in length, a hunting or fishing knife carried for hunting, fishing, sports or other recreational uses or a knife designed for use as a tool or household implement shall not be included within the term "knife" as defined herein unless such knife is knowingly used or intended to be used to produce serious bodily injury or death.

(4) "Switchblade knife" means any knife having a spring-operated blade which opens automatically upon pressure being applied to a button, catch or other releasing device in its handle.

(9) "Deadly weapon" means an instrument which is designed to be used to produce serious bodily injury or death or is readily adaptable to such use. The term "deadly weapon" shall include, but not be limited to, the instruments defined in subdivisions (1) through (8), inclusive, of this section or other deadly weapons of like kind or character which may be easily concealed on or about the person. For the purposes of section one-a, article five, chapter eighteen-a of this code and section eleven-a, article seven of this chapter, in addition to the definition of "knife" set forth in subdivision (3) of this section, the term "deadly weapon" also includes any instrument included within the definition of "knife" with a blade of three and one-half inches or less in length. Additionally, for the purposes of section one-a, article five, chapter eighteen-a of this code and section eleven-a, article seven of this chapter, the term "deadly weapon" includes explosive, chemical, biological and radiological materials. Notwithstanding any other provision of this section, the term "deadly weapon" does not include any item or material owned by the school or county board, intended for curricular use, and used by the student at the time of the alleged offense solely for curricular purposes.

(10) "Concealed" means hidden from ordinary observation so as to prevent disclosure or recognition. A deadly weapon is concealed when it is carried on or about the person in such a manner that another person in the ordinary course of events would not be placed on notice that the deadly weapon was being carried. For purposes of concealed handgun licensees, a licensee shall be deemed to be carrying on or about his or her person while in or on a motor vehicle if the firearm is located in a storage area in or on the motor vehicle.

§ 61-7-3. Carrying deadly weapon without license or other authorization; penalties

(a) Any person who carries a concealed deadly weapon, without a state license or other lawful authorization established under the provisions of this code, shall be guilty of a misdemeanor, and, upon conviction thereof, shall be fined not less than one hundred dollars nor more than one thousand dollars and may be imprisoned in the county jail for not more than twelve months for the first offense; but upon conviction of a second or subsequent offense, he or she shall be guilty of a felony, and, upon conviction thereof, shall be imprisoned in the penitentiary not less than one nor more than five years and fined not less than one thousand dollars nor more than five thousand dollars.

(b) It shall be the duty of the prosecuting attorney in all cases to ascertain whether or not the charge made by the grand jury is a first offense or is a second or subsequent offense and, if it shall be a second or subsequent offense, it shall be so stated in the indictment returned, and the prosecuting attorney shall introduce the record evidence before the trial court of such second or subsequent offense and shall not be permitted to use discretion in introducing evidence to prove the same on the trial.

§ 61-7-6. Exceptions as to prohibitions against carrying concealed handguns; exemptions from licensing fees

(a) The licensure provisions set forth in this article do not apply to:

(1) Any person:

(A) Carrying a deadly weapon upon his or her own premises;

(3) Any law-enforcement officer or law-enforcement official as defined in section one, article twenty-nine, chapter thirty of this code;

(4) Any employee of the West Virginia Division of Corrections duly appointed pursuant to the provisions of section eleven-c, article one, chapter twenty-five of this code while the employee is on duty;

(5) Any member of the armed forces of the United States or the militia of this state while the member is on duty;

(6) Any resident of another state who holds a valid permit or license to possess or carry a handgun issued by a state or a political subdivision subject to the provisions and limitations set forth in section six-a of this article;

(7) Any federal law-enforcement officer or federal police officer authorized to carry a weapon in the performance of the officer's duty;

(8) Any Hatfield-McCoy Regional Recreation Authority Ranger while the ranger is on duty; and

(9) Any parole officer appointed pursuant to section fourteen, article twelve, chapter sixty-two of this code in the performance of their duties.

(b) On and after July 1, 2013, the following judicial officers and prosecutors and staff shall be exempted from paying any application fees or licensure fees required under this article. However, on and after that same date, they shall be required to make application and satisfy all licensure and handgun safety and training requirements set forth in section four of this article before carrying a concealed handgun in this state:

(1) Any justice of the Supreme Court of Appeals of West Virginia;

(2) Any circuit judge;

(3) Any retired justice or retired circuit judge designated senior status by the Supreme Court of Appeals of West Virginia;

(4) Any family court judge;

(5) Any magistrate;

(6) Any prosecuting attorney;

(7) Any assistant prosecuting attorney; or

(8) Any duly appointed investigator employed by a prosecuting attorney.

§ 61-7-8. Possession of deadly weapons by minors; prohibitions

Notwithstanding any other provision of this article to the contrary, a person under the age of eighteen years who is not married or otherwise emancipated shall not possess or carry concealed or openly any deadly weapon: Provided, however, That nothing in this section shall prohibit a minor from possessing a firearm while hunting in a lawful manner or while traveling from a place where he or she may lawfully possess a deadly weapon, to a hunting site, and returning to a place where he or she may lawfully possess such weapon.

A violation of this section by a person under the age of eighteen years shall subject the child to the jurisdiction of the circuit court under the provisions of article five, chapter forty-nine of this code, and such minor may be proceeded against in the same manner as if he or she had committed an act which if committed by an adult would be a crime, and may be adjudicated delinquent.

§ 61-7-10. Display of deadly weapons for sale or hire; sale to prohibited persons; penalties

(a) A person may not publicly display and offer for rent or sale, or, where the person is other than a natural person, knowingly permit an employee thereof to publicly display and offer for rent or sale, to any passersby on any street, road or alley, any deadly weapon, machine gun, submachine gun or other fully automatic weapon, any rifle, shotgun or ammunition for same.

(b) Any person who violates the provisions of subsections (a) or (c) of this section shall be guilty of a misdemeanor, and, upon conviction thereof, shall be fined not more than five thousand dollars or shall be confined in the county jail for not more than one year, or both fined and confined, except that where the person violating the provisions of said subsections is other than a natural person, such person shall be fined not more than ten thousand dollars.

(c) A person may not knowingly sell, rent, give or lend, or, where the person is other than a natural person, knowingly permit an employee thereof to knowingly sell, rent, give or lend, any deadly weapon other than a firearm to a person prohibited from possessing a deadly weapon other than a firearm by any provision of this article.

(e) Any person who violates any of the provisions of subsection (d) of this section is guilty of a felony, and, upon conviction thereof, shall be fined not more than $100,000 imprisoned in a state correctional facility for a definite term of years of not less than three years nor more than ten years, or both fined and imprisoned, except that where the person committing an offense punishable under this subsection is other than a natural person, such person shall be fined not more than $250,000.

§ 61-7-11. Brandishing deadly weapons; threatening or causing breach of the peace; criminal penalties

It shall be unlawful for any person armed with a firearm or other deadly weapon, whether licensed to carry the same or not, to carry, brandish or use such weapon in a way or manner to cause, or threaten, a breach of the peace. Any person violating this section shall be guilty of a misdemeanor, and, upon conviction thereof, shall be fined not less than fifty nor more than one thousand dollars, or shall be confined in the county jail not less than ninety days nor more than one year, or both.

§ 61-7-11a. Possessing deadly weapons on premises of educational facilities; reports by school principals; suspension of driver's license; possessing deadly weapons on premises housing courts of law and in offices of family law master

(a) The Legislature hereby finds that the safety and welfare of the citizens of this state are inextricably dependent upon assurances of safety for children attending and persons employed by schools in this state and for persons employed by the judicial department of this state. It is for the purpose of providing assurances of safety that subsections (b), (g) and (h) of this section are enacted as a reasonable regulation of the manner in which citizens may exercise the rights accorded to them pursuant to section twenty-two, article three of the Constitution of the State of West Virginia.

(b)(1) It is unlawful for a person to possess a firearm or other deadly weapon on a school bus as defined in section one, article one, chapter seventeen-a of this code, or in or on a public or private primary or secondary education building, structure, facility or grounds including a vocational education building, structure, facility or grounds where secondary vocational education programs are conducted or at a school-sponsored function.

(2) This subsection does not apply to:

(A) A law-enforcement officer acting in his or her official capacity;

(B) A person specifically authorized by the board of education of the county or principal of the school where the property is located to conduct programs with valid educational purposes;

(C) A person who, as otherwise permitted by the provisions of this article, possesses an unloaded firearm or deadly weapon in a motor vehicle or leaves an unloaded firearm or deadly weapon in a locked motor vehicle;

(D) Programs or raffles conducted with the approval of the county board of education or school which include the display of unloaded firearms;

(E) The official mascot of West Virginia University, commonly known as the Mountaineer, acting in his or her official capacity; or

(F) The official mascot of Parkersburg South High School, commonly known as the Patriot, acting in his or her official capacity.

(3) A person violating this subsection is guilty of a felony and, upon conviction thereof, shall be imprisoned in a state correctional facility for a definite term of years of not less than two years nor more than ten years, or fined not more than $5,000, or both.

(c) It is the duty of the principal of each school subject to the authority of the State Board of Education to report a violation of subsection (b) of this section discovered by the principal to the State Superintendent of Schools within seventy-two hours after the violation occurs. The State Board of Education shall keep and maintain these reports and may prescribe rules establishing policy and procedures for the making and delivery of the reports as required by this subsection. In addition, it is the duty of the principal of each school subject to the authority of the State Board of Education to report a violation of subsection (b) of this section discovered by the principal to the appropriate local office of the Division of Public Safety within seventy-two hours after the violation occurs.

(d) In addition to the methods of disposition provided by article five, chapter forty-nine of this code, a court which adjudicates a person who is fourteen years of age or older as delinquent for a violation of subsection (b) of this section may, in its discretion, order the Division of Motor Vehicles to suspend a driver's license or instruction permit issued to the person for a period of time as the court considers appropriate, not to extend beyond the person's nineteenth birthday. Where the person has not been issued a driver's license or instruction permit by this state, a court may order the Division of Motor Vehicles to deny the person's application for a license or permit for a period of time as the court considers appropriate, not to extend beyond the person's nineteenth birthday. A suspension ordered by the court pursuant to this subsection is effective upon the date of entry of the order. Where the court orders the suspension of a driver's license or instruction permit pursuant to this subsection, the court shall confiscate any driver's license or instruction permit in the adjudicated person's possession and forward to the Division of Motor Vehicles.

(e)(1) If a person eighteen years of age or older is convicted of violating subsection (b) of this section, and if the person does not act to appeal the conviction within the time periods described in subdivision (2) of this subsection, the person's license or privilege to operate a motor vehicle in this state shall be revoked in accordance with the provisions of this section.

(2) The clerk of the court in which the person is convicted as described in subdivision (1) of this subsection shall forward to the commissioner a transcript of the judgment of conviction. If the conviction is the judgment of a magistrate court, the magistrate court clerk shall forward the transcript when the person convicted has not requested an appeal within twenty days of the sentencing for the conviction. If the conviction is the judgment of a circuit court, the circuit clerk shall forward a transcript of the judgment of conviction when the person convicted has not filed a notice of intent to file a petition for appeal or writ of error within thirty days after the judgment was entered.

(3) If, upon examination of the transcript of the judgment of conviction, the commissioner determines that

the person was convicted as described in subdivision (1) of this subsection, the commissioner shall make and enter an order revoking the person's license or privilege to operate a motor vehicle in this state for a period of one year or, in the event the person is a student enrolled in a secondary school, for a period of one year or until the person's twentieth birthday, whichever is the greater period. The order shall contain the reasons for the revocation and the revocation period. The order of suspension shall advise the person that because of the receipt of the court's transcript, a presumption exists that the person named in the order of suspension is the same person named in the transcript. The commissioner may grant an administrative hearing which substantially complies with the requirements of the provisions of section two, article five-a, chapter seventeen-c of this code upon a preliminary showing that a possibility exists that the person named in the notice of conviction is not the same person whose license is being suspended. The request for hearing shall be made within ten days after receipt of a copy of the order of suspension. The sole purpose of this hearing is for the person requesting the hearing to present evidence that he or she is not the person named in the notice. If the commissioner grants an administrative hearing, the commissioner shall stay the license suspension pending the commissioner's order resulting from the hearing.

(4) For the purposes of this subsection, a person is convicted when such person enters a plea of guilty or is found guilty by a court or jury.

(f)(1) It is unlawful for a parent, guardian or custodian of a person less than eighteen years of age who knows that the person is in violation of subsection (b) of this section or has reasonable cause to believe that the person's violation of subsection (b) is imminent, to fail to immediately report his or her knowledge or belief to the appropriate school or law-enforcement officials.

(2) A person violating this subsection is guilty of a misdemeanor and, upon conviction thereof, shall be fined not more than $1,000, or shall be confined in jail not more than one year, or both.

(g)(1) It is unlawful for a person to possess a firearm or other deadly weapon on the premises of a court of law, including family courts.

(2) This subsection does not apply to:

(A) A law-enforcement officer acting in his or her official capacity; and

(B) A person exempted from the provisions of this subsection by order of record entered by a court with jurisdiction over the premises or offices.

(3) A person violating this subsection is guilty of a misdemeanor and, upon conviction thereof, shall be fined not more than $1,000, or shall be confined in jail not more than one year, or both.

(h)(1) It is unlawful for a person to possess a firearm or other deadly weapon on the premises of a court of law, including family courts, with the intent to commit a crime.

(2) A person violating this subsection is guilty of a felony and, upon conviction thereof, shall be imprisoned in a state correctional facility for a definite term of years of not less than two years nor more than ten years, or fined not more than $5,000, or both.

(i) Nothing in this section may be construed to be in conflict with the provisions of federal law.

§ 61-7-14. Right of certain persons to limit possession of firearms on premises
Notwithstanding the provisions of this article, any owner, lessee or other person charged with the care, custody and control of real property may prohibit the carrying openly or concealing of any firearm or deadly weapon on property under his or her domain: Provided, That for purposes of this section "person" means an individual or any entity which may acquire title to real property.

Any person carrying or possessing a firearm or other deadly weapon on the property of another who refuses to temporarily relinquish possession of such firearm or other deadly weapon, upon being requested to do so, or to leave such premises, while in possession of such firearm or other deadly weapon, shall be guilty of a misdemeanor, and, upon conviction thereof, shall be fined not more than one thousand dollars or confined in the county jail not more than six months, or both: Provided, That the provisions of this section shall not apply to those persons set forth in subsections (3) through (6), section six of this code while such persons are acting in an official capacity: Provided, however, That under no circumstances may any person possess or carry or cause the possession or carrying of any firearm or other deadly weapon on the premises of any primary or secondary educational facility in this state unless such person is a law-enforcement officer or he or she has the express written permission of the county school superintendent.

§ 61-2-27. Required reporting of gunshot and other wounds

(a) Any medical provider who provides medical treatment to a person suffering from a wound caused by a gunshot or a knife or other sharp or pointed instrument, under circumstances which would lead a reasonable person to believe resulted from a violation of the criminal laws of this state, shall report the same to a law-enforcement agency located within the county within which such wound is treated. The report shall be made initially by telephone and shall be followed by a written report delivered to such agency within forty-eight hours following the initial report: Provided, That where two or more persons participate in the medical treatment of such wound, the obligation to report imposed by this section shall apply only to the attending physician or, if none, to the person primarily responsible for providing the medical treatment.

(b) Any medical provider person who in good faith reports a wound described in subsection (a) of this section shall be immune from any civil liability which may otherwise result solely from reporting the same.

⊹ WISCONSIN ⊹
KNIFE RIGHTS MOVEMENT RATING
★ ★ ★ ☆ ☆

CUTTING TO THE CHASE

Wisconsin bans switchblades, gravity knives, balisongs, and any "…knife having a blade which opens … by a thrust or movement." This last part arguably puts many folding knives in question. Concealed carry of a "dangerous weapon" is also prohibited. "Dangerous weapon" includes "…any device designed as a weapon and capable of producing death or great bodily harm…" and "…any other device or instrumentality which, in the manner it is used or intended to be used, is calculated or likely to produce death or great bodily harm." These broad definitions make it difficult for an honest citizen to know for sure what is lawful.

Quick Points Concerning Wisconsin's Knife Law*

KNIFE TYPE	POSSESSION	(Open/Concealed) CARRY	SALE	MANUFACTURE
Assisted Opening	Gray	Gray /Gray	Gray	Gray
Automatic/Switchblade	Prohibited	Prohibited/Prohibited	Prohibited	Prohibited
Ballistic	Legal	Legal/Gray	Legal	Legal
Bayonets	Legal	Legal/Gray	Legal	Legal
Bowie	Legal	Legal/Gray	Legal	Legal
Butterfly/Balisong	Prohibited	Prohibited/Prohibited	Prohibited	Prohibited
Combat/Survival	Legal	Legal/Gray	Legal	Legal
Dagger	Legal	Legal/Gray	Legal	Legal
Dirk	Legal	Legal/Gray	Legal	Legal
Disguised	Legal	Legal/Gray	Legal	Legal
Fixed	Legal	Legal/Gray	Legal	Legal

KNIFE TYPE	POSSESSION	*(Open/Concealed)* CARRY	SALE	MANUFACTURE
Folding	Gray	Gray /Gray	Gray	Gray
Gravity	Prohibited	Prohibited/Prohibited	Prohibited	Prohibited
Hunting/Fishing	Legal	Legal/Gray	Legal	Legal
Machete	Legal	Legal/Gray	Legal	Legal
Razor	Legal	Legal/Gray	Legal	Legal
Stiletto	Legal	Legal/Gray	Legal	Legal
Sword	Legal	Legal/Gray	Legal	Legal
Throwing	Legal	Legal/Gray	Legal	Legal
Undetectable	Legal	Legal/Gray	Legal	Legal

Pre-emption (Only State Law May Regulate, No Local Laws Permitted) – NO
*See all information above and below for more details.

SHARP TIPS ABOUT WISCONSIN'S KNIFE LAWS

A license to carry a concealed weapon is available. Open carry of legal knives is permitted. No dangerous weapons for minors or on school premises. Wisconsin does not have pre-emption, so beware of local laws.

EDGE –U- CATIONAL --- WISCONSIN'S KNIFE LAWS

939.22. Words and phrases defined

(10) "Dangerous weapon" means any firearm, whether loaded or unloaded; any device designed as a weapon and capable of producing death or great bodily harm; any ligature or other instrumentality used on the throat, neck, nose, or mouth of another person to impede, partially or completely, breathing or circulation of blood; any electric weapon, as defined in s. 941.295(1c)(a); or any other device or instrumentality which, in the manner it is used or intended to be used, is calculated or likely to produce death or great bodily harm.

941.23. Carrying concealed weapon

(1) In this section:

(ag) "Carry" has the meaning given in s. 175.60(1)(ag).

(c) "Former officer" means a person who served as a law enforcement officer with a law enforcement agency before separating from law enforcement service.

(d) "Law enforcement agency" has the meaning given in s. 175.49(1)(f).

(e) "Law enforcement officer" has the meaning given in s. 175.49(1)(g).

(g) "Qualified out-of-state law enforcement officer" means a law enforcement officer to whom all of the following apply:

1. The person is employed by a state or local government agency in another state.

2. The agency has authorized the person to carry a firearm.

3. The person is not the subject of any disciplinary action by the agency that could result in the suspension or loss of the person's law enforcement authority.

4. The person meets all standards established by the agency to qualify the person on a regular basis to use a firearm.

5. The person is not prohibited under federal law from possessing a firearm.

(2) Any person, other than one of the following, who carries a concealed and dangerous weapon is guilty of a Class A misdemeanor:

(a) A peace officer, but notwithstanding s. 939.22, for purposes of this paragraph, peace officer does not include a commission warden who is not a state-certified commission warden.

(b) A qualified out-of-state law enforcement officer. This paragraph applies only if all of the following apply:

1. The weapon is a firearm but is not a machine gun or a destructive device.

2. The officer is not carrying a firearm silencer.

3. The officer is not under the influence of an intoxicant.

(c) A former officer. This paragraph applies only if all of the following apply:

1. The former officer has been issued a photographic identification document described in sub. (3) (b)1. or both of the following:

a. A photographic identification document described in sub. (3)(b)2.(intro.).

b. An identification card described in sub. (3)(b)2.a., if the former officer resides in this state, or a certification described in sub. (3)(b)2.b., if the former officer resides in another state.

2. The weapon is a firearm that is of the type described in a photographic identification document described in subd. 1.(intro.) or a card or certification described in subd. 1.b.

3. Within the preceding 12 months, the former officer met the standards of the state in which he or she resides for training and qualification for active law enforcement officers to carry firearms.

4. The weapon is not a machine gun or a destructive device.

5. The former officer is not carrying a firearm silencer.

6. The former officer is not under the influence of an intoxicant.

7. The former officer is not prohibited under federal law from possessing a firearm.

(d) A licensee, as defined in s. 175.60(1)(d), or an out-of-state licensee, as defined in s. 175.60(1)(g), if the dangerous weapon is a weapon, as defined under s. 175.60(1)(j). An individual formerly licensed under s. 175.60 whose license has been suspended or revoked under s. 175.60(14) may not assert his or her refusal to accept a notice of revocation or suspension mailed under s. 175.60(14)(b)1. as a defense to prosecution under this subsection, regardless of whether the person has complied with s. 175.60(11)(b)1.

(e) An individual who carries a concealed and dangerous weapon, as defined in s. 175.60(1)(j), in his or her own dwelling or place of business or on land that he or she owns, leases, or legally occupies.

(3)(a) A qualified out-of-state law enforcement officer shall, while carrying a concealed firearm, also have with him or her an identification card that contains his or her photograph and that was issued by the law enforcement agency by which he or she is employed.

(b) A former officer shall, while carrying a concealed firearm, also have with him or her one of the following:

1. A photographic identification document issued by the law enforcement agency from which the former officer separated that indicates that, within the 12 months preceding the date on which the former officer is carrying the concealed firearm, he or she was tested or otherwise found by that law enforcement agency to meet the standards for qualification in firearms training that that law enforcement agency sets for active law enforcement officers to carry a firearm of the same type as the firearm that the former officer is carrying.

2. A photographic identification document issued by the law enforcement agency from which the former officer separated and one of the following:

a. A certification card issued under s. 175.49(2), if the former officer resides in this state.

b. A certification issued by the state in which the former officer resides, if the former officer resides in another state, that indicates that, within the 12 months preceding the date on which the former officer is carrying the concealed firearm, he or she has been found by the state in which he or she resides, or by a certified firearms instructor if such an instructor is qualified to conduct a firearms qualification test for active law enforcement officers in that state, to meet the standards for qualification in firearms training for active law enforcement officers to carry a firearm of the type he or she is carrying, that are established by his or her state of residence or, if that state does not establish standards, by any law enforcement agency in his or her state of residence.

(c) A person who violates this subsection may be required to forfeit not more than $25, except that the person shall be exempted from the forfeiture if the person presents, within 48 hours, his or her license document or out-of-state license and photographic identification to the law enforcement agency that employs the requesting law enforcement officer.

(d) This subsection does not apply to a licensee, as defined in s. 175.60(1)(d), or an out-of-state licensee, as defined in s. 175.60(1)(g).

175.60. License to carry a concealed weapon
(1) Definitions. In this section:

(j) "Weapon" means a handgun, an electric weapon, as defined in s. 941.295(1c)(a), a knife other than a switchblade knife under s. 941.24, or a billy club.

941.24. Possession of switchblade knife
(1) Whoever manufactures, sells or offers to sell, transports, purchases, possesses or goes armed with any knife having a blade which opens by pressing a button, spring or other device in the handle or by gravity or by a thrust or movement is guilty of a Class A misdemeanor.

(2) Within 30 days after April 16, 1959, such knives shall be surrendered to any peace officer.

948.60. Possession of a dangerous weapon by a person under 18
(1) In this section, "dangerous weapon" means any firearm, loaded or unloaded; any electric weapon, as defined in s. 941.295(1c)(a); metallic knuckles or knuckles of any substance which could be put to the same use with the same or similar effect as metallic knuckles; a nunchaku or any similar weapon consisting of 2 sticks of wood, plastic or metal connected at one end by a length of rope, chain, wire or leather; a cestus or similar material weighted with metal or other substance and worn on the hand; a shuriken or any similar pointed starlike object intended to injure a person when thrown; or a manrikigusari or similar length of chain having weighted ends.

(2)(a) Any person under 18 years of age who possesses or goes armed with a dangerous weapon is guilty of a Class A misdemeanor.

(b) Except as provided in par. (c), any person who intentionally sells, loans or gives a dangerous weapon to a person under 18 years of age is guilty of a Class I felony.

(c) Whoever violates par. (b) is guilty of a Class H felony if the person under 18 years of age under par. (b) discharges the firearm and the discharge causes death to himself, herself or another.

(d) A person under 17 years of age who has violated this subsection is subject to the provisions of ch. 938 unless jurisdiction is waived under s. 938.18 or the person is subject to the jurisdiction of a court of criminal jurisdiction under s. 938.183.

(3)(a) This section does not apply to a person under 18 years of age who possesses or is armed with a dangerous weapon when the dangerous weapon is being used in target practice under the supervision of an adult or in a course of instruction in the traditional and proper use of the dangerous weapon under the supervision of an adult. This section does not apply to an adult who transfers a dangerous weapon to a person under 18 years of age for use only in target practice under the adult's supervision or in a course of instruction in the traditional and proper use of the dangerous weapon under the adult's supervision.

(b) This section does not apply to a person under 18 years of age who is a member of the armed forces or national guard and who possesses or is armed with a dangerous weapon in the line of duty. This section does not apply to an adult who is a member of the armed forces or national guard and who transfers a dangerous weapon to a person under 18 years of age in the line of duty.

948.61. Dangerous weapons other than firearms on school premises

(1) In this section:

(a) "Dangerous weapon" has the meaning specified in s. 939.22(10), except "dangerous weapon" does not include any firearm and does include any beebee or pellet-firing gun that expels a projectile through the force of air pressure or any starter pistol.

(b) "School" means a public school, parochial or private school, or tribal school, as defined in s. 115.001(15m), which provides an educational program for one or more grades between grades 1 and 12 and which is commonly known as an elementary school, middle school, junior high school, senior high school, or high school.

(c) "School premises" means any school building, grounds, recreation area or athletic field or any other property owned, used or operated for school administration.

(2) Any person who knowingly possesses or goes armed with a dangerous weapon on school premises is guilty of:

(a) A Class A misdemeanor.

(b) A Class I felony, if the violation is the person's 2nd or subsequent violation of this section within a 5-year period, as measured from the dates the violations occurred.

(3) This section does not apply to any person who:

(a) Uses a weapon solely for school-sanctioned purposes.

(b) Engages in military activities, sponsored by the federal or state government, when acting in the discharge of his or her official duties.

(c) Is a law enforcement officer or state-certified commission warden acting in the discharge of his or her official duties.

(d) Participates in a convocation authorized by school authorities in which weapons of collectors or instructors are handled or displayed.

(e) Drives a motor vehicle in which a dangerous weapon is located onto school premises for school-sanctioned purposes or for the purpose of delivering or picking up passengers or property. The weapon may not be removed from the vehicle or be used in any manner.

(f) Possesses or uses a bow and arrow or knife while legally hunting in a school forest if the school board has decided that hunting may be allowed in the school forest under s. 120.13(38).

(4) A person under 17 years of age who has violated this section is subject to the provisions of ch. 938, unless jurisdiction is waived under s. 938.18 or the person is subject to the jurisdiction of a court of criminal jurisdiction under s. 938.183.

⁙ WYOMING ⁙
KNIFE RIGHTS MOVEMENT RATING
★ ★ ★ ★ ☆

CUTTING TO THE CHASE
Wyoming would receive a five on the knife freedom rating if its concealed carry law was not so vaguely written. Open carry is fine in Wyoming. Other knife freedoms are strong. There are no knife possession prohibitions based solely on knife features.

Quick Points Concerning Wyoming's Knife Law*

KNIFE TYPE	POSSESSION	(Open/Concealed) CARRY	SALE	MANUFACTURE
Assisted Opening	Legal	Legal/Gray	Legal	Legal
Automatic/Switchblade	Legal	Legal/Gray	Legal	Legal
Ballistic	Legal	Legal/Gray	Legal	Legal
Bayonets	Legal	Legal/Gray	Legal	Legal
Bowie	Legal	Legal/Gray	Legal	Legal
Butterfly/Balisong	Legal	Legal/Gray	Legal	Legal
Combat/Survival	Legal	Legal/Gray	Legal	Legal
Dagger	Legal	Legal/Gray	Legal	Legal
Dirk	Legal	Legal/Gray	Legal	Legal
Disguised	Legal	Legal/Gray	Legal	Legal
Fixed	Legal	Legal/Gray	Legal	Legal
Folding	Legal	Legal/Gray	Legal	Legal
Gravity	Legal	Legal/Gray	Legal	Legal
Hunting/Fishing	Legal	Legal/Gray	Legal	Legal
Machete	Legal	Legal/Gray	Legal	Legal
Razor	Legal	Legal/Gray	Legal	Legal
Stiletto	Legal	Legal/Gray	Legal	Legal
Sword	Legal	Legal/Gray	Legal	Legal
Throwing	Legal	Legal/Gray	Legal	Legal
Undetectable	Legal	Legal/Gray	Legal	Legal

<u>Pre-emption</u> (Only State Law May Regulate, No Local Laws Permitted) – YES
*See all information above and below for more details.

SHARP TIPS ABOUT WYOMING'S KNIFE LAWS
A knife may qualify as a "concealed deadly weapon" and the exceptions to the law all appear to pertain only to firearms. Whether a knife is a deadly weapon will depend on "… the manner it is used or is intended to be used is reasonably capable of producing death or serious bodily injury…" This is may well boil down to what a jury collectively believes about any particular knife.

EDGE –U- CATIONAL --- WYOMING'S KNIFE LAWS
§ 6-1-104. Definitions
(a) As used in this act, unless otherwise defined:

(iv) "Deadly weapon" means but is not limited to a firearm, explosive or incendiary material, motorized vehicle, an animal or other device, instrument, material or substance, which in the manner it is used or is intended to be used is reasonably capable of producing death or serious bodily injury;

§ 6-8-104. Wearing or carrying concealed weapons; penalties; exceptions; permits

(a) A person who wears or carries a concealed deadly weapon is guilty of a misdemeanor punishable by a fine of not more than seven hundred fifty dollars ($750.00), imprisonment in the county jail for not more than six (6) months, or both for a first offense, or a felony punishable by a fine of not more than two thousand dollars ($2,000.00), imprisonment for not more than two (2) years, or both, for a second or subsequent offense, unless:

(i) The person is a peace officer;

(ii) The person possesses a permit under this section;

(iii) The person holds a valid permit authorizing him to carry a concealed firearm authorized and issued by a governmental agency or entity in another state that recognizes Wyoming permits and is a valid statewide permit; or

(iv) The person does not possess a permit issued under this section, but otherwise meets the requirements specified in paragraphs (b)(i) through (vi), (viii) and (ix) of this section and possession of the firearm by the person is not otherwise unlawful.

§ 6-8-401. Firearm, weapon and ammunition regulation and prohibition by state

(a) The Wyoming legislature finds that the right to keep and bear arms is a fundamental right. The Wyoming legislature affirms this right as a constitutionally protected right in every part of Wyoming.

(b) Repealed by Laws 2010, ch. 108, § 3, eff. March 11, 2010.

(c) The sale, transfer, purchase, delivery, taxation, manufacture, ownership, transportation, storage, use and possession of firearms, weapons and ammunition shall be authorized, regulated and prohibited by the state, and regulation thereof is preempted by the state. Except as authorized by W.S. 15-1-103(a) (xviii), no city, town, county, political subdivision or any other entity shall authorize, regulate or prohibit the sale, transfer, purchase, delivery, taxation, manufacture, ownership, transportation, storage, use, carrying or possession of firearms, weapons, accessories, components or ammunition except as specifically provided by this chapter. This section shall not affect zoning or other ordinances which encompass firearms businesses along with other businesses. Zoning and other ordinances which are designed for the purpose of restricting or prohibiting the sale, purchase, transfer or manufacture of firearms or ammunition as a method of regulating firearms or ammunition are in conflict with this section and are prohibited

KNIFE LIBERTY
IN THE UNITED STATES

★ ★ ★ ★ ★

**ALASKA, ARIZONA, GEORGIA, KANSAS,
NEW HAMPSHIRE, TENNESSEE, UTAH (7)**

★ ★ ★ ★

**ALABAMA, ARKANSAS, FLORIDA, IDAHO, INDIANA, KENTUCKY,
LOUISIANA, MAINE, MISSISSIPPI, MISSOURI , MONTANA, NEBRASKA,
NEVADA , NORTH DAKOTA, OKLAHOMA, SOUTH CAROLINA ,
SOUTH DAKOTA, UNITED STATES OF AMERICA, VERMONT,
WEST VIRGINIA, WYOMING (21)**

★ ★ ★

**CONNECTICUT, HAWAII, ILLINOIS, IOWA, MARYLAND, MICHIGAN,
NORTH CAROLINA, OHIO, OREGON, RHODE ISLAND, VIRGINIA,
WASHINGTON, WISCONSIN, TEXAS (14)**

★ ★

**COLORADO, DELAWARE, DISTRICT OF COLUMBIA, MASSACHUSETTS,
MINNESOTA, NEW JERSEY, NEW MEXICO, PENNSYLVANIA (8)**

★

CALIFORNIA, NEW YORK (2)

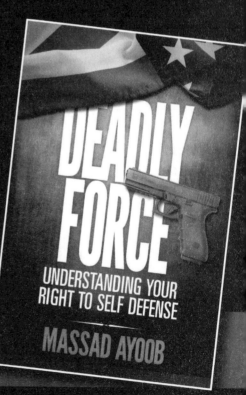